MARIE CHARLES JOSEPH

MAURICE DE WULF

An Introduction to Scholastic Philosophy

MEDIEVAL AND MODERN

[Scholasticism Old and New]

TRANSLATED BY P. COFFEY

DOVER PUBLICATIONS, INC., NEW YORK

PREFATORY NOTE.

My object in translating Professor De Wulf's *Introduction à la Philosophie Néo-scolastique* has been fourfold : firstly, to give the advocates and supporters of " modern " systems of philosophy, as opposed to " scholasticism"—whether in its medieval or in its modern form—an opportunity of obtaining better and more authentic information about the latter system than books in English are usually found to contain ; secondly, to help students of scholastic philosophy to take in the main principles of scholasticism in one connected view, and to equip them with a more accurate historical and critical appreciation of the system than they are ever likely to derive from an unaided study of stereotyped manuals ; thirdly, to give all English readers interested in philosophy of whatsoever kind an insight into the meaning, the spirit and the progress of the movement which has been developing during the last quarter of a century for the revival of scholastic philosophy ; fourthly, to prepare the way for translations or adaptations of the Louvain *Cours de philosophie,* and to draw attention to the value of the work already done and likely to be done in the well-known Belgian centre of the new scholasticism.

For information on this latter point I may be permitted to refer the reader to the Appendix at the end of the present volume.

The utility of the book will, it is hoped, be further enhanced by the Index and the Analytical Table of Contents.

The reader's kind indulgence is claimed for the many defects of a work accomplished during irregular intervals in the discharge of more pressing duties.

THE TRANSLATOR.

MAYNOOTH, August, 1907.

AUTHOR'S PREFACE.

UNDER the title of *Introduction to Philosophy* there have been published in recent years, and more especially in Germany,[1] works of a general character, some of which merely deal with questions preparatory to the study of philosophy, while others contain a doctrinal *resumé* as well. From the nature of things those " Introductions " serve to introduce only one definite system of philosophy—that which has the author's preferences.

It seems likely that a work of this kind, devoted to both medieval and modern scholastic philosophy, will interest not merely those who are already acquainted with scholastic doctrines, but even all who are trying to follow the march of contemporary thought. Whatever may be its extent and duration, the scholastic revival represents at the present time, and will represent in the annals of the Twentieth Century, an intellectual movement that may not be ignored. We still encounter quite a crowd of prejudices regarding modern scholasticism, and many

---

[1] For example : *Einleitung in die Philosophie* by Paulsen (7 Aufl., Berlin, 1901) ; by Külpe (2 Aufl., Leipzig, 1898) ; by Wundt (2 Aufl., Leipzig, 1902) ; by Jerusalem (2 Aufl., Leipzig, 1902) ; by Hans Cornelius (Leipzig, 1902) ; *Einleitung in die Philosophie der reinen Erfahrung* by J. Petzoldt (Leipzig, 1899) ; *Einleitung in die Philosophie der Gegenwart* by Riehl (Leipzig, 1903).

talk about it without understanding it.   On the
other hand, much that is exact and even suggestive,
in its regard, has gained currency at different times
and places of late ; and it is not altogether easy to
collect and compare these later views and to weigh
their respective merits.

The object of the present work is to meet and
combat false conceptions, to co-ordinate true notions,
and so to furnish the reader with some *general
information* on the new scholasticism.   The author has
adopted quite a summary method.   He has merely
traced the outlines, raised and stated the problems,
but he does not claim to have noticed all the points
of view which the subject-matter admits of.   *Introduction to Scholastic Philosophy* being here synonymous
with *presentation, preparation,* the developments of
the different questions treated or simply referred
to, must be sought in special treatises.   He earnestly
hopes that the present volume may prove an effica-
cious *invitation* to its readers to undertake a personal
and deeper study of modern scholastic philosophy.

To form an idea of what *the new scholastic philosophy*
is, one must evidently know what the *scholasticism
of the Middle Ages* was, for the former is only a
revival and adaptation of the latter.   The two parts
of the present work are therefore called for by the
very nature of the subject.

The first part, strictly historical, will " introduce "
the reader to this old scholastic monument—to the
discredit of which so much has been spoken and
written, but which, resembling in so many ways the

majestic cathedrals of the Middle Ages, decidedly gains by being visited and seen in detail.

The second part will point out the meaning of the attempted restoration and adaptation of this edifice to our own time.

In 1899 we published a *brochure* entitled : *What is Scholastic Philosophy?* [1] which we have been requested on many sides to reprint. Most of the ideas in that little work will be found here completely recast and developed. We also reproduce, in different places, the theories expressed in an article in the *Revue Philosophique* of June, 1902, entitled : *Notion de la scolastique.* At the same time we have taken occasion to reply to various criticisms,[2] and to give an appreciation of recent works that have put forth general views on the Middle Ages. The reader will accordingly find a fair number of additional ideas on medieval philosophy, supplementing our previous publications.

The two parts of this work correspond like diptychs : the author has tried to compare, point by point, the ideas of the past with those of the present. The new scholasticism is more extensive than the old, being a development and growth of its doctrine : *Vetera novis augere.* But, on the other hand, though the new scholasticism is already constructed in its main outlines it has yet to be perfected in numerous

---

[1] " *Qu'est-ce-que la philosophie scolastique ?* "

[2] Directed against our manner of comprehending scholastic philosophy, *à propos* of our *Histoire de la philosophie médiévale* (Louvain, 1900 ; 2nd edition, enlarged and revised, 1905).

details.   For those two reasons the second part of the work contains a larger number of separate sketches than the first.

Many of the doctrines here dealt with form the subject-matter of the teaching and publications of our colleagues of the Philosophical Institute.   We have been happy to make use of those works.   Certain developments of Section 15 are borrowed from the conferences of M. de Lantsheere on the sources of Modern Philosophy.   Sections 26, 28, 29, 30 are inspired by the recent well known and widely appreciated works of MM. D. Mercier and D. Nys : footnotes will remind the reader in those places.

We may say in conclusion that our exposition of the new scholastic doctrine contains at the same time the programme of instruction which the Louvain Institute of Philosophy has outlined for itself and is endeavouring to carry out.

M. DE WULF.

Louvain,
     Christmas, 1903.

CONTENTS

PART I

MEDIEVAL SCHOLASTIC PHILOSOPHY

CHAPTER I
INTRODUCTORY NOTIONS

CHAPTER II

DOCTRINAL DEFINITION

CHAPTER III

THE DECLINE OF SCHOLASTICISM

PART II

MODERN SCHOLASTIC PHILOSOPHY

CHAPTER I

SOME EXTRA-DOCTRINAL NOTIONS OF THE NEW SCHOLASTICISM

CHAPTER II

THE DOCTRINES OF THE NEW SCHOLASTICISM

CHAPTER III

THE FUTURE OF THE NEW SCHOLASTICISM

APPENDIX

PART I.

MEDIEVAL SCHOLASTIC PHILOSOPHY.

CHAPTER I.

INTRODUCTORY NOTIONS.

SECTION 1.—THE COMMON ACCEPTATION OF THE TERM
SCHOLASTICISM, VAGUE AND UNFAVOURABLE.

1. The term *scholasticism* is, in the language and
writings of many, a *vague* designation of the philosophical or theological speculation of the Middle Ages.
It sums up for them the mentality of a backward
civilisation. "Scholasticism" is the glimmering
and uncertain light of "the long night of a thousand
years." This unsatisfactory vagueness is aggravated
by an *unfavourable* sense of the word. We are
accustomed to depreciate the wisdom of antiquity,
and to regard it as the product of a credulous age,
with which only the monks and clergy of that time
could have been satisfied. And so *scholastic* has
become a synonym for the out-of-date, the naive,
the scientifically worthless.

2. This contempt for the scholarship of the Middle
Ages dates from the Renaissance. And certainly the
decadent productions of the fifteenth and sixteenth
centuries were calculated to provoke criticisms and
reactions ; but then both of these latter were excessive
(v. Section 19). Laurentius Valla reprobates that
superstitious and senseless race of professors (*genus
hominum superstitiosum et vecors*) who make their
pupils swear never to contradict Aristotle.[1] Ludovicus

---

[1] *Dialecticæ Disputationes*, Præfatio (Opera, Paris, 1540), p. 643.

Vives mercilessly scoffs at the *sophismata* and
dialectical dissoluteness of the University of Paris,
whose masters "rave and invent absurdities, and
a new sort of language that only they themselves
can understand." [1]

Those severe strictures grounded the convictions
of the succeeding generations; and these latter,
improving on the Renaissance, included under one
common expression of contempt not only the
decadents of the fifteenth, sixteenth and seventeenth
centuries, but all the scholastic philosophers *in globo.*
Their science, writes Bacon, degenerated into subtile,
vain and unwholesome questions like a decomposing
organism (solvitur in subtiles, vanas, insalubres, et,
si ita loqui liceat, vermiculatas quæstiones [2]). The
encyclopedists of the eighteenth century expressed
their pity for all "who devoted themselves to those
miserable scholastic subtilities that consist more in
words than in things"; they made merry over Duns
Scotus in whom they found only "vain subtilities
and a metaphysic which every man of common sense
rejects," and of whom it might be said that "a man
who would know fully all he had written would know
nothing." [3]

And when, in the second half of the eighteenth
century, Brucker published his great *Historia Critica
Philosophiæ,* he had recourse to no other sources, for
his estimate of scholasticism, than to those works of
its pitiless detractors. Need we be astonished, then,
that this critical history,—far too impassioned to
deserve its name,—represents the introduction of the
western scholars of the twelfth century to the writings

---

[1] "Sominant et confingunt sibi ineptias ac novam quamdam
linguam quam ipsi soli intelligant." *In Pseudo-dialecticos* (Opera,
Ed., 1782), t. iii., p. 38.
[2] *De augmentis scientiarum,* l. i, c. 9. Quoted by Brucker, *Historia
Critica Philosophiæ,* iii., 877.
[3] *Encyclopédie des sciences, des arts et métiers,* published by
Diderot and d'Alembert, under the word "Aristote" (t. i., pp. 663-4).

of Aristotle as the beginning of a universal stulti-fication ? [1]

An honest search after truth, the same author concludes, was never the spirit of scholasticism. It contains nothing but a tissue of *velitationes philo-sophicæ*, forming an undigested logomachy.[2] 'Dia-lectica ista non rationalis philosophia fuit, sed ars rixosa—Metaphysica inani dialecticæ juncta, malum hoc auctum, indeque exortæ logomachiæ innumeræ—Subtilitas affectata nimia et inutilis—Juncta bar-baries sermonis cum barbarie cogitationum ' : these are a few of the choice rubrics under which Brucker groups his diatribes against a movement of ideas that he condemned without understanding.

Such an attitude, on the part of a man whose name is first on the roll of the great modern historians of philosophy, could not fail to create a widespread distaste for medieval scholasticism. Amongst our contemporaries even, some have rehearsed the same summary condemnations and the same contemptuous prejudices. Taine, for example, considers the epoch of the great doctors of the thirteenth century as an age of " imbecility " worthy only of contempt. " Three centuries at the bottom of that gloomy abyss did not add a single idea to man's intellectual inheritance." [3] Others are of opinion that it is better to " jump clean " across those Middle Ages, regarding them as a disgrace to human thought. The Germans have a name for this indifferentism : *Der Sprung über das Mittelalter.* So from the closing of the Greek schools by Justinian in 529 to the

---

[1] " Cui (dialecticæ) cum accederent sæculo xi metaphysicæ specu-lationes, præcisiones mentales, et varia alia mentis otiosa deliria, sæculo vero xii Aristotelis metaphysica his elegantiis plena innotuisset, ita hominum horum subtilitas aucta est, ut plane ab humani intellectus natura degeneraret."—*Historia Critica Philosophiæ* (Leipzig, 1766), t. iii., p. 712.
[2] *Ibid.,* pp. 870-871.
[3] History of English Literature, v. i., pp. 223 and 225.

publication of the *Discours de la Méthode* in 1637, slumbering humanity would have ceased to think, or to bring up before its sovereign reflection the great problems of philosophy !   With such naive prejudices it was certainly only natural to take Descartes for a ' saviour ' from whom the seventeenth century and modern society once more learned how to philosophize. So, for example, thinks M. Penjon : " If philosophy is, as we have defined it, a free search, we may say that from the edict of Justinian (529) to the Renaissance in the fifteenth century there is a sort of interval during which there is, properly speaking, no philosophy. For, during all that period, western humanity was subject, in the region of speculation, to the dogmas that constitute the Christian teaching, and, in the region of morals, to the ecclesiastical discipline founded on those dogmas.   We should, therefore, in a history of philosophy, simply skip that interval of eight or nine centuries and pass directly to study the researches that prepared the way for modern philosophy." [1]

Great was the astonishment of the moderns when those pseudo-degenerate Middle Ages began to reveal treasures of philosophic thought to the numerous recent explorers who are still occupied in shovelling away the rubbish of centuries from around that whole epoch.   Victor Cousin and his school were the initiators of this modern historical research movement.   They made people understand by slow degrees that there was no such thing as a medieval " interlude," and that the sequence of thought was nowhere and no while interrupted. Stöckl, Hauréau, Ehrle, Denifle, Bæumker, Erdmann, Ueberweg-Heinze, Picavet, Willmann, Mandonnet, Baumgartner, Delacroix—these, to mention only contemporaries—have shown that scholasticism constitutes a movement of ideas as complex and as well worthy of attention

[1] Précis d'histoire de la Philosophie, Paris, 1897, p. 165.

as even the finest syntheses of antiquity. The thread of tradition extending from ancient to modern philosophy is now for all time reknotted. Nothing in the world seems less like an intellectual lethargy than the activity of the Middle Ages.

3. And now that the prejudice which has weighed so heavily against medieval philosophy is being gradually dissipated, and what was so long only sneered at is at length being taken seriously, it is high time to get rid of the vagueness that attaches to the word *scholasticism*. For if it be true that the progress of a science can be judged from the precision of its terminology, a first condition for the progress of Middle Age philosophical history is the exact determination of the meaning we are to attach to the words it is constantly making use of. What then, speaking scientifically, is the meaning of the term "scholasticism"? Many replies have been formulated. A critical examination of them will form the matter of the pages that follow.

SECTION 2—THE POINT AT ISSUE—A MISTAKE TO BE AVOIDED.

4. People philosophized in the Middle Ages. And it is of *philosophical* doctrines there is question when we speak of scholastic *philosophy*. It may seem quite superfluous to insist on this, but it is the only way to make intelligible the discussions we are about to deal with. Now, all philosophy consists in *a rational study of all or some of the problems arising from our attempts to explain the universal order of things by their ultimate causes or principles*. And hence : either scholastic philosophy is not a *philosophy*, and then those who talk of it mistake the covering of words for the kernel of reality ; or it

justifies, on some title or other, the general idea just
outlined ; that is to say, its content represents some
attempts, good or bad, superficial or profound,
convergent or divergent, to solve the perennial
enigmas of the universe.

5. That the latter is the fact, we shall see with all
evidence.   And that is just why we must not confound, as happens too often, *scholastic philosophy*
with *scholastic theology*.   Theology is not a study
of the universal order by the light of human intelligence ; it is, at least in its dogmatic portion,
a systematization of certain doctrines that a positive
revelation has delivered to us.   To confound scholastic
philosophy with scholastic theology is to confound
the examination of natural truths by reason with
the study of Christian dogma—as if scholasticism
were only, as Brucker expresses it, a discussion of
revealed mysteries by the light of the badly understood principles of Aristotelianism.[1]   What a number
of modern authors fall into the same error and think
that " the content of the ideas being fixed by dogma,
no liberty remained except in the method of
explaining and applying them." [2]   If scholasticism
be no more than that, we may truly call it no longer
a *philosophy*, but an exegesis of belief, a commentary
on the faith, a mere plea *pro domo*.

This confusion, so easily introduced, between
scholastic philosophy and scholastic theology, is due
to the wrong interpretation of a group of specific
relations that were established by the Middle Ages

---

[1] " Philosophia hæc scholastica quæ Aristoteli male intellecto
revelationis mysteria subjiciens, de eorum sensu juxta illius præcepta
disputabat." *Op. cit., p.* 712.

[2] Fouillée, *Histoire de la Philosophie*, Paris 1883, p. 198, etc.   The
same confusion is evident in a most recent work : " Unter
Scholastik verstehen wir diejenige Philosophie welche die Kirchenlehre
als wissenschaftliches Schulsystem zu begründen und auszubilden
sucht."   (By scholasticism we understand the philosophy that the
Church teaching seeks to establish and develop as a scientific school
system).   Vorländer, *Geschichte der Philosophie*, Bd. i., Philos. des
Altertums und des Mittelalters (Leipzig, 1903), p. 233.

between those two branches of speculative study, and which will form the subject of a full investigation further on (Section 7). It perverts the very meaning of an historical study of medieval philosophy, by making that study a mere department of the history of religions.[1] It is expressly condemned by the scholastics themselves. Their unanimous declarations on the subject cannot leave the least room for doubt. This is the point we have now to establish.

What determines the proper individuality of each of the various sciences, what furnishes us with a test of their diversity, is not, the scholastics tell us, the identity or diversity of the materials which they treat (the material object of the sciences), but the treatment itself of those materials (formal object of the sciences). The distinction between two sciences is altogether due to the distinction between the *points of view* from which they regard things, of their principles and of their methods of procedure. Just as two architects can build, by different arrangements of the same stones, the one a Roman temple, the other a Gothic cathedral, so can two sciences deal with the same realities provided they approach them from different standpoints. The astronomer, remarks St. Thomas, studies the rotundity of the earth, no less than the physician ; but the former draws his proofs from mathematics, the latter from the laws of matter.[2]

So it is with theology and philosophy. Each presents under every respect the characteristics of that independence which is proper to a distinct science. The one is based on the revealed word,

---

[1] The administrative regulation of the *École des Hautes Études* at Paris, which places works bearing on medieval scholasticism in the *section of religious sciences*, is inspired by this unfortunate confusion.

[2] " Diversa ratio cognoscibilis diversitatem scientiarum inducit. Eandem enim conclusionem demonstrant astrologus et naturalis ; puta quod terra est rotunda. Sed astrologus per medium mathematicum, id est, a materia abstractum ; naturalis autem per medium circa materiam consideratum." *Summa Theologica*, 1ma Pars., q. i. a. 1.

the other on the light of reason ; the one is built up by the way of authority, the other proceeds by scientific proofs.   Thomas of Aquin, Henry of Ghent, Bonaventure, Godfrey of Fontaines, Duns Scotus— in a word, *all* the scholastics, have given expression to the same view regarding *the distinction between theological science and philosophical science.*

It is of scholastic *philosophy* there is question here, and of it alone.   The author avows his incompetence in the domain of the history of dogmatic and mystic theology.   He will take account of the latter only in so far as may be necessary to understand certain relations which are found to have existed in the Middle Ages, as indeed in every other epoch, between philosophy and the other great divisions of human knowledge.

6. *Defining* is a different function from *naming.* To *define*, strictly speaking, we must penetrate, as it were, to the depths of the reality, and circumscribe its sphere of being (definire).   *Naming* is simply attaching a name to a thing known in any way whatever.   And moreover, names are defined as well as things : all logicians distinguish the *nominal* and the *real* definition.   The nominal definition is an explanation of the etymological or conventional meaning that attaches to the *name.*   It clears up ideas and prevents equivocations.   But obviously it needs to be followed by a *real* definition—a definition of the thing.   To define a *thing* is to tell what the thing is, and what accordingly distinguishes it from every other thing.[1]   Real definition is all the more perfect the more deeply it penetrates the nature of the thing to be known.   If we could grasp in an adequate manner the more fundamental realities of the proper object of a science we should possess that science in its entirety in two or three definitions.

---

[1] Aristotle, *Anal. post* ii., 3—Cfr. Mercier, *Logique*, pp. 330 to 333. (Louvain, 1902 ; fourth edition, 1905).

Unfortunately that is an ideal which the human mind, while always aiming at, can never fully reach. This test of the relative perfection of real definitions enables us to appreciate at their true value a double group of them : *intrinsic* and *extrinsic* definitions. Everything can be subjected to a twofold process of definition, according as we explore what the thing is *in itself*, what are its constituent elements and their characteristics—in which case we reach the thing to be defined just as it is, in an absolute and intrinsic way ; or, on the contrary, content ourselves with observing the *relations of the thing in question with another thing*—in which case we reach only its relative and extrinsic aspects. To form for ourselves an idea of the planet on which we dwell we may describe the *complexus* of elements of which it is composed ; or we may consider it in its relations with the sun which gives it light. So far from mutually excluding, the absolute and relative notions complete each other. But it is evident that the former are more important than the latter, and that they alone can lead us to an adequate knowledge of the object to be defined— apart from the case of things which consist entirely in mere relations.

7. Let us apply these elementary notions of Logic to the matter in hand. We may define either the name " scholasticism " or the thing which it designates, arriving thus at verbal or real definitions. The latter in turn will be either intrinsic or extrinsic.

Now, since a philosophy is constituted by its doctrinal content we may designate as *intrinsic* or *absolute* such notions or definitions of scholasticism as are based on its solutions and doctrines. To look for *extrinsic* or *relative* notions of scholastic *philosophy* is to turn one's back on this doctrinal content and to neglect its peculiar and characteristic significance, for the sake of pointing out the relations, in themselves very numerous, no doubt, and very instructive,

which exist between *elements foreign to its doctrine*
and that doctrine itself.

Most of our historians of scholastic philosophy
have confined themselves either to elucidating its
nominal definition or to establishing relations extrinsic
to its doctrine. Amongst the latter, some have fixed
upon the relations of scholasticism with the language
and the schools which have transmitted its ideas, or
with the methods that have favoured its teaching ;
others have characterized it by the epoch in which
it flourished ; others again by its relations with the
Middle Age sciences or with scholastic theology or
with ancient philosophy.

There are those also who have deciphered some
pages of the doctrinal code of scholasticism with a
view to discovering inner and differentiating features ;
but instead of reading the book to the end, they have
closed it too soon, or turned over its pages too rapidly.

And so we have a collection of notions or definitions
of scholasticism that present a curious mixture of
true and false, of commonplace and striking, and
many of which are often adopted successively by one
and the same author. We must try to sift them
and to determine what elements from amongst them
we ought to retain.

The following scheme sums up what has just been
said, and will serve as a plan for the subsequent
sections :—

A.—Nominal definitions (sec. 3).

B.—Real definitions
  I.— Extrinsic to the doctrine : Study of its relations with :
    1° the schools (sec. 3),
    2° language and methods (sec. 4 & 5).
    3° the medieval epoch (sec. 6).
    4° scholastic theology (sec. 7).
    5° ancient philosophy (sec. 8).
    6° medieval science (sec. 9).
  II. — Intrinsic to the doctrine
    1° incomplete (sec. 10).
    2° integral (sec. 11-18).

SECTION 3.—SCHOLASTICISM, THE 'DAUGHTER OF THE SCHOOLS.'

8. According to etymology (σχολή =otium), the *scholasticus* is the man of leisure, the man who is free from the cares of material life or public affairs, and devotes himself—or is thought to devote himself —to the culture of the mind. Greek pedagogy was acquainted with the σχολαστιχός,[1] but the Middle Ages received the word from classic and patristic latinity, which had already given it manifold significations. For Quintilian the *scholasticus* is a rhetorician or professor of eloquence[2]; St. Augustine calls the pleader at law a *scholasticus;* St. Jerome applies the name to all distinguished scholars.[3]

From the sixth century the sense of the word *scholasticus* becomes more and more restricted to the didactic function (*scholasticum officium*) which was honoured by Charlemagne, and received its own proper privileges and insignia.[4] The custom becomes common of calling *scholasticus* or *scholar*, the titular of any teaching office whether in an abbey school or in an episcopal school.[5] The science imparted

---

[1] Ueberweg-Heinze (*Geschichte der Philosophie*, ii., 1898, p. 149) remarks the term in a letter of Theophrastus to Phanias (*Diogenes Laertius*, v. 50).

[2] Quoted by Forcellini, *Totius Latinitatis Lexicon*, under the word *scholasticus*.

[3] St. Augustine, *Tr. 7 in Joh. 1* "Qui habent causam quærunt aliquem scholasticum, jurisperitum."—St. Jerome, *De viris illustr.* cap. 99 (Migne P. L. 23, 738): "ob elegantiam ingenii cognomen scholastici meruit."—Cfr. Pseudo-August., *Principia dialectica*, 10. "Nam cum scholastici non solum proprie, sed et primitus dicantur ii qui adhuc in schola sunt, omnes tamen, qui in litteris vivunt, nomen hoc usurpant."

[4] Fulbert of Chartres offers Hildegaire the rod and tablets of the schools, *scholarum ferulam et tabulas.*—Clerval, *Les écoles de Chartres au moyen âge, du Ve. au XVIe. siècle* (Paris, 1895), p. 31.

[5] Ducange, *Glossarium ad scriptores mediæ et infimæ ætatis*, under the word *Scholasticus*. "Dignitas ecclesiastica, qua qui donatus est, scholis ecclesiasticis præest." The *scholæ palatinæ* created by Charlemagne were teaching institutions. See under the word *Scholæ*.

in those schools was called scholastic science or
scholasticism, and had for its object either theology
or the liberal arts—and amongst these, chiefly
philosophy.   Does this notion, borrowed from
etymology and history furnish adequate elements
for a definition of " scholastic philosophy " ?   We do
not think so.

9. What, for example, should we know about
Greek Philosophy, were it defined : " the philosophy
taught at the agora, at the squares of the Greek
cities, later on in special establishments called
Lyceums, Gymnasiums, Academies, from the foundation to the decline of those schools, that is, down to
the period when a new spirit, the modern spirit.
giving birth to imperial decrees, began to encounter
the old philosophy and to wrest from it the office
of forming and guiding the human intelligence " ?

Now, it is just in such terms, *mutatis mutandis*,
that M. Hauréau expresses himself on the first page
of his *Histoire de la Philosophie scolastique*.   " Scholastic philosophy," he says, " is the philosophy professed
in the schools of the Middle Ages from the foundation
to the decline of those schools, that is, down to the
period when the extern philosophy, the new spirit,
the modern spirit, liberating itself from the shackles
of tradition, began to encounter the old, and to
snatch from it the office of forming and guiding the
human intelligence." [1]   And, regarding the decay
of scholasticism as quite a final and accomplished
fact, the learned historian thinks that the art invented
by Gutenberg dealt it the *coup de grace*.   Up to that
time, in fact, the rarity of the manuscripts obliged
studious people to undertake long journeys to follow
the lessons of the public schools.   " As soon as the

[1] Hauréau, *Histoire de la Philosophie scolastique*, v. i. (Paris, 1872),
p. 36.   Similarly in the *Dictionnaire des sciences philosophiques*, he
writes, under the word *Scolastique :* " Scholasticism is the philosophy
taught in the schools of the Middle Ages."

Press had multiplied copies of the ancient texts, and even of more modern glosses, a person might follow up his studies to the limits of the science without frequenting the public schools. . . Heretofore people flocked to Paris from all parts of Europe to follow the courses of the most famous masters ; now, however, deserted by the scholars, the public chairs were soon deserted by the professors themselves, and their numbers were seen gradually to diminish. So ended oral or scholastic teaching. Philosophy will be no longer taught didactically, except in convents and colleges, nor will it be accorded the favour of a refuge in those institutions controlled by the Church except on condition of an entire dependence." [1]

Before discussing the definition of M. Hauréau, let us refer, just to show its inexactness, to the corollary he draws from it. If scholasticism be merely the philosophy professed in the schools, it seems strange, *a priori*, that it should have been smothered by the progress of an art so eminently calculated to increase tenfold the power of oral teaching. For, as a matter of fact, the invention of printing has not synchronized with the decay of the Western schools. In every country in Europe numerous universities have been seen to spring up posterior to the sixteenth century. And even to-day the growing influence which perfected machinery assures to the Press is far from anything like depopulating the centres of learning. The publication of works will never prevent the youth from assembling around the professor's chair no more than it will ever draw the crowd away from the orator's tribune ; the spoken word is endowed with a persuasive power for which even in the very best of books we may search in vain.

10. Accordingly we are not surprised to find that M. Picavet of the Paris *Ecole des Hautes Etudes*,

[1] *Ibid.*, p. 38

while attaching himself to M. Hauréau [1] draws the
contrary conclusion from the principle laid down
by his master. Scholasticism remains with him the
"daughter of the schools." [2] It is the "theology or
philosophy that is taught, that is sometimes invented
or developed, and that sometimes also dies in the
schools." [3] But whilst for M. Hauréau the schools,
and with them scholasticism, would have ceased to
exist at the end of the Middle Ages, for M. Picavet
they have survived the invention of printing ; and
scholasticism outsteps the Middle Ages just like the
school teaching of which it is the "daughter."
"There are Platonic, Peripatetic, especially Neo-
Platonic scholasticisms. There is a Protestant
scholasticism and a Catholic, a Hegelian, a Cousinian,
a Schopenhauerian, etc. But scholasticism in the
most ordinary sense of the term is the medieval
philosophy that we find among the Byzantines,
among the Arabs and the Jews, and among the
Western Christians." [4] The extension thus given
by M. Picavet to the notion of scholasticism is more
conformable to Logic than the restriction of M.
Hauréau. But is it any happier ? Would Hegel,
Cousin, Schopenhauer [5] have been pleased to hear
themselves called *scholastics*. Not only does every
teacher of philosophy—Kant as well as Thomas
Aquinas, Wundt as well as Boutroux, Paulsen as
well as Bergson, M. Picavet himself—become
scholastic ; but scholasticism reaches beyond the
confines of philosophy and theology and embraces
every science that can claim a leading exponent and
an oral teaching.

[1] M. Picavet, *Nos maîtres,* I. M. Hauréau (*Revue internationale de
l'Enseignement,* Decr. 16th, 1900).
[2] *Revue Philosophique,* 1902, p. 185.
[3] *Grande Encyclopédie,* under the word "Scolastique."
[4] *Ibid.*
[5] See Valentiner, *Schopenhauer als Scholastiker* (Leipzig, 1901) with
the sub-title "Ein Kritik der Schopenhauerischen Philosophie mit
Rücksicht auf die gesammte kantische Neuscholastik." What can
this author mean by *scholastic ?*

11. Now all this is simply an abuse of language—a sin against scientific terminology. For everybody without exception, scholasticism simply is a *medieval thing*; and it is only in the measure in which the notions brought forward by MM. Hauréau and Picavet refer, to the Middle Ages that they can be of any interest at all in the present study. The capital vice of the formula that makes scholasticism "the daughter of the schools" is that it is devoid of real meaning. It tells us nothing and it cannot tell us anything about the *content* of the teaching delivered from the medieval chairs. The oral teaching of the Middle Ages was the vehicle of the most widely opposite philosophical doctrines; not to mention the fact that, all teaching being then oral, scholasticism—"the daughter of the schools"—is no more a philosophy or a theology than it is a medical or juridical discipline. The *oral* character of the teaching being *common* to all branches of science, that circumstance is useless when we are looking for a *differentiating* character of scholasticism. No doubt, it is intelligible that *schola* meant the teaching κατ᾽ ἐξοχήν (8), and *scholasticus* the teacher of the two sciences which at that time universally marked the crowning perfection of human knowledge. But that trite notion can hardly serve as the basis for an understanding of the philosophy or theology themselves as taught in the schools of that epoch.

12. Moreover, if we only press matters a little, all these purely verbal and etymological definitions become tautologies. Scholasticism coming from *schola*, to say that scholasticism is the "philosophy taught in the schools," is it not simply to say that scholasticism is scholasticism?

It is interesting to compare the present definition with the one commonly given of the Middle Ages themselves. "There is no term," writes M. Godfrey Kurth, "on whose definition there is a more perfect

agreement than on that of the *middle ages*. The
middle ages, we are told on all sides, form an intermediate epoch between antiquity and modern times.
That is the definition of all the dictionaries and
encyclopedias, of all the manuals and resumés. You
must not look for any other from the most learned
medievalists.   However their points of view may
differ in their appreciation of the middle ages, they
are unanimous when there is question of the definition,
and all reply, with an unanimity difficult to find on
any other question, that the middle ages are an
intermediate epoch." [1]

That is to say, in other words, that *the middle ages
are middle ages*.

M. Kurth points out that such a verbal definition
is due to the transposition of a *philological* classification into the domain of *history*.   In studying the
development of the Latin language from its beginnings
down to their own time the philologists of the sixteenth century distinguished three phases: the phase
of classical Latin, extending from the beginnings of
Roman Society to Constantine the Great; the phase
of barbarous Latin, embracing, according to their
view, not only the disfigured Latin spoken by the
Germanic peoples, but even the Latin of the learned
as it was preserved in writing after the creation of
the modern languages; and, finally, the phase of
the Renaissance or of Latinity as regenerated by
Humanism.

To distinguish those three ages of Latin, they were
called respectively, "the high or superior age, the
middle age and the final or latest age." [2]   Modelling
their divisions on those of the philologists, historians
came habitually to regard as intermediate, from the
general point of view of *civilization*, the centuries

---

[1] G. Kurth, *Qu'ést ce que le moyen age ?* (Paper read at Fribourg at
the international scientific Congress of Catholics, August 19th, 1897).
Brussels, 1898, p. 3.
[2] *Op. cit.*, pp. 14 to 16.

that had been made intermediate in point of view of *latinity*.

It is just such an identification that vitiates the definition of scholasticism we have been considering. In the history of philosophy, no less than in general history, we are unconscious legatees of an arrogant and unjust age. The pedagogues of the sixteenth century judged scholastic philosophy *en bloc :* the sum total of what used to be taught in the schools of the Middle Ages. And they regarded those teachings as the *withered fruits* of a barbarous and bygone mentality. Some of those puerilities have outlived the Renaissance.

SECTION 4.—SCHOLASTIC METHODS.

13. Method (μέθοδος) is the way followed in order to arrive at an end. When there is question of philosophy, this end is either its *construction* or *its communication*. During the Middle Ages the system of philosophy called scholastic had its inventive or constructive methods, and its pedagogic or.didactic procedure. We will outline these very briefly.

14. CONSTRUCTIVE METHODS.—Every science takes its constructive methods from what constitutes its formal object or special point of view, the latter giving to the science its specific character (5). Now, scholastic philosophy was not in possession of its ways and means from its very outset. We observe in the formation of its methods a historical progress parallel to the accumulation of its doctrinal patrimony. The early Middle Age period was smitten with an overweening attachment to the *synthetic* or *deductive* method. This latter, starting from very general and very simple principles, deduced from them relations more and more special and complex.

Scholastics and anti-scholastics alike, dearly loved that descending march of the human mind. "It is my purpose," wrote Bœthius, "to build up a science by means of concepts and maxims just as is done in mathematics." [1]   St. Anselm of Canterbury draws from the idea of God not only a proof of the real existence of an Infinite, but even a whole collection of theorems relative to His attributes and to His relations with the world.   Two centuries before Anselm, John Scotus Eriugena, the father of anti-scholasticism, stands forth as the purest type of the deductive reasoner.   His metaphysic is a long description of the Divine Odyssey, inspired by the monistic, Neo-Platonic conception of the *déchéance* of the One through successive generations.   And even at the threshold of the thirteenth century, Alanus of Lille trys to apply to philosophy a mathematical method which reminds one of the *morê geometrico* demonstrations of Descartes and of the theorems of Spinoza. [2]

Though we find traces of the *analytic* method in the eleventh and twelfth centuries—notably with Abelard, and with those who, in the controversy about the universals, insisted on the predominance of the psychological point of view—yet we must come down to the brilliant philosophical achievements of the thirteenth century to witness the complete triumph of the method of observation.   It impregnates and fertilizes the works of the great thinkers of the thirteenth century, the treatises of Alexander of Hales, of Bonaventure, still more so of Albert the Great, of Thomas Aquinas [3] and of Duns Scotus. The new method asserts itself in psychology, where

---

[1] *De Hebdomadibus*, Prol.
[2] Baumgartner, *Die Philosophie des Alanus de Insulis* (in the *Beiträge zur Geschichte der Philosophie des Mittelalters*, edited by Bäumker, ii., 4. Münster, 1896, pp. 29 and foll.)
[[3] Cf. an article on "St. Thomas' Physiological Psychology, by Dr. J. Gasquet, in the *Dublin Review* of April, 1882—*Tr.*]

an exact investigation of the activities of the soul, and principally of the phenomena of sense, intellect and will, is taken as the solid basis of all theories on the nature of man ; in cosmology, where the physical and chemical facts brought to light by common observation or by the employment of the scientific processes of the age, give rise to doctrines explanatory of the universe ; in ethics, where all is based on the study of the free act ; and the same may be said of logic, of theodicy, and even of metaphysics. (Sections 12-17).

Not that the scholastics of the thirteenth century burned what their predecessors had adored. For the ideal of philosophy—of wisdom—is to go back upon the results obtained by observation, and to subject analytic knowledge to the unifying work of some synthesis that sets out from the first cause to come down again to ultimate effects. In all the philosophic matters treated by the thirteenth century, general views abound. The theory of exemplarism studies created essences in their relations to the creating intelligence ; cosmic teleology follows out in all their applications the adaptations of beings to the ends they must attain ; doctrines such as that on individuation are treated successively from the analytic and from the synthetic points of view. Examples of this kind might be multiplied.

In its definitive and most highly perfected form, such as may be found above all in the thirteenth century, scholasticism employed an *analytico-synthetic* method—the only one that harmonizes fully with the solutions offered us on the philosophical problems dealt with.

The history of philosophy helps the constructive philosopher in his analyses as well as in his syntheses ; and it was for that reason that the scholastics questioned the representatives of the Greek and Patristic philosophies upon the ever abiding problems of human

thought.   But history was for them a pedagogical
process also, as we shall see further on when we come
to deal *ex professo* with their conceptions on this
matter.

15. PEDAGOGICAL METHODS.—It is one thing to
build up a science, another thing to *teach* it.   The
Middle Ages employed didactic methods which bear
very little resemblance to the pedagogical procedure
of modern times.   Those methods were remarkably
unified in the West, though with a uniformity that
did not imply immobility.   Scholastic pedagogics
are not moulded in stereotyped forms.   On the
contrary, we witness the rapid spread of innovations,
and a continued and universal progress.   Amongst
the chief causes of internationalism in methods were
the intercommunication between the various intellectual centres and the unity of scientific language.

The wanderings of the principal teachers of the
eleventh and twelfth centuries bear witness to the
great frequency of academic changes.   At the great
monastic or capitular schools of Bec, Laon, Tours,
Auxerre, Chartres, Paris, etc., students, collected
together from every corner of Europe, may be seen
in crowds around masters of world-wide renown.
Adelman of Liège and Berenger of Tours go to
Chartres to hear the illustrious Fulbert.   John of
Salisbury is in touch with all the notable philosophers
of his time.   Manuscripts travelled then no less than
books do now.   *Codices* were passed from monastery
to monastery, to be copied ; some of their fortunate
proprietors used to carry them with them through
all their long peregrinations.

The multiplicity of those travels backwards and
forwards across vast tracts of country—long and
costly journeys by sea as well as by land—grew at
length to enormous proportions, when, at the close
of the twelfth century, Paris saw erected the first
university of the Middle Ages.   From all sides came

a rush to Paris, the *sapientiæ fons ;* and from it streamed forth teachers to spread the light abroad through all Western Europe.

In all the schools philosophy was taught in one and the same—Latin—language. Philosophical works were written in Latin ; and so the expression of delicate shades of thought demanded the creation of a special vocabulary and of a specific latinity.[1] Halting as it was in its beginnings, and disfigured in its later days by the barbarisms and dross of the epoch of decadence, yet the scholastic Latin of the great philosophical writers of the thirteenth century, while wanting in the elegance of the language of Cicero, is nevertheless, sober, lucid and pure in form. It is a language of the initiated. If its formulas are complex, they possess in turn the advantage of precision and richness. Thinkers of the stamp of Leibnitz have paid the highest tribute of praise to that terminology, and those who try to translate it into a living language have reason to know the extent of its resources and of its power.

16. To uniformity of language corresponded uniformity of the philosophical programme. Down to the end of the twelfth century, the seven liberal arts, divided into the well-known twofold group of the *trivium* (grammar, rhetoric, dialectic) and *quadrivium* (arithmetic, geometry, astronomy, music), formed the basis of intellectual culture in all scientific circles. And just as the quadrivium group opened out gradually into various other sciences, so, too, dialectic developed to such a point as to eclipse the two other branches of the trivium ; and to this dialectic universal philosophy became attached by certain ties whose nature we shall investigate more fully later on (Section 9).

[1] See, for example, the *Thomas-Lexicon* of Schütz (2nd ed. Paderborn, Schöningh, 1894) ; the *Lexicon Bonaventurum* of Joannes of Rubino and Antonius Maria a Vicetio (Venice, typ. Emiliana, 1880).

From the beginning of the thirteenth century, when the faculty of arts at Paris prescribed the philosophical works to be taught, and the order of teaching them, uniformity of studies became still more marked : the University of Paris was the great philosophical metropolis of the thirteenth and fourteenth centuries, and upon its regulations were modelled those of the other universities.

17. The programme of studies must not be confounded with the method of teaching : it determines the materials to which the method is applied. Here are some details of the pedagogical system of scholastic philosophy : the commentary, the schematization, the use of the syllogism and of historical arguments, the mixing together of matters philosophical and theological.

Commentary on some text was the chief and natural form of teaching. It was in honour throughout the Middle Ages ; and in order to insure its observance, the faculty of arts in the Paris University determined not only the texts to be commented on, but also the time to be devoted to each commentary. *Legere* is the consecrated term for such a task. The *lectio* is the lesson *par excellence :* the German word *Vorlesungen* recalls its historical etymology. Of course the commentary was not necessarily servile. The master might enlarge at will the outlines of the manual, and raise new questions on those suggested by the letter of the text. The works of Aristotle furnished the chief material for such commentary. But the language of the Stagirite is hoary, technical, and often hard to understand—apart from the fact that most of the scholastics, ignorant of Greek, had to be content with translations from the Greek or oftener from the Arabic. For those various reasons Aristotle needed to be explained, and that circumstance of itself contributed largely to keep the commentary long in vogue.

18. Side by side, however, with the commentary, teachers also had recourse to the *systemátic treatise*, and we find this form followed in quite a number of book-like productions. Still it must be borne in mind that these latter works are not philosophical treatises in the modern sense of the word—devoted *ex professo* to the study of some branch such as metaphysics or psychology. Works like the *Heptateuchon* of Thierry of Chartres, a veritable manual of the seven liberal arts, are the exception rather than the rule of that age. On the contrary, most of the productions of the time have each its own proper plan, and each author has his own independent method of treatment. The *Monologium* of Anselm, the *Quæstiones naturales* of Adelard of Bath, the *Sic et Non* of Abelard, the *Polycraticus* of John of Salisbury, the *De Potentia* of Thomas Aquinas, the *De Unitate Formæ* of Giles of Lessines, the *Reportata Parisiensia* of Duns Scotus, etc., are no more restricted to a uniform plan than the numerous philosophical works that form our libraries of contemporary philosophy. There were, of course, and especially from the thirteenth century onwards, works modelled on a certain uniform type : the *Summæ Theologicæ*, systematic treatises of theology and scholastic philosophy with numerous divisions and subdivisions into parts, chapters, articles, numbers, etc. ; the *Questiones Quodlibetales*, collections of solemn conferences given by the University doctors once or twice a year, towards the approach of Easter or of Christmas. But the plan followed, and the order of the questions treated, are not the same in the *Summa Theologica* of Thomas Aquinas as in that of Albert the Great, or in that of Henry of Ghent. And as for the *Quodlibeta*, these show the very greatest variety ; so that it is quite impossible to try to reduce to any unity the grouping of the questions treated in them. Hence, there is no such

thing as a regular systematization of scholastic
work if we are to understand by that term an
assemblage of problems treated according to a stereotyped plan.

19. On the other hand, both professors and writers
applied to the study of *each individual question* a
triadic process which became general in the thirteenth
century.   It consists in a prefatory statement of
the pros and cons (*videtur quod non ; sed contra*)
of the thesis ; next comes the solution of the question
(*respondeo dicendum*) forming the body (*corpus*) of
the article ; and finally, the replies to the objections
(*ad primam, ad secundam,* etc.).

This method has a logical connection with the
Aristotelian doctrine of the ἀπορία. Aristotle, imbued
with the spirit of investigation which he had
inherited from the Socratic dialectic, insisted on
the necessity of collecting all the arguments and
doctrines in opposition to a given thesis, and of
discussing and refuting them in regular order.   It is
the καλῶς διαπορῆσαι of which the *Metaphysics* and
the *Nicomachian Ethics* make mention.[1]   This labour
serves as a preparation for personal research ; it
defines the points of view and brings out the force
of the difficulties.   St. Thomas Aquinas appreciates
those wise recommendations of the *Metaphysics* in
the following terms : " Consuetuto Aristotelis fuit,
fere in omnibus libris suis, ut inquisitioni veritatis
vel determinationi praetermitteret dubitationes emer-
gentes " [2] ; and again, commenting on the passage of
the *Nicomachian Ethics* just referred to : " Positis his
quæ videntur probabilia circa prædicta, prius indu-
camus dubitationes, et sic ostendemus omnia quæ
sunt maxime probabilia circa prædicta . . . quia
si in aliqua materia dissolvantur difficultates et

---

[1] *Metaph.* iii., 1 ; *Eth. N.* vii., 1.
[2] *In* iii., 1. *Metaph.*, l. 1.

derelinquuntur quasi vera illa quæ suut probabilia, sufficienter est determinatum." [1]

The first application of this didactic method appears in Abelard's *Sic et Non* and *Summa Dialecticæ*. The former treatise submits to the judgment of beginners all the texts of the Fathers relating to the same question and apparently presenting some disagreement with one another. The latter undertakes the same work for dialectic, laying not only sacred, but, this time, profane authors under contribution. Abelard, however, stops short at this contradictory exposition; he leaves the reader in suspense, or rather lets him try to reconcile the conflicting opinions as best he can for himself.

Alexander of Hales perfects this didactic method and gives it its definitive form. While drawing his arguments from the twofold source of authority and of reason, he at the same time uses the abundant materials transmitted by the Greeks and Arabians. Above all, he dissipates the apparent contradictions of the expositions by way of pro and con in the *resolutiones* that follow. These *resolutiones* contain a developed and co-ordinated system of philosophy. From those two points of view Alexander is an improvement on Abelard; and the great doctors of the thirteenth century only perpetuate this method. [2] It permeates all the works of the thirteenth century.

20. To this formal schematization is intimately attached the use of the syllogism and of historical arguments. The syllogism is a didactic procedure of the first order, of which Leibnitz has been able to say: " I am persuaded that if we acted oftener so,

---

[1] *In* vii., l. *Ethic. ad Nicomachum*, l. I.

[2] On the origin of this method, see Endres, *Ueber den Ursprung u. die Entwickelung der Scholastischen Lehrmethode* (Philosophisches Jahrbuch, ii., I), and Picavet, *Abélarde et Alexandre de Halès, créateurs de la methode scolastique* (Biblioth. École des Hautes Études, sciences religieuses, t., vii.).

if we sent one another syllogisms and prosyllogisms
with the replies in form, we could very often, in the
most important scientific questions, get at the bottom
of things, and dispel a great many imaginations and
dreams.   By the very nature of the procedure we
should cut short repetitions, exaggerations, digressions,
incomplete expositions, voluntary or involuntary
omissions, mistakes of order, misunderstandings, and
all the annoying results that follow from those
things." [1]

The syllogistic form appears most frequently in
the summary *exposé* of the pros and cons where
it has the advantage of resuming and pointing the
argument.   It is taken up again in the final replies
to the objections where it brings to light the defects
of the major or minor of those objections.   But it
also finds a place even in the " body " of an article,
and there it enables the author to condense, strengthen
and compress his thought as in a vice.   Thomas
Aquinas and Duns Scotus make the greatest use
of it.

21. One of the best means of finding the pros
and cons of a question is by consulting the great
thinkers of past ages, and weighing their doctrines,
" for there is a presumption that they have a real
foundation." [2]   The numerous appeals of the scholastics to the Greek philosophers known at their time,
to the Fathers of the Church and to earlier scholastics ;
the attention they devote to those of their contemporaries who do not share, or who even positively
attack, their doctrines, are inspired by no other
motive than this.   For them the history of philosophy has a double advantage : it enables them to
make capital out of other people's ideas, and to meet
their errors.   It is then a valuable instrument in

[1] *Letter to Wagner*, quoted by Mercier, *Logique* (Louvain, 1902), p. 171.
[New edition, 1905—*Tr.*].
[2] Aristotle, *Divin. in* s. c., 1 ; *Ethic.* i. 8.

the service of true philosophical doctrine; that is its sole *raison d' être*. Such an absolute subordination of history explains up to a certain point why the scholastics were not sufficiently exact in fixing the historical fact as such. The fault is not peculiar to the scholastics; it is the result of a habit of mind —quite general in the Middle Ages—which did not apply to history a method of strict historical criticism. That is why the historical attainments of the philosophers of this period are not free from error; and we might apply to not a few of them what Henry of Ghent wrote on the subject of St. Augustine: " Philosophia Platonis imbutus, si qua invenit in ea fidei accomodata, in scriptis suis assumpsit; quæ vero invenit fidei adversa, *quantum potuit in melius interpretatus est.*" [1] This desire to find the truth in the writings of the ancients was a stumbling-block to the right interpretation of their texts.

Then, again, literary authorship was not surrounded by sufficient guarantees in those days, and certain epochs seem to have had no scruple about putting in circulation new treatises under apocryphal titles, or about mutilating and interpolating texts. Alcuin, even at so early a date, speaks of the *defloratio* or pillage of other people's ideas. [2] Hence the very serious difficulties that beset the work of restoring and assigning to their respective authors the writings of the Middle Ages. Moreover, they did not all read at first hand the works from which they quoted. A whole crowd of texts, notably of Aristotle and St.

---

[1] Summa theol. (Edit. 1646, Ferrara), art. I. q. 1, No. 26.
[2] The treatise *De Immortalitate Animæ* of William of Auvergne is an almost literal reproduction of the *De Immortalitate Animæ* of Gundisalvi. V. Baumgartner, *Die Erkentnisslehre des Wilhelm von Auvergne* (Münster, 1893). In the full light of the thirteenth century we see two religious of the same name (Johannes de Colonia) dispute the literary proprietorship of a work on the *Sentences*, and the question was fought out before the general Chapter of the Dominicans or Friars-Preachers, in 1269, at a meeting at which Thomas Aquinas was present. Mondonnet, *Siger de Brabant et l'Averroïsme latin au* XIIIᵉ *siècle* (Fribourg, 1899), p. 97.

Augustine, and of certain scholastics then in vogue, such as Boethius and Gilbert de la Porrée, and also of the great Arabian commentators, Avicenna and Averroës, formed the common patrimony of the schools. These are to be found stereotyped in the writings of all, and were quoted most frequently from memory. But men like Albert the Great and Thomas Aquinas must have had recourse to the sources, for in their writings we find exegetical discussions in abundance.

Whenever there is question of contemporaries the state of affairs is different and we generally find the authors well informed. Here, the controversy assumes a character of actuality and its interest decidedly grows. Alanus of Lille is perfectly familiar with the theories of the Cathari and of the Albigenses ; Thomas Aquinas lives in permanent contact with the Averroïst, Siger of Brabant. During an author's lifetime he is rarely referred to save by anonymous designations such as *unus doctor dicit, aliqui dicunt.* Albert the Great is one of the few philosophers of the thirteenth century who are exceptions to this rule. If those covert allusions were transparent for contemporaries, they are none the less a source of considerable embarrassment for the historian.

22. The mixture of philosophical and theological questions and arguments is another peculiarity of the scholastic methods. Pure philosophical questions were discussed side by side with theological questions, somewhat as if we found the same book treating both of physical and of chemical theories. A more typical example could not be mentioned than the group of eighteen questions to be found in the *Summa Theologica* of Thomas Aquinas, devoted to an investigation of the nature and activities of the human soul.[1] They constitute a veritable treatise on psychology which, some have ventured

[1] I^{ma} Pars., qq. 75-94.

to say, " may be taken as complete." [1] And
we find this treatise inserted between a study on
the work of the six days of creation, on the one
side, and a study on the state of innocence of the
first man, on the other. To bring to light, therefore,
the philosophical ideas of a medieval writer, it will
not suffice to put under contribution his strictly
philosophical works ; we must also have recourse
to his theological productions—as, for example, to
the *Sentences* of Peter Lombard. Nay, more, the
quodlibetic disputations often contain, in addition
to philosophy and theology, controversies on canon
law, ecclesiastical discipline, education, or questions
of actual interest at the time.

The origin of this characteristic mixing of philosophy and theology must be traced to the peculiar
circumstances that affected the beginnings of scholastic philosophy, and to the disciplinary relations
established during the Middle Ages between those
two sciences ; but this mixture, as such, in no way
compromises the distinction between philosophy and
theology themselves.

SECTION 5.—DEFINITION OF SCHOLASTICISM BY ITS
METHODS.

23. What we have just said will supply us with
the necessary *data* for an examination of the group
of definitions of scholastic philosophy drawn from
the method of teaching it : definitions which choose
as differentiating characteristic some one process
or other of a pedagogic nature.

And, firstly, a definition of scholastic philosophy
is sought for in the language, or in the use of numerous
terms and formulæ which must be penetrated before
arriving at the doctrine. " Scholasticism," it is

[1] Hauréau, *Hist. de la philosophie scholast.*, II'., p. 345 (Paris, 1880).

said, "is a philosophy borrowing the peripatetic
tongue"; so that there exists a "contradiction
between the matter and the form, since platonic
ideas are clothed in peripatetic language."[1] Or again :
Scholasticism requires an initiation, a sojourn at the
school, a technical explanation. "To understand
it," writes Dr. Hogan, "we have only to remember
that, among the causes which contributed most to
the diffusion of the Cartesian Philosophy, was the
fact that its author and followers took up and dealt
with the highest questions in the language of everyday life. All technical terms were discarded, so that
educated persons could, without any special training,
follow the developments and discussions to which
the new system gave birth. Since then philosophy
has ceased to be scholastic in the original sense of
the word ; that is, confined to the schools. In its
various shapes it has gone abroad and impressed
itself on the literature of the day. It has formed
the conceptions and the language of society[2] . ."
Are those various judgments well founded ? Does
it not seem, on the contrary, that any language at
all that is sufficiently pliable can give expression
to any sphere whatever of ideas ? A system of philosophy is not constituted by formulæ of initiation,
or by conventional vocabularies; nor is the tie
which unites the latter with the former indissoluble.
History furnishes us with significant information on
this point. Stoicism had the rare merit of creating
a new and precise terminology, adapted to an original
manner of conceiving the universe. Yet the historians
of Stoicism do not define it by its use of a technical
language, but by its dynamism, at once monist and
materialist, which made it a doctrine *sui generis,*

---

[1] Huet, *Recherches historiques et critiques sur la vie, les ouvrages et
la doctrine de Henri de Gand,* p. 95 (Ghent, 1838).
[2] "Clerical Studies" by the V. Rev. J. B. Hogan, S.S., D.D., p. 67.
(Boston, Marlier, 1898).

creating an epoch in the evolution of Greek philosophy. The language of the Stoics has survived Stoicism ;[1] it has served other systems, especially Neo-Platonism, and many of its terms have passed over into medieval and even into modern philosophy. Such also was the lot of more than one scholastic formula to be found under the pen of a Descartes, a Leibnitz, and others.[2] Now, it is clear that in those different cases the language is an accessory to the doctrine. It is not the servant who gives his name to the master ; on the contrary, the former is seen to don successively the liveries of those in whose service he is engaged.

As to Dr. Hogan's assertions about the difference between medieval and modern philosophy, they are contestable from more than one point of view. These two philosophies were, of course, propagated in different channels. But this phenomenon is easily explained by the different material and social conditions in which men of science found themselves in the thirteenth and seventeenth centuries. Notably the invention of printing achieved a revolution in the propagation of ideas. And for the purpose of discriminating two philosophical epochs, it is hardly necessary to attach to the presence or absence of a formulary such importance as Dr. Hogan does.

The language of the scholastics is a language of ideas, but then every well-constructed science has

---

[1] Let us recall, amongst many others, the words :—Τονος, λογος σπερματικος, φωναι, σημᾶιον, λεκτον, καταληπτικον.

[2] The influences of scholastic Latin are to be found in modern French. The latter " underwent, during the Middle Ages, the influence of the low Latin, that new language which theology and scholasticism produced from the classical Latin by modifying it to make it suit new mental requirements, and in which the most eminent thinkers and philosophers of our epoch have written. . . . This barbarous offshoot of the classical Latin is at once an original language, serving to give expression to ideas and sentiments heretofore unknown, and also one of the sources of modern French, in all that concerns the expression of abstract, philosophical, religious, scientific, and juridical ideas."—Hątzfeld and Darmesteter, *Dictionnaire générale de la langue française, etc.* Introd., p. 7.

its vocabulary. Besides, it is a mistake to think that modern philosophy has not its technical terminology, though indeed with the drawback of its not being very precise. Descartes has his formulæ (*esprits animaux, pensée*) ; Leibnitz has his also (*monades, apperception, petites perceptions,* etc.) ; Kant is unintelligible without the aid of a vocabulary[1] fuller than the scholastic one (*a priori forms, Ding-an-sich, transcendental esthetic, categorical imperative,* etc.). This want of uniformity in the language of modern philosophers is creating a confusion for which there seems to be no hope of remedy. At all events the scholastic formulæ are intelligible without any master's explanation from the professorial chair ; and many excellent treatises of all sorts enable anyone with the inclination, to familiarize himself with the sound philosophy of the thirteenth century without leaving his desk or his library.

Besides, even granting that its formulæ were accessible only through the commentaries of a professor " in a school," that circumstance would leave us still in ignorance of the thought expressed in those formulæ.

24. Others define scholasticism by its syllogistic procedure, with the attacks and defences, distinctions and sub-distinctions, which such procedure implies. " Scholasticism," says Diderot, " is not so much a special philosophy as a certain dry, stiff sort of arguing, to which Aristotelianism, incrusted by hundreds of puerile questions has been reduced." [2] And nearer home, M. Fouillée regards scholasticism as a heap of empty formulæ, " without ideas, drawing consequences *ad infinitum* without verifying

---

[1] Cf. Wegner, *Kantlexicon* (Berlin, Peters). See, especially for the " *Critique of pure Reason,*" the *Sach-Register* in Dr. Vorländer's edition (Halle, Hendel), or the important commentary of Dr. Vaihinger (in four vols., Stuttgart and Leipzig, 1881-1892).

[2] Works, t. 19, p. 362.

principles, these remaining above examination." [1] Or,
again, scholasticism means "any mode of thought
characterized by excessive refinement and subtlety ;
the making of formal distinctions without end and
without special point." [2]

To show how superficial those notions are, we need
only consider that the doctrine of Kant may be
condensed into syllogisms as well as that of St.
Thomas. Would Kant be called a scholastic had
he given his transcendental idealism to the world
in serried lines of sorites ? Is Leibnitz a scholastic
because he highly esteemed the resources of the
syllogism, and because he himself, in a dispute with
a great mathematician, urged the argument as far
as the fourteenth polysyllogism ? (20) Or, again,
is Wolff a scholastic because he adheres to the
syllogism and the schema, in those well-known
manuals from which all Germany of the eighteenth
century learned its rudiments of philosophy ?

25. Sometimes also, scholasticism is defined, not
by identifying it with any definite procedure, but by
signalizing as its distinctive characteristic, *systematization* aimed at for its own sake. Whilst the scientific
materials accumulated by the Fathers of the Church
exist in a state of disorder, scholasticism arranges
them in a strictly defined setting. Scholasticism,
we read, is *Schulwissenschaft*, the adaptation of science
of whatever sort to the needs of pedagogy. [3]

That fact is indisputable, but it will not afford us
ground sufficient for a definition. In the first place,
the uniformity of systematization in scholasticism

---

[1] History of Philosophy, p. 198 (Paris, 1883).

[2] *Dictionary of Philosophy and Psychology*, published by Baldwin
(Macmillan, 1902), v. 2, p. 492, under the word "Scholasticism,"
signed by J. Dewey. Later on we shall meet yet another meaning
given to the word in the same article.

[3] Willmann, *Geschichte des Idealismus*, t. 2, section 67, numbers 2
and 4 (Brunswick, 1896). We can understand how historians who
take this point of view can call J. Scotus Eriugena "the first scholastic,"
the palatine philosopher having systematized earlier and better than
St. Anselm (see next Section). Cf. Willman, *ibid.*, p. 339.

does not embrace the order of the questions treated, but regards principally the line followed in the study of any definitely fixed question (18 and 19). Then, too, such systematization is not peculiar to scholastic philosophy, and hence the definition inspired by it no longer suits " omni et solo definito." In fact, whether they deal with questions of theology or of civil or canon law, or with scientific questions, or with disciplinary controversies or even simple questions of actuality, the publicists of that age had recourse to the same methods.   Speaking of the dialectic method inaugurated by Abelard, M. Langlos writes : " This manner of teaching and exposition, well suited to develop a taste for argumentation and for the formal ' dispute,' spread rapidly through all Northern Europe, and into Italy ; for the *Decree* of Gratian of Bologna, entitled *Concordantia discor-dantium canonum,* was no less deeply influenced by the *Sic et Non* than the Lombard *Sentences* were."[1] When Godfrey of Fontaines discusses the point of Feudal law which used to give rise to so many quarrels between lords and peasants, " utrum licet habere columbarium," he follows the same plan, and uses the same distinctions as when he studies " utrum mundus possit esse ab æterno."   It was a plan deliberately chosen ; it is in keeping with the logic of the scholastics who subject not only philosophy, but every branch of human knowledge, to the same laws of method (17).   In a word, to define scholastic philosophy by its methods is to mistake its labels for its contents : it is going around the edifice and describing its facade instead of visiting its interior. All the definitions we have hitherto examined present this common defect, *that they stop short at the formal setting of the doctrine without penetrating to the doctrine itself contained within this setting.*

[1] Lavisse and Rambaud, *Histoire générale du 4me siècle à nos jours,* t. 2, pp. 550 and 551.

SECTION 6.—SCHOLASTIC PHILOSOPHY AND MEDIEVAL
PHILOSOPHY.

26. People have been accustomed to understand
by scholasticism the sum total of the philosophic
thought of a distinct epoch, and so to identify *scholastic* with *medieval* philosophy. Accordingly, all
who lived and philosophized in the Middle Ages
would be scholastics. This identification, found
already in Cousin,[1] and openly admitted by Hauréau,
Ueberweg-Heinze and Erdmann,[2] is formulated in
the following terms by M. Picavet : " Scholasticism,
in the strict sense of the word, denotes the speculative
researches of the ninth to the fourteenth centuries,
in which, side by side with certain scientific data,
philosophy and theology predominate."[3]
The origin of this identification is easily accounted
for. Historical studies in medieval philosophy are
of a very recent date. It was customary to regard
all the speculations of that age as a homogeneous
whole, of a very vague and general character ; and
to apply to that whole the no less vague denomination of *scholasticism.* That description has been
retained even by those who have shown by their
works that the homogeneity of medieval thought is
only apparent, and, on closer examination, admits
of considerable divergences.
One all-important fact has been brought to light.
During the Middle Ages there flourished *manifold*

---

[1] Cousin, *Histoire générale de la Philosophie* (Paris, 1864), p. 189.
Cf. Cesar Cantu, *Storia universale. Documenti* (Torino, 1863), t. 2, p.
295 : " La scolastica . . . non è . . . una forma particolare
della filosofia, ma propriamente la filosofia di un certo tempo."
[2] Hauréau entitles the history he has written of medieval philosophy :
Histoire de la philosophie scolastique. So also Ueberweg-Heinze,
op. cit., p. 146 ; Erdmann, *Grundriss der Geschichte der Philosophie*
(Berlin, 1896), t. 1, p. 263. All the Middle Age philosophers and
philosophies studied by those authors, are called scholastic. Nowhere
do we find in them a classification of medieval systems into scholastic
and non-scholastic, nor any trace of such classification.
[3] Picavet, *Abélard et Alexandre de Halès* (Paris, 1896), p. 3.

systems of philosophy, some inter-related, others foreign to one another ; and, among these latter, many were involved in inevitable conflict by the assertion of contradictory principles. *Viewed in its totality*, the philosophical output of the Middle Ages may be compared to a chaos, a mosaic of systems : there is no *doctrinal* unity to be found in its productions. That is the only plausible meaning to be found in such statements as that " scholasticism, as generally understood, is less a system than a chaotic compound of all systems.[1]

After all, we should naturally expect such a state of affairs. The Middle Ages, in the wider sense of the term, comprise the first fifteen centuries of our era ; in the narrower sense of the history of ideas, they embrace the period extending from Charlemagne to the Renaissance (ninth to fifteenth centuries). It is not likely that, during such a long lapse of ages, humanity would have settled down contentedly into accepting one single philosophical conception of the universe, the *scholastic* conception, and that not a discordant voice should have marred the intellectual concert. Such a phenomenon would .have been unique in history. The more we study any given civilization, the more clearly does it present itself to us as a complexus of thought-movements, which meet and combine, or conflict and repel one another.

In literature as in painting, in politics as in religion, in science as in philosophy, there have been at all times *dominating*, but never *monopolizing* systems. The romantic and the classic in art, in politics the democratic and the aristocratic, in religion the heterodox and the orthodox, have been ever and always at war ; and it was not in the region of

---

[1] Lindsay, *Scholastic and Mediæval Philosophy* (*Archiv f. Geschichte der Philosophie*, 1901, p. 43).—Cf. Hauréau : " All systems are represented in Scholastic Philosophy, which, therefore, is not itself a system " (*Dictionnaire des sciences philos.*, under the word *Scolastique*).

philosophy that the struggle lacked determination during the Middle Ages.

This new fact which ought to dominate a history that deals, not with a mere nomenclature of philosophical names and events, but with the logical evolution of ideas, must likewise inspire the terminology by which divergent systems are to be designated. Beyond the problem of terminology arises that of the interpretation itself of Middle Age philosophy. The two problems are inseparable. But as soon as we set ourselves to the task of determining the relations between scholastic philosophy and medieval philosophy we are brought face to face with an alternative : Either we must make the term " scholastic " a huge label to cover the whole complex collection of medieval systems, like the trade marks of promiscuous merchandise, or we must adopt an *a potiori* denomination by restricting the meaning of the word to *one* of those systems, or to *one group* of systems, to the exclusion of all the others. It is the second alternative we stand by,[1] both because it enables us to avoid serious difficulties, and more especially because it puts us on the way to a right interpretation of two or three great facts that dominate the history of medieval philosophy, and which would be otherwise inexplicable.

28. Let us first refer to some of the difficulties that arise from confounding *scholasticism* with *all medieval philosophy.*

(*a*) Such identification is *arbitrary.* That the expression " medieval philosophy " should describe a collection of doctrines is intelligible. But it is hard to see why " scholastic philosophy " should be synonymous with medieval philosophy.

---

[1] Setting out from a different point of view, Windelband, we are glad to see, arrives at the same conclusion : Es erscheint somit nicht angemessen, der mittelalterlichen Philosophie den Gesammtnamen der " Schololastik " zu geben. *Geschichte der Philosophie* (Freiburg, i. B. 1892), p. 210.

(*b*) To adopt such an identification, by applying one and the same name to different things, would be to approve of the vague notions with which people have heretofore been satisfied.

The fact is that no matter what side we turn, the doctrinal horizon grows ever larger. Western philosophy resolves itself into manifold systems. From the eleventh century onward, we find a clearly marked pantheism, renewed from the Neo-Platonic, in conflict with many more or less complete forms of Aristotelian individualism. John Scotus Eriugena (ninth century) and Anselm of Canterbury (1033-1139) are at the opposite poles of thought, and they personify the work of the ninth to the eleventh centuries. In the twelfth century, Alanus of Lille combats the psychology of the Cathari and the Albigenses, who are propagating the ideas of Lucretius and Epicurus. The influences of John Scotus Eriugena are emphasized in the pantheism of Chartres ; still more amongst the Amauritian pantheists, who are openly attacked (towards 1210) by a scholastic, Garner of Rochefort ; and in the pantheistic materialism of David of Dinant (late in the twelfth century), of whom St. Thomas writes : " Error fuit Davidis de Dinanto, qui stultissme posuit Deum esse materiam." [1] This monism, under all its forms, is in irreconcilable opposition with the philosophy of an Abelard (1079-1142) or of a John of Salisbury (thirteenth century).

With the thirteenth century commences the long drawn out struggle between the Averroïst system, which had already found its defenders, and the great systems to which Albert the Great, Bonaventure, Thomas Aquinas and Duns Scotus have attached their names. This fight against Averroïsm passes through various phases, some of them very exciting.

[1] Summa Theologica, I^ma Pars, q. 3, a. 8, *in corp.*

In the University of Paris it is taught in " the schools of the Rue de Fouarre," whilst in the neighbouring schools every effort is made to refute it and to under- mine its influence.   The Averroïstic leader makes a direct attack on the leader of the opposing party. In 1270, St. Thomas Aquinas writes his treatise *De unitate intellectus* against the *De anima intellectiva* of Siger of Brabant.   Along with the doctrinal controversy, both parties carry on a campaign of personalities and intrigues, ending in official pro- hibitions, periodically renewed, and all alike fruitless. Averroïsm survives the thirteenth and fourteenth centuries : in the universities of Northern Italy during the fifteenth century, the name of Averroës is on every tongue ; and it is to hear his theories against personal immortality and a future life that enthusiastic audiences hail the arrival of their pro- fessors with cries of " Speak to us on the soul, tell us about the soul."   In proportion as we advance from the thirteenth century the conflict of ideas becomes more heated, until finally the combined forces of the Renaissance—the German mysticism, the theosophy of Bovillus and of Giordano Bruno, the Platonism of Bessarion and of Marcilius Ficinus, the Pseudo-Aristotelianism of Achillinus and of Niphus, the cabalistic Pythagorism of Reuchlin, and various other doctrines—make a fatal attack on the philosophy whose sway had extended over so many centuries.

Would it not foster confusion of ideas to identify *the one* Scholastic Philosophy with the *numerous* and *irreconcilable* philosophies of the Western Middle Ages ?   " A Philosophy " ought to mean *one* system ; it ought not to mean a *chaos* of systems (11.)   It is agreed to describe as *scholastic* the philosophy pro- fessed by certain great men of thought, by an Anselm of Canterbury, an Alexander of Hales, a Bonaventure, a Thomas Aquinas, a Duns Scotus—by those exactly who, alone from amongst the crowds, emerged like towering mountain tops from the mist and darkness of the Middle Ages. And is it not an abuse of received language to apply the same family name to men who waged open war against the most cherished convictions of those doctors[1] ?

Nor is that all. Besides the Western philosophy, other currents of ideas pass down the Middle Ages, pursuing a course of their own ; and these may not be neglected : Byzantine philosophy on the one hand, and on the other the Asiatic philosophies.

Banished from Athens and Alexandria, Greek philosophy was transplanted into the capital of the Eastern empire, and flourished there throughout the Middle Ages. Its development was slow and irregular like the Byzantine genius itself. Although Byzantium could gather the inheritance of the ancient wisdom in its own native tongue, yet the infiltration of Greek philosophy was less marked there than in the Arabian civilization, where the Greek inheritance was soon incrusted with a large Arabian deposit. But withal, Byzantine philosophy is the product of a distinct civilization. Compare, in the ninth century, the patriarch Photius with the palatine Scotus Eriugena ; or, in the twelfth, Michael Psellus, professor at the Academy of Constantinople, Prime Minister of Michael Parapinakes—with John of Salisbury, familiar figure in the Paris schools, trusted

---

[1] It is likewise this identification of scholastic with medieval philosophy that has led almost all historians of Middle Age philosophy to put John Scotus Eriugena among the scholastics. See, for example, Penjon, *op. cit.*, p. 175 ; Rehmke, *Grundriss der Gesch. d. Philosophie*, Berlin, 1896, p. 89 ; Ueberweg, *op. cit.*, p. 150. " Remarkable thing ! Not only is Scotus Eriugena the father of scholastic philosophy, but he even seems to comprise in his work all its developments." St. René Taillandier, *Scot Érigène et la philosophie scolastique*, Paris, 1843. Nothing could be more deceptive than such a classification, for we find in J. Scotus Eriugena the beginnings of currents of ideas which *enter into conflict* with the doctrines of Anselm, Alexander of Halès, Thomas Aquinas, Duns Scotus, etc., etc. J. Scotus Eriugena is, in our opinion, the father of antischolasticism. See our *Histoire de la philosophie médiévale* (Louvain, 1900), p. 182.

friend at the Vatican and at the English Court ; and you will vividly realize how vast a difference there is between the pompous and oftentimes empty genius of Byzantium, and the cold, speculative reason of the West.

And what is to be said of the bundle of various doctrines gathered together under the title of Asiatic philosophy ?—the Armenian tradition, illustrated by David the Armenian ; the current of Persian ideas initiated by the Greek philosophers, refugees at the Court of Chosroes Nushirvan, and at the academies of Nisibis and of Gandispora ; Syrian culture so flourishing in the schools of Resaina, of Chalcis and of Edessa ; and, above all, the brilliant outburst of Arabian peripateticism both in Asia and in Spain ? All those peoples, who are the heirs of the Greek ideas, have their own distinct turn of philosophic thought, resulting from their constitution, from their scientific relations, from their religious, political and social institutions, nay, even from their very climate and physical surroundings.

Now, during the whole period prior to the thirteenth century, the Western, the Byzantine and the Arabian currents developed in absolute independence : Paris, Byzantium, and Bagdad are three intellectual centres unknown to one another ; and we find in the ninth century three personalities—John Scotus Eriugena, Photius, Alkindi—each professing a distinct philosophy apparently without a suspicion that any other existed. Are all those philosophies to be integral parts of *the* scholastic philosophy ? And must we also admit the Chinese and Indian philosophies, since in the land of Buddha all philosophical tradition had not yet quite disappeared in the Middle Ages ?

The truth is that those syntheses, which abound in the Middle Ages, are so many irreducible products. Even if particular theories are found to be identical in two or more of the various opposing systems—

as, for example, the solution of the universals'
problem by Avicenna and by St. Thomas—they
show, notwithstanding, the general impress of each
system as soon as we cease to regard them separately
and place them in their respective contexts. And
that is why, from a *doctrinal* point of view—which
alone considers a philosophy *by that which it has
in it philosophical*—we cannot hope to find, in the
medieval variety of systems, Western, Byzantine,
or Asiatic, a common spirit which might serve as
basis for the one common title of " scholastic." To
discover characteristics common to so large a group,
we should be obliged to fall back upon *extra-doctrinal*,
or, in other words, upon *non-philosophical* notions ;
upon those vaguer elements which have their value
indeed as marks of a civilization, but do not afford
an adequate basis for a philosophical definition.
So much we admit to be just and accurate in a
criticism with which M. Picavet has honoured us,
and in which he pleads for the identification of two
titles which we feel bound to keep separate :
" *Scholastic* thus ' becomes the exclusive epithet
of those who, in philosophy, hold Thomist doctrines
or doctrines akin to Thomism ; just as *Roman Catholic*
is applicable only to those who give full and complete
adherence to the theology of St. Thomas. But
those classifications are equally arbitrary. There
are scholastics amongst the Neo-Platonists, or in the
time of Kant, Hegel and Cousin, in this sense that
they propagate or imbibe their doctrines in the
schools . . . but in the Middle Ages . . . all
alike, whether orthodox or heterodox, . . . are,
accordingly, *scholastics*. And this is not a mere
etymological and esoteric definition : it implies
characteristics to be found in them all, and
distinguishing them from all other philosophers.

' That is, in our theory.

Christians of the East and Christians of the West, Arabians and Jews alike, belong to a theological epoch, and give a systematic conception of the world and of life, in which God and Immortality hold the foremost place, and which embodies in varying proportions, religion and theology, Greek and Latin philosophy, especially Neo-Platonism, together with the scientific affirmations of antiquity and of contemporary explorers."[1]

29. But if, on the other hand, we restrict the meaning of the term "Scholastic Philosophy" to *one* medieval system, tautology and equivocation disappear.   Far from falsifying, we should be only fixing the fluctuating meaning attached to the epithet "scholastic" at a time when no attention was devoted to the opposition movements that filled the Middle Ages.

Names are conventional substitutes for things. When a thing denoted by a name is simple and single, the name is intelligible to all and adequately fulfils its function as substitute.   But as soon as we discover that apparent simplicity disguises real complexity, we must improve and enrich our vocabulary.   So, for example, the terminology of biologists grew and developed according as the microscope revealed new bodies in a cell that was first believed to be of a homogeneous nature.   The historian of medieval philosophy yields to the same necessity.   By giving different names to different systems he is only respecting the law that governs the development of scientific nomenclature.

We may add that the choice we shall make, when we come to select the particular medieval system that deserves to be called the *scholastic* system, will be in keeping with the language of tradition.   It will be rightly held that, *ceteris paribus*, those who

---

[1] Picavet, *à propos* of our *Histoire de la philosophie médiévale*, in the Review *Le Moyen Age*, 1902, p. 34. See above, p. 16.

have been called the princes of scholasticism by the
custom of centuries, and are still so called at the
present day, have the first right to an *a potiori*
denomination by retaining the title they have always
enjoyed.   Let us respect that custom.   The term
" scholasticism," applied to the doctrine of their
adversaries, is an abuse of language.

And this permits us also to point out that our
suggested solution of the above problem of historical
terminology, not only avoids serious inconveniences,
but also explains several important facts of history
which we may summarize as follows :—*There is a
philosophical synthesis common to a group of the
leading doctors of the West.—That synthesis does not
sterilize originality of thought in the case of any one
of them.—It is predominant in the Middle Ages:* to it
belongs the name of " Scholastic Philosophy."

30.   There is a synthesis common to a group of the
leading doctors of the West, amongst whom may be
mentioned   the   prominent   names   of   Anselm   of
Canterbury, Alexander of Hales, Thomas of Aquin,
Bonaventure,   Duns   Scotus,   William   of   Occam,
and a long line of other distinguished personalities.
These men, in fact, show very pronounced family
resemblances ;   they   are   in   agreement   on   a   considerable   number   of   fundamental   theories—those
precisely   that   form   the   essentials   of   a   system,
because they have for object the capital problems of
all philosophy (11).

That synthesis is not the work of one day, or of
one man.   It was not born of the genius of an
Albert the Great, or a Thomas of Aquin ;   only
centuries could have built up such a vast body of
doctrine   as   scholasticism.   Sparse at first, and
scattered through many glosses and commentaries
up   to   the   eleventh   century,   scholastic   thought
became conscious of its power for the first time with
St. Anselm of Canterbury.   The logical controversies

of the time soon led to metaphysical debates. With Abelard, who gave such an impetus to the problem of the universals, psychological themes began to assert themselves ; and it can be said that in the last years of the twelfth century, the works of Alanus of Lille and of John of Salisbury indicate, by their synthetic tendencies, the approach of an age of maturity.   Neither of these two writers knew of the rich Arabian literature that was to communicate to scholasticism, about ten years later, such an incomparable splendour.   We may ask ourselves how it would have fared with scholasticism, had it pursued an autonomous development, left to its own forces, and deprived of all contact with the rich inheritance of ideas bequeathed by the Arabians. Perhaps it would have brought forth with greater labour, but also with greater glory, the master-thinkers of whom it is so justly proud.

However that may be, less than thirty years after the appearance of the new Aristotle in the West, Alexander of Hales, and more especially Albert the Great, achieved a systematization of ideas, such as the widest circulation of the works of any one philo-sopher would have been unable to call forth in a medium not prepared to receive it.

The unity of scholasticism is seen even in the fifteenth century, the age of its decline, when the regents of the Italian universities rise up in arms against the Averroïstic materialism.   It reappears yet once again, during the sixteenth century, in the revival so nobly attempted by such men as Suarez, Vasquez, and the professors of the college of Coimbra.

At all times we find its common patrimony defended against invaders : from the very beginning the fight goes on ; and this defence, energetic and triumphant in the centuries of its greatness, cowardly and disastrous in the ages of its decay, accounts for the fact that men like Thomas of Aquin, Bonaventure, Henry of Ghent, whilst engaged in interminable controversies among themselves about special questions, join hands at once whenever there is question of defending their common convictions against the common enemy.

31. The unity of the scholastic system does not sterilize originality of thought in its various representatives.

A monument in ideas, scholasticism resembles those monuments in stone that were erected during the same period, and had several generations of men as their architects and builders. The comparison is an apt one : the directive rules of the corporation left every stone-cutter free to follow his own artistic inspirations in the executing of the work entrusted to him. That is why the Middle Ages, while preserving unity of plan in those cathedrals, could yet invite the very lowliest even of its artisans, to contribute something or other stamped with the mark of his own distinct personality.

In scholastic philosophy, similarly, we meet with unanimous agreement in the solution of vital, essential questions—a certain doctrinal minimum which differentiates the scholastic system from that of a Plato, of a Leibnitz, or of a Kant.

But if unity of principle asserts itself in the solution of individual problems, it does not prevent shades of difference, variety in development, and diversity of interpretation : therein lie the differences between the syntheses of an Alexander of Hales, a Bonaventure, a Thomas Aquinas, a Duns Scotus, a William of Occam.

It is needless to add that the common element of scholasticism, apart from its historical setting, is the product of an abstraction, and that the living reality was always this or that definite scholasticism. This fact must never be lost sight of by anyone

who would follow fruitfully the development of the
scholastic controversies.   And hence it would be
misconceiving the debates of the time to imagine
a clan of monks and seculars quarrelling over trifles.
It is only ignorance of the scientific surroundings
in which scholasticism developed that could have
gained currency for those unreasoning prejudices
that caricature it.   Nothing could be more remote
from barren hair-splittings than those episodes in
the clash of scholastic systems.

One single example will suffice.   When St. Thomas
came to teach in Paris, towards 1269-1271, he fell
foul of the older scholastic school of Alexander of
Hales and St. Bonaventure, to which he opposed
a new peripateticism, better developed and more
logical.   While agreeing with his illustrious opponents
on all the fundamental theses of philosophy, he
separated from them on a whole crowd of questions
that were relatively secondary, but yet sufficient in
number and importance to give to *his* scholasticism
quite a characteristic impress.   To plurality of forms
in the individual, he opposed unity of substantial
principle ; to the theory of the *rationes seminales*,
that of the *privatio ;* to the hylemorphic composition
of spiritual substances, the doctrine of subsisting
forms ; to the Augustinian theory of the identity of
the soul and its faculties, that of their real distinction,
etc.   It is precisely in that divergence of views that
the perspicacity of the innovating genius of St.
Thomas reveals itself.   But his contemporaries—
not excepting his brethren in religion—heard his
teaching with a deep distrust.   The documents of
the time introduce us to a series of public debates,
personal intrigues and official prohibitions.   We
witness a general *mêlée* which provokes quite a
storm of pamphlets and polemical works, and brings
on the scene all the striking personages of the time ;
a giant conflict of ideas, forming a perfect parallel

with the most exciting episodes in the history of modern philosophy.[1]

Those discussions show that there were various sections in the scholastic family, and that some amongst them surpassed others in their unity of doctrine and in their understanding of fundamental principles.

They also reveal certain weaknesses.

32. Oftener than once, in fact, in the course of its history, scholasticism witnessed *deviations* from its principles.   Enthusiasts, like Raymond Lully, so far exaggerated the compenetration of theological and philosophical truth as to lead philosophy to the confines of theosophy.   Others, like Roger Bacon, too independent or too narrow, made compromises with Averroïsm, or emphasized the rights of empirical observation so far as to give an apparent footing to modern historians in search of precursors for positivism.   Such men as those were far from being *enemies* of scholasticism ; they tarnished its purity, but in good faith.   Hence it is only right to make a place apart for those " rash disciples." If the scholastics are a party, is it any wonder that the party should have its troublesome members whom it distrusts, as well as its open adversaries on whom it wages an unending war ?

33. Finally, the above-mentioned synthesis is *dominant in the Middle Ages.* In the West, it can lay claim to *the greatest names.* It can also vindicate for itself a *vast majority* of all the suffrages ; for, prior to the twelfth century, most of the philosophers are preparing it in various ways, and subsequent to the thirteenth century, it still draws around it hundreds of advocates who perpetuate and popularize its fundamental solutions.

[1] We have published, with a historical introduction, one of the most curious of those products of passing events, the controversial treatise *De unitate formæ,* of Giles of Lessines (vol. i. of the collection *Les Philosophes du moyen age,* edited by the *Institut supérieur de philosophie,* Louvain, 1901).

On the other hand, Eriugenian Pantheism and Latin Averroïsm, the two chief forms of the opposition, fall into a secondary place, if we compare their prestige and value with those of the great synthesis they tried to undermine.

From which we conclude : Scholastic Philosophy will denote, not all the philosophies of the Middle Ages, but *one* definite synthesis, the most widespread, the most ably defended, and the best constructed, in the intellectual history of the Western Middle Ages.[1] It is, if you will, its philosophy *par excellence*, but not its *only* philosophy.

34. Thus to fix the meaning of *scholasticism* is to fix, at the same time, that of *anti-scholasticism ;* that is to say, of those systems that opposed the fundamental principles of scholasticism, or of certain conceptions animated by other principles irreconcilable with the former ones. If one of the terms is legitimate, both are. " The distinction between scholasticism and anti-scholasticism seems arbitrary (writes M. Valmy), at least for the time previous to the thirteenth century and the formation of the doctrinal synthesis. It leads to representing Scotus Eriugena as the adversary of a system that was not yet in existence in the ninth century, and to separating masters and disciples, as in the case of Thierry of Chartres and Bernard of Tours." [2] No

---

[1] In his *Histoire de la philosophie*, vol. i. (1896), M. Elie Blanc says, on the subject of scholasticism : " It is not precisely *a system*, for most systems were upheld by some people or others during the Middle Ages ; and it is evident, moreover, that scholasticism profits much by all that is best among the philosophers and their schools," p. 378. We confess we are unable to understand M. Blanc's reservations, for he himself writes, p. 381 : " The scholastics succeeded in demonstrating a collection of truths closely allied with one another : in a word, they built up a *system*, without, however, falling a prey to the systematizing spirit." Does the author not contradict himself ? He goes back on the same line of thought in the *Université Catholique* (1902, p. 145), to contrast his view with the theory developed in the text above.

[2] In a criticism of our *Histoire de la philosophie médiévale* (*Études*, published by the Jesuits, 1902, p. 266.)

doubt the scholastic synthesis was not fully finished until the thirteenth century, but it was in process of formation in the ninth and tenth centuries, in the glosses of a Rhaban Maur or an Eric of Auxerre. But the monistic principles of J. Scotus Eriugena were directly opposed to the individualistic realism that lay hidden in those glosses and treatises, and developed as a matter of fact into doctrines whose hostile character hardly escaped the notice even of contemporaries. Then as regards masters and disciples, do they always follow the same paths ? And if the disciple turns his back on the route followed by his master, must they not inevitably arrive at opposite points ? And if so, how are we to avoid placing them in different categories ?

On the other hand, M. Delacroix recognises the justice of a classification of medieval systems into *scholastic* and *anti-scholastic ;* but he adopts it for reasons of another order : " We believe," he writes, " that the division is a correct one. It is easy to detect, throughout all the periods of medieval philosophy, two great currents moving in opposite directions ; but the opposition springs less perhaps from the philosophic content of the systems than from their attitude towards dogma and their relations with theology. We think, in opposition to M. De Wulf, that the essential characteristic of the systems he calls anti-scholastic, is their spirit of independence and of freedom in regard to dogma. . . . The distinction between scholastic and anti-scholastic systems is a precious one, but to us it does not seem appropriate except as referring to the spirit rather than to the content of each of those philosophies." [1] M. Delacroix has recourse to a new criterion : the dependence or the independence of the respective systems in regard to dogma.

---

[1] *La philosophie médiévale latine jusqu'au 14me siècle* (in the *Revue de synthèse historique*, August, 1902, p. 102).

This brings us to a new order of researches in which we shall encounter the opinion of the learned professor of Montpellier.

SECTION 7.—SCHOLASTIC PHILOSOPHY AND SCHOLASTIC THEOLOGY.

35. Of all the current notions of Scholastic Philosophy assuredly the most widespread is the one inspired by its relations with Christian dogma. Some would have it the handmaid, others the spouse or honoured working companion; but for all alike, scholasticism is simply philosophy placed under the power or under the guidance of Catholic theology. To believe those who understand this subordination in the sense of a veritable servitude, medieval philosophy was built up simply and solely to defend Catholicism. The extreme language employed by such authors to express that dependence, exposes them to the unfortunate confusion of ideas already referred to; and many have been unable to avoid it (5). " The Middle Ages," says Cousin,[1] "mean simply the absolute reign of the Christian religion and of the Church. Scholastic philosophy could not be anything else than the product of thought in the service of the reigning *Credo*, and under the supervision of ecclesiastical authority." The same verdict, slightly toned down, is given by Ueberweg-Heinze: " Scholasticism is philosophy in the service of the existing Church doctrine, or at least in such dependence on it that, in a common domain, the latter holds the ruling place as supreme standard."[2] And in like manner Freudenthal writes: " However lively may

---

[1] *Histoire générale de la philosophie* (Paris, 1864), p. 189.
[2] " Die Scholastik ist die Philosophie im Dienste der bereits bestehenden Kirchenlehre oder wenigstens in einer solchen Unterordnung unter dieselbe, das auf gemeinsamen Gebiete diese als die absolute Norm gilt." Ueberweg-Heinze, *op. cit.*, p. 146.

have been the debate concerning the nature and meaning of Scholasticism, one thing was agreed upon by all, friends and foes alike : its complete subordination to Church dogma." [1]   With these very similar definitions, which might be quoted indefinitely, let us finally compare the opinion of one of our most notable historians, Windelband.   He regards scholasticism as a " scientific systematization of Church doctrine, fully expounded, examined and developed." [2] From this so-called slavery, which appears to have been acknowledged even by scholastics themselves (*Philosophia ancilla Theologiæ*), people generally concluded that the rights of reason were violated, and that the Middle Age intellectual movement was, as a necessary consequence, completely sterilized. [3]

Side by side with this first group of historians, there are others who keep closer to the real facts of the time.   These latter writers speak of a " collaboration " or " union " of philosophy and theology, in this way laying claim to esteem and consideration as rightly due to the former, and demurring to the despotism of the latter.   " The deepest and widest characteristic of scholasticism," writes Gonzalez, " is the union of philosophy with theology, or, to

---

[1] " Wie heftig der Streit über Wesen und Bedeutung der Scholastik auch geführt ward, eines war von Freund und Feind zugestanden : ihre vollständige Abhängigkeit von der Kirchenlehre." Freudenthal, *Zur Beurtheilung der Scholastik* (Archiv für Geschichte der Philosophie, Bd. 3, p. 23).

[2] " Der Augustinismus concentrirt sich um den Begriff der Kirche ; für ihn ist die Aufgabe der Philosophie in der Hauptsache darauf gerichtet, die Kirchenlehre als wissenschaftliches System darzustellen, zu begründen und auszubilden : insofern als diese Aufgabe verfolgt, ist die mittelalterliche Philosophie die kirchliche Schulwissenschaft, die Scholastik." Windelband, *op. cit.*, p. 209. In Baldwin's Dictionary of Philosophy and Psychology (Cf., p. 35, n. 2), Dewey speaks of *scholasticism* as " The name of the period of medieval thought in which philosophy was pursued under the domination of theology, having for its aim the exposition of Christian dogma in its relations to reason."

[3] Freudenthal (*op. cit.*, p. 23), criticising a work of Ritter (*Geschichte der Philosophie*, Bd. 7, p. 123), notes as a " singular and incredible " opinion of the author, the thesis maintaining that the Church of the Middle Ages did not interfere in any way with freedom of thought.

express it otherwise, of human and natural science with divine and revealed science."[1]   Two scholars of high repute in Germany, Erdmann[2] and Otto Willmann,[3] and in France two others, Blanc[4] and Picavet, have adopted the same view. The latter has candidly protested, in the name of historical truth, against the fable that scholastic philosophy was subjected to any excessively rigorous *surveillance*. " The works of the scholastics," he says, " bear witness to a *collaboration* between philosophy and theology."[5]   We find the same idea developed in a study presented by the same writer to the International Philosophical Congress (1900), on " The Value of Scholasticism."   After emphasizing the essentially theological character of the Middle Ages, M. Picavet goes on to say : " But just as in positive or metaphysical epochs—to use the formula made current by Comte—there is room for religion, or for theology which is its systematized conception, so, in like manner, the Middle Ages had their philosophical conceptions, as well as researches and theories of a scientific character.   Accordingly, scholasticism is a mixture of theological, philosophical and scientific doctrines.   Nor must we imagine that the famous formula '*Philosophia* (comprising *Scientia*) *ancilla Theologiæ*' represents as accurately, as succinctly the mutual relations of the three factors.   Hagar, the handmaid of Abraham and the type of philosophy, was considered by the Moors as the equal, if not the superior, of Sarah, the type of theology.   The Christians themselves regarded her as a spouse, and not as

---

[1] Gonzalez, *History of Philosophy* (French translation, Paris, Lethielleux) vol. ii., p. 419.
[2] *Op. cit.*, vol. i., sections 150 and 151, p. 264.
[3] " Es ist also ein durch die Ideen und zuhöchst durch den Glauben orientierter Realismus, der die echte Scholastik charakterisiert." Otto Willmann, *Geschichte des Idealismus* (Brunschwig, 1896), vol. ii., p. 323.
[4] *Histoire de la Philosophie* (Lyons and Paris, 1896), vol. i., p. 381.
[5] Report published by the *Revue de métaphysique et de morale*, 1900, p. 650.

a servant in the lower and ordinary sense of the word.
Then, too, St. Thomas sometimes uses the word
vassal instead of *servant* : and we know that some
vassals were the peers or equals of their suzerains.
Moreover, if we examined the systems, the theological
or philosophical works of the time, we should sometimes find ourselves very much embarrassed as to
whether philosophy or theology had the main part
in them.   Of this we can very easily find a practical
proof by studying St. Thomas's commentary on the
Sentences of Peter Lombard—a commentary which
formed a sort of first edition of the *Summa Theologica*." [1]   For the rest, it matters little, from our
present point of view, what those writers may think
about the value, scientific and doctrinal, of that union
of theology with philosophy.   Cardinal Gonzalez,
Erdmann and Willmann are convinced of its fecundity.
Picavet does not take sides.   Others, as Eucken,
for example, infer the bankruptcy of the medieval
conception—the temple of nature built by Aristotle
being so different in style of architecture from the
temple of grace erected by Christ, that their juxtaposition (*Nebeneinander*) resulted necessarily in an
incongruous, uninviting edifice, altogether lacking in
unity of design. [2]

36. Some authors submit the second class of the
above-mentioned formulas to an ingenious widening
process, like what we have already encountered (10)
in reference to " scholasticism."   Just as scholasticism was the proper title of any and every " daughter
of the schools," so might it be similarly applied to
every philosophy subject to any dogma.   The
scholasticity of a system would be measured by the

[1] Picavet, *La valeur de la scolastique*, in the Library of the International Philosophical Congress, vol. iv. (Paris, 1902), pp. 244-246.
Cf. Picavet, *Le moyen age*, etc., p. 64.   This latter study is published
in a volume called *Entre camarades* (Paris, 1901).
[2] *Thomas von Aquino und Kant. Ein Kampf zweier Welten.*   In the
Kantstudien, 1901, vol. vi., part 1, pp. 1-19.

degree of its subjection.   It is in this sense that
M. Carra de Vaux says of the Arabian philosophy
that the capital problem in the minds of its culti-
vators was the *scholastic problem*, meaning the
alliance of philosophy with the Koran.[1]   And he
is able to say of Alfarabi that he "jumped clean
across" the scholastic problem.[2]   In like manner,
too, M. Blanc writes : "These various scholasticisms
would consist in the agreement of the philosophies
in question with such and such religious creeds. . .
The spirit of scholasticism must be sought in this
very accord of faith and reason, rather than in this
or that abstract, ill-defined system, or, indeed, even
in any definite system."[3]   Dogma thus determines
scholasticism.   The Middle Ages produced a Mahom-
metan scholasticism in the East, as well as a Catholic
scholasticism in the West.   The Vedanta embodies
a Brahminical scholasticism, the writings of the
Jewish Philo, a Jewish scholasticism,[4] and nearer
home nothing would hinder us from speaking of a
Protestant scholasticism.

Now, in order to discuss the grounds of those
definitions, and to sift the true from the false, we
must give some outline of the code of relations
established in the Middle Ages between philosophy
and theology.   We shall find these relations in the
parallel *formation* of both sciences, in their *pedagogical organization* and in the *subordination* and
co-ordination of their doctrines.

37. Amongst the problems of scholastic philosophy,
very many had their origin in theology in this sense,
that they arose *on the occasion of* theological controversies.   In the ninth and tenth centuries, the

---

[1] *Avicenne* ("Les grands philosophes," Alcan, Paris, 1901), p. 273.
[2] *Ibid.*, p. 116.
[3] *Ibid.*, p. 115.   Compare with this quotation the statements
referred to above, p. 51, n. 1.
[4] The expression used by Zeller, *Die Philosophie der Griechen*, vol. .
p. 341.

quarrel about Predestination raised the question of Human Liberty and its relations to Divine Providence and Divine Justice ; the Paschasian controversy on the Real Presence of Jesus Christ in the Eucharist brought forth dissertations on Substance and Accident ; the dogma of the Trinity suggested discussion on the notions of Nature and Person and Individual ; Transubstantiation and the Divine Simplicity provoked the study of Change. But all that is not saying that the two spheres of research were confounded (5) ; for the genesis of a philosophical controversy is one thing, its intrinsic value and significance quite another.

Scholastic philosophy and scholastic theology ran parallel in the Middle Ages ; they went through a common rhythmical movement of progress, culmination and decay.[1] If the fortunes of the two sciences were so intimately bound up together, it is simply because religious faith inspired the medieval civilization with a teaching system that was *sui generis*, a system whose fundamental principle was the convergence of all human knowledge towards the study of theology. This abiding tendency is visible in all the programmes of studies that were in use in the monastic and abbey schools. Everyone's ambition, after studying or while continuing to study philosophy, was to become a theologian. Later on, in the universities, degrees in arts were a necessary qualification for degrees in theology. To be a bachelor, licentiate, or master in theology, was the end ; to study philosophy, the means—just as at the present day, in the *regime* of many universities, a diploma in philosophy and letters gives access to the other scientific branches of study. The honour rendered to the masters of the sacred faculty is an index of the esteem in which the science of theology was held. The theologians took precedence not only of the

---

[1] Cf. Willmann, *op. cit.*, vol. ii., section 68, pp. 342 and foll.

" arts " but also of the " law " and of the " medicine " professors. One should examine in detail the minute prescriptions which laid down the uncontested prerogatives of the sacred faculty, at Paris and elsewhere, to see how faithfully that organization of studies reflected the spirit of the whole medieval society.[1]

38. The relations just referred to are extradoctrinal ; they arise from the genius of medieval civilization, from a peculiar organization of public and private life. But we also find a collection of laws which express relations of *subordination* and *coordination* between the *contents* of the two sciences— relations, too, that are just as clear in the minds of scholastics as the very distinction itself between theology and philosophy. Those laws had been already tacitly admitted by the philosophers of the early Middle Ages, were expressed in main outlines by St. Anselm, and were finally codified in the introductions to most of the great theological *Summœ* of the thirteenth century.

Scholastic philosophy is recognised to be subordinate to theology. This dependence—unanimously admitted though differently interpreted by all the historians of the Middle Ages—is summed up in a formula which needs some explanation : *The subordination is material, not formal.* That is to say : while the two sciences preserve their *formal* independence, or independence as regards the principles that direct their investigations, there are certain *matters* in which philosophy cannot contradict the conclusions of theology. The medieval scholastics justified this subordination, because they were profoundly convinced that in Catholic dogma they found the word of God, the infallible expression of the truth. *Supposing to be admitted as certain* any

---

[1] See on this subject, Thurot, *De l'organisation de l'enseignement dans l'Université de Paris* (Paris, 1850), and the documents published by Denifle and Chatelain, *Chartularium Universititis Parisiensis* (Paris, 1889-1894)—and the *Auctuarium Chart. Univ. Paris* (Paris, 1894).

proposition whatsoever, that two and two are four, for example, logic absolutely forbids every other science to arrive at any conclusion that would overthrow that judgment of mathematics. There, simply, is the whole reasoning of the scholastics. It is an application of a universal law of solidarity that is true of all the sciences, whether rational or experimental. We see it in our own days applied to the manifold relations between physics, chemistry, astronomy, mechanics, and in general all the sciences that approach a common subject-matter (*material* object) from different points of view (*formal* objects).[1] The truth or otherwise of the hypothesis—the existence, namely, of a Divine Revelation—does not fall within the competence of the philosopher. But *granted that hypothesis*, the consequence of the conditional is beyond all debate : reason *must avoid* running counter to a dogma *supposed* to be certain, for truth cannot contradict truth. "*Supposito* quod huic scientiæ (that is to say, theology) non subjacet nisi verum . . . supposito quod quæcumque vera sunt judicio at auctoritate hujus scientiæ, falsa nullo modo esse possunt judicio rectæ rationis. *His inquam suppositis*, cum ex eis manifestum sit quod tam auctoritas hujus scientiæ quam ratio . . . veritati innituntur, *et verum vero contrarium esse non potest*, absolute dicendum quod auctoritati hujus scripturæ nullo modo ratio potest esse contraria, immo omnis ratio recta ei consonat"[2]

Such then is the special point of view from which the doctors of the Middle Ages proclaimed the primacy of theology. It is a point of view that the historian ought to understand and respect. Now, what is the nature and extent of this control to which scholastic philosophy submitted ? A certain scholastic

---

[1] We see yet another application of the law in the condition for a scientific hypothesis, that the latter must not contradict any conclusion demonstrated as certain.

[2] Henry of Ghent, *Summa Theologica*, 10, 3, n. 4.

formula has been much abused in this connection. *Philosophia ancilla theologiæ* would seem to deprive the former of all independence of action. Nor is it without interest to recall the fact that St. Peter Damian, who gave it currency in the eleventh century, belonged to the school of those exclusive theologians who thought little of philosophy (40). The formula is therefore suspect, and expresses only very imperfectly the conception of the scholastics.

Imagine a traveller left to himself in a vast forest which he wishes to explore ; nothing to hinder him in his movements and searchings : he wanders about at will, up and down, left and right. But at certain points that are near precipices, some friendly stranger's hand has erected warning notices, that such and such a direction leads to some abyss or impassable ravine. The comparison does not come to us from the Middle Ages, but it conveys their thought : the control which theology exercises over rational research is rather of a negative and prohibitive kind. Theology does not at all interfere with the characteristic outlines and principles and method of philosophy, but *in certain questions* it warns the latter not to reach conclusions in contradiction with its own. We need hardly mention that this prohibitive attitude is conceivable *only where both sciences meet on a common ground :* an observation that will soon lead us to an important conclusion. Moreover, the theologian's prohibitive attitude does not necessarily give any positive direction to the philosopher's researches ; seeing that Revelation contains dogmas that are mysteries, surpassing the power of reason, and that even those of its truths that are accessible to reason can assume a philosophical character only on condition of being demonstrated.[1]

---

[1] The above theory on the subordination of philosophy to theology is very clearly set forth by Henry of Ghent, *Summa Theologica*, art. 7, De Theologia in comparatione ad alias scientias.

39. Besides that dependence, of which we have just outlined the principles and indicated the limits, history also reveals another relation between scholastic philosophy and scholastic theology, an interchange of scientific services redounding to the profit of both sciences, a *positive co-ordination* of both—something quite different from the simple mixture of philosophical and theological matters already referred to (22). As regards *philosophy*, its very character of " scientia subalternata " implies a certain indirect limitation, by the " scientia subalternans," on certain delicate problems, such as, for example, the notions of person and nature. But what we have already said about the subordination of the two sciences finds its application here also ; such limitation supposes that they meet on common ground. Now this borderland is more restricted than is commonly believed ; in quite a multitude of departments all co-ordination of the two branches of knowledge is precluded by the very nature of the matters dealt with (43). As regards *theology*, the question is : did it have recourse to philosophy for a rational justification of its dogmas, for an apologetic of Revelation ; or, as it is usually put, did it make use of the *dialectic method ?*—a question of great importance in the history of theology, one that also indirectly interests scholastic philosophy, and whose solution, moreover, will clear up a question already touched upon.

40. An autonomous science, medieval scholastic theology had its own autonomous constructive methods, just as philosophy had its own too. Those methods are proper to theology, to the content of the Christian Revelation. They have to do chiefly with the interpretation of the Scriptures and the Fathers . . . At the same time, however, the more important group of medieval theologians had recourse, *in addition,* to a subsidiary method, the

dialectic method.   In virtue of that method, theology
seeks the aid of its sister science, philosophy, and
gets from it those motives of credibility that constitute
the preliminaries and lay the foundations of the
sacred science itself.   Furthermore, whenever it lays
down a dogma it endeavours—not indeed to demonstrate it from reason, but—at least to show its
rational character ;   and so the authority of the
Scriptures is supplemented by a veritable apologetic.
The introduction of this dialectic method gave rise
to stirring controversies amongst the *theologians,*
and will serve as a basis of division for the various
parties whose origin and general significance are all
that concern us here.

The argumentative theology that made use of
dialectics, and thus built up " scholastic theology "
proper, developed largely along two great lines, shown
clearly to be divergent by the recent researches of
Denifle and Gietl.[1]   Those were the schools of
Abelard and of St. Victor, respectively.   Though both
these schools alike laid reason largely under contribution, alongside the fundamental study of the
Scriptures and the Fathers, yet they contributed
differently to the final triumph of that method which
was to achieve such brilliant results in the hands of
the great theologians of the thirteenth century.
While the school of Abelard exaggerated the
importance of dialectics, and often applied them
imprudently, forgetting that they play only a subsidiary role in theology, the school of St. Victor
confined the method within the boundaries of perfect
orthodoxy.   The two schools, therefore, played
quite different parts.   " They did not need," as Fr.
Portalié very well says, " to set up as a principle
the introduction of philosophy into theology : that

---

[1] Denifle, *Abaelards Sentenzen und die Bearbeitung seiner Theologia,*
in the " Archiv fur Litteratur und Kirchengeschichte des Mittelalters,"
1885, vol. i.—Gietl, *Die Sentenzen Rolands nachmals Papstes Alexander III.* (Fribourg, 1891).

had been already done by Anselm, and—a little
reluctantly—by Lanfranc. Hugh of St. Victor, like
Abelard, adopts the principle, and both display the
same zeal in its application.   It is entirely false
that the school of St. Victor impeded the scientific
development of the faith by an excess of mystical
symbolism. . . .   But, on the one hand, it is
certainly to the school of Abelard that we are chiefly
indebted for the three essential improvements of
the new theology : the idea of condensing into a
Summa worthy of the name a complete synthesis
of theology, the introduction of a more exact dialectical procedure, and the fusion of Patristic erudition
with rational speculation. . . .   On the other
hand, it is to the school of St. Victor alone that the
glory belongs of saving the credit of the new method
when it was seriously imperilled by the doctrinal
temerities of Abelard." [1]

The thirteenth century profited by those experiments, and the two currents that issued from the
school of St. Victor and from that of Abelard united
in the great theological works of the princes of scholasticism.   According to the teaching of St. Thomas
Aquinas the authority of the Scriptures supplies
theology with its proper and cogent proofs, while
the authority of philosophical reason is of a subsidiary
and accessory kind. [2]

It must be borne in mind that this *Dialectic Method*
to which theological reasoning has recourse, belongs to
theology rather than to philosophy.   That is because

---

[1] Portalié, *Ecole théologique d'Abélard*, in the Dictionary of Catholic
Theology, published by Vacant (Paris, 1899), vol. i., pp. 54 and 55.
For the rise of this theological method, see also Féret, *La faculté de
théologie à Paris* (Paris, 1894), vol. i., pp. 18-22. Torreilles, *Le mouvement théologique en France depuis ses origines jusqu'à nos jours* (Paris,
1902), pp. 8 and fol.
[2] See the Prologue of the *Commentary on the Sentences*, art. 5.   Fr.
Gardeil has clearly expounded the nature of the relations between
these two methods in a study on the *Reform of Catholic Theology ı
The documentation of St. Thomas* (*Revue thomiste*, May-June, 1903),
pp. 199 and fol.

of its *avowed object :* to make the resources of human
reason subserve the *direct apologetic of a dogma
fixed beforehand.*   So much was admitted by the
philosophers themselves.   We find, in 1272, a mani-
festo issued by the vast majority of the masters in
arts against a turbulent faction of Averroïsts, formally
forbidding both masters and bachelors of the Faculty
to " determine " or even " dispute " matters theological.   That would be, says the document, to
outstep the boundaries prescribed for philosophers.
But, as Aristotle says, he who is not a geometrician
cannot, without grave disadvantages, discuss
geometry.[1]   Such texts must be peculiarly embar-
rassing to those who will insist on denying the
existence of a philosophy distinct from theology in
the Middle Ages.

On the other hand—there is hardly need to mention
it—those same theologians who advocated the application of dialectics to matters of revelation, had
been, and continued to be sincere philosophers as
and whenever occasion demanded ; discussing, in that
capacity, theories offered in explanation of the natural
order of things, as, for example, the notions of movement and of efficient cause, and the problem of the
origin of ideas : questions entirely unconnected with
scriptural and patristic studies.   While that is true,
however, there was also another section of theologians
who did not share those views, either on the rights
of the dialectic method in theology, or even on the
autonomous value of dialectics and philosophy in
themselves.   There was always a party of *reactionaries*
who took fright at the spectacle of the heresies to
which the abuse of dialectics had led, and who would

[1] " Statuimus et ordinavimus quod nullus magister vel bachellarius
nostræ facultatis aliquam questionem pure theologicam, utpote de
Trinitate et Incarnatione sicque de consimilibus omnibus, determinare
seu etiam disputare presumat, tanquam sibi determinatos limites
transgrediens, cum sicut dicit philosophus non geometram cum geome-
tra sit penitus inconveniens disputare."   Denifle and Chatelain,
Chartularium Universitatis Parisiensis, vol. i., p. 499.

prevent the repetition of such heresies by condemning the method itself whence they had sprung. Of their number were St. Bernard and Stephen of Tournai. What is more : certain rigorist and exclusive theologians were in the habit of declaring war against *all* profane science, and *their* influence, too, had to be counted with. Arnold of Bonneval, Hugh of Amiens, Peter of Rheims or Peter the Chanter, not to mention the more exalted mystics like Walter of St. Victor, would recognise but one form alone of knowledge, to wit, the revealed word ; and their lamentations on the subjection of theology to dialectics found an echo in the full scholastic turmoil of the thirteenth century.[1] Others again give evidences of a tendency that was more moderate. Peter Lombard, for example, takes up a sort of hesitating attitude. In the Book of Sentences philosophy is for him a mere instrument, of which moreover he makes but little use. He does not regard it as an autonomous science interpretative of Reality.[2] A century before him, St. Peter Damian had depreciated the rôle of philosophy in a similar way ; in his view, it ought " velut ancilla dominæ quodam famulatus obsequio subvenire."[3]

41. To sum up and conclude :—

(*a*) The most remarkable personalities of the Western Middle Ages were both philosophers and theologians,[4] and this double rôle is in a certain way alternately manifested in their works (5, 22). As

---

[1] Mandonnet, *Siger de Brabant*, etc., pp. 46 and 70. There were, therefore, theologians who refused to be philosophers ; there were not, to our knowledge, any philosophers who did not grapple with some or other question of theology.

[2] Cf. J. N. Espenberger, *Die Philosophie des Petrus Lombardus und ihre Stellung im zwölften Jahrhundert* (Beiträge zur Gesch. der Philos. iii., 5, Münster, 1901).

[3] *Opusc.* 36, Quoted by Espenberger, p. 36, n. 2.

[4] Deutsch, *Petrus Abelard* (Leipzig, 1883), p. 427, brings out very clearly this distinction between the *philosophy* of Abelard and his *theology*. Fr. Portalié, in the articles referred to, is evidently of the same way of thinking.

philosophers their pre-occupation was to find an explanation of the order of Nature by the sole light of reason. For that they had recourse to the intellectual legacies of Greek antiquity and of the Patristic epoch (Section 8). They were all the time mindful of Catholic Theology, and professed a submission, not " formal," but " material," to its dogmas. As dogmatic theologians, their purpose was to give a systematic exposition of Catholic belief ; and in doing that they used the argument from authority as the principal proof. Moreover, by employing the dialectic method and extolling its utility, as most of them did, they claimed for philosophy the place of an auxiliary science, and thus admitted it to a unity of a higher order.

(b) Philosophy, therefore, figures in medieval speculation on a two-fold title : It has, firstly, an autonomous value ; and this is mainly the point of view from which it occupies the attention of the historian of philosophy. Then, secondly, it inspires the dialectic method, and, accordingly it forms also the object of an important chapter of the history of theology.

Now, apparently, the majority of historians overlook this autonomous value of *scholasticism* and see in it nothing more than an apology for dogma.[1] They forget that the Middle Ages expected *something further* from philosophy, and built up a complete synthesis of conceptions about God, Nature, and Man, that is to say, *a philosophy proper*, distinct

---

[1] Such, for example, is the view of Fr. Tyrrell : " By Scholasticism we understand the application of Aristotle to Theology, or the expression of the facts and realities of Revelation in the mind-language of the peripatetics." Still the author does not confound, as so many others do, scholasticism (meaning : scholastic theology) with the co-existing philosophy (which we call scholastic philosophy). For he adds : " It was the error of the scholastics to put too full a reliance on the *secular philosophy*, history, physics and criticisms of their own day." Tyrrell, *The use of scholasticism*, in *The Faith of the millions* (London, 1902), pp. 224 and 225.

from the theological monument.   That forgetfulness
we believe to be the cause of the widespread confusion
of those two sciences, and of the consequent depre-
ciation of scholastic philosophy.[1]

Scholasticism is not a mixed science, half-theologi-
cal, half-philosophical.   There is no such thing as a
mixed science, for every science derives its specific
nature and character from its formal object, and
the concept of *mixed formal object* implies a contradiction.   When scholasticism simply is spoken of,

---

[1] We must, therefore, distinguish : (*a*) theology and its methods
of authority ; (*b*) the dialectic method in theology ; (*c*) philosophy
as an autonomous science.   M. Delacroix shares, we believe, in this
view : "M. De Wulf," he writes, " blames us for neglecting the distinction
between scholastic philosophy and theology ; we freely admit that
the medieval philosophers distinguish these two domains (*a* and *c*) ;
but, for them, the first—or, if you will, the last—problem of all philosophy, is that of the relations of Reason and Faith, of philosophy and
theology, and it is on that point their philosophy and theology unite."
La philosophie médiévale latine jusqu'au XIVe. siècle (Revue de synthese
historique, August, 1902), p. 102, n. 1.

On the other hand, M. Picavet wrongly accuses us of " reducing
medieval philosophy to an orthodoxy " under the name of scholasticism
(*Revue philosophique*, 1902, p. 184).   Analysing our *History of Medieval
Philosophy*, he writes :   " For M. De Wulf, therefore, scholasticism
is the agreement of the teachings of the Catholic religion with the
results of philosophical investigation. . . .   So, he really reduces
medieval philosophy to an orthodoxy which he calls scholasticism."
(*Ibid.*, p. 184).   We are surprised at such a judgment.   M. Picavet
has overlooked what appears to us all-important in scholasticism : the
evolution of its doctrinal content.   And he reproaches us for the
very fault of which we accuse himself : the fault of seeing in scholastic
philosophy only its relations with theology.   In reality, according
to our view, it is something altogether different from an orthodoxy
or an apologetic.   If we give Thomism the place of honour, it is not
because " philosophical Thomism in league with theological Thomism
is the philosophy that excels all others and must be the standard for
judging them " (p. 184), but simply because it is in itself the most
complete expression of the scholastic synthesis.   Far from us the
thought of depreciating the value of other similar syntheses.   Finally
the criterium of the distinction between *scholasticism* and *anti-scholasticism* is by no means Catholicism, as M. Picavet asserts (" from this
scholasticism, from this orthodox and Catholic philosophy, M. D. W.
distinguishes the doctrines, etc.," p. 184)—but the antagonism of
the philosophical systems themselves ; and if it is evident to him that
such a division is valueless except for Catholics (p. 185), we believe
that it has nothing whatsoever to do with the personal religion of the
historian, who must always distinguish—no matter what religion he
belongs to—between the philosophical conception of J. Scotus Eriugena
and that of St. Thomas of Aquin.

it must mean *either* theology *or* philosophy, not *both together*.[1]

42. The general relations between scholastic philosophy and dogmatic theology, hold good also, *mutatis mutandis*, between that same philosophy and mystic theology. This latter is a department in the supernatural order, and has therefore nothing in common with philosophical research. To realize this, one has only to see that the " mystic ways," the raptures and ecstasies which encompass the union of the soul with God, and which are described in such glowing terms by a Hugh of St. Victor or a Bonaventure, are *essentially* different from the analogical and negative knowledge of God, arrived at by philosophical speculations (70, 71). They are the steps of a steeper ladder which it is not given to man to climb without new stores of energy imparted by grace from on high. If, then, the great leaders of medieval philosophy had their hours of mystic elevation, we must not infer any *real* confusion of scholasticism and mysticism, but simply a co-existence of mystic knowledge and scholastic thought in the minds of certain doctors. They are at the same time mystics and philosophers, because they are theologians as well as philosophers. If St. Thomas wrote a treatise *De Ente et Essentia* and also hymns to the Blessed Sacrament, it is because there were really two men in him, as it were, obeying two distinct inspirations. In the famous fresco of Taddeo Gaddi at Florence, symbolizing the cardinal virtues, the old and new Testaments, the seven liberal arts, civil and canon law, theology at once speculative and mystic, the artist does not mean to portray the confusion of all the intellectual studies of the Middle Ages in *one*

---

[1] "Scholasticism,"writes M. Elie Blanc,'has this peculiar to it, that it harmonizes philosophy and theology . . . it is, if you will, and it must necessarily be, a mixed science, theology if it proceeds from faith, philosophy if it proceeds from reason." In the *Université Catholique*, 1901 (p. 114).

single science—scholasticism. Rather, he wants
to express the harmonious convergence brought
about by medieval culture between *distinct sciences*,
under the queenly primacy of theology. The fresco
is a fitting commentary on the Bible text transcribed
by the painter on the book that lies wide open on
the knees of the saint : " Propter hoc optavi et
datus est sensus, et invocavi et venit in me spiritus
sapientiæ, et præposui illam regibus et sedibus." [1]

43. In the light of these historical facts it will be
easier to decide whether the subordination of philosophy to theology (38) or the primacy of the latter,
can yield a satisfactory definition of scholastic philosophy. We think it cannot—whether we make the
scholasticity of a philosophy a generic notion, to be
differentiated by this or that regulating dogma, or
whether we apply the term only to philosophies in
harmony with the religions of the Middle Ages, and
notably with the Catholic religion. And here are
our reasons :—

Firstly—Although the *reality* of that subordination
of philosophy to medieval theology is incontestable,
and although it characterizes scholasticism far more
than the method of teaching in use at that epoch
(Section 3), still the present definition no less than
the former is open to the ·same general objection
that it does not point out what constitutes scholastic
philosophy as such, that is to say, in its *doctrinal
content*. It embraces only *attributes extrinsic to the
thing to be defined* (7) ; and of necessity these attributes
are secondary. Hence :

Secondly—Whatever be the cause, the extent and
the nature of the subordination of scholasticism to
theology, is it not evident that this philosophy will
have a meaning in itself—abstracting altogether
from the dogma on which it is the commentary—*in
the measure in which it will offer a rational explanation*

[1] Sap., 7, 7.

of things? From this point of view, the Upanishads contain a pantheist or subjectivist philosophy; the scholasticism of the thirteenth century an individualist and objectivist philosophy. The former might be compared with the systems of Kant and Fichte; the latter with that of Aristotle.

Similarly, if you speak of an Arabian scholasticism with M. Carra de Vaux, or of a Jewish scholasticism with M. Zeller, must you not also admit that such theories as the procession of the spheres, the unity of the intellect, the dualism of God and the λόγος, give to Avicenna's synthesis or to Philo's syncretism a meaning profoundly different from that contained in the synthesis of Thomas Aquinas? To understand the philosophical personality of those three leading representatives of three great races, it will not suffice to say that they are *scholastics;* we must go farther and look at their philosophy *in itself.* And again, Reuchlin also has sought to reconcile philosophy with the Cabal, and Melanchton with the reformed dogma; but independently of their religious leanings, the two systems have also their own proper individualities, because they offer each a rational explanation of the universal order, capable of being appreciated as such.[1] We see, then, that even in *theories expressly related to dogma*, there is room, and there must be room, for other test-elements *besides their dependence on dogma.*

Thirdly—This will become all the more evident when we consider that medieval scholasticism is composed of quite a crowd of doctrines *having no*

---

[1] There is a Protestant scholasticism, writes M. Blanc (*Université Catholique*, Sept., 1902, p. 144), *à propos* of an article we published in the *Revue Philosophique* (June, 1902). We do not deny that the Protestants have a philosophy in harmony with the reformed dogma. But that is not the question.   Our contention is that that philosophy has *its own* signification *as a philosophy*, irrespective of its relation to Protestant dogma.   To deny that would be to deny its claim to be called a *philosophy* at all.   M. Blanc has not, we think, sufficiently appreciated the point at issue.

direct connection with Catholicism.   And this is what
we should expect.   To be in the condition of servant
implies being under the master's roof, or in the same
profession, in the same administration, or at the
very least, being occupied with the master's business.
But scholastic philosophy is occupied with a vast
number of problems that are no concern of Catholic
dogma.   To deny this would be to confound philosophy with apologetics, which have no *other object*
and no *other raison d'être* than the justification of
dogma ; it would be to lie against history and convict
one's self of culpable narrowmindedness in the study
of the great medieval systems.

Nothing, in fact, in the written or traditional
sources of dogma obliged the philosophers of the
thirteenth century to explain the enigma of the
constitution and changes of material nature by primal
matter and substantial form.   So true is this that
Aristotle, who initiated that doctrine, took no trouble
to harmonize his cosmology either with Catholicism
—and for a good reason—or with any other religion
whatever, and that several philosophers of the early
medieval period adhered to the atomic theory *notwith-*
standing their Catholicism.   And will it be said that
the theory of matter and form, so fundamental in
scholasticism, ought not to be taken into account
in forming an estimate of the scholastic conception
of the cosmos ; or that even in Aristotle this doctrine
has no intrinsic philosophical significance ; or perhaps
that this Aristotelian doctrine loses its value in
scholasticism by the mere fact of its being transferred
to the Middle Ages and co-ordinated in a common
synthesis with theories controlled by dogma ?   Moreover what is true of matter and form is true of the
theory of the *potentiæ activæ et passivæ,* of the
principle of individuation, of the distinction between
essence and existence, of the theory of the *rationes*
seminales, of the unity or plurality of the substantial

principle in things ; of the whole logic, psychology and ideogeny of scholasticism, notably of the formation and function of the *species intentionales ;* of the subordination of will to intellect, of the manner of exercising volitional activity, etc.[1] The territory that is common to scholastic philosophy and theology is much narrower than these sciences themselves : and outside that common territory the subordination of one of them to the other would have no meaning (38). Hence that subordination is incapable of defining scholasticism as such.

Finally, what are we to think of the more abstract conception that would make scholastic philosophy a philosophy subordinated to any dogma whatever, and which would see in *Catholic* scholasticism a *variety* analogous to Indian, Arabian, Protestant and other scholasticisms ? Here again the same difficulties recur in a more general way. The distinctive element of each variety is a *religious* and dogmatic element, an *extra-philosophical element*, therefore ; and so we continue to characterize *a philosophy* by *that which is not philosophical* (see *first reason*)—an unscientific procedure. Furthermore, whether the ruling dogma be Brahminism or Mahommedanism, or Catholicism or Protestantism, we forget that the philosophical theories subordinated to such dogmas will nevertheless possess a meaning of their own, looked at from a properly philosophical or rational point of view (see *second reason*). Finally, where there is question of a real synthesis, it will include a multitude of solutions beyond the control of dogma, the latter having nothing to do with the questions that called forth those solutions (see *third reason*).

[1] M. Blanc disputes those facts, which nevertheless appear to be well founded, especially when we consider that many of those questions were taken from Aristotle (in a note in the *Université Catholique,* 1902, p. 145, n. 1).

Fourth reason—Then, in the last place, if we were to define scholasticism as a philosophy in harmony with dogma, we should arrive at this unexpected consequence, that we might and should distinguish in one and the same scholasticism—the Catholic, for example—manifold and contradictory types. Would anyone say that the Augustinian ideology may be reduced to the Thomistic ? And yet is St. Augustine less a Catholic in his theology, or otherwise a Catholic than St. Thomas ? [1]

Even the pantheists, thanks to their allegorical or symbolic method of interpreting the Scriptures, even the Averroïsts, thanks to their doctrine of the two truths, safeguard or imagine they safeguard their orthodoxy ; nay, many of them even boast of having the true spirit of the Gospels.[2]   On the threshold of the Renaissance, Nicholas of Cusa, a Cardinal of the Church of Rome, could discover ingenious means of reconciling his dangerous doctrine of the *coincidentia oppositorum* with his Catholicism. Descartes, Gassendi and Malebranche professed the same faith as Thomas Aquinas, and accommodated their philosophy to their belief.   The accommodation, no doubt, is not so happy, but that is due to the structural weakness of their philosophy itself, and does not affect our argument.

We say, therefore, that to call the philosophies of Augustine, Thomas, Descartes and Malebranche, *scholastic*, is to close one's eyes to history ; for history

---

[1] It is on the solution of the ideological problem that M. Blanc makes all philosophy depend (*op. cit.*, p. 139).

[2] In the Middle Ages no one opposed dogma, but each one explained it for himself.   See, for example, the efforts of J. Scotus Eriugena to reconcile his pantheism with the Catholic faith.   M. Delacroix has found evidences of the same spirit in the mystic pantheists, of whom he has made such a brilliant study (*Essai sur le mysticisme spéculatif en Allemagne au XIVe. siècle*, Paris, 1900).   That is why we think, in opposition to him, that a classification of medieval systems into scholastic and anti-scholastic, on the basis of their submission to dogma or revolt against its yoke, is devoid of utility and at variance with the facts.   See above, p. 52.

represents those systems as occupying opposite
positions and engaged in endless conflict. You
might as well identify the different political groups
of a Parliament on the plea that they are all alike
citizens of the same country. And moreover, if such
an identification of philosophies were possible, it would
be an obstacle to any analysis of the differentiating
qualities of those scholasticisms themselves: unless
indeed an appeal be made *to elements foreign to dogma,*
and specifically Augustinian, or Thomist, or Cartesian,
etc.—a procedure which leads to another definition,
to be discussed later on (Section 11).

Section 8.—SCHOLASTIC PHILOSOPHY AND ANCIENT PHILOSOPHY.

44. A hoary prejudice, sown by the Renaissance
(2), sees in scholasticism a mere counterfeit of
the ancient Greek, and especially of the peripatetic,
philosophy. Brucker speaks of the Αριστοτελομανία
of the scholastics[1]; he accuses them—always on
the strength of Vivès—of having failed to understand
Aristotle,[2] and makes fun of their " supreme reason "
for admitting or rejecting a thesis : " videlicet
Aristoteles dixerat."[3]   Fr. Bulliot, of the Catholic
Institute of Paris, seems to subscribe to those out-
of-date views, when he considers scholasticism as a
mere *phase* of Aristotelianism.[4]

45. It cannot be denied that the scholastic philosophy is most closely allied to the peripatetic, and
that " the logical and metaphysical organism which
is the creation of the founder of the Lyceum, also

[1] *Op. cit.,* vol. ii., p. 885.
[2] In Section XII.: Aristoteles a scholasticis non intellectus,*ibid.,* p. 886.
[3] p. 885.
[4] See Report of the International Philosophical Congress (Paris,
1900), published by the *Revue de métaphysique et de morale,* 1900,
p. 601.

characterizes scholastic philosophy, though only in an accessory way." [1] None of the ancients enjoyed such medieval renown as Aristotle. Even before the West had heard of his three famous treatises on Physics, on Metaphysics and on the Soul, John of Salisbury could write :

> Si quis Aristotelem primum non censet habendum,
> Non reddit meritis præmia digna suis,

and with the exception of the exclusive theologians (41) who accused him of the worst errors of heterodoxy, these eulogiums were ratified by all. We may add too that a number of the great doctors of the thirteenth century—Albert the Great, Thomas Aquinas, Henry of Ghent, Godfrey of Fontaines, Duns Scotus—possessed such a knowledge of Aristotle as many of our moderns might envy.

But there is a long road between the Aristotelianism of the scholastics and the plagiarism of which they are accused. As early as 1840, Ritter regarded this allegation of the historians as a " deep-rooted prejudice " which " he believed he had fully extirpated." Willmann refers and subscribes emphatically to this testimony. [2] Moreover, is it possible that an entire epoch would have abdicated, for one man however great, the right of reflection and investigation ? No thinking man could follow in the footsteps of another with such servility as not to leave after him some mark or other of his own personality.

Perhaps it is because the scholastics themselves were so obstinate in clinging to Aristotle that they are accused of following the Stagyrite like so many sheep ? But let us not be too credulous when we hear the medieval doctors boast of " commentating " Aristotle. For those commentators cannot avoid

---

[1] Gonzalez, *op. cit.*, v. ii., p. 127.
[2] H. Ritter, *Geschichte der Philosophie*, Bd. vii., p. 9.—Willmann, *op. cit.*, Bd. ii., p. 339.

interpreting Aristotle in their own sense, nor do they make any scruple of doing so (21). The Aristotle of St. Thomas, no less than the Aristotle of Andronicus of Rhodes, of Alexander of Aphrodisias, of Themistius, of Simplicius, of Averroes, is an Aristotle clothed after the taste of his commentator. It is quite certain that the doctrines of the Stagyrite were subjected to critical verification. "To set up Aristotle as infallible would be to make a divinity of him," said Albert the Great. "But as he is only a man, he is, like the rest of us, subject to error." [1] Hence it is that scholasticism freely rejects certain of Aristotle's doctrines, such as the divinity of the stars, the absolute quietism of the Pure Act, the necessary eternity of the world. It removes the doubts that clouded his conception of the personality and life of God. It corrects and completes such theories of his as that of matter and form. Several doctrines regarding theodicy, ideology, efficient causes, personal immortality and beatitude, are, from many points of view, veritable victories of medieval genius over Aristotelianism. A detailed analysis, beyond the scope of the present work, would bring to light, in almost every question treated by the scholastics, divergences separating them from Aristotle. [2] In any case, whatever Aristotelian theories may have been borrowed by scholasticism, and whether it appropriated them unchanged, or modified or completed them, it always submitted them to a process of original criticism that redounded to its own advantage as a new and distinct method of philosophizing.

46. Then, too, scholasticism was influenced by other philosophies besides the peripatetic. Pythagorism, Atomism, Platonism, Epicurianism, Stoicism,

---

[1] "Qui credit Aristotelem fuisse Deum, ille debit credere quod nunquam erravit. Si autem credit ipsum esse hominem, tunc procul dubio errare potuit sicut et nos." Phys., lib. viii., tract. i., cap. xiv.
[2] See some efforts in this direction in Talamo, *L'Aristotélisme de la scolastique* (Paris, 1876).

Neo-Platonism, the new ideas of the Patristic philosophy and notably Augustinism, occupy a place
which has been for ages unacknowledged in Western
medieval controversies.   Plato and St. Augustine
excited a degree of admiration which rivalled the
enthusiastic homage paid to Aristotle.   So much
so that in the thirteenth century we find, in opposition
to the peripateticism of the Thomist school, an
important group of scholastics inspired chiefly by
Augustinian sympathies (31).   If a fanatical "ipse-
dixitism" was the reproach of the decadence, the
philosophers of the great scholastic century are free
from it.   *Locus ab auctoritate quæ fundatur super
ratione humana est infirmissimus.*[1]   What guided
the scholastics in borrowing from the past was by no
means their blind cult of some great figure of history,
but their thirst after truth for its own sake (21).
As one of themselves is represented to have said,
they climbed on the shoulders of the giants of
antiquity in order to discern a *still vaster stretch* of
the intellectual horizon.[2]   Scholasticism asks light
of all previous philosophies, but it is the slave of
none of them.   In its perfect form it is the issue
of a specific eclecticism.   Its borrowed materials
are arranged in a new setting and incorporated into
an independent and original structure.

SECTION 9.—SCHOLASTIC PHILOSOPHY AND THE
MEDIEVAL SCIENCES.

47. Scholastic philosophy was made to harmonize
not only with Catholic dogma, but also with the
rational and natural sciences,[3] in conformity with

---

[1] St. Thomas Aquinas, *Summa Theol.*, I a, q. i., art. 8, ad 2.
[2] " Nos esse quasi nannos gigantium humeris insidentes, ut possimus
plura iis et remotiora videre." Quoted by Willmann, *Didaktik* (Brunswick, 1903), v. i., p. 272.
[3] See, for example, definition quoted on p. 44.

the all-pervading spirit of systematization that marks the intellectual work of the Middle Ages. To understand these relations between philosophy and the sciences, we must take notice of the then existing general classification of human knowledge. On this question, as on many others, we can say that notwithstanding numerous divergences the general attitude of scholasticism has remained unchanged. The thirteenth century consciously and explicitly formulated a system whose fragmentary outlines were all that existed in the early Middle Ages. We may accordingly recognise two principal periods in the history of the classification of the sciences.[1]

From the time of Alcuin the trivium and quadrivium furnished the materials for all scientific teaching (16). It is well known that the arts of the quadrivium were never able to rival in popularity the trilogy of Grammar, Rhetoric and Dialectic, and that the latter of these three was not long about eclipsing the other two branches of its group.[2] But dialectic is only the vestibule of philosophy, or at the very most one of its divisions and not the principal one. How then did universal philosophy find a place within the pedagogic framework of the liberal arts ? The problems of metaphysics, theodicy, psychology and ethics, almost entirely unknown in the eighth century, and raised by degrees afterwards, form a very considerable body of doctrine. Was this *a development, an offshoot from dialectic,* so that all philosophy should be found in the trivium ; or are *all* the liberal arts no more than a *preparation for philosophy,* which accordingly, from the beginning of the eleventh century (to fix an approximate date), would assert itself between the quadrivium and trivium below, and theology above ? The former

---

[1] See an interesting work by J. Maritain, *Problème de la classification des sciences d'Aristote à saint Thomas* (Paris, 1901).

[2] See Willmann, *Didaktik* (Brunswick, 1903), v. i., pp. 266 and fol.

of these explanations, commonly admitted and even generalized,[1] will be found to suit well enough the beginnings of Western pedagogy, and the unsettled notions accepted by the earlier generations of teachers, contemporaries of Alcuin.[2]   But the second interpretation is more in keeping with the genius of scholasticism.   It points to a tendency that took shape with Scotus Eriugena (ninth century), asserted itself in Abelard (eleventh century), and finally triumphed in the twelfth century in these views of Hugh of St. Victor : " Sunt enim (septem artes liberales) quasi optima quædam instrumenta et rudimenta quibus via paratur animo ad plenam philosophicæ veritatis notitiam."[3]   Then finally it falls in with the systematization of sciences adopted in the thirteenth century.

48. This systematization took its final shape as soon as the introduction of the greater works of Aristotle gave a new impetus to scholastic studies. The liberal arts are not removed from the programme, but their role as preparatory studies is clearly established,[4] and much of their subject-matter reappears in the wider classification now adopted.   This latter is peripatetic in spirit and origin ; it turns on the Aristotelian conception of *sapientia*, or of *scientia* in the fullest and deepest sense of the word.   Its general outline is as follows : The special sciences are devoted to a detailed study of nature ; each of them deals with some single category of the objects

---

[1] See, for example, Ferrère, *La division des sept arts libéraux* (*Annales de Philosophie chretienne*, 1900, p. 282).

[2] This is, we believe, the view of M. Mariétan.   See *op. cit.*, pp. 86 and 805.

[3] *Erud. didasc.* l. 3 (Migne's edit., v. 176), col. 768.   Quoted by Mariétan, *op. cit.*, p. 841.

[4] In proof of which we may quote this text of St. Thomas, written *a propos* of an expression of the same view by Hugh of St. Victor : " *his* (that is, the liberal arts) *primum erudiebantur qui discere volebant philosophiam* ; et ideo in trivium et quadrivium distinguuntur eo quod his quasi quibusdam viis vivax animus ad secreta philosophiæ introeat." *In lib. Boetii de Trinitate*, q. v. a. 1 (ed. Vives, p. 528, v. 28).

that come under our observation, and approaches them from some one special point of view which constitutes the formal object of that science, gives it its specific character, and determines its principles and method.   An example given above to illustrate the difference between astronomy and what we now call physics, will make this perfectly clear (Sect. 5).

That the full course of philosophy in the thirteenth century included scientific matters, will be evident to anyone who consults the regulation issued by the Faculty of Arts at Paris, on the 19th of March, 1255, *de libris qui legendi essent.*   These comprise commentaries on the various scientific treatises of Aristotle, especially on the first book on meteors, on the treatises on the heavens and on the world, on generation, on the senses and sensation, on sleep and waking, on memory, on plants and on animals.   There the *magistri* had certainly sufficient data for instructing the " artists " on astronomy, botany, physiology and zoology—not to mention the fact that Aristotle's *Physics,* the recognised classic text, opened up numerous questions on physics and chemistry in the modern acceptation of these terms.

But this analytic glance at the various departments of the world of sense does not embrace all that is knowable in it, and the mind is by no means satisfied with such a disconnected and encyclopedic view of things.   Science *par excellence*—that is, philosophy—being, in the Aristotelian and scholastic conception of the matter, a knowledge of the very inner nature of things, demands a *regressive* movement of thought. " It has for its object, not the discovery of any new objects of knowledge by way of analysis whether direct or indirect, but the *synthetic* explanation of the results already reached by analysis."[1]   When the study of nature in detail is carried far enough, " a more mature reflection on the results may suggest

[1] Mercier, *Ontologie* (Louvain, 1903), p. 18.

investigations of a new order : May not the beings and groups of beings observed separately, be perhaps examined together to see what they have in common ? And if, by an effort of abstraction, a common intelligible aspect be found in them, may we not be able, *by means of that common intelligible aspect*, that is to say, *synthetically*, to understand more fully the results obtained by our previous work of analysis ? That, precisely, is the object of *science properly so called*, of what Aristotle defines as the knowledge of things by their causes or principles—of what we nowadays prefer to call philosophy."[1]

Philosophy thus becomes the science *par excellence*, because it seeks a synthetic and deductive explanation of things.   In a way, it knows all things—inasmuch as its way of knowing, its reason for knowing, includes and rules over all things.   *Sapientia est scientia quæ considerat primas et universales causas.*[2]

49. Now the scholastics, following up the Aristotelian conception, brought out the nature of this synthetic process : as abstraction is the law of the human mind (Section 16), they came to discern in the world of knowable things, three common or all-embracing intelligible aspects or objects, fruits of a threefold process of abstraction, each effort of which surpassed the preceding one by the wideness and depth of the reality it seized.   The division of speculative philosophy into physics, mathematics and metaphysics, is based on these three steps in the synthetic or regressive consideration of the totality of things.   It is found on the first page of Avicenna's metaphysics as well as in practically all the works of St. Thomas.[3]   No other scientific classification can ever rival it in endurance, seeing that it has reigned supreme from Aristotle to Descartes, and that

---

[1] *Ibid.*, pp. ii.-iii.
[2] Thomas Aquinas, *In Metaph.*, I, 2.
[3] Avicenna, *Metaphysica*, Venice edition, 1495, fol. I, R.A—St. Thomas Aquinas, *In Lib. Boetii de Trinitate*, q. 5, a. 1, and elsewhere.

it can still compare favourably with even the most popular of our modern classifications.

Physics, in the older and etymological meaning of the word φύσις, studies the sense world as subject to change or movement. Botany and Zoology, for example, pass over the characteristics peculiar to *this* or *that individual* plant or animal—for science is of the *universal* only—but the realities which these two sciences fix upon in *the* plant or in *the* animal, or in the various classes of plants and animals, are of necessity restricted to some group or groups of *living* things. Physics, on the contrary, lays hold of a reality which is not confined to any special class of bodies, but one which is common to all bodies as such : corporeal change and the inner nature of corporeal things as subject to that universal law of evolution or change.

But throughout its ever-varying forms of change, there is one persisting fundamental property which every body retains—its quantity. To follow up the study of that one property, separating, in thought and by thought, the quantity itself from the body which it quantifies, and looking only at the quantity itself as such, quantity as intelligible, therein lies the whole work of *Mathematics*.

Metaphysics or *Transphysics*, sometimes also called *Theology*, rises one degree higher still in abstraction and consequently also in generalization. It passes over the reality of change by which bodies reveal themselves to the physical scientist, and reaches beyond the fundamental attribute of quantity, that inseparable property of bodies,—in order to grasp the substance itself of them, the very being of things. And even if the things which the metaphysician studies are of a sensible, material nature, he studies them apart from their materiality ; so that the science of *being* came to be called without distinction the science of the *immaterial*.

Physics, Mathematics, Metaphysics : such is the trilogy of speculative philosophy, of the synthetic knowledge of the universal order of things. These ideas will be further developed when we come to pass in review the fundamental doctrines of each of those branches (Sections 12-17).

To complete this tableau of the classification of philosophy, we must add to the group of speculative sciences in which disinterested knowledge is its own end, a group of practical sciences in which knowledge is subordinated to our conduct or to our activity. " Theoreticus sive speculativus intellectus in hoc proprie ab operativo sive practico distinguitur, quod speculativus habet pro fine veritatem quam considerat, practicus autem veritatem consideratam ordinat in operationem tamquam in finem." [1] *Logic* which regulates the acts of the understanding so as to secure by their normal functioning the acquisition of truth, and *Moral* which directs our free acts towards our last end, are the two practical sciences that were mainly cultivated. The preliminaries of logic are grammar and rhetoric, and their official teaching was organized by the Paris Faculty of Arts on the lines of the ancient *trivium*. On the other hand, moral was accompanied by historical studies, chiefly by Bible History and a part of that wide department nowadays covered by the name of Social Sciences. [2]

The subjoined scheme indicates the relations to philosophy, of the sciences that received most attention from the philosophers of the thirteenth century:—

Philosophy.		Special Sciences connected.
A.—Theoretical Sciences	1. Physics.	Astronomy, Botany, Zoology, Chemistry, Physics (in the modern sense).
	2. Mathematics.	
	3. Metaphysics.	
B.—Practical Sciences	4. Logic.	Grammar, Rhetoric.
	5. Moral.	Bible History, Social and Political Sciences.

---

[1] Thomas Aquinas, *In Lib. Boetii de Trinitate*, q. v. a. 1 (Vives edition, vol. 28, pp. 526 and 527.)

[2] Willmann, *Gesch. d. Idealismus*, vol. ii., p. 418.

50. This hierarchical conception of the various branches of human knowledge is the source of the relations established in the Middle Ages between philosophy and the special sciences. In the first place, the special sciences were not marked off from one another nor separated from philosophy as they are to-day. They were in process of formation. They rested on rudimentary observations, and the distinction between ordinary and scientific knowledge was unknown. They had their *raison d' être* as a preparation for philosophy rather than as independent branches of study.[1] In the second place it was inevitable that scholastic philosophy should assume a scientific character. How could it be otherwise, seeing that the detailed analytical data furnished by the special sciences that deal with physical nature are the indispensable materials for those synthetic views and large conceptions that form the proper object of philosophy ? In the sciences no less than in philosophy one and the same fundamental law governs the ideological process : the closest possible knowledge of the material world is the proper, adequate and natural object of the human intellect (Section 16). Therefore ought not every interpretation of the world, including the synthetic explanation sought by physics, mathematics, metaphysics even, rest on observation at every moment, and at every single step by which its progress advances ? Without such abiding contact with the living facts of the experimental sciences, what could the whole structure hope to be but a mere chimera devoid of all reality ? In the third place, medieval scholars recognised no *distinction of nature* between the special sciences and philosophy, since both are built up by one and the same intellectual process of abstraction. There

---

[1] Hence the current notion that in the Middle Ages the sciences formed an integral part of philosophy. " Die Naturwissenschaft ist den Scholastikern als Physik ein Teil der Philosophie." Willmann, *op. cit.*, vol. ii., p. 416.—Cf. Hogan, *op. cit.*, p. 48.

is only a difference of *degree*, resulting from the
degree of abstraction to which the world is submitted
in each : while the particular science selects for itself
ontological aspects special to *one* group of things,
the synthetic science of philosophy embraces pro-
founder aspects that are common to *all* material
things.

51. This *principle* of the convergence of philosophy
and the sciences, as understood in the Middle Ages,
gives unity and solidarity to the various departments
of human knowledge.   It has many excellent reasons
to recommend it.   The same, however, cannot be
said of all the *applications* of the principle in the
Middle Ages.   We shall not be in a position to determine exactly how far those applications were war-
ranted or unwarranted until we have tabulated from
special monographs the numerous scientific theories
of that time.   This detailed study, though scarcely
better than begun,[1] has already shown that even in
this direction the thirteenth century made considerable advances.   When we shall have separated the
elements of observation and experiment on the one
hand from the philosophical theories based upon them
on the other, we shall be able to assign their true
value to each.

The scientific observations made in the Middle Ages
vary much in value.   Some are correct though
superficial ;   others are prejudiced, *à priori*, ill-
conducted and trivial.   When the scholastics saw
that the change of wine to vinegar, or of food to flesh
and blood, was a substantial change, they started

---

[1] Works have been published on the sciences of the Middle Ages.
For example : Jessen, *Botanik der Gegenwart und Vorzeit* (Leipzig,
1864)—Carus, *Geschichte der Zoologie* (Munich, 1872)—Günther, *Studien
zur Geschichte der mathem. und phys. Geographie*—Berthelot, *Les
origines de l'alchimie* (Paris, 1885)—*Introduction à l'étude de la chimie
des anciens et du moyen âge* (Paris, 1889)—*Histoire des sciences. La
chimie au moyen âge* (Paris, 1893) ; etc.   There are also numerous
monographs, chiefly on Albert the Great and Roger Bacon.   On the
former, see also E. Michaël, *Geschichte des deutschen Volkes* (Fribourg,
1903), v. iii., pp. 396, 445, etc.

from *data* that were no doubt superficial—seeing that they were ignorant of the chemical constitution of bodies—but nevertheless from facts faithfully observed. On the other hand, when they relied on the faith of antiquity to infer from the apparent immutability of the stars that the matter of the heavenly bodies can be neither generated nor corrupted, they were accepting a fanciful *datum* on the strength of its traditional character rather than of any claim it could have to truth (78). If roses could reason they should infer the immortality of gardeners, "because never in the memory of a rose was a gardener seen to die!" The medieval encyclopedias compiled by such men as Isidore of Seville, Rhaban Maur, Herrad of Landsberg, Hugh of St. Victor and Vincent of Beauvais are full of extraordinary allegations, strange mixtures of fact and fancy, curious in the extreme, and bearing ample evidence of an utter carelessness about verifying observations and experiences.[1] Even the more distinguished of these men,—Albert the Great, for example, whose scientific knowledge was remarkable,—were not above such puerilities. Great mechanical inventions like the telescope and microscope could alone give men that passion for the natural sciences which is characteristic of modern times. But the thirteenth century made none of those discoveries : what wonder then that it did not largely use or profit by inductive methods ? The fault is due to a variety of causes which we are not called upon here to investigate ; assuredly, however, *Philosophy* cannot reasonably be blamed for failing to perform a task that was not within its competence.

But, like science, like philosophy. Observations, accurate though commonplace, could and did lead to legitimate synthetic views : Phenomena like the transformation of wine support the hylemorphic

[1] Willmann, Didaktik, v. i., pp. 275 and fol.

theory of a twofold constitutive element in bodies, primal matter and substantial form.   On the other hand, erroneous conceptions of fact engendered false, fanciful generalizations, such as the whole cosmology of the celestial bodies, the theory of the four sublunary elements and all that is involved in it (Section 15). Accidentally, no doubt, such false *data* could have led to true conclusions : *Ex vero non sequitur nisi verum ; ex falso sequitur quodlibet.*

Furthermore—and this is a point that deserves attention—as the forms of all nature appeared to be eminently simple in character, thanks to the childish and superficial observations of that age, those people easily flattered themselves that they had wrested from nature practically all her secrets ! Hence the striking tendency to hasty generalizations, and the mania for making the facts of experience square with the needs of some preconceived theory in order to fit them by force into the current philosophical synthesis.   Such procedure is against the nature of things : it is like trying to build the dome of an edifice before the foundation.

Those vices of observation and generalization reached a climax in the hollow and inflated science of the epoch of the decadence, and exerted there a most fatal influence on the destinies of scholasticism (Section 19).

Section 10.—Scholastic Philosophy and the Problem of Universal Ideas

52. The definitions we have so far examined (Sections 3-9) all contain a " soul of truth."   Those of them that aim at connecting philosophy with some body of doctrine, such as theology or the special sciences (Sections 8 and 9) are deeper in insight and richer in meaning than those which try to define it

by its relation to some superficial non-doctrinal element (Sections 3-7). Still, neither of the two classes alone, nor both combined, can satisfy anyone who wants to understand scholasticism *in itself* and to get at its real genius ; they have all the common drawback of *defining scholastic philosophy by that which is not philosophy* (7). We cannot reach the heart of the system without familiarizing ourselves with the answers which scholasticism has given to the great philosophical questions raised by human enquiry, and seeking in these answers the character of the scholastic system. " It is clear," writes Willmann, " that the principle of development in medieval scholasticism is to be sought, not in its relations with antiquity, or in its theological aspect, but in the domain of its purely philosophical speculations." [1] But there are two senses in which the word *philosophy* is not uncommonly used (4). In its stricter meaning it is a complete and systematic collection of theories explicative of the universal order of things (55). It is, however, also taken to mean not the complete system but one or more isolated doctrines, answering to *one* or *more* of the problems raised by philosophers.

53. It is from this second point of view philosophy is regarded by those who reduce scholasticism to an endless dispute about Universals. Hauréau takes this controversy for the scholastic problem *par excellence*. He wants to know nothing further from the long procession of doctors who pass over his pages, than their opinions on the three questions proposed by Porphyry. The scholastics, says Taine, went mad over the question of the universals, " the only one bequeathed to them," " so abstract, and so confusingly complicated by the hair-splitting

---

[1] " Es wird ersichtlich dass der Nerv der Entwickelung der Scholastik im Mittelalter wider in ihrem Verhältnisse zum Altertume, noch in ihrer theologischen Seite zu suchen ist, sondern im Gebiete des eigentlichen Philosophierens." *Geschichte des Idealismus*, t. ii.. p. 349.

discussions of the Greeks." [1] Or, again, according to
M. Penjon : Philosophy found itself reduced, "in its
ultimate analysis, to controversies like those between
nominalists and realists, so obscure that we can
nowadays scarcely understand the extraordinary
amount of interest at that time attaching to them." [2]
But M. Penjon is sadly mistaken : the problem about
the nature of the Universal is the common inheritance
of all philosophies ; we find it in India as well as in
Greece, in the Middle Ages as in the modern epoch,
amongst Kantians and amongst German pantheists.
Even those, however, who, with Hauréau as against
Penjon, show a juster appreciation of the real interest
and significance of those time-honoured controversies,
do not go far enough by merely pointing to them
as forming "the scholastic problem." To understand
and define a system of philosophy it is not enough
to indicate *the problem or problems* it deals with ; the
solutions offered in it should be also outlined. Willmann, for example, takes account of those solutions,
when he teaches that the dominant note of the
scholastic philosophy is "the reconciliation of idealism
and realism by the immanence of the idea in the
sense reality." [3] The notion conveyed in those few
words by the learned professor of Prague is at once
accurate and profound ; we believe, however, that
it is incomplete. [4]

54. The early medieval philosophers discussed
this problem of the universals according to the well-
known terms in which it was raised by Porphyry
in his *Isagoge*. Now, the Alexandrian philosopher
divides the problem into three parts : (1) Do *genera*
and *species* really exist in Nature, or are they mere

---

[1] *Hist. de la Litter. Anglaise*, t. iii., p. 222.
[2] Penjon, *Précis d'histoire de philosophie*, p. 174.
[3] *Geschichte des Idealismus*, t. ii., p. 322.
[4] It is completed fully by the author's brilliant exposition of scholasticism in Sections 70-73. The author's attitude, moreover, is explained
by the general point of view of the whole work as indicated by the title.

creations of the mind ?   (2) If they subsist really,
are they corporeal or incorporeal things ?   (3) And,
finally, do they exist *apart* from the things of the
world of sense, or are they realized *in* those things ?
" Mox de generibus et speciebus illud quidem sive
subsistant sive in nudis intellectibus posita sint, sive
subsistentia corporalia sint an incorporalia, et utrum
separata a sensibilibus an in sensibilibus posita et
circa hæc consistentia, dicere recusabo."   It is quite
plain that this text of Porphyry's is completely
within the domain of metaphysics.   In the first
question—on which the remaining two hinge—it is
the *absolute reality* of the universals, their *existence* or
non-existence that is in dispute.   It is in this crude
and undeveloped form we find the question treated in
early scholasticism.   Its first disputants directed
their attention exclusively to the *ontological* aspect
of Porphyry's alternative ;   the one party reduced
universals to things pure and simple, the other to
mere fictions or words.[1]

But it would be flying in the face of history to
confine the activity of the early centuries of scholasticism   to   one   monotonous   dispute   about   the
Universals.   What, for example, does history tell us of
Boetius, the great educator of the early Middle Ages ?
That he was not merely a professor of Logic, but also a
master of Physics, of Metaphysics and of Psychology.
His scholars learned a great deal more from him than
the various meanings of the formulæ of Porphyry ;
they   learned   the   distinction   between   sense   and
intellect, the theory of *passio*, the definition of person,
substantial composition, the principle of causality,
and so on.   Many of those theories were of course
wrongly understood, like the matter and form theory ;
others were incomplete, like his theory of causes ;

---

[1] Compare our study on *Le problème des universaux dans son évolution
historique du IXe au XIIIe siècle* (Arch. f. Gesch. d. Philos., 1896),
also our *Histoire de la philosophie médiévale*, pp. 167-173.

and the whole collection of them wanted that unity which the synthetic genius of the thirteenth century was afterwards to give them. But even what the early scholastics knew of them is quite sufficient to vindicate these philosophers from the charge of exclusivism. Neither they nor their successors ever allowed themselves to be hypnotized by a phrase from Porphyry—like those Indian *nirvanists* who lull themselves to unconsciousness by the monotonous repetition of unmeaning formulæ.

Then, if we follow the question of the Universals through the golden age of scholasticism we shall see at once that it entirely shakes off the shackles in which it was bound up by the Alexandrian philosopher, and, after his example, by his earlier medieval commentators also. At the end of the twelfth century the metaphysical point of view was completed by the development of the *criteriological* and *psychological* aspects of the question—the aspects which alone bring out clearly to view the real value of universal notions.[1]

There is nothing more interesting in the history of the ninth to the twelfth centuries than the gradual widening of the scope of this controversy. The full and complete solution of the problem raises, one after another, delicate questions in physics, metaphysics and psychology. It has a very intimate connection with the theories of Essence, Individuation, Abstraction and Exemplarism. The scholastics of the thirteenth century understood all this; and far from lessening the importance of the whole question, they studied its influence upon all the various organic theories of their philosophical synthesis. The question was no longer an isolated one; it became an organic portion of one vast system (65).

---

[1] Many of those who define scholasticism by the problem of the universals have failed to grasp the real meaning of the controversy. This is the case with Mr. Clifford Allbutt, in his brochure, *Science and Medieval Thought* (Cambridge, 1893), p. 31.

But yet it was only *one* element of the system. This latter included a large number of other elements as well : theological speculation on the divine attributes ; metaphysical theories on Being, Substance, Cause, Individuation, Order, Categories ; controversies in Physics about Matter and Form ; discussions on the origin and growth of knowledge, on Morality and Beatitude ; those and many others besides, which could never have arisen out of Porphyry's three questions.   All this will be made more manifest in the course of the following pages.   We can understand, therefore, with what justice it has been described as " a sort of conspiracy against history to single out from scholasticism some special ideological question, the universals, for example, as Cousin has, or the relations of sensation to pure ideas, as M. de Gerando has, and to draw from these a general appreciation of the philosophical movement in the Middle Ages." [1]

[1] Morin, *Dictionnaire de philosophie et de théologie scolastique au moyen âge* (edited by Migne, 1856), p. 22.   To define scholasticism, Morin has recourse to two methods of procedure : (1) he studies the developments of the concepts of Being and Substance in their relation to Dogma ; (2) he interprets the scholastic applications of ontological *data* to the sciences.   *Ibid.*, p. 23.

CHAPTER II.

DOCTRINAL DEFINITION.

SECTION 11.—CONDITIONS FOR A DOCTRINAL DEFINITION.

55. Science is not a mere collection of theories about some special object, a simple juxtaposition of fragments of knowledge, an encyclopedia upon a given subject. It is, strictly speaking, a systematized body of knowledge, that is,—according to the expressive etymology of the word συνίστημι,—whose various parts or elements hold or hang together, harmonize and fit into one another like the cogs and wheels of a piece of machinery. It is only on condition of such harmony that the manifold conclusions of a science can be reduced to *unity,* and thus establish order in the mind.

So it is with all philosophies worthy of the name. The strongest of the great historical systems are those that were most firmly knit—the Upanishad system, the Aristotelian, the Neo-Platonic, the Cartesian, the Leibnitzian, the Kantian systems; and each has had its special character and tendency impressed upon it by the organic unity of its theories no less than by these theories themselves. Scholastic philosophy in its golden age may be justly considered as one of those great convergent solutions of the enigma of things.

56. To raise all the great fundamental questions of philosophy, and to reduce all the answers to unity;

such are the two essential tasks of every philosophical system. *System*, as such, must be defined by the presence of both those elements. In order to define *this* or *that* particular system, Scholasticism, for example, as opposed to Kantism, we must examine into the body of doctrines peculiar to each, and study these doctrines both in themselves and in their mutual relations. It is evident that the solutions of the one system are not those of the other, and that in order to judge of them we must understand them.

Those considerations make it clear that before we can bring together the elements of a doctrinal definition of scholasticism we must first interrogate its teachers on their fundamental theses, and secondly, that a *doctrinal* definition must needs be a *terminal*, not an *initial* one. The reader will therefore find in the following paragraphs an attempt at a brief exposition of scholastic teaching. And since a body of philosophical doctrines presents very great complexity, our definition of the scholastic system will be necessarily complex, even though it be confined to a mere outline. A definition ought to be brief, no doubt, but the logical demand for brevity must be understood in a relative sense.

57. To convince ourselves of the complexity of a body of philosophical doctrine, we need only consider that the characteristics commonly employed to outline a philosophical system, describe in reality only some *particular doctrine* or *group of doctrines* within *the system*. When Victor Cousin, for example, classifies philosophical systems into sensualism, idealism, scepticism and mysticism, the first two groups can have reference only to one single order of philosophical questions, that of the origin and certitude of knowledge.[1]

---

[1] Mysticism in Cousin's thought stands for something too vague to admit of its being discussed as a system of philosophy. As for scepticism, it is not so easy to construct a doctrinal system out of the very denial of the possibility of doctrine !

Similarly, Renouvier's six fundamental oppositions employed as a basis for his *Esquisse d'une classification systématique des systèmes philosophiques,*[1] are far from being each an adequate characteristic of a system. Of these oppositions : materialism and spiritualism ; evolutionism and creationism ; liberterianism and determinism ; endaemonism and obligationism ; rationalism and fideism ; finitism and infinitism ; each regards *one* doctrine alone, replies to *one* question alone. So true is this that the various alternative couples in question are quite compatible with one another in the same system, and that some of them are actually found united in *every* system. For example, scholastic philosophy is at the same time spiritualist, creationist, libertarian, etc. ; while stoicism is materialist, evolutionist, determinist, etc. Not to mention that it is quite possible to multiply such types of fundamental opposition between different philosophical systems.

It is, indeed, true that some determining characteristics seem better adapted to designate a whole system of philosophy than others, as when we speak of pantheism or positivism. Yet this is not because these latter individualize *the synthesis as such,* in the entirety of its principles and doctrines, but rather because they designate *some one or other* of its most salient doctrines. Strictly speaking, pantheism is not a system, for it decides only *one* doctrine of a system, that of the unity or plurality of all being ; but what is true is this, that there are systems which are pantheistic, being at the same time either materialistic like that of David of Dinant, or idealistic like that of Hegel. Similarly, positivism pronounces upon *one* single problem : that of the origin or source of all our knowledge ; but everybody knows that Comte's positivism and Spencer's positivism are full of other equally important doctrines bearing upon

[1] 2 vol., 1885.

problems quite other than the positivity of science. We see then that in order to delineate a system of philosophy in its entirety we must review all its fundamental theories, give a critical estimate of them, and thus distinguish them from those of other systems on the same subjects. The idea of the fundamental antinomies spoken of by Renouvier, may indeed be utilized, but only on condition of applying them to the special questions overlooked by that author, and of insisting that the members of the various couples enumerated are disjunctively compatible with one another in the same system.

58. So long as we regard a number of different systems under one single aspect, we may group them in categories : Lange has written the history of Materialism, Willmann that of Idealism. But if, on the other hand, we take any system in its doctrinal fulness, it will be found to form a *unique* and *individual whole*. We can give it a singular name, call it Platonism, Thomism, Kantism ; but define it we cannot except by specifying its various doctrines by their distinctive characteristics. The ideal thing would be to give a sketch of all the doctrines ; we should then know how and why the system of St. Thomas differs from that of Scotus or from that of St. Bonaventure. But as we have said above and will show in the sequel, there is such a remarkable agreement amongst the great doctors of the thirteenth century upon all fundamental questions, that their respective syntheses may well be considered as so many species of one and the same genus : scholasticism.

59. Let us now endeavour to apply to the common data of the scholastic synthesis the process of definition just outlined ; and for this purpose let us follow scholasticism through the great departments into which its leading exponents have divided all philosophy. Of course our outline can have no pretension

to completeness of exposition; it will not give in a few pages what the ablest authors have expounded in volumes. It will be mainly historical, and will aim at a faithful presentation of the great organic principles of medieval scholasticism. People like Taine who are ignorant of these principles see in scholasticism only a heap of absurdities. Those who understand them only partially are often mistaken about the meaning of scholastic theories; and this is the case with a large number of our modern historians of scholasticism as soon as they approach the study of it in detail.

Section 12.—Metaphysics.

60. Although metaphysics is the product of the highest intellectual abstraction, yet it has for its chief object the substance or essence of the things of sense; and accordingly, so far from resting on the quicksands of fancy, it is anchored to the firm rock of reality. If, however, it deals with the world of sense (as material object)—the world which will forever remain the proper sphere of all human investigation (87)—it is only by ignoring the properties based upon change that it does so, and by grasping the substance alone, the being and the constitutive principles of things (as formal object). " Philosophi erit considerare de omni substantia inquantum hujusmodi." [1]

Secondarily, metaphysics deals with non-substantial being, with adventitious or accidental being. Thus we justify the definition of metaphysics as the science of being that is immaterial by abstraction, of being taken simply as such, of being as stripped of everything with which the purely sensible order endows it.

[1] St. Thomas Aquinas, in IV. Metaph., lect. 5.

61. *Being* may be studied under certain very general aspects which serve to bring out clearly the meaning of so simple and all-embracing a concept. These are called the transcendental attributes of being. Such, for example, are the aspects of unity, goodness and truth (*unum, verum, bonum*).

Furthermore, being is not a something that is changeless and merely static : it must be studied not merely in its state of repose but also in its inception or *becoming,* in its evolution or change (in its *fieri* as well as in its *esse*). The things of experience have only a finite degree of reality, and even that not actualized all at once. The constant evolution or change to which things are apparently subject is an indication that they are continually gaining or losing reality, that they can appear and disappear. Take a thing in any state whatever : that state will evoke the idea of a prior state in which the thing was not what it now actually is. Before *actually* being, it *could* be, what it is. A chemical combination presupposes others, and can lead to still further combinations of matter. Before a man reaches the ripeness of age and knowledge and virtue he must have passed through all the successive stages of their infancy and youth. Now, in order to be able to pass from A to A^1 the being must have already possessed in A some *real* principle of the change ; it was *really* capable of receiving or undergoing a new determination or modification ; it possessed the *capacity*, or *was in* the *capacity* of becoming what it now *actually* is. *Actuality* (actus) is therefore the degree of being (ἐντελέχεια), of actual or positive perfection in a thing ; *potentiality* (potentia), the mere *capacity* of receiving some such complement of being or perfection—it is non-being, therefore, if you will, yet not mere nothingness, but such non-being as implies within itself the real principle of a future actualization. This actualization, this passage from the potential

to the actual state, bears the technical name of
movement, defined by the scholastics after Aristotle
as "the actualization peculiar to a being which is
still formally potential." "Convenientissime Philosophus definit motum dicens quod motus est actus
existentis in potentia secundum quod hujusmodi."[1]

The pair of ideas "potency and act" thus became
synonymous with "being determined and being
determinable." In this general sense it passed
beyond its original signification of a process of
becoming, an organic evolution or *fieri*, and served to
interpret all compositions, without exception, of all
being that is contingent or limited in its reality.
It was regarded as a primordial distinction, of
universal application in the order of the real being,
and thus became an exceedingly fertile conception
in metaphysics. Substance and accident, essence
and existence, specific essence and individual, are
so many examples of the "potency and act" couple.
Nor is this fundamental distinction peculiar to
metaphysics; it effects an entrance into other
domains, into logic, physics, psychology and ethics;
and everywhere it expresses the same elemental
relation of the "determinable" to the "determined":
the genus is to the species, the corporeal matter to
the soul, the passive intellect to the active, the free
act to its subjective end, as "potency" is to "act."

62. The first important application of the "potency
and act" couple is found in the great classification
of things into *substances* and *accidents*. The substance
or substantial being is the being that exists without
needing any other being in which to inhere for its
existence, and which serves as subject or support
for other realities. Man, horse, house, are substances;
whereas the virtue of the virtuous man, the colour
of the horse, the size of the house are accidents.
These adventitious realities (*ac-cidere*) are ontological

[1] St. Thomas, *In III. Phys.*, lect. 2.

determinations (*actus*) of the substance (*potentia*).
Here we touch upon the famous Aristotelian classification of the categories of being. And as a matter
of fact the scholastics took up and developed very
considerably the study of the nine accidental pre-
dicaments, especially those of quality, quantity,
relation, time and space.

The study of *quality* (accidens modificativum
substantiæ in seipsa) raises some important controversies passed over by Aristotle, notably that
regarding the distinction between a substance and
its powers or faculties of action. Can action proceed
directly from the substance in contingent beings,
or do these act through the medium of faculties ?
This question was hotly debated in the thirteenth
century, and its solution is of great importance in
psychology. Opinions were divided. The Thomists
held that there is a real distinction between substance
and faculty, so that the actual operation as such is
a determination or *actus* which affects the substance
not directly but through an intermediary, the faculty :
" operatio est actus secundus." St. Bonaventure,
on the other hand, steers between Thomism and the
old Augustinian doctrine of the identity of the soul
with its faculties ; while Duns Scotus deals with
the matter in a way peculiar to himself, by the
distinctio formalis a parte rei (65).

63. The real distinction between matter and form,
the two constitutive principles of corporeal substances, is likewise a particular application or aspect of
the distinction of "potency " and "act." The doctrine
of matter and form is regarded by the scholastics,
just as by Aristotle, as belonging properly and
primarily to physics (74). Wherever there is change
throughout nature, there must be found matter and
form. The piece of oak is the passive recipient
subject (*materia*) of the shape or figure (*forma*)
introduced by the carver's chisel. But these are

respectively a " second " or " derived " matter and form. For the oak itself one day made its first appearance and grew to be a tree by the gradual assimilation into the acorn of innumerable chemical elements—themselves substantial beings—which were gradually transformed into cells of " oak." And so we may ascend the path of change indefinitely. Now, in order to explain the transformation of substances, their chemical combination and decomposition, Aristotle demanded, in the various substantial realities which appear and disappear, a permanent substrate which he called primary matter (ἡ πρώτη ὕλη) and a specific principle which he called substantial form (εἶδος). The intrinsic union of matter and form gives rise to the corporeal substance. The matter being the principle of indetermination and the form that of determination, there is an unmistakable relation, in the domain of corporeal substances, between these two pairs of ideas, matter and form on the one hand, and potency and act on the other.

But is composition from matter and form applicable outside the *corporeal* order of things ? Does it hold for incorporeal substances, so as to be thus a mark of all contingent being ? Here we reach a point at which the Thomistic and Franciscan teachings bifurcate. The latter completely identify potency and act with form and matter, and therefore represent the latter composition as the all-pervading, necessary property of all created things whatsoever. This is not the view of Albert the Great and St. Thomas. These doctors teach that primary matter enters as a constituent into *corporeal substances only* ; it is the foundation of spatial extension, of multitude, and of the imperfection of bodies generally. In this they are rather followers of Aristotle, as their opponents are of Avicebron*:

There was general agreement in recognising an

*Ibn Gabirol.

existential dependence of matter on form—though some held the contrary opinion (Henry of Ghent, for example). St. Thomas taught expressly that God could not bring primary matter into existence without some substantial form as determining principle : it would be intrinsically impossible to do so, seeing that the potential, *as such*, cannot be in act.

The converse question—whether form is necessarily allied with matter, or whether a form of itself alone may not constitute an incorporeal being[1]— assumed a special importance in scholasticism, on account of its intimate relation with the doctrine on angels. These latter—superior intelligences, free from the imperfections of corporeal life—form an intermediate step between God and man in the hierarchy of essences. Indeed it may be said that scholasticism has constructed, upon the purest principles of intellectual and volitional activity, a psychology, or rather an " eidology " of angels, which has nothing in common with Aristotle's vague conjectures on the intelligences that moved the world's spheres.[2] How did the philosophers of the thirteenth century conceive the composition and nature of the angels ?

There were different theories. Although unanimous in ascribing to the angelic nature a composition of potency and act, which all regarded as the essential note of contingent being, they were divided upon the question of a real composition of matter and form. In opposition to the Franciscans whose views we have just mentioned, the Thomists asserted that the angels are " pure " or " separated " forms. And here is their reason : Since it is the form that actualizes the matter and gives the compound its

---

[1] Or even—in the minds of certain scholastics of a later period— simple corporeal beings, such as they conceived the heavenly bodies to be.

perfection and not *vice versa*, there can be no contradiction in the concept of *forms subsisting* apart from any union whatsoever with matter. Such separated intelligences, moreover, are not only intrinsically possible but also contingent and finite, for their essence is limited by their existence : " quia forma creata sic subsistens habet esse et non est suum esse, necesse est quod ipsum esse sit receptum et contractum ad determinatam naturam. Unde non potest esse infinitum simpliciter." [1]

64. What we have been just saying suggests an examination of the functions attached to the form by scholasticism. Its first function in the real order (whether of corporeal or incorporeal being), is that constitutive causality which we have been explaining (formal cause, *id per quod aliquid fit*) ; it makes the thing what it is ('το τι ἦν ἔιναι, *quod quid est*) ; it gives the thing its natural impress, fixes its specific rank and its degree of perfection. Furthermore, it is in a special way the principle of the activity of the thing (*natura*), and the source of its faculties and operations. The form is also the seat of *finality*, of that objective, innate tendency which impels the being to realize some specific end by the exercise of its activities.

From all this, it is easy to understand that the form is the principle of *unity* in a being. And particularly in *corporeal* being it is the form that gathers up into one unique subsistence the scattered elements of extended matter. But what exactly is the scope of this unitive function of the form ? Or, in other words, can one and the same corporeal being receive the intrinsic determination of more than one form ? The answer of St. Thomas is in the negative, and is therein strictly peripatetic ; we have his fundamental argument in these words of the *Summa Theologica* : " Nihil est simpliciter unum, nisi per formam unam

---

[1] St. Thomas, *Summa Theologica*, 1a, q. 7, a. 2.

per quam habet res esse."[1]   But this solution was novel, for it ran counter to the teaching of Alexander of Hales, of St. Bonaventure and of Albert the Great himself ; and it drew forth the most energetic protests from the Franciscan schools (31).   Most of the thirteenth century scholastics and a considerable number of those of the fourteenth, admitted that the various degrees of perfection found in one and the same being have distinct forms corresponding to them, and this without detriment to the complete and perfect unity of the being.

As for the matter, seeing that it is the recipient of all determinations, it must itself be destitute of all.   It is the form that leavens it from within, as it were ; and every form is some one realization of the inexhaustible potentiality of the recipient.[2]

65. The multiplication of individual beings in one and the same species, gives rise to two problems of fundamental importance : the relation of the individual to the universal, and the question of the principle of individuation.   Now, those two problems were organically connected with the doctrine of the distinction between potency and act.

The " universals " controversy was practically decided before the thirteenth century : scholasticism unanimously accepted the solution arrived at in the twelfth.   " The individual is the real substance ; the universal derives its ultimate form from the subjective work of our minds."   The most subtle dialecticians, not excepting Duns Scotus himself with all his daring differences of view, take no exception to those scholastic conclusions.   No one, however, is more exact and logical in those delicate matters than the Angelic Doctor.   It is as a tribute of homage to his wonderful powers of exposition, and not as

---

[1] 1a, q. 76, a. 3, c.
[2] The " matter and form " couple was of course freely transpor' ed from the *real* to the *ideal* order, where " formalis " is synonymous with " actualis," and " materialis " with " potentialis."

crediting him with a great discovery, that posterity has called this moderate realism by the name of Thomistic realism. In any case, among all the solutions of the famous " universals " problem, it is the one that harmonizes best with scholastic philosophy.

Appropriating a formula which was current in the scholastic repertory, St. Thomas sums up thus the relations of the individual to the universal : The reality of essences may be viewed in three states : *ante, rem, in re, post rem*, or, in the language of Avicenna, *ante multitudinem, in multiplicitate, post multiplicitatem*.[1] The universals *ante rem* are defined in the theory of Exemplarism with an Augustinian largeness of view that borders on the erroneous system of Avicenna. The universals *in re* represent the physical side of the problem, the theory of the *mere subsistence* of individuals with the principle of their individuation.[2] The universals *post rem* are the fruit of a subjective elaboration to which the objective aspects of things are subjected by the activity of the mind when it considers things apart from their individualizing conditions. Formally (*formaliter*) the universal exists only in the mind, but it has its foundation (*fundamentaliter*) in the things.

With the exception of the " terminists " or " nominalists " of the fourteenth century, who denied the real validity of our universal representations, thus showing the first signs of the scholastic decadence, the scholastics generally drew a distinction, in all created substances, between the essential determinations which reappeared identically in every representative of a species, and the individualizing

---

[1] Logic, Venice edition, 1508, fol. 12, V.A.

[2] St. Thomas thus lays bare the fundamental error of exaggerated realism, which was completely eradicated in its extreme form : " Credidit (Plato) quod forma cogniti ex necessitate sit in cognoscente eo modo quo est in cognito, et ideo existimavit quod opporteret res intellectas hoc modo in seipsis subsistere, scilicet immaterialiter et immobiliter." Summa Theol., 1a, q. 84, art. 1.

determinations which distinguished each representative from every other within the species. The former are to the latter as the determinable is to the determinant, as potency is to act. What is the distinction between them? In the view of St. Thomas the concepts of specific essence and of individual essence correspond to different constitutive realities in the individual thing (*distinctio realis*). Others conceived the distinction as a merely logical one. Duns Scotus advocated the existence of a *distinctio formalis a parte rei*, as if, anterior to the act of thought, the object of each universal idea possessed a certain separate unity in the things themselves (*a parte rei*).

66. But there arose another problem which was discussed with the greatest possible ardour in the thirteenth century: what is the principle of the individuation of things? In other words, if we are to reconcile the stability and abiding identity of essences with the endless diversity and wonderful variety of their individual realizations in nature, whence or how does it come that there are innumerable individuals in one and the same species? Here we have a scholastic controversy *par excellence*, for it presupposes, at least in a certain measure, the peripatetic solution of the problem of the universals. The medieval philosophers all admitted that within any species the *basis* of individuation ought to be *essential* and *intrinsic*; but difference of views arose as soon as the question was asked whether it is the matter or the form, or the union of both principles, that accounts for the individuation of things.

We find the Aristotelian system in St. Thomas Aquinas, but so completely amplified and perfected that the new developments almost entirely eclipse the borrowed portion. Aristotle had shown why the form, being an indivisible principle, cannot multiply itself numerically; but he had left in obscurity the individualizing function of the matter. St. Thomas explained that the individualizing principle is not the matter in a state of absolute indetermination—as unskilled or hostile interpreters of Thomism have often alleged, in the hope, perhaps, of discovering a contradiction. It is the *materia signata*, that is to say, the primary matter endowed with an intrinsic aptitude to occupy a definite portion of space.[1]

For St. Thomas, therefore, the question of individuation confines itself to the world of corporeal things. More logical even than the Stagyrite, he holds that in the hierarchy of separated forms each individual constitutes its own species.[2] As regards the heavenly bodies, composed of matter and form, and nevertheless each unique in its species, the view of St. Thomas can only be understood by referring it to the general principles of scholastic physics (78).

Others among his contemporaries arrive at different conclusions. St. Bonaventure finds the principle of individuation in the combined action of both constitutive principles, matter and form; Henry of Ghent, in a negative property of each substance, marking it off from every other substance; Duns Scotus, in a positive disposition of the final form to assume *such* or *such* individuality, *to be this thing*. And as for the multiplication of individuals in supramaterial species, this can have no difficulty for those who admit in them a physical composition of matter and form.

67. A fourth sort of composition in being, not referred to by Aristotle, gave rise to some exceedingly delicate scholastic discussions: the composition of essence and existence. The relation of the *concept* of essence to that of existence was not called into

---

[1] St. Thomas, *Op. IX. De Principio Individuationis.*
[2] Zeller, *Die Philosophie der Griechen*, II., p. 239, n. 3.

question ; nor the relation of a *possible* essence to an existing essence ; between the terms of those comparisons a real distinction was admitted by all. But we may pursue further our analysis of being, and enquire whether, *in an actual being*, its fundamental, constitutive reality (*essentia, quod est*) is one thing, and the actuality or act by which that reality exists (*esse, quo est*), another thing. And on this point opinions differed. St. Thomas advocated the doctrine of a real distinction : in God alone, the Actus Purus, are essence and existence identical ; in created being, on the other hand, whether spiritual or material, the perfection signified by the word " exists " is confined and circumscribed within the limits of the essence which it determines. " Unde esse earum non est absolutum sed receptum, et ideo limitatum et finitum ad capacitatem naturæ recipientis." [1] Essence is to existence what potency is to act.[2] But all being is *actualized* only in the measure in which it is *capable* of actuation ; for the degree of actual being is measured by its corresponding potentiality. Hence a contingent essence can receive existential actualization only within the limits of its contingency.

Looking at the general structure of Thomism, we find this theory of the real distinction very closely connected with some of the most fundamental theses of scholasticism. Moreover, it throws into bold relief the contingency of the creature ; and above all, it safeguards unity of existence in beings composed of matter and form, *i.e.*, of consubstantial, incomplete and mutually irreducible elements, as also in beings that exercise their activities by means of faculties really distinct from their own substance. Nevertheless we find among the various exponents

---

[1] *De ente et essentia*, c. 6.—Cf. the unfinished opusculum *De substantiis separatis*.
[2] See Cajetan's commentary on this passage.

of scholasticism a widespread and energetic opposition to this particular Thomistic thesis. The whole Franciscan school especially denied any real composition of essence and existence.

68. Another theory closely related with that of power and act is the theory of causes. A *cause* is whatever exerts any real and positive influence in bringing anything to pass. Within the cycle of change in the world of contingent things, all being, whether in its substantial constitution or in its accidental states, exists *in its causes* or *in potency*, before it appears *realized* or *in its actual state*. Its realization is its "passage from potency to act." But a thing considered in a potential state as regards any determination, cannot give itself that determination. It must receive it under the influence of some other being already in act. "Quidquid movetur ab alio movetur." This extrinsic principle of change is called an *efficient cause*.

Under its influence, the thing (matter) that is in potency to receive some perfection (form), *i.e. capable* of receiving it, does actually receive it. By their intimate union and intercommunication, the recipient subject and the communicated perfection exert a *constitutive causality* on the new being, or on its new state. They are the *constitutive causes*, either of the substance of the thing itself (*primary material cause, substantial formal cause*), or of some attribute of the thing (*secondary material cause, accidental formal cause*).

Finally the efficient cause is solicited by some good to be realized through its action (final cause), and develops its activity in that direction. This stimulation of efficiency by an end or motive is clearly evident in the wonderful order and beauty of the universe.[1]

---

[1] Beauty is the manifestation of order. Its perception occasions esthetic pleasure. Scholasticism, while not neglecting entirely the study of the beautiful, gave it only a secondary consideration. We shall deal with it in the second part of the present work.

If order were a rare exception it might possibly
be the outcome of a chance coincidence of motor
causes.   But its endurance and its universality can
only be explained by an internal tendency which
co-ordinates the actions of the operative causes, and
thus secures the realization of the designs of nature.
It is this inherent, intrinsic finality that explains
the constant recurrence of natural phenomena and
the preservation of the various species, organic and
inorganic, in the domain of physics ; the innate
tendency of the mind towards truth, in criteriology ;
the natural inclination of the will towards the good,
in ethics.   And so, the theorem of finality appears
in scholasticism as the crowning and perfecting
doctrine of the " philosophy of being."

SECTION 13.—THEODICY.

69. The human mind can have no pretensions to
a *proper* knowledge of what is beyond corporeal
being (87, 42).   Even metaphysics itself, the highest
of all the sciences, has for its primary object the
substances of visible nature : by mental abstraction
it considers their being apart from matter (60).
Still, on the other hand, the profession of an absolute
agnosticism as regards the essentially Immaterial
Being, the Deity, is a philosophical error ; and
scholasticism has successfully avoided it.   The very
same mental operation which attains to being that
is abstract negatively or by abstraction, yields at
the same time a series of concepts which can be
applied by analogy to being that is immaterial
positively or of its very nature.[1]   And this explains
and justifies the title of (rational) *Theology* which
we find in Aristotle (θεολογική), in the Arabians and

[1] St. Thomas, *In Lib. Boetii de Trinitate* q. 5, a. 1.—Cf. Mercier,
Ontologie, p. viii.

occasionally in the scholastics, as synonymous with metaphysics.

70. We find as early as Aristotle the well-known classification of beings into two great categories : on the one hand, *beings partaking of a mixture of potency and act*, beings which, before possessing a perfection actually, exist already in a prior state in which they are destitute of it ; on the other hand, the *pure act, actus purus*, exempt from all potentiality, namely, God. The medieval doctors developed and improved those Aristotelian *data*, employing them in a domain unknown to Aristotle. Uniting them with certain theories of the Fathers of the Church, especially of St. Augustine, they built up a new *theodicy* which is certainly one of the finest contributions of medieval thought to our intellectual inheritance from antiquity. The peripatetic notion of an immovable motor, wrapped up in inaccessible self-contemplation was supplanted by the theory of a *self-existent Being, infinite in Its pure actuality*. Apart from a few weaker spirits in the decadent epoch, the scholastics all admit that the consideration of the actual contingent universe can convince the human mind of the existence of God (*a posteriori* proofs).

71. In like manner, it is by observing creatures that we can know anything about the divine *essence*. Reason tells us that all the perfections found in creatures must be in God also—analogically and eminently (*analogice* and *eminenter*). Furthermore, the study of the divine attributes is but a series of corollaries from the study of His *aseity*. Thus, for example, God is perfect science ; He is also perfect love—contrary to what Aristotle taught ; and there is absolutely no doubt about His personality.

The multiplicity of the divine perfections is swallowed up in the *unity* of the infinite. But the scholastics differ in their conceptions of the kind

of distinction to be admitted between those perfections—just as on the question of their relative
pre-eminence. St. Thomas recognises a virtual
distinction between the divine attributes (*distinctio
rationis cum fundamento in re*) ; and, true to his
intellectualism, he emphasizes the role of the divine
science. Others, under the lead of Duns Scotus,
introduce here the strange *distinctio formalis a parte
rei*, and attribute a preponderating importance to
the divine will.

72. Regarding the relations between God and the
world we notice still further points of difference
between the peripatetic and the scholastic philosophy.
The absolute subordination of the being composed
of power and act to the being that is pure actuality,
does away with the inexplicable dualism of finite
and infinite, so obtrusive in Aristotle in common with
the whole of pagan philosophy. This subordination
is revealed in the three theories of *exemplarism,
creation* and *providence*.

Exemplarism.—In the first place, God knows all
things independently of their existence in time.
Before realizing the universe He must have conceived
the vast plan of it ; for He has done all things
according to weight and measure. God's ideas,
says St. Thomas, have no other reality than that of
the divine essence itself. Since His knowledge
exhausts the infinite comprehensibility of His being,
He not only knows His essence in itself (*objectum
primarium*) ; He also sees the relations between it
and creatures, its far distant imitations (*objectum
secundarium*). If some scholastics have other views
about the nature of the divine ideas, all agree that
they are the supreme ontological foundation of
contingent essences ; not, of course, that we know
things in God (ontologism), but because, in a synthetic
view of all reality from the First Cause downwards,
we see that the attributes of all created things

necessarily reproduce or show forth their uncreated exemplar.   The divine ideas are at once the ultimate reason of the *reality* of things, and the final basis of their *cognoscibility :* it is on them, therefore, that the *certitude* of our knowledge must, in its ultimate analysis, be found to rest.   In harmony with the doctrine of the innate tendency of the intelligence towards truth as the final cause of its acts (68), those synthetic speculations reveal the favourite attitude of the epistemology of the thirteenth century, and points to the direction in which we ought to seek for the two great bases of its criteriological dogmatism. The influence of the Augustinian *rationes æternæ* and of the Pythagorean speculations on numbers, may be easily detected in the theory of exemplarism.

Creation.—According to those divine ideas, the *causæ exemplares* of the world, God produced from nothing, by His creative act, all contingent realities. Scholasticism here improved on Aristotle, not only by its concept of " exemplary " causality, which was incompatible with the immobility of God as conceived by the peripatetics ; but also by its theory of efficient cause (*id a quo aliquid fit*).

In Aristotle, the efficient cause should be rather called the *motor*[1] cause ; for efficiency, in his concept of it, does not regard the production of the first or earliest recipients or *subjects* of movement.   These are supposed to be eternal, as also the world which has resulted from their combination ; and movement results necessarily from their conjunction.

In scholasticism, on the contrary, it is not merely the *movement* of things that falls under the influence of the divine efficient cause, but the very *substance* of those things, even in its deepest reality.   Whether, further, we admit the necessity of a creation in time

---

[1] In modern scientific language a *motor* cause is one that produces *local* motion.   It is taken here in a wider sense to designate the productive cause of *any sort* of movement or change *whatsoever.*—Cf. n. 61.

or, with St. Thomas, fail to find any evident contradiction in the concept of eternal creation—is a matter of minor importance.

Providence.—The Omnipotent Creator retains His sovereign power over the creature He has called into existence out of nothingness by the simple act of His all-producing will. While respecting the proper nature of every created being, He conserves its essence, co-operates with its activity (*concursus congruens naturæ creaturæ*), and rules it by His Providence. He is also the final cause of the universe, but in a deeper sense than with Aristotle. All things tend towards God ; a thesis intimately connected with the doctrine of the future life and happiness of man.

The application of Aristotelian metaphysics to the study of the Divinity gives the theodicy of the thirteenth century a depth and richness which neither the Fathers of the Church nor the early scholastics ever saw in it. It is really one of the most powerful affirmations of theism the world has ever witnessed. The God of the scholastics is no anthromorphic deity, " dwelling away in the clouds," and keeping the world-machine in motion : pantheism makes merry over such fanciful imaginings, but these have nothing in common with the sublime conceptions of the thirteenth century.

SECTION 14.—GENERAL PHYSICS.

73. The object of general physics in the ancient meaning of the word, is the synthetic study of the *corporeal* world. The great, striking phenomenon which enables the physician to rise above the endless details of nature, and to embrace it in one comprehensive view, is the *movement* or change of bodies. Metaphysics deals with *movement* as such (61) ;

physics, with corporeal *movements*. These latter, as Aristotle taught, are of four kinds : the appearance and disappearance of substantial compounds (γένεσις and φθορά) ; qualitative change (αλλοίωσις) ; growth and decay (αὔξησις and φθίσις) ; and, finally, local motion (φορα), the movement *par excellence*, which the three other kinds presuppose. The concept of local motion occasioned controversies on time and space.

74. The theory of substantial change gives us a very characteristic explanation of the evolution of nature. Difference of properties reveals a *specific* difference between corporeal substances. On the other hand, these substances change into one another and combine with one another to produce new compounds, specifically distinct from the generating factors ; and these latter compounds in turn, under the unceasing action of surrounding agencies, are again resolved into their elementary constituents ; the abiding identity of the primary matter through all the varying stages of the process, together with the diversity of specific forms, yields an adequate explanation of the visible facts (65).

In all the scholastic systems, the primary matter of the body is endowed with a fundamental relation to quantity. Quantity, or passive diffusion in space, is the first attribute of bodies, and it is regarded as a function of the primary matter—just as the reduction of the corporeal elements to unity is a function of the form.

The abiding identity of the primary matter does not offer any obstacle to its real diversification in the innumerable substances of the universe. To understand fully the mind of the scholastics on this subject we must remember that the transformations of substances follow a rhythmic gradation the stages of which are regulated by the finality of the cosmos.

75. This theory of the rhythmic evolution of

substantial forms is beautifully developed in scholasticism. Matter is, no doubt, a treasure-house of potentiality, a pliable thing which assumes a succession of forms throughout any given series ot compositions. But this plasticity has its limits; it follows certain lines. Nature will not change a stone into a lion; in its evolution it obeys a law of progress, the detailed application of which it is the mission of the special sciences to study, while the physician views it only in its generality. Or, in scholastic language, the primary matter is not deprived of one form to assume any other form indifferently, but only to be united to *that particular form* which corresponds with the immediately neighbouring type *in the natural hierarchy of things.* By reason of a special predetermination, the different stages traversed by matter are thus fixed in a very perfect way. Hence the teaching of St. Thomas that, antecedent to its union with the spiritual soul, the human body assumes a certain number of intermediary forms, until nature's work has thus raised the embryo to a state of perfection which demands the supreme informing principle, the spiritual soul, infused by Almighty God. This is simply the " *natura non facit saltum* " expressed in philosophical language: a simple but striking interpretation of the principle of cosmic evolution. Here also we are led into the full meaning of the formula: *corruptio unius est generatio alterius.*

This process productive of forms (*eductio formarum e potentiis materiæ*) is rightly regarded as one of the most difficult questions of scholasticism. Its greatest teachers are unanimous in admitting the intervention of a triple factor: the First Cause exerting the *concursus generalis ;* the pre-existing matter disposed to receive the new form and give birth to the new compound; the natural agent or active principle, which actualizes the receptive subject. But there is little or no agreement as to the respective rôle of each of these three factors.   St. Thomas lays stress on the *virtus activa* of the natural agent, and on the passivity of the matter.   He simply reduces the problem of the appearance and disappearance of forms to that of the actualization of a potency in a pre-existing subject (61).   The Thomistic teaching is thus opposed to the more ancient theory of the *rationes seminales,* defended by St. Bonaventure and by most of the earlier scholastics of the thirteenth century.   The advocates of this latter cosmological hypothesis would maintain that God endowed matter from the beginning with certain active forces which are the seminal principles of all things, and whose gradual development in the bosom of the material universe accounts for the appearance of the innumerable material substances of nature.

76. However that may be, finality rules the whole series of substantial changes, and the universal order of things, just as it rules the activities of each individual being (68).

With the exception of a few realists of the twelfth century who were led into error by the poetical descriptions of the *Timæus,* the scholastics never regarded nature in the light of a real, individual, physical organism, after the manner of the ancients. As regards the ultimate term of the cosmic evolution, scholasticism finds an explanation, unknown to Aristotle, in the relation of the world to God.   The existence of the creature can have no other end than the glory of its Creator.   That glory finds its first manifestation in the contemplation of the universe by the Infinite Intelligence ; secondly, in the knowledge which other intelligent beings can acquire of the marvellous order of creation.   Such is the elucidation of an enigma which Aristotle had encountered without being able to offer a satisfactory solution of it : how is God the final cause of the material universe ?

Section 15.—celestial and terrestrial physics.

77. The spectacle of the heavens is imposing; chiefly because of the unending revolutions and apparent immutability of the stars. Influenced by the popular beliefs which held the stars for divinities, Aristotle regarded them as *more perfect* substances than those of the earth. He set up a *distinction of nature* between the former as being exempt from the laws of change, and the latter as being manifestly plunged in an ocean of change. Medieval philosophy espoused this *a priori* principle; and its vitiating influence is revealed in the three thirteenth century departments of special physics: physical and mechanical astronomy; the theory of sublunary matter; and the action of the heavens upon terrestrial substances.

78. The superior perfection of the starry universe is revealed firstly in its constitution and secondly in its local motion. The heavens are complete strangers to birth and death alike: the astral substance is immutable, exempt from generation and corruption. In philosophical language the theory runs thus: the heavenly bodies are indeed composed of primary matter and substantial form, but these two constitutive elements *are here indissolubly united to each other.*[1] And as primary matter, that receptive subject of those original determinations, cannot assume a new substantial form without losing the one it has (*corruptio unius est generatio alterius*), the indissolubility of that union explains both the impossibility of all transformation and the permanence of the starry bodies; that is, of the fixed stars and planets: for the comets, whose irregular motions would not fit in with the theory, were regarded as a sort of atmospheric will-o'-the-wisps.

[1] Some scholastics, posterior to the thirteenth century, attributed the immutability of the stars to their supposed simplicity.

But the scholastics did not infer the eternity of the stars from their immutability, as Aristotle had done : their teaching on this point was an application of their general doctrine of creation (72) ; and they still more emphatically repudiated the view that would see in the star a divinity. On the other hand, however, they accepted this other corollary that *each siderial type is unique :* since the form here determines all the matter it is capable of informing, each star or heavenly body must be unique of its kind.

Just as their astronomical physics were adapted to their general principles on the constitution of bodies, so also were their celestial mechanics inspired by *a priori* considerations on the perfection of circular movement. The only sort of change observable in the stars is the local displacement due to their revolutions. And in fact, since local motion was regarded by both ancient and medieval physicists as *a necessary manifestation of all corporeal essences,* each specific substance should possess its own specific movement : here we have the theory of *natural movements and natural places,* one of the old antitheses to our modern mechanics. The theory simply means that if a body be displaced by an efficient cause, it will determine and direct its movement, according to its nature, towards the *place* which is *natural* to it.

The heavenly body, superior in its constitution to the earthly, has also a nobler sort of motion : its movement is circular. This is the most perfect of all motions, for the circle has neither beginning, middle, nor end ; it is complete in itself, without further addition.

Without attempting a detailed explanation of the revolutions of the heavenly bodies, let us merely note that all the astronomical theories of the thirteenth century were based on the geocentric system of Ptolemy. The stars are fixed in concentric spheres whose revolution around the earth accounts for their diurnal motion. But who sets them in motion ? Not astral souls, as Aristotle had taught—intelligent and divine forms, "unchangeable actualizations of the Nature-soul, identical with itself everywhere, yet also everywhere differentiated by the greater or less degree of docility of the body it informs "[1]; but intelligent motors, as St. Thomas taught, *extrinsically* related to the spheres which they set in motion mechanically.[2] To explain the complex motions of the planets various hypotheses were put forward : homocentric cycloids, excentric cycloids and epicycloids. Of the planets, the moon is the nearest to the earth. Hence the term *sublunary* applied to earthly substances.

79. Whilst the heavenly bodies move in a circle, earthly bodies move in a straight line ; and this is indicative of their inferiority. Fire which is " absolutely " *light*, and air which is light " relatively," move naturally upwards ; earth which is absolutely *heavy*, and water which is relatively so, tend naturally downwards. So that each of the four sublunary elements possesses its own proper place : fire fills the upper regions ; earth fills the depths ; water and air come between, water next the earth, air next the fire. These, with the ether or fifth essence (quintessence), which constitutes the heavenly bodies, form the whole stock-in-trade of the medieval cosmogony. The ancients inferred the unity of the world from the tendency of each element towards its own natural place ; from the property of weight in the heavy elements they inferred the central position of our earth in the universe, its spherical shape and its immobility.

[1] Piat, *Aristote* (Paris, 1903), p. 129.
[2] " Ad hoc autem quod moveat, non oportet quod uniatur ei ut forma, sed per contactum virtutis, sicut motor unitur mobili." *Summa Theol.*, I., q. 70, a. 3.

The earthly bodies are moreover mutually opposed in regard to their sensible qualities : warm and cold (active qualities), dry and moist (passive qualities). As every body is both active and passive, each element is endowed with a combination of some two qualities taken one from each pair : warm and dry (giving fire), warm and moist (giving air), cold and dry (giving earth), cold and moist (giving water). By reason of such oppositions the elements can be changed into one another ; but more especially do they give rise, by chemical combination, to the " mixtum " or chemical compound, which the science of the Middle Ages distinguished perfectly well from the mechanical mixture. The formation and dissolution of " mixta " explain the constant change that is going on in the inorganic and organic kingdoms.

80. This incessant change implies the uninterrupted activity of efficient causes.   And as these latter are arranged in hierarchical order, the efficiency of the earthly forces is ultimately traceable to the heat and other active powers of the heavenly bodies : on the abiding continuity of these celestial forces depends the continuity of all terrestrial change. " All multitude," says St. Thomas, " proceeds from unity.   Now what is unchangeable or immovable has one sole mode of being ; while what is movable can have many.   And hence we see that throughout all nature motion comes from something immovable. Hence, too, the more immovable a thing, the more is it a cause of motion.   But the heavenly bodies are the most unchangeable of all bodies, for they are subject only to local motion.   Therefore the manifold and varied motions of mundane bodies are to be referred to the motions of the heavenly bodies as to their cause." [1]   In this view the heavens are

---

[1] " Cum omnis multitudo ab unitate procedat, quod autem immobile est uno modo se habet, quod vero movetur, multiformiter, considerandum est in tota natura, quod omnis motus ab immobili procedit. Et ideo quanto aliqua magis sunt immobilia, tanto magis sunt causa

made the source of all terrestrial change; they effectuate the union of forms with matter, and are thus the cause of all generation.

This theory explains the exaggerated importance attached to the stars in the later Middle Ages, as well as the vogue of the many arts which professed to study their influence : *magic* which interrogated the occult powers of the heavens ; *astrology* which explored the ruling influence of the stars over human destinies ; *alchemy* which sought to supplant the ordinary course of terrestrial change in bodies by an artificial method under man's control, and so to direct the mysterious transforming power of the heavens as to make primal matter pass through all sublunary forms.[1]

SECTION 16.—PSYCHOLOGY.

81. According to the medieval classification of the sciences psychology is merely a chapter of special physics, although the most important chapter ; for man is a *microcosm ;* he is the central figure of the universe. The full development of psychology synchronizes with the culmination of philosophical culture in the thirteenth century. The fragmentary and imperfect treatises of earlier times give place to complete and comprehensive studies, published as separate works on psychology (22). Conformably with the plan usually followed in the Middle Ages, we may divide the problems of scholastic psychology

eorum quæ sunt mobilia. Corpora autem cælestia sunt inter alia corpora magis immobilia : non enim moventur nisi motu locali. Et ideo motus horum inferiorum corporum, qui sunt varii et multiformes, reducuntur in motum corporis cælestis, sicut in causam." *Summa Theol.*, 1a. q. 115, a. 3.

[1] The medicine taught at the time was also coloured by the theory of the four elements. These were supposed to be found in the body in the form of humours (bile, spleen, blood, black bile) whose respective predominance accounted for the four temperaments, and whose harmonious blending constituted health.

into two groups, according as they treat of the
nature of man, or of his *activities*. In the former
group we find three leading theories : the soul is
the substantial form of the body ; it is spiritual and
immortal ; it is created by God.

82. Not the soul alone, but the whole man is the
object of scholastic psychology. Now, man is a
substantial compound, of which the soul is the
substantial form, and the body the primal matter.
Thus we have the most intimate conceivable relation
established between the two constitutive elements
of our being ; and we have these relations explained
by the general theory of hylomorphism as set forth
above (63, 64). For example, the soul gives the
body its substantial perfection, its actual existence
and its life[1] ; in the human nature (*id quod agit*)
the soul is the formal principle (*id quo agit*) of all
activities.

This is an Aristotelian theory, and breaks with
the earlier medieval theories which were all of a
Platonic tendency. The pseudo-Augustinian treatise
De Spiritu et Anima, which the twelfth century
adopted as its manual of psychology, illustrates the
union of body and soul by the comparison of the
ship and the pilot, and infers the *juxtaposition* in
man of two substantial beings. Alanus of Lille
(1128-1202) was a philosopher who summed up and
systematized the intellectual work of four centuries ;
and he represents the human soul as an independent
substance associated to the body through a sort of
connubium or *copula maritalis*, effected by the agency
of a *spiritus physicus*[2]. Thirty years later these
conceptions were supplanted by that of the peripatetic anthropology which gained universal acceptance
among scholastics from the time of Alexander of

---

[1] " Anima dicitur esse primum principium vitæ in his quæ apud nos
vivunt." St. Thomas, *Summa Theol.*, 1a, q. 75, a. 1.

[2] Baumgartner, *Die Philosophie des Alanus de Insulis*, Münster,
1896, pp. 102, and foll.

Hales. The thirteenth century did indeed accept and hand on the theory of the *spiritus physicus,* bequeathed to the Middle Ages by Greek antiquity ; but it did not follow Alanus of Lille by making this *spiritus* a third factor acting as connecting link between soul and body ; neither did it on the other hand identify the *spiritus* with the human soul, like Telesius and the Renaissance naturalists in their materialistic psychology ; but it saw in the *spiritus* an emanation from the informing principle, an agency which disposes the brute matter for the activities of organic life.

If, however, all the great scholastics were agreed in explaining human nature by the hylemorphic theory, each of them was guided by his own metaphysics (64) in deciding whether the spiritual soul, by informing the body, does or does not exclude the presence of other substantial forms, especially that of the " plastic mediator " or *forma corporeitatis,* in the compound. It was of course on this psychological application of the general question that the respective supporters of the unity and of the plurality of forms carried on their warmest discussions. The Thomist thesis finally prevailed, though the other opinion was never condemned ; and, indeed, if we except some extreme and ill-framed formulæ—such as that of Peter Olivi (Petrus Joannis Olivi), for example,[1]— the recognition of a plurality of forms is not regarded as incompatible with the fundamental principles of scholastic psychology and metaphysics.

83. If scholasticism renounced Plato and St. Augustine in its enquiries into the composite nature of the human being, it availed of their assistance in

---

[1] Peter's teaching was, moreover, not recognised in his own order. Among those who disowned him was Richard of Middleton, himself a supporter of the plurality of forms. On Olivi and the Council of Vienne, see a series of articles by Père Ehrle, in the *Archiv. f. Litter. u. Kircheng. d. Mittelalters.* II. and III. Cf. our *Histoire de la philosophie médiévale,* 1st edit., p. 304.

establishing the *spirituality* of the soul.[1]   Those
who claimed for human reason the power of demonstrating the spirituality of the human soul—and they
were the vast majority among scholastics—appealed
by preference to its independence as regards matter
in its highest operations.   Differing from Aristotle,
the scholastics attributed immateriality not merely
to the active intellect or any other faculty, but to
the very substance of the soul.   And since
immortality has no other intrinsic reason than the
immateriality of our intellectual cognitions and
volitions, it is not merely the active intellect in a
state of cold and barren isolation (Aristotle) that will
survive the body, but the whole soul in the enjoyment
of its conscious and personal life, and in the full
exercise of all its nobler activities.   This new theory,
put forth against the erroneous or misleading statements of Aristotle, should of itself suffice to vindicate
scholasticism from the charge of undue servility to
tradition in the department of psychology.

Duns Scotus, as is well known, threw doubts on
the demonstrative force of the arguments brought
forward by the Stagyrite in favour of the immateriality
of our intellectual life.   Those doubts were collected
by William of Occam, and subsequently exploited
against the scholastic system by the Averroïsts and
the philosophers of the Renaissance.   But it is well
to bear in mind that the attitude of Scotus was purely
negative ; and that his criticism was moreover not
absolute, but merely *relative* to the Aristotelian
argument.   Neither Scotus nor Occam ever claimed
to have discovered any *positive* reasons against the
spirituality of the soul ; their psychological teachings
differ essentially from the materialist views of the
fifteenth and sixteenth centuries.

---

[1] " Animam considerando secundum se, consentiemus Platoni ;
considerando autem secundum formam animationis quam dat corpori,
consentiemus Aristoteli." *Albert the Great, Summa Theol.*, II., 348.

84. St. Augustine's perplexities about the origin of human souls—by generation or by creation—had percolated down to the twelfth century; but from the beginning of the thirteenth we find scholastics unanimous in teaching that the direct and continuous intervention of the Creator can alone bring into existence the human souls destined to animate the bodies of infants. There can be scarcely any need to observe that creationism has nothing in common with the Platonic theory of pre-existence, nor with the nondescript Aristotelian theory which would account for the origin of the human body and of the passive intellect by the laws of natural generation, while attributing an ill-defined extrinsic (θύραθεν) origin to the active intellect.

85. The activities of the soul can be divided into fundamentally different groups. The faculties from which they come can acquire an ever greater facility of action by repeated exercise; and this abiding tendency to act in a given direction is called a *habit*. As to whether the faculties have a reality distinct from the soul, or are merely different modes of one and the same energy applied to different objects—that depends on the issue of the metaphysical discussions which determine the general relations of the contingent substance to its powers of action (62).

Whichever opinion they espoused on this point— one of secondary importance in psychology—the scholastics classified the vital functions of man into three groups: the lower or vegetative functions, such as nutrition and reproduction; the cognitive functions; and the appetitive functions. The two latter groups occupied most attention, as they include the whole psychic life proper. Then, further, the scholastics were true to their spiritualist principles in distinguishing carefully two irreducible orders of psychic activity, the sensible and the suprasensible;

so that we must recognise two orders both of knowledge and of appetition.

86. A leading authority on scholastic philosophy, Fr. Kleutgen, S.J.,[1] sums up its teaching on both kinds of knowledge in three general principles, which underlie all the ideological theories of scholasticism on the nature and origin of our mental representations.

Firstly : The known object is in the knowing subject as a mode of being of that subject. " Cognitum est in cognoscente secundum modum cognoscentis."

Secondly : All cognition takes place after the manner of a representative image of the thing known in the knowing subject. " Omnis cognitio fit secundum similitudinem cogniti in cognoscente."

Thirdly : This representation is effected by the co-operation of the known and the knower. And this co-operation guarantees the real objectivity of our knowledge.

87. In *sensation,* the known *object* is reproduced (psychically), in the representative act, in all its concrete conditions : it is a material thing existing at a perfectly definite time and place. We see an individual oak-tree, for example : it meets our gaze with its whole retinue of actual properties, and these we attribute to it and to it alone, here and now present at this instant of time and at this point of space. Hence we say that sensation seizes on its objects in all their *individual* conditions.

And this is so in all sensation. The scholastics, with Aristotle, distinguish the senses into external and internal. The former (hearing, seeing, smell, taste, touch) reveal to us some external object which either some one of them (*sensibile proprium*), or many together (*sensibile commune*) perceive. The informations of the internal senses, on the other hand,

---

[1] Kleutgen, *La philosophie scolastique* (French trans. from German, Paris, 1868). V. I., pp. 30, and foll.

come from within—as the name itself indicates. These are : the *common sense,* which makes us aware of our external sensations and distinguishes between them ; the *imagination* and the *sense memory,* which store up the traces of past sensations, recall and combine them (*phantasma*), and can thus contribute to the production of thought in the absence of an external object ; the *vis œstimativa* (instinct) in the animal, or *vis cogitativa* in man—a power which, blindly in the former, and directed by intelligence in the latter, appreciates the utility or harmfulness of the sense properties of an object.

The *seat* of sense knowledge is the organism, that is to say, the body "informed" by the soul. The Western medieval philosophers were inclined to emphasize unduly the physiological side of sensation. This was owing to the influence of a twofold current of Arabian thought, coming through Monte Cassino (in the eleventh century), and through the Arabian schools of Spain (in the twelfth) : an influence that led more than one scholastic to conclusions bordering on materialism. But the thirteenth century masters set things to rights : in addition to the physiological, they bring out the psychological aspect of sensation ; they proclaim the two phases of the total process to be mutually irreducible ; and they assert the interdependence of these phases as a fundamental law not only of sense life but of all perceptive and appetitive activities whatever.

The study of the *origin* of sensation brings to light the causal co-operation of object and subject. Here the scholastics give proof of their remarkable powers of psychological analysis. A representative faculty is described as *passive* ;[1] that is to say, in order to

[1] A technical expression, often misunderstood. Froschammer, for example, a recent biographer of St. Thomas, failing to grasp its meaning, accuses the latter of making knowledge a purely passive phenomenon. Same error in Erdmann, *Geschichte der Philosophie,* I., p. 452 (Berlin, 1892) ; in Werner, *Joannes Duns Scotus* (Vienna,

pass into a state of action and to produce that immanent perfection commonly called " knowing," it must receive from some external source or agency a something to determine and complete it in its very being.   This stimulation by the external object is in the nature of an initial impulse, without which the senses should remain in a state of perpetual inaction.   When the disturbance from without reaches the passive faculty, the latter reacts, and this reaction completes the cognitive process. Impressed and expressed *species* or image (*species impressa, expressa*), or, to vary the phrase, representation impressed from without and revealed or shown forth from within—are the terms most commonly used to describe this double aspect of the one single phenomenon which is accomplished wholly and entirely within us.

It is of interest to note, in this connection, the growth of a *physical* theory from this *psychological* teaching—the theory of the *medium*.   The science of the thirteenth century would have the external object act upon the sense organ not by direct contact but through an intermediary.   In the process of vision, for example, the object influences the air, and produces the psychic determination through its agency.   But whether the external agent that immediately excites the cognitive faculty be the object itself, or some second factor of the physical order, the difficulty remains all the same : in the one case as in the other a material agent contributes to the production of a psychic phenomenon, and the mystery is there still.

All the leading scholastics—St. Thomas and Duns

1881), p. 76.   A passive faculty is not a *non-acting* faculty, but simply one which is *passive* before being *operative*, which must be determined or " informed " by something other than itself before exercising an activity ; in opposition to an *active* power which has no such need of any outside influence, and which passes into action as soon as the requisite *conditions* are present.

Scotus, to mention no others—had a full appreciation of this difficulty, for they draw a sharp and clear distinction between the psychic *immutatio* wrought by the object in the sense, and the physical phenomena which take place in the *medium*. We must regret the fact, however, that the exact bearing of their analysis in this matter was not fully grasped by many of their contemporaries ; not a few of the latter were led astray by the distorted interpretation of the " species sensibilis " to be found in so many of Aristotle's commentators. For these the " species " was not a determinant of the *psychic order*, an action excited by the object and elicited and terminated in the faculty ; it was rather a miniature of the external thing, a tiny image that traversed the intervening space and entered the organ, a sort of substitute for the reality, a proxy that established contact with the sense, was assimilated by the latter, and thus provoked conscious knowledge : an absurd conception entertained by certain Aristotelians of the time of William of Auvergne, and to which we shall have occasion to recur.

88. On the *object* of the human *intellect* and its essential difference from the sense faculties, the teaching of scholasticism is peripatetic. While sense knowledge attains only to the particular and contingent (87), the intellect reaches realities whether substantial or accidental, *by stripping them of the individualizing features that characterize the objects of sense*. That is to say, the concept is *abstract*, and accordingly its object, looked at by the intellect, can be *universalized* or referred to an indefinite multitude of individual things. Our eyes see *this* oak, *this* colour ; our intellect conceives oak, colour, tree, being in general.

According to St. Thomas, our cognitions are abstract not only when they regard the world of sense, which is the proper object of our intellects, but even when they have for object the *nature* of the soul.   The *existence* of the *ego* is the only intuitive *datum* we have : this is given in every single conscious activity of ours, according to the expression of St. Augustine : *ipsa (anima) est memoria sui.*

But if the understanding conceives only the abstract and universal aspects of things, must we therefore deny it all direct knowledge of the individual ?   St. Thomas thinks we must, and his conclusion is logical.   And to meet the objections which at once arise, he grants the intellect a certain sort of knowledge of individual things, a knowledge got by a kind of *reflexio* or *applicatio* whose nature is one of the obscure points of Thomism.   In their anxiety to leave to the human intellect an immediate perception of the individual, the Angelic Doctor's rivals would not follow him in these bold deductions ; they preferred to introduce into their complicated psychologies a lot of new apparatus, not easy to explain or to justify.   Duns Scotus, for example, and William of Occam, not content with the abstract and universal representation, which, they say, results from *distinct* knowledge, recognise in addition an intuitive knowledge which *vaguely* reveals to us the concrete and individual existence of things.   But it may well be asked in what does this intuitive intellectual knowledge differ from sense perception ; and whether the distinction does not regard the degree of clearness rather than the *nature* of the mental process.

We see then that abstraction remains the key-stone of scholastic ideology.   It supplies us, moreover, with the final solution of the criteriological problem, and of the time-honoured enigma of the universals.   We have already referred to the metaphysical aspect of the question, and to the " three states of the essence."   There is a second formula which bears more directly on the psychology of the problem : The essence may be submitted to a three-fold subjective consideration, " secundum esse in natura, secundum se, secundum esse in intellectu." *Secundum esse in natura*, it is individual ; *secundum se*, it is simply the essence of things, abstracting from their mental or extramental existence ; *secundum esse in intellectu*, it is universalized, conceived in relation with an indefinite multitude of things of the same species. The process of universalization, as such, is subjective ; it is superadded to a previous process of abstractive segregation, which grasps the objective being of things.

89. How are those abstract and universal representations formed in our minds ? This was another favourite subject of research in the thirteenth century. A well-known adage sums up the results : *Nihil est in intellectu quod prius non fuerit in sensu.* This formula asserts the sensible origin of all our ideas, and the dependence of our highest intellectual operations on the organism. The intelligible object must somehow affect or determine the " passive faculty of the understanding." This is obviously essential for the genesis of all intellectual thought. And to bring about this determination, two things are absolutely necessary : the presence of a sensible image of some sort (*phantasma*), and the operation of a special abstractive faculty (*intellectus agens*). Nor are the scholastics less unanimous in maintaining, against the Arabian philosophers, that all those various thought-principles are *within* the soul, and that the hypothesis of an *external* or " separate " active intellect cannot be reasonably entertained. When, however, they approach the study of those principles more closely, and try to determine the part played by each factor in the total process—by the active intellect, the passive intellect and the phantasm, respectively—they espouse different and conflicting opinions.

The question is a delicate one : on the one hand, the understanding is like a virgin page on which the outside world is somehow to be traced ; on the other, it would seem that there is nothing fit to actuate this understanding, since its proper object, the abstract and universal, does not exist as such in nature (65). According to St. Thomas and Duns Scotus, it is the sensible reality that acts on the passive intellect, by means of the *phantasma*, but this latter can exert a merely instrumental causality under the efficient influence of an immaterial faculty, the active or acting intellect (*intellectus agens*). Under the influence of this higher power, the sensible image, or in ultimate analysis the external object itself, sets the passive intellect in action (*species intelligibilis impressa*) : this action, which is immanent and representative in character, completes the intellectual process of abstract cognition (*species intelligibilis expressa*). Here, as in the study of sense knowledge, we see the theory of the psychic determinant supplementing the simple notion of a passive power.

The " terminists " or " Occamites " of the fourteenth and fifteenth centuries, and at a later period, Malebranche, Arnauld, Reid and others, tried to throw ridicule on the doctrine of the *species intelligibiles*, regarding them as a purely fanciful apparatus uselessly introduced into the process of ideation. But curiously enough, all their polemics arise out of a misunderstanding of the doctrine. As a matter of fact, immediately after the introduction of the new text of Aristotle into the West, a false interpretation of the *species intelligibilis* became current—an error analogous to that already referred to in connection with the *species sensibilis*. William of Auvergne (d. 1249), Bishop of Paris, one of the most renowned philosophers and theologians of his time, informs us that several of his contemporaries defended the theory of the *spiritualized phantasm*, or of the *transformation* of the *species sensibilis* into a *species intelligibilis*, under the purifying influence of the *intellectus agens*.[1] Here the *species intelligibilis* plays the same rôle in the understanding as the *species sensibilis*, for it is a simple prolongation of the latter : a substitute for the external world, which comes before the faculty as before a photographic camera, acts upon it and thus enables it to know the external thing of which the *species* is a mere image. This is not the place to examine critically such an untenable hypothesis ; but we may remark that the supposed transformation of a material effect (the sense image) into an immaterial one (the spiritualized image), uproots the very foundations of scholastic spiritualism.[2]

It would be interesting to know who were those contemporaries of William of Auvergne who had the complete text of the *De Anima* in their hands, and still supported the false view of the *species intentionalis* bequeathed to them by the Arabian commentators of Aristotle. Their mistake was widespread in the Middle Ages. William, in refusing to accept it, gives proof of his exceptional grasp of the ideological problem. And when, later on, we find William of Occam urging difficulties against the doctrine of the *vicarious species*, we cannot blame him for it. But his objections do not touch the *genuine* doctrine on the *species intentionalis*. And the best proof of this is that he himself admits a determination of the intelligence from without, and conceives the genesis of our representative states in practically the same way at St. Thomas and Duns Scotus.

[1] Cf. Baumgartner, *Die Erkenntnisslehre des Wilhelm von Auvergne* (Münster, 1893), pp. 49 and 67.

[2] Malebranche expresses himself as follows : " Those *impressed species*, being material and sensible, are rendered intelligible by the *intellectus agens*. The *species thus spiritualized* are termed *expressed*." *De la recherche de la vérité*, L. III., ch. 2. Cf. our article : *De speciebus intentionalibus dissertatio historico-critica (Divus Thomas*, Plaisance, 1897).

90. The appetitive life is regulated by the universal law : *Nihil volitum nisi præcognitum.* All desire or appetite pre-supposes a knowledge of the thing desired. The sense appetite is the inclination or tendency of the organism towards a *concrete* object presented by the senses as an individual good. The intensity of this inclination is the source of the sense passions : and these furnish a fertile field for commentaries and classifications, wherein the scholastic genius finds free scope.

The rational appetite or will is moved to action by the presentation of good in the *abstract.* Here, likewise, the mainspring of the appetitive inclination is the perfecting or developing of the appetitive subject or being : *Bonum est quod omnia appetunt.* According to St. Thomas, the action of the will is *necessary* when the latter is placed in presence of the absolute good, for this fully and completely satisfies the appetitive faculty ; it is, however, *free* when the good presented is contingent, and accordingly insufficient to satisfy fully the will's capacity for enjoyment. But even this free choice of a particular good presupposes the irresistible straining of the rational appetite after the good in general.

Henry of Ghent, Duns Scotus and William of Occam take a somewhat different view of *liberty* and of our *manner of exercising volitional activity,* from that of St. Thomas. They look upon liberty as the primordial and essential attribute of volition, and ascribe to the will an absolute power of self-determination ; the spontaneity of the act involves its liberty. In none of its volitions is the will *necessitated* by the good presented by the intellect : even in presence of the universal good the will preserves its freedom both of exercise and of specification, for, says Scotus, it has the power of turning aside from the intellectual presentation. This absolute indeterminism of the will reveals the mode of action of the latter faculty : the appreciation of the value of a given good by the intellectual faculty, is merely a *conditio sine qua non*, but never exercises any *causal influence proper* on volition.[1]   While St. Thomas regards the will as a *passive faculty* in the technical sense of the word, Scotus and Occam hold it to be *purely active* like the *intellectus agens*.

Emphasizing those divergences between medieval intellectualism and voluntarism, many modern historians have professed to find a proclamation of the *primacy of the theoretical reason* in the Thomist theory, and in the Scotist and Occamist theories an affirmation of the *primacy of the will*.[2]   And they refer, in support of their view, to the numerous articles in which the medieval doctors examine the various relations of co-ordination and subordination between the intellectual and volitional activities in order to decide for the superiority of either one of these faculties over the other.

But since the time of Kant, the *primacy of one faculty over another* is to be understood in a very special sense, and imparts to a system of philosophy a definite criteriological colouring, so to speak, a well and clearly marked attitude.[3]   It is a formula which may not be transported into medieval philosophy without changing its meaning.   For those scholastic discussions on the primacy of the spiritual faculties were of very minor importance : the scholastics never dreamed of a " dogmatism of the practical

[1 See, however, an important study on this subject by Dr. Minges, O.F.M., *Ist Duns Scotus Indeterminist ?* (*Beiträge zur Geschichte der Philosophie des Mittelalters*, Band V., Heft 4 ; Munster, 1905), in which the Subtle Doctor is defended against the charge of having taught the absolute indeterminism of the will.   Cf. also, review of same work in the *Philosophisches Jahrbuch*, B. 19 (1906), H. 4, pp. 502-506.—*Tr.*]

[2] Among others, Windelband, *Geschichte der Philosophie* (1892). p. 259.

[3] Kant propounds the *primacy* of the will or practical reason over the pure or theoretical reason because the former reveals to us the existence of noumenal realities (liberty, immortality and God), which are beyond the reach of the theoretical reason and its certitude.

reason," nor of the encroachment of volition upon knowledge. Even among the medieval *voluntarists,* the adage *nihil volitum nisi præcognitum* is fully recognised. As Henry of Ghent expresses it, the hierarchical relations of the will and the reason are analogous to those of master and servant, but it is none the less true that the servant goes before his master and bears the torch to light him on his way.[1]

SECTION 17.—MORAL PHILOSOPHY AND LOGIC.

91. The scholastics of the thirteenth century approached the philosophical side of moral questions : previously these had been studied mainly from the theological point of view. A system of moral philosophy essentially implies a theory on the *end of man* and on the *human act.* It is, in fact, the study of human acts or conduct (material object) in their relation to man's last end or destiny (formal object). The human act *par excellence* is the *free act :* this alone is moral or immoral. The *last end* of man is God : to possess Him is the object of the natural tendencies of all our highest psychical activities. Aristotle knew little or nothing about the natural happiness of man. The scholastics on the contrary have proved that knowledge (*visio*) and love (*delectatio*) of the Creator constitute the most perfect activity of which man is capable : that the actual securing and enjoying of beatitude, as such, is accomplished by an act of knowledge (St. Thomas) or of love (Duns Scotus) or of both combined (St. Bonaventure). Accordingly, the free act which tends towards the possession of God will be moral, or morally good ; that which draws us away from Him, immoral, or morally evil.

On *moral obligation* the scholastics propounded a

---

[1] Henry of Ghent, *Quodl.,* I., 14, *in fine.*

theory unknown in Greek philosophy. Moral obligation has its foundation, as St. Thomas teaches, in the very nature of our acts ; for this nature serves as basis for the *lex naturalis* with which our consciences are impregnated, and from which all positive law derives its binding force. But ultimately it is to the divine order we must look for the binding force of all law.

Since human nature is morally bound to tend towards its own good, it is likewise bound to utilize the means that are necessary for this purpose. We are led into the knowledge of these means by that *habitus principiorum rationis practicœ* which the scholastics called *synderesis*. Under the guidance of this *synderesis* the intellect formulates the general regulative principles of the moral life ; while *moral conscience* is merely the application of these universal principles to some particular case.

It is interesting to remark that the constitutive elements of the moral goodness of an act (object, circumstances and end), those in virtue of which it tends towards its proper end, are identically the principles of the *ontological perfection* of the act. The degree of ontological or real perfection in an act is likewise the measure of its morality : a further example of the consistency and solidarity of the great leading ideas of scholasticism.

92. The scholastics addressed themselves again, after the example of Aristotle, to a detailed study of the moral virtues, analyzing exhaustively the various grooves into which our moral activity runs in the varying circumstances of life. Their teaching on the nature of morality in general is followed by a body of doctrine dealing with the several relations, domestic, religious and civil, which specify our moral activities in the concrete.

Private property and monogamous and indissoluble marriage are dictated by the natural law. Social life has its *raison d'être* in human nature itself, and ultimately in the will of God. For all authority is of divine origin. St. Thomas does not seem to have troubled about the origin of authority in a society coming newly into being. But he does discuss the various forms of government in an existing state : and he declares them all to be legitimate so long as those in power govern with a view to the common good. After the manner of the ancients, especially of Plutarch, the different classes of society are compared to the various members of a living body, but nobody ever thought of ascribing to this analogy the *real* significance attributed to it by certain organicists in our own time. We also find in the social ethics of the Middle Ages some traces of the communal and feudal organizations of society.[1] Finally, the thirteenth century justifies the subordination of the temporal to the spiritual power ; but already in the fourteenth we find certain writers influenced by the hostile spirit that animated the princes of the time against the papacy.

93. Aristotle is the undisputed master of logic, and the scholastics merely comment on his teaching. Logic is understood to be *the body of laws to which the mind must conform in order to acquire science.* But what are we to understand by *science ?* It is knowing what a thing is, in a necessary and universal manner. *Scientia est universalium.* It is not concerned with the individual, particularizing characteristics of things. By *scientific demonstration,* and *syllogism* which is its basis, we discover the essences, properties and causes of things. Hence the importance attached by Aristotle to those processes : they form the chief subject-matter of the *Analytics,* his principal logical treatise. But the investigation of both processes implies the preparatory study of

---

[1] See on this subject Max Maurenbrecher, *Thomas von Aquinos Stellung zum Wirthschaftsleben seiner Zeit,* I. Heft (Leipzig, 1898).

the simpler operations into which they may be resolved, namely, conception and judgment.

The *concept* represents things to us under abstract and general aspects, some proper to a single species of things, others common to the several species of a common genus. Logic deals with the concept only in so far as it is an element of the judgment. And accordingly, when the scholastics transport into logic the *categories* of being, they take the latter not in the sense of classes of existing realities but of *objective concepts* capable of standing as predicate or subject in a judgment.

Judgment or enunciation is the union of two concepts, of which one (the predicate) is affirmed or denied of the other (the subject). The *De Interpretatione* studies the quality of judgments (affirmation, negation), their quantity (universality, particularity), and their modality (necessity, possibility, contingency).

It is the syllogism that almost monopolizes the attention of medieval logicians. They study at great length this process by which the human mind, while not perceiving immediately the relation between two concepts, the possible terms of a judgment, compares them successively with a third or middle term. The *demonstrative syllogism*, which alone leads to scientific knowledge, arranges our ideas by deducing the particular from the general; it co-ordinates and subordinates our mental notions according to their degree of universality. But demonstration has its limits, for the mind must stop at some indemonstrable first principles which it sees to be self-evident as soon as it has abstracted them from the data of sense. In like manner, *definition* (ὁρισμός) and *division* must reach a limit, for it is impossible to define everything, or to analyze things *ad infinitum*.

Those sciences are deductive or rational which

can be built up independently of experience, by the simple drawing out of the objective relations between our concepts : the mathematical sciences, for example. The inductive or experimental sciences are those that offer us an explanation of the facts of sense experience. The nature of the science will determine the sort of method to which it ought to have recourse (14).

94. In the general economy of the scholastic system, logic is regarded as merely an instrument of knowledge, but it is very closely allied to metaphysics and psychology.   Albert the Great and his successors laid down clearly the relations of the science of concepts to the science of reality.   For St. Thomas's master, logic is a *scientia specialis*, the *vestibulum* of philosophy : preliminary to the latter as drawing is to painting.   Thus the golden age of scholasticism put an end to the absurd and ruinous despotism exercised by dialectics in the early Middle Ages.   Towards the end of the twelfth century we find in the poetic language of Alanus of Lille the comparison of logic to a pale maiden, emaciated and exhausted by too protracted vigils.

Unfortunately those excessive subtleties of the logicians were destined to reappear (96).   But this was when scholasticism had begun to degenerate ; and such decays and failings as that to which we must presently call attention, cannot in any way detract from the real value of the great doctrinal synthesis we have been trying to outline.

SECTION 18.—CONCLUSION.

95. After the sketches we have just given, let us recall for a moment the question raised above : in what should a *real* and *intrinsic* definition of scholasticism consist ? (7) It should be derived from within, and should give the fundamental doctrines

of the system itself. Now to get at these essential
features we need only to take up in detail the solutions
it offers, and to study the distinctive marks of these
latter. Each mark will differentiate and individualize
scholasticism in some special way ; and the whole
collection of them will portray the essential nature
of scholasticism (57, 58). Any *one* of these signs
taken by itself may possibly be common to scholasticism and some other historical solutions ; but the
sum-total of them taken together will be found in
scholasticism and in it alone.[1]

The chief of those great leading features of scholasticism might be indicated as follows : In the first
place scholasticism is not a *monistic* system. The
dualism of the purely actual being of the Divinity
on the one hand, and creatures composed of act and
power on the other, erects an impassable barrier
against all pantheism. Moreover, the compositions
of matter and form, of individual and universal ;
the real distinctions between the knowing subject
and the known object, between the substance of
the soul in heaven and the substance of God who
fills and satisfies its faculties : those are all doctrines
manifestly incompatible with monism. Scholastic
theodicy is *creationist* and *personalist*. The scholastic
metaphysic of the contingent being is at once a
moderate dynamism (act and power, matter and form,

---

[1] A point lost sight of by M. Laplasas in his criticism of our view.
This author's pamphlet (*Ensayo de una Definicion de la Escolastica*,
Barcelona, 1903) reviews an article published by us in the *Revue
philosophique* (June, 1902), and shows a grave want of acquaintance
with scholastic *teaching*. Further, we believe M. Blanc to be wrong
in thinking that the scholasticism common to St. Bonaventure, Scotus,
Suarez and others, " is in no way distinct from any other Christian
philosophy whatever, from Caro's, for example, or even from Cousin's
in the later editions of *Le Vrai, le Beau et le Bien*." (*Université
cathol.*, 1901, p. 114). Not to mention the fact that several theories
of this " common scholasticism "—its ideology, for example—will ever
remain irreconcilable with the corresponding theories of a Caro or a
Cousin, the *whole collection* of the doctrinal characters of scholasticism
belongs to it *alone*, and the accidental agreement of scholasticism and
French eclecticism in occasional, isolated conclusions cannot destroy
the specific oneness of the medieval system.

essence and existence) and a frank avowal of *individualism*. This same *dynamism* governs the formation and dissolution of natural substances; while from another standpoint the material world is interpreted by scholasticism in an *evolutionist* and *finalist* sense. Then, again, scholastic psychology is not materialist but *spiritualist*, not idealist or *a priori* but *experimental*, not subjectivist but *objectivist :* its very definition of philosophy implies that the intellect is capable of seizing an extramental reality. Its logic, based on the data of psychology and metaphysics, advocates the use of the *analytico-synthetic* method. Its ethical teaching derives its principal features from psychology : it is *eudemonist* and *libertarian*.

By varying our standpoint and examining the scholastic system in other ways we might find other intrinsic features for our definition. An integral definition would embrace them all. They are all connected with one another, and they all complete one another : and so they ought, for the different doctrinal departments defined by them are bound closely together in a compact organic unity.

CHAPTER III.

THE DECLINE OF SCHOLASTICISM.

---

96. Very much still remains to be written about the decline of scholasticism from the commencement of the fifteenth century—about the causes of the decay, its different stages and its general significance. Valuable data for such a work have been already collected ; and these point to the conclusion that the decline in question must not be regarded as the *death-agony of a philosophical system* killed by modern discoveries, but rather as a very complex intellectual movement laden with many injurious influences *quite other than the philosophical doctrine itself.* An impartial study of these factors would go to show that the sterility of the period in question is to be laid at the door of the philosophers rather than of the philosophy. This is the first important reserve we are forced to make when we hear and read of the " end of scholasticism," and of its annihilation by modern ideas. And we shall try to justify this contention in the pages that follow.

Yet another reserve, of a different kind, may be merely mentioned here ; the works of specialists would need to be quoted in justification of it. It is this : Notwithstanding the general bankruptcy of

scholasticism in the West, there was a real and profound revival in Spain and Portugal during the
sixteenth century, a return to the great, leading
principles of scholasticism, an intellectual awakening
which bears eloquent testimony to the vitality of
its doctrines in the hands of really capable men as
distinct from petty, unenlightened quibblers.   In
the midst of the barren wastes this branch was seen
to blossom forth and to bear abundant fruit.   There
were certain extrinsic causes, however, which mili-
tated against the new scholasticism of such men as
Suarez and Vasquez.   Moreover, its failure to adapt
itself to contemporary forms of thought accounts
quite sufficiently for the ephemeral character of its
influence.   At the same time it must not be forgotten
that the tradition of scholasticism was never entirely
interrupted—even down through the seventeenth and
eighteenth centuries and up to the commencement
of the neo-scholastic revival that will be dealt with
in the second part of the present volume.   Ever
and anon we see great names arise above the level
of an almost universal mediocrity, to form occasional
brilliant links in the long chain that connects the
sixteenth with the twentieth century.

97. Amongst the reproaches heaped upon the
dethroned sovereign by the philosophers of the
Renaissance and their successors, were, first of all,
her linguistic barbarisms and her barren and obsolete
methods.   The Latin of the fifteenth century and
subsequent scholasticism shows a lamentable disregard
for even moderate accuracy : and the humanists, in
their well nigh idolatrous cult of literary elegance and
style, laid this intolerable and most grievous fault
at the door of the philosophy itself.   The prevalent
contempt for literary form had certainly been dis-
graceful : it extended even to ignorance of ordinary
orthography.   It was in vain that a few of the most
enlightened members of the University of Paris—

Peter D'Ailly and John Gerson—protested and pleaded for reform : the Philistine current was too strong to be arrested in its rapid rush to destruction ! Then, too, there were vexatious and inexcusable faults of method : the endless multiplication of distinctions and sub-distinctions and divisions and classifications, on the plea of clearness ; until finally all thought became mystified and muddled in an inextricable maze of schemes, systems and departments ! Nothing could have been better calculated to foment those abuses than the dialectic formalism that poisoned all the philosophical writings of the sixteenth century. This excessive hair-splitting tendency, already latent in the terminism of William of Occam (in the fourteenth century), admitted into logic, under the guise of purely subjective notions, a multitude of theories that had been ousted from the domain of metaphysics. And these proved a *damnosa hereditas*, introducing still further confusion into the already tangled discussions of the logicians.

98. Another and more fatal influence at work was the widely prevalent ignorance of the real meaning and character of the scholastic system. They still, no doubt, talked and wrote of matter and form in the scholastic manuals of the seventeenth century, but they commonly compared the union of those two principles with that of a man and woman who would meet and marry, and then get divorced in order to contract other matrimonial alliances.

When Malebranche and Arnauld ridiculed the " species intentionales ", their scoffs and sarcasms were justified by the fantastic notions of those scholastics who had inherited only a deformed caricature of the ideology of the thirteenth century (89).

When Molière concocted his quodlibets against the theory of faculties, or made fun of the " virtus dormitiva " of opium, his bantering sallies were not undeserved ; for many of his contemporaries who stood by those scholastic formulæ, either gave them a merely verbal meaning or mistook their real meaning, betraying equally in both cases the sane and rational metaphysics of the thirteenth century which they thought they were defending.

Add to all this that the leading spirits of the time had, for the most part, lost the habit of thinking for themselves : so much so that their works have been justly described as " commentaries on commentaries." We can easily understand, therefore, that the scholastic manuals and compilations of the later Middle Ages are no better than mere counterfeits of the masterly productions of the philosophic thought of the thirteenth century.

99. Nowhere was the culpable ignorance of the scholastics regarding contemporary thought so disastrous as in the domain of the natural sciences. Great discoveries were everywhere revolutionizing physical and mechanical astronomy, physics, chemistry and biology,—and the mathematical sciences as well. The geocentric system of Ptolemy gave place to the heliocentric system of Copernicus ; and Galileo's telescope had begun to reveal the secrets of the heavens. But the paths of the stars careering through the immensities of space gave the theory of solid celestial spheres its death blow ; the displacement of the sun-spots on the solar disc revealed a rotatory motion in the sun itself ; the moon displayed its mountains and plains, Jupiter its satellites, Venus its phases, Saturn its ring. In 1604, a hitherto unknown star was discovered in the sign of the Scorpion. Later on it was shown to evidence that the magnificent comet of 1618 was not an atmospheric will-o'-the-wisp but a heavenly body moving through the interplanetary regions of space. Then Kepler formulated the laws of the elliptical motion of the planets, and Newton inferred from Kepler's laws the

law of universal gravitation which unified all astronomical phenomena. In another department, Torricelli invented the barometer and discovered the weight of the air; heat and cold were registered by the thermometer not as distinct and contrary properties but as different degrees of one and the same property of matter; light was decomposed and water analyzed; Lavoisier laid the first foundations of modern chemistry. At the same time Descartes, Newton, Leibnitz and others devoted their genius to mathematical researches; and, enriched by their contributions, those sciences made rapid and giant strides.

Man's scientific conception of the universe was reconstructed on altogether new lines, and many of the scientific theories which the medieval mind had incorporated in its synthetic view of the world were now finally and completely discredited. To mention only a few: There was an end of the idea that circular motion is the most perfect, and of the theory that the heavenly bodies are exempt from generation and corruption. If there are spots on the sun, the immutability of the heavenly bodies becomes a respectable myth. Nor were the new mechanics long about exploding the theory of the *locus naturalis* of bodies (15). In short, there was much that needed to be reconstructed or modified.

Now, the traditional astronomical, physical and chemical theories were bound up with the principles of general metaphysics and cosmology by ties that were centuries old—though often indeed of a frail and fanciful character. Were not the principles dependent upon the theories, and did not the overthrow of the ancient science involve the ruin of the ancient philosophy? Not necessarily; and that for this reason: amid the debris of the demolished science there remained untouched quite sufficient data to support the constitutional doctrines of scholasticism.

It is sufficiently obvious that philosophers and scientists alike should have closely watched and studied the scientific progress of the time in order to be able to pronounce upon the possibility or impossibility of adapting the new discoveries to the traditional philosophy.   That is certainly what the princes of scholasticism would have done had they lived at such a critical turning point in the history of the sciences.   We are aware from well-known and oft-quoted texts that they never meant to give all the scientific theories of their own time the value of established theses, but rather of more or less probable hypotheses whose disproof and rejection would in nowise compromise their metaphysics. So, for example, St. Thomas, when, speaking of the movements of the planets, he makes use of these significant words : " Licet enim talibus suppositionibus factis apparentia salvarentur, non tamen oportet dicere has suppositiones esse veras, quia forte secundum aliquem alium modum, nondum ab hominibus comprehensum, apparentia circa stellas salvantur." [1]   And his disciple, Giles of Lessines, gives frequent expression to the same view.

But, unfortunately, the reverse of all this was what actually took place.   The deplorable attitude of the seventeenth century peripatetics towards the science of their day was just the opposite of what it ought to have been.   Far from courting or welcoming a possible alliance between their cherished philosophy and the new scientific discoveries they turned away in terror from the current theories lest they should be compelled to abandon their own out-of-date science.   It is said that Melanchthon and Cremonini refused to look at the heavens through a telescope. And Galileo speaks of those Aristotelians who, " rather than alter Aristotle's heavens in any particular, obstinately deny the reality of what is visible

[1] In Lib. II. De Coelo et Mundo, l. xvii.

in the actual heavens." The Aristotelian teaching they regarded as a sort of monument from which not a single stone could be extracted without upturning the whole. This it is that explains the obstinacy with which they tried to defend the discredited astronomy and physics of the thirteenth century, and the ridiculous attitude of the " Aristotelians " in their widespread university controversies with the Cartesians.[1] Those philosophers were shortsighted ; they were apparently unable to distinguish the essential from the accessory ; they failed to realize the possibility of abandoning certain arbitrary applications of metaphysics in the domain of the sciences without abandoning the metaphysic itself.

Is it any wonder that they drew upon themselves the ridicule of the scientists ? And these latter in turn made the scholastic *philosophy* responsible for the errors of medieval *science*, from which *the former had been declared inseparable.* When we remember that for very many scholasticism meant merely the old systems of astronomy and physics we can understand at least to some extent why they should treat it with such sarcasm. They were not long about discrediting a system that defended such mistaken views. The necessity of making a clean sweep of the past became more and more apparent. And some, not satisfied with condemning all scholasticism *en bloc,* went even so far as to condemn *all* philosophy. It is from this epoch of unparalleled progress in the sciences of observation that we may date not only the sharp distinction between common and scientific knowledge but also the divorce of the latter from philosophy. The more moderate among the scientists, while repudiating scholasticism with scorn,

---

[1] See an article of Feret, *L'aristotélisme et le cartésianisme dans l'Université de Paris au XVIIe. siècle* (Annales philos. chrét., April, 1903), and the interesting work of Mgr. Monchamp, *Galilée et la Belgique. Essai historique sur les vicissitudes du système de Copernic en Belgique* (Brussels, 1892).

gave their adherence to some system or other of modern philosophy; for the latter had always professed its respect from the very commencement for the sensational scientific discoveries of the seventeenth century.

To sum up : The contest that arose in the seventeenth century between the peripatetics and the scientists had no real bearing on the essential content of the scholastic teaching, but regarded mere side issues and secondary matters. The misunderstanding was indeed inevitable : it was almost if not altogether irremediable, and unfortunately it exists even still.[1] The scholastics and the scientists of those days were both alike responsible for it : the latter would cut down the powerful oak-tree of centuries on the pretext that it bore some rotten timber under its spreading foliage; while the former stupidly contended that its hoary head must not be touched at any cost—that by stripping it of a few withered branches it would be deprived of its very life.

100. Francis Bacon reproached the scholastics of his time with ignorance of the sciences and neglect of history; and he was justified in doing so. "Hoc genus doctrinæ minus sanæ et seipsum corrumpentis invaluit apud multos præcipue ex Scholasticis, qui summo otio abundantes, atque ingenio acres, lectione autem impares, quippe quorum mentes conclusæ essent in paucorum auctorum, præcipue Aristotelis dictatoris sui scriptis, non minus quam corpora ipsorum in cœnobiorum cellis, *historiam vero et naturæ et temporis maxima ex parte ignorantes*, ex non magno materiæ stamine, sed maxima spiritus, quasi radii, agitatione operosissimas telas, quæ in libris eorum extant confecerunt."[2]

---

[1] According to M. Deussen, Galileo and Copernicus destroyed not only the old astronomy, but also, without knowing or wishing it, the personal God of the scholastics. *Jacob Boehme* (p. 20).

[2] Quoted by Brucker, *Historia crit, Philos.*, vol. III., pp. 877, 878.

The new philosophical syntheses, elaborated *independently* of scholasticism and built upon Baconian empiricism or on Cartesian rationalism, soon directed their attacks *against one another*.   The scholastics no longer counted for a force to be reckoned with. Indeed, apart from the value of their doctrines, what general social influence could these men hope to wield who closed their doors and windows against the outside world, and philosophized without the least heed or concern for the dominant ideas of their time ?

101. The story of the decline of scholasticism would seem to point to a conclusion of considerable importance for all who have any interest in the new scholasticism of the nineteenth and twentieth centuries : *the corrosive action of the causes that encompassed the ruin of medieval scholasticism did not attack its great organic doctrines ; so that its vital parts are still sound and healthy.*

Neither barbarisms of language, nor abuses of method, nor faults of dialectic, disprove the substantial soundness of a philosophical system.   Nor can the ignorance of those who make a clumsy defence of it in any way lessen its intrinsic value.   And if the *savants* of the sixteenth century neglected to compare scholasticism with the rival philosophies that surrounded it on all sides, scholasticism is not entirely to blame for that negligence, nor can such omission raise any prejudice against the possible issue of a comparison which anyone is at liberty to institute at any time.   Exactly the same holds true of the attitude of scholasticism at the present day towards the modern sciences : the question of their compatibility with medieval scholasticism *is still an open question, for it has never yet been seriously investigated.*

We were justified, therefore, in saying that scholasticism lapsed not for want of ideas but for want of men, and that the fact of its decay should in no way militate against an attempt at its revival.   But if such an effort is to prove successful we must avoid what was formerly so fatal to its progress ; and thus, once more, we will allow the past to dictate its great and salutary lessons to the future.

PART II.

MODERN SCHOLASTIC PHILOSOPHY.

CHAPTER I.

SOME EXTRA-DOCTRINAL NOTIONS OF THE NEW SCHOLASTICISM.

Section 20.—the word and the thing.

102. During the last half century many a philosophical system of ancient or of modern date has had both its matter and its form dressed up and refurbished, to suit the changed and changing mentality of the age we live in.[1] We find that convenient prefix, the serviceable " neo," attached to all sorts of titles in contemporary terminology ; and no one dreams of protesting against such descriptive epithets as *Neo-Cartesianism, Neo-Spinozism, Neo-Hegelianism Neo-Kantism, Neo-criticism, Neo-idealism,* etc. Quite indifferent to the master it serves, the particle sometimes even does duty for sufficiently far-fetched and fanciful doctrines—such as that of Neo-Socratism to quote only one example.[2] Indeed the pleasure of creating a *neologism* would seem to have been the only excuse for inventing certain systems devoid of any great positive value or significance.

Why is it then, we may ask, that the term *neo-scholastic* is regarded with such suspicion and hostility,

[1] Cf. L. Stein, *Der Neo-Idealismus unserer Tage* (Archiv. f. system. Philos., 1903, pp. 265, and foll.)

[2] Cf. H. Gomperz, *Grundlegung der neusokratischen Philosophie* (Leipzig, 1897). The author informs us in the introduction that " the Socratic school . . . founded by Leo Haas in 1890 . . . is a community of believers who make it their profession of faith that for a man of goodwill there is no evil whether in life or in death."

although it is even " making its way out of the purely
specialist reviews into books, periodicals and the
ordinary currency of the Press."[1]   It is simply
because this new word, having been adopted as a
rallying cry by the few, still remains a bugbear in
the eyes of the many.

In the first place, it is a scandal to all those who
still entertain the old stock prejudices against medieval
scholasticism, and who seem to take it for granted
that a prejudice must be well-founded simply because
it can boast of a hoary antiquity.   A name that
recalls so many unpleasant old charges and controversies naturally excites repugnance and distrust :
the revival of a past so thickly strewn with errors
would seem to be of necessity a retrograde step ;
it would be the rehabilitation of a narrowly clerical
thought-system, manacled by the restraints of the
Roman Church ; it would oppose the modern spirit
and ignore the scientific discoveries and methods of
which our century is so justly proud.

Secondly, the word is a stumbling-block to those
exclusive admirers of the past who would fain amass
all the best traditions of the Middle Ages and transmit
that sacred deposit to posterity, unchanged and
unchangeable ;—extreme partisans of tradition, for
whom all change seems to imply betrayal of truth
or else doctrinal decay, and to involve in either case
the unpardonable crime of what for want of a better
name we will call *scholastic sacrilege*.   So the priests
of ancient Egypt argued when they systematically
excluded all foreign influences from their traditional
teaching, and symbolized its abiding and immutable
stability in those uncanny sphynxes that defy the
work of time with their rigid, stony stare.

And, thirdly, the new compound grates intolerably

[1] Hubert Meuffels, *A propos d'un mot nouveau* (La Quinzaine,
February, 1901, p. 521).

on the ears of those lovers of fine language who show more concern for the sound of a word than for the idea that underlies it : to their delicate sensibility such an incongruous combination of old and new is little short of a positive torture. " Neo-scholasticism," exclaimed one of them to us recently, " No, no, impossible, impossible ! " And so we find friends of the new movement influenced by esthetic considerations of consonance to substitute the title of *Neo-Thomism* for that of *Neo-scholasticism.*

Now, without defending the musical superiority of the word *Neo-scholasticism*, we prefer it, in the absence of a more harmonious substitute, to the term " Neo-Thomism." And our reason is a simple and intelligible one. " Neo-Thomism," or " Neo-Scotism," or indeed, any other title reminiscent of any one great medieval philosopher, labours under the obvious disadvantage that it likens the new philosophy too exclusively to the thought-system of *some particular individual*, whereas in reality this new philosophy is sufficiently large and comprehensive to pass beyond the doctrinal limitations of any individual thinker [1] and to draw its inspiration from the whole field of scholastic philosophy as outlined in some of the preceding Sections (12-17). Moreover, Neo-scholasticism is not the same as Neo-Thomism, as we shall show later on; and hence the former expression must have our preference. The function of words is not to misrepresent but to express accurately the things they denote—and that even at the expense of a little musical consonance.

M. Meuffels has no hesitation in advocating this view of the matter in a French periodical,[2] and we agree with him both on his decision itself, and on

---

[1] From this point of view we may follow with an equal degree of interest the restoration of the teachings of St. Bonaventure and of those of St. Thomas. See, for example, the articles of Fr. Evangelist, in the *Études franciscaines* (1902 and 1903).

[2] *La Quinzaine*, article referred to above.

the convincing reason he gives for it : *the Neo-scholasticism of the present day, like the scholasticism of the Middle Ages, is a body of doctrines, and by its doctrines it must be judged.*   Both those who anathe-matize the Middle Ages and those who adore them, have to be cured of certain optical illusions before they can see the significance of quite a number of ideas that are developing under our very eyes and have already taken their place among the most dominant factors in contemporary thought.

103. When the father of a family dies, his children do not squander away his estate on the pretext that they can assert their own personality in the world only by carving out their own fortunes independently, or that their father's property is useless for the needs of their generation.   On the contrary, the son receives the patrimony bequeathed to him, as a sacred inheritance ; he regards these stored-up fruits of ancestral toil as a precious capital by the use of which he can render his own labour more productive than it otherwise could be.   Now, the transmission of philosophical ideas is in many points analogous to the transmission of goods of fortune.   Every epoch inherits from the preceding and bequeathes to the succeeding epoch.   Even systems which react against tradition, themselves contain *traditional elements.*   Without going farther back than the earlier of the modern philosophers—men who gloried openly in demolishing tradition and scourging pre-judices and preconceived ideas of all sorts—even those have been clearly convicted, so to speak, of having borrowed much, perhaps unconsciously, from the Middle Ages ; and they have been justly likened by La Bruyère to ungrateful children who direct their first attacks against their own nurses.   Nobler and abler men, of the stamp of Leibnitz, have bestowed on the worth and excellence of scholastic philosophy encomiums that deserve to be more widely

known.[1]   It would be worth while, from a critical
point of view, to re-edit a book published in 1766
by an eclectic disciple of the Hanoverian philosopher,
L. Dutens, under the curious title : *Recherches sur
l'origine des découvertes attribuées aux modernes, où
l'on démontre que nos plus célèbres philosophes ont
puisé la plupart de leurs connaissances dans les ouvrages
des anciens.*[2]

When the new scholastic philosophy proclaims by
its very name its continuity with a glorious past,
it is merely recognising this incontestable law of
organic relationship between the doctrines of
centuries.   It does more, however.   Its endeavour
to re-establish and to plant down deeply amid the
controversies of the twentieth century the principles
that animated the scholasticism of the thirteenth
is in itself an admission that philosophy cannot
completely change from epoch to epoch ; that the
truth of seven hundred years ago is still the truth
of to-day ; that out and out relativism is an error :
that down through all the oscillations of historical
systems there is ever to be met with a *philosophia
perennis*—a sort of atmosphere of truth, pure and
undiluted, whose bright, clear rays have lighted
up the centuries even through the shadows of the
darkest and gloomiest clouds.   " The truth for
which Pythagoras, Plato and Aristotle sought, is
the same as that pursued by St. Augustine and St.

[1] See, *e.g. Lettre à Wagner*, Op. phil. ed. Erdmann, p. 424 ; *De stilo
phil. Nizolii*, Op. phil. p. 68 ; *Théodicée*, II., n. 330.   Cf. Willmann,
Gesch. d. Idealismus, Vol. II., p. 533.

[2] Paris, 2 vols.—Among the principal works on the relations between
modern and scholastic philosophy, we may mention Glossner, *Zur
Frage nach dem Einfluss der Scholastik auf die neuere Philosophie
(Jahrb. f. Phil. u. sp. Theol.*, 1899) ; Von Hertling, *Descartes' Beziehungen zur Scholastik* (Sitzungsberichte d. philos.-philol. u. histor.
Klasse d. München. Akad. d. Wiss, 1899) ;   J. Freudenthal, *Spinoza
und die Scholastik* (in Phil. Aufsätze Ed. Zeller gewidmet, Leipzig,
1887) ;   Nostitz-Rieneck, *Leibniz u. die Scholastik (Philos. Yahrb.*,
1894) ;   Jasper, *Leibniz u. die Scholastik* (Diss), Leipzig, 1898 ; Rintelen,
Leibnizens Beziehungen zur Scholastik (Archiv. f. Gesch. d. Philos.,
1903).

Thomas. . . . In so far as it is elaborated in
the course of history, truth is the child of time;
but in so far as it embodies a content that is independent both of time and of history, it is the child
of eternity."[1]   For "if reason be aught but a
deceptive aspiration after the absolutely inaccessible,
surely whatever has been brought to light, whatever
our ancestors have unearthed and acquired in their
pioneer labours, cannot have proved entirely worthless to posterity. . . .   Instead of eternally commencing over again the solution of the great enigma
of nature and of consciousness, would it not be wiser
to preserve our traditional inheritance, and go on
perfecting it ?   Can it be better to let the intelligence
live on its own personal and ever-incipient thought
than on the accumulated wisdom of centuries ?
Should we not be better employed in adding to that
common fund of doctrine than in changing it every
day—in the hope of attaching our names to some
new system ? "[2]   Such is obviously the postulate
that must be either explicitly or implicitly recognised by all of us who find in scholasticism, and in
the wealthy store of Greek thought assimilated by
scholasticism, a remarkably close approximation to
absolute truth—closer perhaps to the ideal of true
wisdom than any of the contemporary forms of
positivism or of Neo-Kantism.[3]

[1] Willmann, *op. cit.*, V. II., p. 550.   Cf. Commer, *Die immerwæhrende
Philosophie* (Vienna, 1899).
[2] Van Weddingen, *L'Encyclique de S. S. Léon XIII. et la restauration
de la philosophie chrétienne*, 1880, pp. 90 and 91.
[3] Cf. De Wulf, *Kantisme et néo-scolastique :* " For our part we believe
that extreme evolutionism, which is losing ground every day in the
special sciences, is an unsound hypothesis when applied to philosophy.
No doubt, history shows that systems adapt themselves to their
surroundings, and that every age has its own proper aspirations and its
own special way of approaching problems and solutions ; but it also
lays before us, clearly and unequivocally, the spectacle of ever-repeated
beginnings *ab initio*, and of rhythmic oscillations between contrary
poles of thought.   And if Kant has found a new formula for subjectivism and the *reine Innerlichkeit*, it would be a mistake to imagine
that he has no intellectual ancestors.   Even at the first dawn of history

At the same time, let us hasten to add, the new scholasticism inscribes on its programme, side by side with this respect for the fundamental doctrines of tradition, *another essential principle*, of equal importance with the first—which it supplements— and expressed with equal clearness by the name it has chosen for itself : the principle of *adaptation to modern intellectual needs and conditions*. The heir to a fortune accumulated a century ago does not treat it in the same way as its compiler would in his day. For the better employment of it he avails of all the advantages to be derived from new and improved economic surroundings. He invests his capital in industrial enterprises, delivering it up to a vast and complicated currency that has little in common with the simple investments through which it earned interest for his forefathers. So it is, too, with the riches of the mind. *Absolute* immobility in philosophy, no less than *absolute* relativism, is contrary both to nature and to history. It leads only to decay and death. *Vita in motu*. To have scholasticism rigid and inflexible, would be to give it its death-blow, to make of it a mere *caput mortuum ;* an interesting relic, no doubt, but only a relic, fit indeed to figure respectably at an international exhibition of bygone systems, but fit for nothing else.

we find some of them, for M. Deussen has unearthed in the *Upanishads* to the Vedic hymns the distinction between the noumenon and the phenomenon, and has been able to recognise in the theory of the Māya " Kants Grunddogma, so alt wie die Philosophie."

No, it is by no means proven that all truth is relative to a given time or a given latitude ; nor that philosophy is the product of the natural and necessary evolution of purely economic forces. The materialist conception of history is as groundless as it is gratuitous. Alongside the changing elements that are peculiar to any given stage of development in the life of humanity, there is at every stage and in every system an abiding soul of truth—a small fraction of that full and immutable truth which hovers around the mind in its highest flights and noblest efforts. This soul of truth it is that the new scholasticism hopes to find in certain fundamental doctrines of Aristotle and St. Thomas ; and it is precisely in order to test their value that they must be cast into the crucible of modern thought and confronted with the doctrines opposed to them." (*Revue Néo-Scolastique*, 1902, pp. 13 and 14.)

We have been more than once accused of com-
mitting a gross anachronism : of transporting bodily
into the twentieth century the conceptions of the
thirteenth.   J. Frohschammer, the not over critical
author of a work entitled : *Die Philosophie des
Thomas von Aquino kritisch gewürdigt*,[1] justifies the
publication of his views in the following combative
language :—" In the actual circumstances," he writes,
" we are called upon not merely to criticize a theoretical system but to destroy the practical influence
which the philosophy of Thomas has acquired since
he has been proclaimed commander-in-chief of the
scholastic forces.   The papacy, allied with Jesuitism,
is utilizing these forces to the utmost for the purpose
of carrying on a struggle to the death against all
modern philosophy, all modern science and even
against civilization itself ; and that, in order to erect
upon their ruins the temporal supremacy of the papacy
as well as the scholastic science and civilization
of the Middle Ages."[2] (!)   Professor Eucken, while
freely admitting the *historical* value of Thomism,
thinks that it has no permanent or *absolute* value,
and that an attempt to rehabilitate its leading
doctrines would be tantamount to denying the
progress of humanity and trying to reverse the
wheel of time (das Rad der Weltgeschichte
zurückdrehen).[3]   Maurenbrecher naively jokes at
the Neo-Thomism, " which fails to see how utterly
impossible it would be to resurrect the social organism
of St. Thomas' age."[4]   And M. Secretan pronounces
the following prejudiced and summary condemnation
of the new movement :   " There can be no possible
understanding," he writes, " between science and a

---

[1] Leipzig, 1889, in 8vo of 535 pp.
[2] Vorrede, p. v.
[3] *Thomas v. Aquino u. Kant. Ein Kampf zweier Welten* (Kantstudien,
1901, Bd. VI., pp. 10-11 and 18).
[4] *Thomas von Aquinos Stellung zum Wirthschaftsleben seiner Zeit*
(Leipzig, 1898), p. 50.

school of philosophy that proclaims every question already settled as it turns up, or settles it then and there by an appeal to authority." [1]

Quotations might be multiplied indefinitely. But we may assure such writers that there is no need for alarm : that they have only to disillusion themselves and make their minds easy. The promoters of the new scholastic movement will have none of that puerile psittacism which contents itself with repeating lessons learned by heart ; they are quite aware that an archaic renaissance is not unlike a death-agony. From the fruitless efforts of the fifteenth century philosophers to revive, in their original form, Platonism or Aristotelianism, Stoicism or Atomism, history has gathered a lesson that ought to open the eyes of the blindest. Besides, we find that those who have pronounced on the meaning and scope of the new scholasticism in recent years are all unanimous in declaring that if this philosophy contains a soul of truth in it it should be able to fit in with all the advances made, and all the progress realized, since the Middle Ages, and to open wide its arms to all the rich fruits of modern culture.

Talamo advocates this work of modernization.[2] Gutberlet, the learned Fulda professor, outlines a similar programme in an article in the *Philosophisches Yahrbuch*, espousing the philosophical system of St. Thomas, in order to complete and improve and correct it.[3] As Dr. Ehrhard of Strassburg has so well expressed it : " St. Thomas of Aquin should be a beacon (*Lichtthurm*) to us, but not a boundary (*Grenzstein*). . . . The needs of any epoch are peculiar to that epoch, and will never repeat

---

[1] *La restauration du thomisme* (*Revue philosophique*, 1884, V. II., p. 87).

[2] *L'Aristotélisme de la scolastique dans l'histoire de la philosophie* (Paris, 1876), Conclusion, p. 531.

[3] *Die Aufgabe der christlichen Philosophie in der Gegenwart* (Phil. Jahrb., 1888, pp. 1-23.)

themselves."[1]   Like declarations have been frequently
repeated by the professors of the Louvain Philosophical Institute, and by their official organ, the
Revue Néo-Scolastique.[2]   They have been echoed
over and over again by Mgr. d'Hulst,[3] Kaufmann,[4]
Hettinger,[5] Meuffels,[6] Schneid,[7] etc., all of whom
refer to the well-known advice of Leo XIII. : " We
proclaim that every wise thought and every useful
discovery ought to be gladly welcomed and gratefully
received by us, whatever its origin may have been."[8]

104. To sum up : The whole aim and object of the
new revival of ideas to be treated in the subsequent
pages of the present work, is just simply the realization

---

[1] *Der Katholicismus und der zwanzigste Jahrhundert im Lichte der kir-
chlichen Entwicklung der Neuzeit* (Stuttgart, 1902), p. 252.

[2] See especially 1894, p. 13 ; 1899, p. 6 ; 1902, p. 5.—Cf. Mercier,
Les origines de la psychologie contemporaine, pp. 440 and foll.

[3] *Mélanges philosophiques* (Paris, 1892), *passim*.

[4] *Schweizerische Kirchenzeitung* (March 14th, 1902).

[5] *Timotheus, Briefe an einen jungen Theologen* (Frèiburg, 1897),
pp. 192, and foll.—Cf. *La Quinzaine* (December 1st, 1902) : *Comment
faire ?*

[6] " Rightly understood, therefore, the new scholasticism is no mere
re-editing, no mere systematic and uncritical justification of everything that has been, rightly or wrongly, labelled with the elastic title
of ' Scholastic Philosophy.'   The new scholasticism has all that is
best in medieval scholasticism, enriched and completed, moreover,
by modern science, adapted to the needs of our times, directed in its
tendencies by the spirit and teaching of the Papal Encyclical.   In
other words : the aim and object of the new scholasticism is ever to
go on increasing and adapting to present needs the patrimony of
truths bequeathed to us by those who have gone before us, and
especially by St. Thomas Aquinas."   *A propos d'un mot nouveau*,
p. 527. [See also a series of four articles in the *Irish Ecclesiastical
Record* (Jan., Feb., May and June, 1905), in which we have discussed
the scholastic view of the relations between philosophy and the sciences,
and described how these relations are realized in practice in the teaching
of the Philosophical Institute of the Catholic University of Louvain.—
Cf. Appendix, *infra.—Tr.*]

[7] *Die Philosophie d. hl. Thomas und ihre Bedeutung für die Gegenwart*
(Wurzburg, 1881), p. 74.

[8] Encyclical *Aeterni Patris*. Picavet, who is no scholastic, makes
this candid plea for the new movement : " Why, if there be a new
Cartesianism, a new Leibnitzianism, a new Kantism, should there
not be also a new Thomism ?   We think we have shown clearly enough
that the millions of Catholics who with Leo XIII. proclaim their
allegiance to Thomism, have not the slightest intention to become
mere echoes of the thirteenth century, nor to leave out of account, in
constructing their systems, the researches and discoveries of modern
science."   (*Revue philos.*, 1893, vol. 35, p. 395.)

of that characteristic and perfectly justifiable union of a borrowed element—the traditional *scholasticism*—with a *new* and original element. Just as in the Middle Ages scholasticism grew and developed from its own inner vital principle, after assimilating Greek and Patristic ideas, so will the new scholasticism be animated by its own proper spirit all the while that it feeds on medieval ideas in the full light of the twentieth century. And what are the factors of this new spirit, or how far is the new scholasticism likely to modify the old ? We shall try to outline an answer to these questions in the paragraphs that follow. By keeping to the order of Part I. we shall be able to compare the past with the present, and so to meet all the questions of more particular interest in the study of contemporary scholasticism. This first chapter deals mainly with the external relations (6) of the new scholasticism (Sections 20-24). The second will treat of the doctrine itself (Sections 25-33).

SECTION 21.—MEASURES FOR TEACHING AND PROPAGANDISM.

105. Is the new scholasticism the " child of the schools " ? Just as much as, but no more than, positivism or Kantism or pantheism or the philosophy of immanence. It is propagated by teaching, but also by all the manifold forms of modern printing : books, pamphlets, reviews, even newspapers have helped to spread its doctrines. Quite a large bibliography of the new scholasticism has grown up within the past two decades.

A person would certainly provoke a smile at the present day, if, under pretext of reviving the past, he tried to propagate his ideas through the sole medium of manuscripts, refusing to have anything

whatever to do with the printing-press. The most
extreme reactionaries would scarcely venture to push
absurdity so far. Neither would they venture to
rehabilitate the ancient *trivium* and *quadrivium*
(16 and 17), nor to put into force once more in our
modern universities the edict issued in 1255 by the
faculty of arts in Paris (48). Moreover, the historical
continuity of teaching methods has been completely
interrupted. Far-reaching innovations have been
introduced. And these in a certain measure reflect
the progress of the doctrines themselves conveyed
by them.

The commentary, which formed the chief vehicle
of instruction in the thirteenth century (17), has
been long since abandoned in favour of a systematic
exposition of the various branches of philosophy.
The latter method is much better calculated to give
the student a unified view of all philosophy, while
at the same time it prevents useless repetitions.
It also makes it easier for us to enrich the new scholasticism with doctrines borrowed from other systems
whenever that may be necessary, as well as to make
better use of the findings of the various special
sciences. We could count on our fingers those who
would limit the work of restoration to a simple
exposition of the philosophy of St. Thomas " in all
its fulness and in the order he himself followed."
In the opinion of Fr. Janvier, any other method than
the latter would be a *misguided advocacy* of Thomism.
" The most enlightened and right-minded scholastics,"
he writes, " took the Encyclical of Leo XIII literally,
and proceeded to expound the whole teaching of
St. Thomas following both the method and the style
of the Angelic Doctor himself."[1] But Fr. Janvier's
expression of opinion called forth numerous protests,
even unexpected protests ; and we have every reason
to be glad that it did so.

---

[1] *L'action intellectuelle et politique de Léon XIII* (Paris, 1902), p. 49.

At the same time the commentary will still prove useful, whether for the thorough investigation of special questions in which the explanation of isolated texts could easily be of the greatest importance, or in the more advanced studies for the doctorate when an exhaustive analysis of some Aristotelian or scholastic treatise is prescribed. This, in fact, is the method of teaching followed in most of our modern universities, and it shows excellent results. The formal setting of a question by the application of the well-known triple process " Videtur quod—Sed contra—Respondeo dicendum," as also the use of the syllogism, are too valuable as didactic methods to allow them to lapse, or to deprive the new scholasticism of their services (19, 20). But the continuance of such methods does not exclude their adaptation to the modern mind. Nothing can redeem the monotony of dissecting human thought after a stereotyped method, and by a constant repetition of the same rigid formulæ. The inevitable outcome of such a system is an arid and barren formalism that provokes weariness if not disgust. The exposition of reasons for and against, the answering of objections, the vigorous syllogistic demonstrations : all these processes gain immensely in attractiveness, without losing a particle of their force, when they are stripped of their medieval garments and presented to the twentieth century in a somewhat more modern dress. The matter is simply beyond discussion so far as works in philosophy are concerned ; the idea of writing a treatise on criteriology or a book on contemporary psychology, after the manner and style of the *Summæ Theologicæ* or the *Quodlibeta,* would be simply barbarous.

And so, too, of oral teaching. That students should be taught by means of discussions and practical exercises to put an argument " in form " and to answer it ; that they should learn, by the searching application of distinction and sub-distinction, to detect the latent vice or weakness of a doctrine: by all means ; that is most essential. But let them learn also to despise mere sophistry and to avoid the intolerable abuse of juggling and trifling with formulæ (Section 33). Let them learn to grapple with reality and to shake off the delusion that all knowledge is crystallized in the phrases of their daily lessons.

106. There are, besides, certain new didactic methods which custom has universally established in other domains : it would be very unwise not to employ those methods, which are the fruits of modern progress, for the benefit of the new scholasticism. The thirteenth century had thoroughly organized and availed of public discussion ; this is supplemented nowadays by the *monograph* and the *dissertation*, at certain stages of the student's course. For the latter, by putting his hand to such work, learns to think for himself—and to express his thoughts. Above all, our teaching methods would profit immensely by the introduction and use of *laboratories* and of what the Germans call the *Seminar*, or class for practical tuition.

The idea of a " laboratory " in connection with the teaching of philosophy may possibly provoke a smile. Nevertheless, alongside the libraries and reading rooms, which might be called the laboratories of the speculative departments of philosophy, there is really a place and a demand for experimental science laboratories (psycho-physiology, physics, chemistry)—once you admit that the new scholasticism ought to refresh and reanimate itself by contact with the experimental and rational sciences (Section 24).

The " practical seminary "—where a small circle of students devote themselves, with the help and direction of their professor, to the study of some special question—can be employed with profit in all departments of philosophy : its good results have been everywhere in evidence.   In work of this kind, where each contributes his share to the achievement of some common purpose, each will have the benefit of the others' researches ;   the right methods of investigation and the proper use of instruments and means of research will be learned by actual practice ; the student will be brought into contact with the *constructive* or *inventive methods* in use in the various branches of his studies ;   and in this way his tastes will often be fostered for some particular line of work, and his intellectual vocation often definitely decided by some success that may have crowned his initial efforts.

107. In regard to teaching methods there is a final question which divides even the most sincere and well-meaning among scholastics : in what language should the new scholasticism be taught ?   Must we retain the philosophical Latin of the Middle Ages, the language of the great scholastics themselves whose deep and wholesome doctrines we would fain perpetuate ?   Or should we boldly translate into the living languages the exact and delicate formulæ which make the scholastic idiom unintelligible except to the initiated ?

The sermons of Master Eckhart (*circa* 1260-1327), who, with all his peculiar views, was really a scholastic, may be regarded as the first beginnings of a German literature ;   and, in common with the works of Raymond Lully, they are among the earliest applications of a living language to philosophy.   But for long after their time Latin remained the common language of all educated people in the West.   Then the Humanism of the Renaissance came along and gave it a new lease of life which lasted for two centuries.   The philosophy of the fifteenth century became the battle-ground of two kinds of latinity :

the scholastic Latin which became more and more
barbarous, corrupted as it was by the decay of the
doctrine itself (except in the Spanish and Portuguese
authors of the sixteenth century), and the classical
Latin, cultivated for its own sake by a group of
writers less concerned for the thought itself than for
the expression of it.   The earliest of the " modern "
philosophers, Descartes, Bacon and Leibnitz, wrote
partly in Latin and partly in their vernacular ; but
in the eighteenth century the various vernaculars
almost universally supplanted their common rival.
The nineteenth century confirmed the modern usage :
at the present day very little philosophy is written
in Latin, and the speaking of it in Latin is practically
confined to the public displays of defending theses
for academic degrees.

108. As an exception to this general movement
we must recognise the existence of a large and influential group of scholastics who boldly undertook
the revival of the medieval doctrines in the second
half of the century just elapsed, and whose vigorous
propaganda has certainly contributed much to the
restoration which has now become so widespread.
Their example has been followed by most professors of
scholastic philosophy—especially in the ecclesiastical
seminaries and colleges where special reasons, the
force of which we freely recognise, oblige the students
to familiarize themselves with the official language
of the Church.

Apart from those considerations of tradition and
ecclesiastical discipline which we do not wish to mix up
with this dispute,[1] the reasons which the " latinists "

---

[1] The question has been discussed from this point of view by M.
Meuffels in the Revue Néo-Scolastique of February and November,
1903 ; and by Hogan in his Clerical Studies.   The same aspect of
it has also been dealt with by Count Domet de Vorges in the Revue
Néo-Scolastique, 1903, p. 253.—See also: Kihn, Encyclopædie u.
Methodologie der Theologie (Fribourg, 1892), pp. 95-99, and Mgr. Latty,
De l'usage de la langue latine dans l'enseignement de la théologie (Chalons,
1903).

bring forward are mainly drawn from the pedagogic excellence of the Latin language in the matter of scholasticism : this philosophy, they tell us, is so closely bound up with the phrases and formulæ, the expressions and idiom, in which it was embodied in the Middle Ages, that these are practically inseparable from the doctrine itself. From which they infer that we must continue to teach and to write scholastic philosophy in the twentieth century in the self-same Latin which was its natural vehicle in the thirteenth.

To that which is their main argument, they add this other consideration : that the propagation of the doctrine itself will be helped on by the employment of one common " language of learning," which, being intelligible to all, will surmount the obstacles arising from differences of race and country, and facilitate intellectual intercourse between all who take part in the common work of scholastic reconstruction.

In theory, no one has ever denied the very great value of Latin, *as a historical fact*, in scholastic pedagogy ; and the employment of that language, were it accepted by all, would probably render as much service in the twentieth century as it rendered in the thirteenth. But the question, formulated in such terms as these, belongs to the *abstract* and *ideal* order ; and it might have quite another solution were it made *concrete* and *practical*. And as a matter of fact the supporters of vernacular teaching insist that the new scholasticism must take into account the age and the surroundings in which it has to live and to assert itself, and, above all, the intellectual atmosphere breathed by the learned men of our time—an atmosphere which is the outcome of certain factors peculiar to modern life. To ignore all these considerations would be simply to work not for our contemporaries but for the vanished figures of history ; it would be sowing the living word in the desert.   But the moment we take these new elements into consideration the whole pedagogical problem of the language of philosophy assumes a totally different aspect.

In the first place, this at all events is clear, that if we take the latinists' contention in the exclusive sense of denying the *possibility* of teaching scholastic philosophy in any modern language, the contention is certainly extreme and unjustifiable.   It rests' on a confusion of ideas.   Seeing that the scholastics have written in Latin, of course an intimate acquaintance with their latinity is an essential condition for *understanding* their doctrine or encompassing its revival—just as one must understand Sanscrit or Greek in order to speak with authority on the Upanishads or on Aristotle.   In fact, we must strongly insist on the necessity of a thorough-going *scholastic philology*, for it is an indispensable aid to the study of medieval philosophy.   It is precisely for want of such an equipment—which can be had only through special training and initiation—that many of our modern historians of medieval institutions commit such deplorable mistakes.[1]   Missing the technical meaning of a word or of a phrase, they credit the scholastics with absurd and unmeaning theories, and accuse them of errors for which their own ignorance alone is accountable.

Therefore a thorough knowledge of scholastic Latin is of the first importance.   But it is one thing to *understand the language* in which an author has written, and another thing altogether to make use of that same language to *express* that author's ideas, to discuss their meaning, their origin, their merits and their defects, with all the developments that such a work of exegesis implies.   If a philosopher undertake to explain the theory of the *ātman* or

---

[1] See, for example, p. 129, n. 1.

of the εἶδος he should be fully conversant with the
meaning of the Sanscrit or of the Greek term, but he
need not necessarily write or deliver his lectures on
those subjects in Greek or in Sanscrit. Any language
of normal development will furnish the materials
needed for the expression of any idea whatsoever,
provided they are managed by skilful hands and
suitably chosen for the ideas they are intended to
embody.   Every normal language will be found
capable of expressing any stock of ideas.   That many
of our modern languages do combine the requisite
conditions of richness and flexibility—who will
venture to deny ?   We have a sufficient proof of it in
one single work : Fr. Kleutgen's well-known volumes,
which have done so much for the spread of scholastic
ideas, were written originally in German *(Die Philosophie der Vorzeit vertheidigt)*,[1] and afterwards
translated into French and Italian (*La philosophie
scolastique exposée et défendue ; La filosofia antica
esposita e difesa*).[2]   And personal experience—which
others will still confirm with theirs—has amply
proved the superiority of that work over many a
Latin treatise, even from the simple point of view
of doctrinal interpretation.   Other examples might
be added.   In short, the facts have already proved
that scholastic thought is by no means immovably
embedded in its medieval setting.   Latin is not a
sort of epidermis that may not be removed without
flaying or disfiguring the doctrine itself.   Hence,
at the very least, it cannot claim a *monopoly* in the
teaching of scholastic philosophy.'
  Then, furthermore, those who would support the
strange contention that an author must be expounded in the language in which he wrote, would be
putting the scholastics of the Middle Ages in a very
awkward position.   For the world knows that their

---

[1] Second edition, 2 vols. Innsbruck, 1878.
[2] Four vols., Paris, 1868-1870 : five vols., Rome, 1866-1868.

commentaries on Aristotle are not in Greek but in
Latin ; nay, even that they had to use Latin translations in studying Aristotle themselves : we could
count on our fingers the Western scholars who could
read Greek between the ninth and the fourteenth
centuries.   And yet who will venture to say that
the medieval scholastics did not thoroughly understand and expound Aristotle ?

As to the advantages of having one common
language of learning, they are too obvious to be
disputed.   But here again we are only chasing
shadows : contact with actual facts will give a
rude shake to our fancies.   We are not now living
in the conditions that obtained in the Middle Ages.
The modern languages have been built up slowly
and gradually ; and they have inherited a long lease
of life from deep and wide divergences of national
manners and customs, ideas and traditions.   Moreover there is not one of the four or five great European
languages that has not been most successfully
employed in the service of philosophic thought by
men of the highest genius ; and their imitators are
simply legion.   The repeated deplorable failures
both of individual and of organized effort to secure
the recognition of some one *common language of
learning*, should be a sufficiently clear index to the
sort of results likely to be achieved by the promoters
of such an utopia : especially seeing that the men who
are trying to stem such an irresistible current must
at the same time struggle against a multitude of other
difficulties which have hitherto prevented sincere
and unprejudiced minds from appreciating the real
value of the new scholasticism.   Practically it will
come to this in the long run, or rather indeed it has
come to this already, that we simply must familiarize
ourselves—and it is not a very difficult task—with
at least the more important of the modern languages.

109. So far, we have been suggesting considerations

more of a defensive nature against a claim which is, to say the very least, exaggerated. On the other hand, the claim of those who support the modern languages gains enormously in force and persuasiveness, when we begin to reflect on the many serious disadvantages connected with the use of Latin nowadays in our schools. If we would secure an abiding vitality and influence for the new scholasticism, we must force an entrance for it, at any cost, into those indifferent or hostile circles from which its very name has hitherto sufficed to exclude it. It is not by shutting itself up in secluded class-halls, nor by receiving the incense of a small coterie of select admirers, that modern scholasticism is to accomplish the important mission intended for it by those who are devoting their lives to its propagation. It must be brought into touch with the modern mind, with all the main currents of ideas that are shaping the mentality of the age we live in. We must give it an opportunity of stating and supporting its reasons and arguments, of opposing its solutions to rival solutions; in a word, we must secure currency for it in the world of contemporary thought.

Now, is it by the use of Latin that it is likely to force an entrance into those quarters from which it has been so long exiled? It certainly is not. It will knock in vain at the library door of the Positivist or Neo-Kantian if it finds its way thither embodied in ponderous Latin volumes. It will meet with the reception usually accorded to inconvenient visitors. It will be considered an anachronism—as archaic and out of date as the cut of its clothing—and put aside with the simple remark that it can have no use or interest except for Church folk.

So true is this that if certain modern publications on scholasticism have attracted attention and provoked serious and earnest discussion in quarters where quite other doctrines were holding undisputed

sway, these publications must be sought, not amongst
learned Latin treatises, but among the works that
breathe a modern spirit and are written in a living
tongue.   Nor would it be anything short of an
illusion to imagine that at least those who are friends of
the Middle Ages and restorers of its philosophy should
find in Latin a special help, an additional stimulus
to work.   Here again the dead language of another
age is only a source of trouble and delay.   Indeed
with the exception of a few remarkable personalities
belonging for the most part to Roman or Italian
centres of learning, where by force of national
tradition the study of Latin was held in honour,
it must be admitted that quite a multitude of philosophical manuals are written in a style that is only
very remotely reminiscent, we will not say of Cicero's
elegant latinity, but even of the standard philosophical
latinity of the Middle Ages.   And what are we to
say of the Latin spoken in the class-halls both by
professors and by students ?   Does it not, for the
most part, reach the low level of what we might
fairly describe as jargon ?   Then, does anyone
seriously believe that the beginner, while yet quite
a stranger to the effort and the habit of philosophical
thought, can possibly feel at ease within the cramping
confines of an unfamiliar language ?   A teacher of
ripe experience, who has had abundant opportunities
of judging the tree by its fruits, has spoken in the
following terms of the difficulties of the youthful
student : " A second difficulty, of the most serious
kind and common to all beginners, arises from the
utter strangeness of the new field that is opened up
to their activity. . . .   All is new and difficult
—the notions, the terms, the methods and the
language. [The student] is suddenly introduced into a
world of abstract ideas hitherto unknown.   And then,
Latin, as a vehicle of thought, is unfamiliar to him.
Even the old, well-known truths assume strange

and, to him, unnatural forms, whilst the terminology of the schools is obscure and bewildering. He is soon lost, as in a fog. . . . Some never emerge from the gloom, and even those who do always remember it as the most trying period of their intellectual formation."[1] And further on, he says: "It has been the experience of the writer for many years that, of those who have been taught philosophy, and especially scholastic philosophy, only in Latin, not more than one in half a dozen had brought away with him much more than a set of formulas, with only a very imperfect notion of their meaning, though not unfrequently accompanied by a strong determination to cling to them all, indiscriminately and at any cost."[2]

Dr. Hogan, the late venerated president of the Boston Seminary, refers in those passages only to *ecclesiastical* students, who have such incentives, apart altogether from philosophy, to preserve and to utilize their store of latinity. In the case of *lay* students, therefore, who are attracted to the study of philosophy only by a strong, disinterested love for truth, and a praiseworthy ambition to explore the great problems of the world and of life, this anachronism of language becomes, unfortunately, a disastrous and insurmountable obstacle. Of that we have had sad experience in the Louvain Philosophical Institute, to which the writer has the honour to belong. From 1895 to 1898, the courses were given in Latin: the experiment had practically the effect of an interdict; the lay students withdrew,

---

[1] Hogan, *Clerical Studies*, pp. 64, 65.
[2] *Ibid.*, p. 70.—Similarly, Count Domet de Vorges very justly remarks that "Oftentimes students imagine they have grasped an idea when they are only repeating a formula. And even professors are not exempt from this danger. They may think they have the solution of a question in certain high-sounding phrases which make an impression because uttered in a strange language. It has often occurred to us, in reading modern manuals, that the author would not have dared to defend his thesis in the vernacular." *Revue Néo-Scolastique*, 1903, article referred to above, p. 172.

leaving in the class-halls only the ecclesiastics, who were obliged to follow the lessons. The withdrawal of the regulation in 1898 just saved the institution which had been led to the brink of ruin.

It is also for reasons analogous to those that certain works in Latin, by men of the highest ability, have attained to such scanty publicity, scarcely finding their way beyond a quite restricted professional circle ; while if they had been written in a living language they would have undoubtedly secured a widespread and favourable reception.

In philosophy, just as in every other domain of thought, the author or professor, whether he likes it or not, must take account of the tastes and tendencies of the public ; because these are simply indications of the mental attitude of a given state of society. The dry and stilted forms of language that satisfied the medieval philosophers will not be tolerated at the present day. The moderns have trained us to expect and to demand a literary clothing for even the most abstract ideas—the French, especially, who have in Descartes a master of style no less than a leader of thought. Unless the new scholasticism caters for those requirements in educated circles it will not be received there. Not that we are to write literature instead of philosophy, but at least that we ought to please and respect our public by addressing them in language sufficiently clear and pure and simple to make even the most abstruse and abstract of our theories easily intelligible.

For that reason, then, Latin has little chance of fixing the attention of the public in philosophical circles. There is furthermore this additional reason : we have a whole department of ideas in which the disadvantages of Latin are so manifest that even the most extreme " latinists " are disposed to bend their principles to the needs of the case : the department

of the history of philosophy, including the consideration of modern scientific researches.   (Sections 22
and 24).   How could we deal in Latin with Kant,
Hegel, Spencer, Taine, Renouvier, Boutroux, Wundt ;
or treat of psychophysiology, sociology, etc., without
coining a vocabulary of strange and displeasing
neologisms ?

110. The contradictory positions we have so far
outlined, together with their respective lines of
defence, will be found to involve ultimately the very
essentials of the new scholastic programme ; for
they spring from two widely different conceptions
of the nature and scope of the revival in question.
If we are simply and solely to take up and teach
once more the scholastic synthesis of the thirteenth
century, then indeed a dead language will best suit
a dead system—a system far removed from all the
actual influences of the present age.   But if on the
contrary the revival of that ancient synthesis is to
be a real revival, if we are to breathe into it a genuine
and healthy vital energy by adapting it to our actual
and present needs—and there is absolutely no other
way of vitalizing it—then must the new scholasticism
speak the language of the twentieth century.

Surely, it is the latter of these two ideals we ought
to aim at realizing ?   And if so, the teaching of
scholastic philosophy, in book and in pulpit alike,
must be modernized.   A sound philological study
of the great authors of the thirteenth century—an
exegesis of their terminology, together with the
reading and explanation of some texts—will amply
supply for the Latin pedagogy of the past.   Those of
us who have been led by this method into a knowledge of the scholastic authors—we ourselves are of
the number—have only to congratulate ourselves on
the suitability and general excellence of such a mode
of procedure.

SECTION 22.—THE NEW SCHOLASTICISM AND THE HISTORY OF PHILOSOPHY.

111. The history of philosophy was not altogether unknown in the Middle Ages (21). But within the last fifty years history has taken such an important place among higher studies that we must define exactly the attitude of contemporary scholasticism towards this particular department of scientific research.

Many causes have contributed to bring about the present-day enthusiasm for historical studies. There is, for example, the influence of Cousin's eclecticism in France, and of Hegel's idealistic evolutionism in Germany; the history of philosophy was employed by both these writers, though in different ways, as an essential constituent part of their philosophical systems. Then also, historical research is in no small measure the outcome of that irresistible craving for knowledge which is so characteristic of our time, and which has been the mainspring of the natural, as it now is of the historical sciences.

Every human fact in past history possesses its own proper interest; for it may one day become an important item in some great work of systematization. And if it has any connection, remote or proximate, with philosophical conceptions, it may account more or less fully for the influence of some personality in the formation or filiation of systems, or for the effects of a certain trend of thought on a given state of society, and so for several other things. The study of the history of philosophy, like the study of any other science, is a department of the general search after truth; and that alone is enough to justify its existence. Enough also to justify us in expecting from the historian of philosophy the full use of those critical methods which the second half of the nineteenth century has proved to be indispensable for the scientific study of history.

However, this all-important rôle of the history of philosophy escaped the notice of the medieval scholastics. Hence the defects already referred to : a want of exactness in registering the historical fact as such, a certain carelessness in attributing an opinion or a text to its real author, looseness and consequent inaccuracy of quotation, etc. (21). At that time, history was regarded as serving another purpose : as embodying for us the soul of truth contained in every philosophical system ; as helping to refute anti-scholastic theories, and in this way confirming the doctrinal soundness of scholasticism itself. This second motive for cultivating the study of the history of philosophy was of the first importance from the medieval point of view. Moderns, on the other hand, regard it as of minor importance ; though, of course, as a matter of fact, any system of philosophy is bound to derive the greatest possible advantages from the criticism and control of an historical audit.

This remarkable difference of standpoint between medievals and moderns arises rather from the mental attitude of the latter than from any purely historical cause ; most of our modern historians of philosophy have no philosophical convictions themselves, and are careful not to have any. So great is the chaos of modern ideas and systems that few have the courage to take up a definite attitude and defend it. The majority are reluctant to commit themselves to any even moderately comprehensive system, because the world of thought is perhaps more than ever a prey to contradictions ; and perhaps, too, because it is not always easy to square one's life with one's principles—especially if these be of a dogmatic and decided character. Hence it is that nowadays we so commonly find an easy-going sort of scepticism supplanting all conviction, and that instead of trying to build up some system or other of philosophy for themselves so many are content with criticizing the systems of others. The modern attitude, therefore, on this matter, is the very antipodes of that of the medieval writers. This opposition, however, does not spring from the nature of things, but rather from the mental outlook of a certain group of historians ; the two principal reasons for the study of the history of philosophy—the reasons just referred to—so far from excluding, actually supplement and complete each other ; and both alike will have their weight with the scholastics of the twentieth century.

112. For should these latter hold aloof from the great works of historical research that are being carried on in all departments of study ? Or should they allow the history of philosophy to be written without them ? They should not. If they ignored this important instrument of scientific progress and perpetuated the defects that were excusable in the Middle Ages, but are not so at the present day, they would be showing a culpable narrowmindedness and fostering a prejudice that might prove very injurious to the new scholasticism. To do good work in the history of philosophy, one must be a philosopher no less than an historian. Let modern scholastics, therefore, take part in this work ; let them step resolutely into the great movement and bring to light the truth at any cost. Above all, let there be an end, once and for all, to the petty and illiberal attitude shown in certain quarters towards historical studies.[1] Let us

[1] It will scarcely be believed that up to a few years ago no history of philosophy was taught at the Gregorian University. It is still a dead letter in multitudes of seminaries. Orti y Lara, of Madrid, regards the historical study of philosophy as an idle bibliomania. See Lutoslawski, *Kant in Spanien* (Kantstudien, 1897, Bd. I. pp. 217-231). Cornoldi (*Filosofia scolastica speculativa di S. Tommaso d'Aquino*, p. 22, French edition) describes the history of modern philosophical systems as "the history of the intellectual aberrations of man . . . the pathology of human reason." Dealing with

give up condensing the doctrines of others into a few syllogisms for the purpose of refuting it by a few distinctions.   Those synoptic refutations of Cartesianism,[1] Positivism or Kantism, adorned with

those despisers of history the Abbé Besse gives utterance to these bitter truths : " Defenders of tradition," he writes, " they have become its prisoners, and that not a little blindly—seeking to know it only in its official framework.   And they have scarcely a glimmer of the historical sense.   They seem to have no idea of all that is to be gained by an intimate familiarity with the whole train of events and ideas that have accompanied each successive step in the systematization of thought, each new contribution to the expressive powers of language. Their philosophy is without either topography or chronology./   It seems to belong to no age ; but simply to issue from the darkness of night and to vanish into it again."   *Deux centres du mouvement thomiste : Rome et Louvain* (Revue du Clergé francais, 1902.   Reprint, p. 34).   [Cf. *Irish Ecclesiastical Record*, May, 1905, *Philosophy and the Sciences at Louvain*, p. 400. Cf. Appendix, *infra.—Tr.*]

[1] We cannot resist the temptation to quote the passage from the *Journal d'un évêque*, where M. Fonsegrive, the learned editor of the *Quinzaine*, gives a brilliant pen-picture of a performance of this kind : " From the heights of his professorial pulpit, to an audience of some forty youths in soutane and seated on benches before him, a priest of about thirty years was expounding a Latin textbook—in Latin— and the unfortunate man, instead of endeavouring to speak the simple, technical Latin that would have been fairly easy to understand, was actually trying to improve on it, to beautify it, as he thought, by plentifully sprinkling it with *Jam enim's* and *Verum enim vero's*, and winding up his periods with *Esse videatur's*.   In fact, he was merely repeating—less clearly—the text that lay before him, without adding to it a single example or a single idea.   Yet the pupils seem to drink in his words without taking a note, some of them bent conscientiously over their textbooks, others sitting bolt upright with their eyes fixed on the professor—except when they stealthily cast them on ourselves.   The subject of the lesson was the question of the Cartesian doubt ; and the professor followed the author through his exposition of the six reasons—neither more nor less, for he proved even that—on account of which the Cartesian doubt could not be accepted.   *Refellitur, refutatur Cartesius*, repeated the professor again and again, apparently without ever dreaming of taking the trouble to point out the reasons that influenced Descartes to formulate his doubt in such terms, or to explain the rôle assigned by Descartes to his *hyperbolic* doubt in the process of acquiring scientific knowledge. *Refellitur, refutatur Cartesius* —they did not get beyond that.   The pupils went away convinced that Descartes' whole conception of things was fundamentally unsound, that he was himself utterly absurd, and must have been animated with the most perverse and incurable antipathy towards truth.   That day, they excommunicated Descartes for ever from the world of thought ; indeed their professor proceeded more by way of anathema than of discussion.   For, discussion implies an understanding of what is discussed : elementary good faith demands so much : and under- standing implies study.   But this professor who had just so airily refuted Descartes had never read him—not even the *Discours de la méthode*.   I saw that at once when talking to him immediately after class."   Yves le Querdec, *Journal d'un évêque* (Paris, 1897), p. I., pp. 116-118.

a goodly number of uncomplimentary epithets, only
reveal the ignorance of the pseudo-critics. We know
of a certain treatise on Theodicy in which Fichte
is accused of claiming for man the power of creating
God as a "thing-in-Himself," whereas according
to the *Wissenschaftslehre* the non-ego is evidently
produced not as a 'thing-in-itself," but merely as
a representation !

It is only fair, however, not to make the picture
unduly dark.   We gladly and respectfully recognise
the existence of an important and growing group of
scholastics who are thoroughly devoted to historical
studies   Bäumker, Ehrle, Denifle, Willmann, Mandonnet, Domet de Vorges, and many others besides,
have completely broken with the old, cramping
conditions.

113. Moreover, it can be scarcely necessary to
remind the reader that the study of the history of
philosophy is in perfect accord with the spirit of
scholasticism.   If devotion to historical fact is its
own justification, it also furnishes those who believe
in the possibility of certitude with the additional
doctrinal advantages which recommended it to the
ancients.   Greek philosophy had in a manner
evolved, by a gradual process, all the main solutions
of the great philosophical problems ; and its influence
was profoundly felt by medieval scholasticism. It
must be of the greatest importance, therefore, to be
able to recognise and appreciate the peculiar and
specific manner in which the genius of the Greeks
conceived the various theories and arguments put
forth by them : to trace through all their eddying
currents and cross-currents the development of those
great ideas that were destined to live on amid all
change, to survive all decay, and to vitalize philosophy for the Fathers of the Church, for the medieval
scholastics and for the founders and exponents
of modern systems.

The history of medieval philosophy has a special interest for those of us who aim at expounding, perfecting and popularizing its principal system—scholasticism. It trains us to discriminate between what is essential and what is merely accessory in the latter; it teaches us—as nothing else can—that principles whose truth is abiding and perennial, can be applied to the new data of the twentieth century no less successfully than they were applied to those of the Middle Ages. The various polemics and controversies of the medieval scholastics lose most if not all their meaning when taken out of their historical setting :[1] those problems have developed from epoch to epoch; and their very evolutions are a proof that scholasticism has steadily moved with the march of thought, however slow may have been the stages of its progress. Finally, those historical studies bring to light the mistakes of the scholastics, their doctrinal errors and the consequences they suffered from them. What an education for those who are wise enough to profit by the salutary lessons drawn from the experience of centuries ![2]

[1] In St. Thomas' psychology there is an argument for the immortality of the soul, which is unintelligible except in the light of the historical development of ideas in the Middle Ages. The Angelic Doctor asserts the principle that the more the soul is liberated from corporeal conditions and limitations the more capable it becomes of those noblest speculations which are the glory and the pride of humanity ; and he accordingly concludes that its complete separation from the body cannot possibly be a cause or occasion of its annihilation. Such an argument is entirely out of joint with the Thomistic theory of the *natural union* between soul and body. But it finds its explanation in the fact that certain Neo-Platonic and Augustinian ideas had percolated here and there into medieval scholasticism : it is based on some of these foreign elements. Elsewhere, too, with history in hand, it would be easy to point out that theories like divine exemplarism in ontology, and arguments like that from the *incommutabilia vera* in natural theology, though accepted by Roman authors and regarded by them as the purest Thomism, were never really accepted by St. Thomas in the form in which they are usually presented. Those authors are Thomist in intention, but anti-Thomist in reality owing to their neglect of history. See further examples in Besse, *op. cit., p. 35.*

[2] The historical exploration of the Middle Ages is, moreover, one of the forms, or, at the very least, an important index, of the contemporary return to scholasticism. See the general outline of those researches given above, pp. 6 and 7.

In the last place, modern and contemporary philosophy should have a liberal share of attention in those historical studies, for this philosophy is the very soul of the intellectual civilization in which the new scholasticism in fighting for a place. This contest and competition of systems is both inevitable and all-important. Unless the new scholasticism were determined to keep closely in touch with living, actual thought, why should it be of the twentieth century any more than of the thirteenth? Or how could it hope to flourish in the face of positivism or of Neo-Kantism unless by vindicating its superiority over them in open intellectual discussion? And if these latter systems do not commence the debate, why should it not take the initiative? Where is the use in being *au courant* with your age if your work is not noticed by the men of your age; and how are you to attract their notice unless you raise the questions they raise, and in the way they raise them, in order to compare and contrast system with system, argument with argument? It is amusing to find philosophers at the present day proving against the ancient Greeks that the soul is neither a circle nor any other species of figure, while they remain in blissful ignorance of the agnosticism of a Spencer or the *idées-forces* of a Fouillée. Here, again, the old-time scholastics are our masters, if we would only learn from them. Thus, St. Augustine breaks a lance not with the ancient mystics of Eleusis, but with the Manicheans who were swarming all the schools of his day; while Alanus of Lille and William of Auvergne address themselves not to the Manicheism of the past, but to the contemporary errors of the Cathari and the Albigenses. So, too, St. Thomas writes against his Averroïstic colleague, Siger of Brabant, in the University of Paris; he loses no opportunity of attacking the theories of the Arabian Averroës and the Jew Avicebron*: and if he were to come amongst us to-day

*Ibn Gabirol.

he would leave Siger, Averroës and Avicebron alone, and join issue with Paulsen, Wundt, Spencer and Boutroux.

This acquaintance with the systems of our adversaries will not only help us to sift the true from the false in what they contain, but will likewise enable the new scholasticism to benefit by many a theory accepted in modern philosophy, to correct its own errors and to make good its own shortcomings. And as to the great leading principles which it will have victoriously defended against modern attacks, how much more mature and reasoned will be our certitude of them, as a result of such serious discussions! Is it not a consoling thing, after all, to have gone the rounds of contemporary thought, and to have found that the explanations others have to offer of the mysteries of life are a much more defective and imperfect lot than the little inheritance of which we ourselves are in possession? Is not that of itself something to reassure us in those hours of darkness when weak human reason grows anxious at the fogs and mists that sometimes overcloud even its most sacred and cherished convictions?

114. All those considerations which we have been putting forward in the present Section would appear then to issue in a conclusion analogous to that of the preceding Section: The reassumption, in the abstract, of a vanished philosophical system, has no need for the history of philosophy; and the little coterie who would adopt it as their credo may put up their library shutters and leave the outer world alone. On the other hand, the accommodation of the new scholasticism to our own time will require a distinct development in historical studies and an advance along the lines laid down by modern historical criticism.

SECTION 23.—THE NEW SCHOLASTIC PHILOSOPHY AND
RELIGIOUS DOGMA.

115. In this connection the effort to harmonize
the new scholasticism with modern thought implies
a considerable departure from the medieval point
of view.   It is not, of course, that we need to establish
a distinction between philosophy and religious dogma,
Catholic or otherwise : such distinction was already
clearly recognised in the Middle Ages (5).   The new
scholasticism is not a theology ; the former might be
entirely renewed, while the latter remained quite
stationary and uninfluenced ; or *vice versa*.   Indeed,
we are just now witnesses to a revolution in theology :
but the very remarkable controversies of modern
times upon Biblical criticism and the Inspiration of
the Scriptures, have little to do with philosophy.

However, the Middle Ages bound up philosophy
with theology in a system of the closest hierarchical
relations : the natural outcome of a civilization in
which religion held undisputed sway over public
as well as private life, and Catholicism enjoyed a
monopoly, in fact and in right, throughout the
entire Western world.   The philosophical *curricula*
of the abbey schools, and afterwards of the faculty
of arts in Paris, are both an index and a product
of this peculiarly medieval view of things (37).

But religious as well as political continuity has
been long since interrupted and broken in society :
the outcome of which fact is a more or less complete
neutrality of the State towards religions.   So also
have medieval pedagogic institutions vanished—
with the spirit of which they were the visible embodi-
ment.   To attempt a reconstruction of them would
be endeavouring to set up a *regime* whose very
foundations have disappeared.   And hence such an
intermingling of philosophical and theological theses

and arguments as is characteristic of the thirteenth century *Summæ*, would be entirely out of place and unmeaning in our courses and treatises on modern scholasticism (37, 45).

At the present day it is not in connection with theology that the problems of scholasticism arise, and the progress of the latter discipline is in no way dependent on that of the former.   Above all, the new scholastic philosophy is *autonomous : it has a value of its own*, a value that is *absolute* and *independent*.   In the Middle Ages, over and above that function, philosophy fulfilled the rôle of a guide or introduction to theology.   The diploma of doctor in philosophy is nowadays something more than a preparatory step towards degrees in the sacred sciences : it stands on its own merits, and its right to do so is recognised universally.   It now invites to its " banquet " not merely those who are destined for the service of the Church in the ranks of the clergy, whether secular or regular, but all, without exception, who have a thirst for knowledge in the better and larger sense of the word.   It even gives a special welcome to those who study it for its own sake, without any religious or professional object ; and it holds out to all who approach it the promise of knowledge and certitude about God and the whole universe, about man and man's destiny, and the meaning of human life.

116. But what are we to say of the *doctrinal*, as distinct from the *pedagogical*, relations established in the Middle Ages between *philosophy* and *theology?* For if extra-doctrinal relations are dependent on circumstances of time and place, surely the doctrinal relations themselves are above and beyond all such conditions ?   Must these, therefore, remain unaltered in the scholasticism of the twentieth century ?   If we are correctly gauging the attitude of contemporary scholastics on this matter, we believe there is nothing

to change *on the side of philosophy*. The independence
of modern scholasticism in relation to all theology,
as in relation to all other sciences whatever, is simply
an interpretation of that unquestionable principle
of scientific progress, as applicable in the twentieth
century as it was in the thirteenth : that *a properly
constituted science derives its formal object, its principles
and its constructive method, exclusively from its own
domain ;* and that in these things, any borrowing
from another science would compromise its very
right to a separate existence (5).

The material subordination of the various sciences
amongst themselves is a law that is logically indis-
pensible for the unification of human knowledge.
" A truth that has been *duly demonstrated as certain*
in any one science will serve as a beacon to all other
sciences." A theory that is *certain* in chemistry
must be accepted in physics : the physicist who
runs counter to it is surely on a false track. In
like manner, the philosopher may not endeavour to
upset the *certain* data of theology any more than the
certain conclusions of the particular sciences. This
reasoning, which we find formulated by Henry of
Ghent, is as sound and cogent to-day as it has ever
been. The manifold forms of scientific activity are
regulated and limited by a mutual subordination of
branches, which is, however, negative and prohibitive,
not positive and imperative. To deny such mutual
limitations would be denying the conformity of truth
with truth : it would be denying the principle of
contradiction, and yielding to a relativism destructive
of all knowledge (38).[1]

[1] Hence a philosophy is *untrue* in so far as it *contradicts* Revealed
Truth ; and he alone possesses the *fulness* of truth—so far as it can
be had in this world—who possesses the Christian Philosophy of Life,
that Philosophy which embraces and harmonizes natural and revealed
truth. As we have written elsewhere in this connection : " However
systems may differ there is only one *true* Philosophy of Life, varied
and manifold as its expressions may be. Life has its departments
of thought and of action ; but these, though distinct, are related.

But when is a theory *certain ?* Here is a question of fact, in which it is easy to make mistakes. In proportion as the principle is simple and absolute, its applications would seem to be complex and variable. It is no more the *philosopher's* business to vindicate the certainty of theological data than of the conclusions of physics or chemistry. On these matters he must look for certitude elsewhere : and so long as it is not to be found he need take little notice of such data or conclusions.

117. From the point of view of philosophy pure and simple, so far is Catholicism from being inseparably bound up with the new scholasticism that during the last century philosophers have been endeavouring, in the very best faith, to adapt the most varied and widely divergent systems of philosophy to the teachings of Christianity—and so we see repeated once more a phenomenon which was observed taking place in the Middle Ages, at the Renaissance, and during the formation and development of the numerous systems of modern philosophy (43, *4th reason*). Several such examples will be easily recalled : Gunther's Dualism, now forgotten, but only after a long spell of popularity in Germany and Austria owing to its unmistakable tinge of Hegelianism ; Rosmini's philosophy in Italy, founded by one who was a saintly priest though an unsafe psychologist, and which can still count numerous sincere disciples ; [1] Traditionalism, so ably defended by De Bonald and Bautain ; Ontologism, which has had no living voice to

The true and the good are standards in all, whether in Nature or above it. If man's mind and heart conform to them fully, he is a philosopher and a Catholic. In so far as he deviates, he falls into error and evil If his philosophy is out of harmony with Revealed Truth, it stands convicted of error. The man who loves truth and seeks it will embrace a philosophy that makes room for Revelation and recognises on earth an Infallible Exponent of that divine message to mankind."—*Thoughts on Philosophy and Religion*, in the *Irish Ecclesiastical Record*, May, 1906, p. 388.—*Tr.*]

[1] The organ of Rosminianism is the periodical *Il Nuovo Risorgimento*, edited by the irascible Mr. Billia.

plead for it since the death of Professor Ubaghs of the University of Louvain ; and, finally and especially, the Cousinian, eclectic Spiritualism which has so long been the " official philosophy " of France, and which is even still to be met with in so many of its semi- naries : between all these systems and scholasticism, whether ancient or modern, there are very profound differences, and nevertheless the supporters of these systems were good Catholics.   " Associated with the names of Descartes, Malebranche, Leibnitz, Balmes, Rosmini, etc. [these doctrines and theories] became as familiar to the new, as pure scholasticism had been to the older generations.   It was a sort of eclecticism, not very deep, or systematic, or strong ; yet it was truly a Christian philosophy, loyal to the faith and to the Church ; and helped, like the theories it superseded, to light up the obscurities of revealed truth, to defend its doctrines, and to establish peace between reason and faith."[1]

The most interesting of those attempts to square a given philosophical system with Catholicism is that which is now being actually made by a group of French Catholics—not merely lay, but clerical—who

---

[1] Hogan, *op. cit.*, p. 38.   The author remarks that " one of the most eloquent panegyrics ever written on Descartes " came from the pen of a Jesuit, Fr. Guenard (*ibid.*, p. 57).

[Neither to the quotation in the text above, nor to the paragraphs illustrated by it, can any reasonable exception be taken ; for they fully recognize the *material* dependence of philosophy on theology, and imply that no theory or system can be true if it contradicts any doctrine established as certainly true by theology.   They do not, however, make it quite clear how far the above-mentioned systems, or any of them, have a right to be called " Catholic," or to be described as " Christian Philosophy."   The author's views on the relation of Philosophy to Religion and Supernatural Theology, his apparent denial (*cf.* below, p. 197) that Catholicism can be exclusively and inseparably bound up with any one system of philosophy (and his alleged definition of Scholastic Philosophy by its content alone, exclusive of its method) have been adversely criticized in the *Etudes- Franciscaines* (October, 1904, pp. 338-355 ; March, 1905, pp. 270, seq. *Libéralisme philosophique : A propos d'un livre récent*) by Père Diégo- Joseph, and defended in the same Review (January, 1905, pp. 36-54.— *Réponse au " Libéralisme philosophique"*) by Père Hadelin.—Cf. p. 192, footnote.—*Tr.*]

are enthusiastic supporters of Neo-Kantism. The movement is of recent date, and is making rapid progress. Its significance is all the greater because it shares the many attractions of a well-known, widespread and fashionable philosophy; and also because it is contemporary with an almost universal coalition of Catholic philosophers—mainly of priests and religious—who profess and advocate allegiance to a modern scholasticism.

The intellectual dictatorship of Kant is nowadays officially proclaimed and acknowledged in most universities, especially in France and Germany. From the calm heights of pure speculation, which are familiar to the philosopher alone, Kant's teaching and theories have also found their way into the prefaces of scientific works and into avowedly popularizing treatises; nay, they have even percolated into our modern dramas and romances.[1] We believe that the explanation of the enormous influence of Kantism lies in its remarkable combination of a theoretical subjectivism with a practical dogmatism. The phenomenism which is the last word of the *Critique of Pure Reason*, and which Bergson has pushed to its logical extremes, would never have caught on without the noumenism of the *Critique of Practical Reason*. Kant's ethics serve as a palliative after his criteriology, for they establish, on the basis of sentiment and will, the existence of God and of the soul, as well as human liberty and immortality: all of which realities or things-in-themselves the intelligence of man is unable to discover, and which are, nevertheless, the indispensable nourishment of moral and social life. Hence, we see, it was mainly on the ground of his ethical teaching that the

---

[1] Witness the *Déracinées* of Maurice Barrès, and more especially the *Nouvelle Idole* of François De Curel. This piece, played some years ago at the Antoine theatre in Paris and the Moliere theatre in Brussels, contains some curious and characteristic assertions of agnosticism and Neo-Kantian voluntarism.

" return " movement " towards Kant " (" *Zürück zu Kant* ") was accomplished. But is there any real possibility of good companionship between the mutilated certitude of a reason that rules a world of *mere representations* and the certitude of a will that goes deeper down into another world of *extramental realities ?* Is it a logical theory, this of the two certitudes ? We doubt it gravely, and that for reasons of a purely philosophical kind ; this, however, is not the question to settle here.

Suffice it to remark that this " voluntarism " will allow a Catholic, *who accepts the two antinomian certitudes of Kantism,* to hold that the objective data on which the Catholic faith is based are illusory in the face of pure reason, and at the same time to hold their reality and affirm their real existence through and for the will.

And there are, in fact, *Catholic Neo-Kantians.* Ollé-Laprune, with his sentimental philosophy, may be said to have prepared the way for them. " Even philosophical knowledge, even rational certitude is not a product of the pure understanding, of the pure reason. Belief is an integral element of science, just as science is an integral element of belief ; that is to say, that the *life of the spirit* is always one and continuous with the *life of the being* himself ; or again, that philosophy is indissolubly a matter both of reason and of soul ; or again, finally, that thought can neither suffice for life, nor can life find in itself alone its light, its strength and its whole law. ' We must discern more than reason in man, and more than man in reason.' " M. Blondel, who sums up in those words the teaching of Ollé-Laprune,[1] has himself improved on his master ; and others have followed these—in a direction leading straight to Neo-Kantism. Indeed, to arrive there nothing more was required than to bring Ollé-Laprune's

---

[1] M. Blondel, *Léon Ollé-Laprune* (Paris, 1899).

attack on reason into *explicit conformity with the Kantian criticism,* and to confine all certitude about the real world to man's volitional activity.

On this peculiar attitude of certain French Catholics the reader will find copious bibliographical information combined with some suggestive comments, in an exhaustive article published in the *Kantstudien*— a periodical which keeps thoroughly abreast of the evolution of Kantism. " Notwithstanding the Encyclical of the 4th of August, 1879, which describes Christian philosophy as scholastic," writes M. Leclère, " and the Encyclical of the 8th of September, 1899, condemning Kantism, there are—in this land of France where the faithful are usually so prompt to hearken to the voice of the Holy See—Catholics and even priests, who have consciously or unconsciously drawn their inspiration from Kant, and continue to do so, in the hope of building up in this wise a new philosophy that may serve as a human basis for revealed faith ; and they contend that they are as free from heresy as the Thomists who are opposing them, or the Cartesians who are left quietly alone." [1]

118. Let us, therefore, freely accept the conclusion that a Catholic may, in good faith, give his allegiance to systems other than the new scholasticism.[2]

---

[1] Albert Leclère, *Le mouvement Catholique Kantien en France a l'heure présente* (Kantstudien, Bd. VII., H. 2 and 3). Reprint, 1902, p. 2.

[2] [This, of course, does not in any way imply that conflicting systems may be true together ; nor is it in any way incompatible with what has been said above regarding that matter (See footnote, p. 194). A Catholic may adhere, *in good faith,* to a system that is on the whole unsound. I have elsewhere gone " so far as to say that if by different philosophical systems are meant presentations and combinations of the same general truth looked at from different points of view, then you can have a number of such systems in accord with Revelation. . . Hence the answer to the interesting question how far Catholics may adhere to different schools or systems of philosophy will depend very largely on the view taken as to the meaning of a ' school ' or a ' system.' In so far as these are merely different expressions or presentations of the same natural truths from different standpoints they are in necessary harmony with Revealed Truth, and a Catholic is free to choose. But in so far as they are contradictory of each other, some of them must be erroneous, and such error *may* be in logical opposition

This being so, it is clear that there can be no such thing as a *Catholic philosophy* any more than there can be a *Catholic science*.[1]   But there are philosophers who in the matter of religion profess definite dogmatic beliefs, just as there are chemists or medical doctors who are at the same time Catholics, or Protestants, or Jews.   Modern scholasticism will progress and develop without meddling in any way with matters of religion ; it would be a fatal blunder to confound it with apologetics.[2]

The following paragraph, taken from one of the most eminent leaders of the new scholastic movement, sets forth clearly and forcibly the proper attitude for Catholic scientists to take up as a safeguard and pledge of freedom in their scientific speculations :

" . . . the false notion is abroad that the Catholic *savant* is always and necessarily defending his faith,

—directly or indirectly—to some revealed truth ; and if it be, just as no philosopher should adhere to it if he saw its erroneous character, so also no Catholic should adhere to it if he saw its opposition to Revelation.   But a Catholic may see neither the error nor the opposition in question ; and, so long as he does not, he may adhere to the system without seeing the logical inconsistency of his position.   All the more so, as he may in good faith interpret Revelation in a sense which he regards as true, and which is *de facto* consistent with his philosophical views.   But all that will not make these latter any less erroneous or any less opposed to the true meaning of the Revealed Truth in question.   St. Augustine, Scotus, Eriugena, Abelard, St. Thomas, Duns Scotus, William of Occam, Nicholas of Cusa, Descartes, Gassendi, Malebranche, Pascal, Rosmini, were all alike Catholics ; but is that any proof that their philosophical systems, which differed so widely, were all substantially true or substantially orthodox, or that some of those mentioned did not remain Catholics rather *in spite of* their philosophy, so to speak, and through *bona-fide* ignorance of the unsoundness of their systems ? "—*I. E. Record, art. cit.*, pp. 387-388. —Cf. above p. 74.—*Tr.*]

[1] [This is quite true, and quite consistent with the negative and material subordination of philosophy to theology insisted on above (p. 192) ; as also with the fact that there can be only one true Philosophy in the larger sense of a Philosophy of Life. (See footnote, p. 192).—*Tr.*]

[2] Biblical criticism and scientific discoveries of all sorts have given a considerable impetus to modern apologetics.   In fact, they have practically made it a new science : unlike medieval apologetics, it appeals not merely to philosophy but to all the special sciences.   Even in the Middle Ages, however, *philosophy proper* was distinguished from *dialectic* or *apologetic* philosophy (39) : a distinction that is more important nowadays than it ever has been.

that in his hands science must needs be a weapon to be utilized for that sole purpose. Indeed, not a few are disposed to regard the Catholic *savant* as living in constant dread of the thunderbolt of an excommunication, as bound hand and foot by distressing and cramping dogmas, as utterly unable either to profess or to feel a disinterested love for science, or to pursue it for its own sake, so long as he remains faithful to his religion. Hence the distrust he encounters on all sides. A publication issuing from a Catholic institution—Protestant ones are received with less disfavour, doubtless because they are regarded as having given some proof of their independence by their revolt from authority— is almost invariably treated as a plea *pro domo*, a one-sided, apologetic affair, to be refused—*a priori*— the right of an impartial, objective examination." [1]
. . . "We must aim at forming, in greater numbers, men who will devote themselves to science for its own sake, without any other or remoter aim of a professional or apologetical character, men who will work at first hand in fashioning the materials of the edifice of science, and so make original con- tributions towards its gradual construction." [2]

It would be an utter mistake to imagine that the new scholasticism was called into existence to do battle for any religious belief; or to imagine with M. Picavet, for example, that "Catholics, identifying it with Thomism . . . contend that it has the same value for them as it had for the orthodox Thomists of the thirteenth century." [3]

---

[1] Mercier, *Rapport sur les Études superieures de philosophie*, presented to the Congress of Malines, September 9th, 1891, p. 9.
[2] *Ibid.*, p. 17.
[3] Picavet, in the *Grande Encyclopédie*, under the word " scolastique " (last paragraph).

SECTION 24.—THE NEW SCHOLASTICISM AND THE
MODERN SCIENCES.

119. The history of the sciences during the last three
centuries, especially during the nineteenth, is like the
tale of one grand triumphal march of the human
mind. In the domain of visible Nature, the inductive
methods have led to astonishing discoveries—
discoveries that have made the world of the twentieth
century almost another world altogether from that
of the Middle Ages; and Nature is being forced to
yield up more of her secrets every day.

From the standpoint of method, or the general
logic of the sciences, three profound differences mark
off the modern from the medieval epoch : the multiplication of the sciences; their separation from
philosophy; and the distinction between common or
ordinary knowledge—*cognitio vulgaris*—and scientific
knowledge.

In the Middle Ages astronomy bordered on astrology, chemistry on alchemy, and physics on magic ;
in our days science has ruthlessly eliminated whatever
is groundless or fanciful. By sifting and searching
the nature of corporeal things in every conceivable
way, new aspects of matter have been revealed in
rapid succession, and each distinct *point of view* has
become the centre and starting-point of a *new branch*
of scientific study. This multiplication of the
sciences has gone hand in hand with a more careful
and exact determination of their respective
boundaries : to take a few examples at random, we
see that crystallography, stereochemistry, cellular
biology, bacteriology, are confined each within the
sphere of a perfectly definite " formal object," which
we might describe as the typical angle at which each
of them approaches the study of a more or less
considerable group of things.

By thus determining their respective boundaries the sciences secured for themselves an autonomous power, and thus loosened the ties which had hitherto bound them so closely to philosophy.   In the Middle Ages they were considered *as mere preliminaries* to the study of rational physics (48, 49); specialized research had no meaning except as a preparation for the synthetic process of philosophy.   To-day the sciences have a meaning and a value of their own : each has its own work cut out for it; and their separation from philosophy is complete.   Unfortunately, the impetus of extreme and prejudiced notions has exaggerated that friendly, mutual independence into a hostile divorce ; the scientists have gone one way, the philosophers another ; and the disastrous old prejudice has too readily taken root— a prejudice so unjust, untrue, and injurious to all branches of knowledge that the results furnished by the work of the one party are incompatible with those yielded by the labours of the other.

The progress of each special science within its own domain has wrought yet another revolution in human knowledge.   Until mechanical instruments for the accurate and detailed observation of phenomena were forthcoming, inductive methods were necessarily restricted in their application ; and it was, as a rule, impossible to get beyond a very elementary knowledge of the workings of Nature. It was well known in the thirteenth century, for example, that wine exposed to the air became vinegar. But what is such knowledge compared with the complex formulas of modern chemistry ?   In those ages Albert the Great or Roger Bacon might boast of having mastered all the sciences of their time ; nowadays any such pretension would provoke a smile.   In every single branch, progress has compelled the distinction between *common* and *scientific* knowledge.   The former is usually the starting-point for the latter; but the teaching and conclusions of the various sciences can be fully understood only after a long and laborious process of initiation in the case of each and every one of them.

120. Do those profound changes in the outlines and contents of the sciences imply a corresponding change in the relations established in the Middle Ages between science and philosophy, in the attitude of each order of studies towards the other? Will modern scholasticism pay no heed to the discoveries of those sciences, or will it rather draw its inspiration from those discoveries?

There should be no mistaking the principle underlying the answer to such a question. The considerations that urged medieval scholasticism to keep in touch with the sciences are a thousand times more cogent nowadays than ever they were. If the deep and all-embracing view *that justifies the separate existence of philosophy* (48) presupposes analytic researches, is it because these latter have been multiplied exceedingly that we are to begin to ignore them?[1] The horizon of specialized knowledge is

---

[1] " All that exists, as contemplated by the human mind, forms one large system or complex fact. . . . Now, it is not wonderful that, with all its capabilities, the human mind cannot take in this whole vast fact at a single glance, or gain possession of it at once.   Like a short-sighted reader, its eye pores closely, and travels slowly, over the awful volume which lies open for its inspection.   Or again, as we deal with some huge structure of many parts and sides, the mind goes round about it, noting down, first one thing, then another, as best it may, and viewing it under different aspects, by way of making progress towards mastering the whole. . . .   These various partial views or abstractions . . are called sciences . . . .   they proceed on the principle of a division of labour. . . .   As they all belong to one and the same circle of objects, they are one and all connected together ; as they are but aspects of things, they are severally incomplete in their relation to the things themselves, though complete in their own idea and for their own respective purposes ; on both accounts they at once need and subserve each other.   And further, the comprehension of the bearings of one science on another, and the use of each to each, and the location and limitation and adjustment and due appreciation of them all, with one another, this belongs, I conceive, to a sort of science distinct from all of them, and in some sense, a science of sciences, which is my own conception of what is meant by philosophy. . . . "   Newman, *Idea of a University :* Discourse III., 3, 4 (pp. 44-51).

ever receding ; all sorts of researches have parcelled out between them the various departments of the visible universe : and is it that philosophy, whose very mission is to explain that universal order by its highest and widest principles—by principles applying not merely to this or that particular group of facts but to the totality of known phenomena— should be unconcerned about the very thing to be explained ! Philosophy is like· a watch-tower from which we gaze out upon the panorama of some stately city. We take in its general outline, the great arteries of its commercial life, its main streets and public places, its most striking monuments, their general appearance and relative positions : in a word, all the many things that a passing visitor fails to see, who merely walks through its streets and laneways, or visits its libraries, churches, galleries and museums. But what if the city gradually grows and stretches away into the dim distance ? Why, evidently all the more reason—if we would still secure a bird's-eye-view of it—to ascend, and, if needs be, to build, still higher, the steps of our tower, and so be able to discern the general plan and the main, outstanding features of the more modern quarters.

Moreover, the new scholasticism is heir to certain theories in explanation of the cosmic order ; and those theories it holds to be as valid and as fruitful at the present day as they were in the days of Aristotle or of St. Thomas, while its opponents declare them to be irreconcilable with the conclusions of modern science. Would it then be wise or opportune to withdraw those principles from the shock of an encounter with current difficulties and from the test of a comparison with the established truths of science, as the weak and the feeble are wont to be sheltered from trying conflicts ? Of two things, one or other : Either the old principles are powerless

to interpret and assimilate the established data of
the modern sciences, in which case modern scholastics
—seeking truth above all things, as they do—will
no longer allow mere chimeras to lull them to a false
security.   Or those old principles will not yield an
inch to the systems invented by modern philosophers,
but will adapt themselves equally well to the new
facts and furnish an equally satisfactory interpretation of them ; in which case the philosophy of the
past will have come out victoriously from the contest
and established a rightful claim to be likewise the
philosophy of the present.   That is exactly the
reason why the wedding of philosophy to the sciences
is not merely one of the striking features of the
present scholastic revival, but even the principal
aim of the promoters and pioneers of the movement.
The principle was clearly and explicitly laid down
by Leo XIII. in the Encyclical *Æterni Patris ;* and the
Louvain Philosophical Institute, founded by his
orders, has consistently carried out its application in
every department of its teaching.[1]

121. It would be almost impossible to enumerate
the men of note who have lent their warm support
to this programme, or to give even a faint outline
of the arguments they bring forward in favour of it.
Two books, chosen at random from a number, will
supply copious information to those who are interested
in the very actual question of the reconciliation of
philosophy with the sciences ; the one, historical :
La philosophie de la nature chez les anciens,[2] by M. Ch.
Huit ;   the other, more theoretical : *Contribution
philosophique a l'étude des sciences,*[3] by Canon Didiot
of the Catholic Faculty of Lille.

Then, moreover, the necessity of a scientific

---

[1] [See Appendix.—*Tr.*]
[2] Paris, 1901.   Crowned by the French Academy of Moral and
Political Sciences.
[3] Lille, 1902. Cf. Baunard, *Un siècle de l'Eglise de France,* 1902, Ch.
" Etudes divines et humaines."

philosophy is admitted everywhere at the present day, not merely by modern scholastics but by all the leaders of thought in the most widely divergent schools of philosophy. M. Boutroux, for example, is constantly insisting on the importance of a good understanding between philosophers and scientists. We have all the more pleasure in quoting some statements of the learned Sorbonne professor, recently made at a few Philosophical Congresses, because they amount to an emphatic expression of Aristotelian and scholastic teaching. " Such a union," he said, " is in fact the classic tradition of philosophy. But there came a psychology and a metaphysics with the claim that they could exist and develop independently of the sciences by drawing their nourishment from the self-conscious reflexion of the human mind. To-day, however, philosophers are all at one in taking scientific data for their starting-point."[1] Of course ; for the essential function of philosophy is to harmonize and unify in some higher synthesis the things that are given to us as separate. " Side by side with the analytical researches in which the positive sciences are almost exclusively concerned, there must be another order of researches wherein the mind will examine, in things, the conditions of their intelligibility, truth, harmony and perfection. Logic, Psychology, Moral should faithfully preserve within them the leaven of Metaphysics, which will some day perhaps take up current experimental theories and breathe a new life into them. . . . . These reflections on the state and scope of philosophy will help to determine the aim and method of philosophical teaching in our universities. Such teaching ought to have both a universal and a special character. In fact, what is peculiar to such training, and what

[1] Opening discourse at the International Congress of Philosophy, organized in 1900 by the *Revue de métaphysique et de morale.*—See same Review, September, 1900, p. 697.

differentiates it from all other mental disciplines, is just this feature of universality. It aims at embracing things and sciences, theory and practice, concrete and abstract, real and ideal, matter and mind, both in their inner mutual relations and in their underlying unity. To accomplish this task, it must have constant recourse to the positive sciences, and it must likewise constantly refresh itself with reflex thought." [1]

Professor Wundt of Leipzig, whose exceptional competence in science and philosophy adds great weight to his authority, is of the same way of thinking. One particular paragraph in his *Einleitung in die Philosophie*,[2] where he deals *ex professo* with the present question, concludes with this significant definition of philosophy : " Philosophy is the general science whose function is to unify in one consistent system all the knowledge brought to light by means of the several special sciences, and to trace back to their first principles the methods in common use in those sciences and the conditions which they in common assume as prerequisites to all knowledge." [3] Yet another well-known scientist of Leipzig, Ostwald, professor of chemistry, writes in an introductory article in the *Annalen der Naturphilosophie*, that under his editorship the review will aim at " exploring the territory that is common to philosophy and the special sciences." Finally, we may quote these interesting words of Professor Rhiel: " Never in the history of science," he writes, " was there an epoch more given to philosophy than the present one.

---

[1] International Congress on Higher Education, 1900, in the *Revue internationale de l'enseignement*, December 15, 1901, pp. 507-509.

[2] Leipzig, 1901.

[3] Section 2, *Philosophie und Wissenschaft :* " Philosophie ist die allgemeine Wissenschaft, welche die durch die Einzelwissenschaften vermittelten Erkentnisse zu einem widerspruchlosen System zu vereinigen, und die von der Wissenschaft benützten allgemeinen Methoden und Voraussetzungen des Erkennens auf ihre Principien zurükzuführen hat " (p. 19).

. . . For we are now coming to see the value and the significance of the inevitable division of labour that has forced itself upon us. . . . This is the age of 'synthetic science,' and synthesis is synonymous with philosophy."[1]

122. The reader will have to pardon us for giving such lengthy quotations. They are needed in view of the attitude of those lovers of tradition who are unrelenting adversaries of everything modern : the testimony of such unimpeachable witnesses as. we have just mentioned, in favour of a philosophy based on the sciences, ought to set those people thinking. *Laudatores temporis acti*, tenaciously conservative of the past, they wish to know nothing about what is going on around them, because they imagine that it is all simply and solely an attack upon their fortress of truth. *Vetera* is their motto : *paleo-scholastic* their name. When we remember that some of them have suggested that the Almighty may have created the fossils in the state in which the geologists have found them, we cannot well refrain from a sceptical smile.[2] The fact is, these men live amid their contemporaries, indeed, but are certainly not of them ; to give samples of their out-of-date knowledge would not be worth the trouble. We shall be better employed examining some of the reasons by which they seek to justify their voluntary ignorance of science. Those reasons are partly of a theoretical, partly of a practical kind.

Ordinary observation, they say, yields an adequate foundation for philosophy. This is proved by the very existence of scholasticism. Seeing that the Middle Ages have been able to rear such an imposing edifice of synthetic thought without the aid of modern scientific theories, why should we now have recourse

[1] A. Rhiel, *Zur Einführung in die Philosophie der Gegenwart* (Leipzig, 1902), p. 247.
[2] Cf. Besse, *op. cit.*, p. 32.

to these latter for the reconstruction of that same
edifice ?

Yes, of course, even ordinary superficial observation
is usually trustworthy in its informations ; and it
will accordingly furnish sound materials for abstract
philosophical thought. Otherwise how would the
ancients have ever known anything at all about the
philosophy of Nature ? But that is not the question
here. The question is whether ordinary observation
will suffice *always* and *everywhere.* Or are there not
whole regions of things quite inaccessible to common,
unaided experience ? And can the philosopher remain
altogether indifferent to these ? Such questions must
be almost superfluous : to ask them is to answer
them. Has not biology let in a flood of light on the
philosophical study of human nature ; and have not
chemistry and crystallography done the same for
that of inorganic nature ? " Would it be wise,"
asks Professor Nys, " to condemn ourselves to use
indefinitely the primitive utensils of our ancestors,
for the sole reason that they had no better for their
purposes in their day ? . . . . All visible nature
is nowadays revealed to our gaze in quite a new light.
Why should the philosopher not take advantage of
this newly known world and interrogate and explore
it for his own special purpose ? "[1] So truly has
every new phenomenon its philosophical side that
" there is not at the present day, in the study of
visible nature, a single branch that is not crowned
with some philosophical hypothesis or other."[2]
More than this. It is just one of those hypotheses
—and one that is seriously entertained—which now
calls into question the very *foundations* of that
common observation on which our old-time scholastics
are still fain to build : the hypothesis that denies all
specific distinction between the various properties

[1] Nys, *Cosmologie* (Louvain, 1903), p. 23.
[2] *Ibid.*, p. 24.

of corporeal things.   Modern atomism would reduce all those properties to mere movements of one homogeneous matter.   And there is little use in trying to answer its arguments by a mere appeal to ordinary common sense or to a long-standing tradition.   For better or worse the question has been pushed back, by an analysis of both common sense and tradition, to the domain of science, and either there or nowhere must it be answered.[1]

123. Besides this theoretical objection, difficulties of the practical order have been urged against the realization of the new scholastic programme.   The special sciences are so extensive, and their growth in recent times has been so rapid, that no individual philosopher can hope even to reconnoitre those vast regions, much less to master them.   " Science," in the Aristotelian sense of the word, is become an Utopia, an ideal not given to mortal to realize.

We will let one of the ablest promoters of the new scholasticism answer that objection.   " At the present day," writes Mgr. [now Cardinal] Mercier, " when the sciences have become so vast and so numerous, how are we to achieve the double task of keeping *au courant* with all of them, and of synthesizing their results ? The difficulty is in truth a serious one, nor is it in the power of any one individual to surmount it. His courage will fail and his unaided effort count for little in presence of the daily widening field of observation.   And therefore it is that the *association* must make up for the insufficiency of the *isolated individual ;* that men of analysis and men of synthesis must come together and form, by their daily intercourse and united action, an atmosphere suited to the harmonious and equal development both of science and of philosophy."[2]

But, then, if all philosophy presupposes a knowledge

[1] *Ibid.*, p. 25.
[2] *La philosophie néo-scolastique* (Revue Neo-Scolastique, 1894, p. 17). [Cf. Appendix, *infra.—Tr.*]

of the sciences, and if on the other hand it is utopian to aim at knowing all the sciences in detail, where are we to draw the line ? Then, too, among those who want to unite the study of scholastic philosophy with the study of the modern sciences, very few are likely to become *genuine research students in the scientific domain :* most of them will be satisfied to take their scientific conclusions on the authority of others.

This must be admitted unless special scientific courses are provided for students of philosophy. All the necessities of the case can be met only by some such special arrangement. For, the general scientific courses in our modern universities contain either too much or too little for students of philosophy : " *too much,* because the professional scientific training which they provide must go into a multiplicity of technical details that are not needed for the study of philosophy ; *too little,* inasmuch as the observation of facts is often the ultimate aim of professional training, whereas from the point of view of philosophy it can be only a means, a starting-point towards the discovery of their highest laws and causes."[1]

M. Boutroux holds the same views upon the teaching of philosophy in universities ; a wide and elastic organization of the philosophical faculty should find a place within it for " all the theoretical, mathematico-physical and philologico-historical sciences."[2] Such special teaching as M. Boutroux advocates, and for the same reasons, has been available—and availed of [3]—for the past fifteen years at the Philosophical Institute of Louvain University.[4]

[1] Mercier, *Rapport sur les études superieures de philosophie*, p. 25. (Louvain, 1891).

[2] *L'Enseignement de la philosophie.* Communicated to the International Congress on Higher Education, 1900 (Revue internat. de l'enseign., 1901, p. 510.

[3] [See Appendix, *infra.—Tr.*]

[4] [To yet another objection, that the instability and imperfection of the sciences do not as yet guarantee us in attempting to base a system of philosophy on them, see the answer given by M. Besse, Appendix, *infra.—Tr.*]

CHAPTER II.

THE DOCTRINES OF THE NEW SCHOLASTICISM.

SECTION 25.—DOCTRINAL INNOVATIONS.

124. The thoughts to which we have been so far giving expression will reveal the sense in which modern scholasticism aims at submitting the great, leading principles of medieval scholasticism to the control of the latest results of scientific progress. The application of this test has modified the doctrinal content of the *new scholasticism* so far that we may distinguish it from its *medieval* ancestor : theories *now known to have been false* are simply ABANDONED ; the great, constitutive doctrines of the medieval system are RETAINED, *but only after having successfully stood the double test* of comparison with the conclusions of present-day science and with the teachings of contemporary systems of philosophy ; new facts have been brought to light, and under their influence a store of new ideas has ENRICHED the patrimony of the ancient scholasticism.

125. In the first place, a single stroke of the pickaxe has stripped the walls of the old scholastic edifice of a whole pile of decayed and mouldering plaster : theories transparently false, inspired by erroneous astronomical physics and applied to the interpretation of Nature (77, 78), and in which arbitrary observations of phenomena were connected by bonds no less arbitrary with cosmological or metaphysical

principles.   Only a fool would nowadays maintain the relative superiority of the substance of the stars compared with that of the earth.   Their incorruptibility, their substantial individuality, their peculiar mode of composition from matter and form, their subjection to extrinsic spiritual movers, their influence on the generation of certain forms of mundane life : these are some of the theories defended by St. Thomas but repudiated by all modern scholastics.   The same applies to numerous theories in " terrestrial physics," such as that of the *locus naturalis*, and that of the four chemically simple bodies with their sets of properties (79) ; and also to numerous views peculiar to medieval psychology, such as the transmission of " species sensibiles " through space, and their reception into the sense organs (87).

Still more of those old scholastic theories, especially in the domain of visible nature, are likely to become discredited according as modern science proves their insufficiency.   Our own friend and colleague, Professor Nys, has shown clearly, for example, that experiments in the vivisection of the higher kinds of organisms compel us to extend our teaching as to the divisibility of essential forms to *all* the animating principles in the animal kingdom, and so to abandon the Thomistic theory on the essential simplicity of the higher forms of organic life.[1]

Then, finally, it is plain that of the vast body of doctrines that are certain to survive scientific tests, all are not of equal importance.   Nowadays, just as in the Middle Ages, there are views and opinions which open discussion or personal convictions are free to introduce or not to introduce into the new scholasticism, without in any way interfering with its broad and distinctive principles (31).

126. This work of renovation and reconstruction

---

[1] Nys, *La divisibilité des formes essentielles* (Revue Néo-Scolastique, 1902, p. 47.)

will show forth the main lines of the edifice and give scope for the application of new designs. The organic principles of the system undergoing restoration must unquestionably form the basis of the new scholasticism. But let there be no mistake about the scope of the contemplated restoration. It will not be brought about insensibly or unconsciously : it will not be merely mechanical or merely *a priori*. Here, above all, it behoves us to form well-reasoned convictions, based on long and ripe reflection. The new scholasticism must assert and make good its claim to live ; and for that it must stand the test of comparison with rival systems (113) and of agreement with scientific conclusions (120). The matter and form theory is an explanation of cosmic change ; but it will not survive the twentieth century unless it compares favourably with mechanical atomism and with dynamism, both of which hypotheses claim to have discovered the true meaning of the facts. Scholastic spiritualism and scholastic ideology offer an interpretation of the facts of consciousness and an explanation of the difference between sensation and thought ; but they must also show us that the explanation offered by the positivists is not any better supported by the results of modern scientific research. The Middle Ages propounded doctrines of the most purely idealistic character regarding happiness and the last end of man ; but perhaps the utilitarianism of the positivists, or the formalism of Kant, or the pessimism of Schopenhauer, have shown those ideals to be chimerical ? Finally, metaphysics was regarded as the perfection and completion of knowledge in the schools of other days ; nowadays, its very possibility is called into question. Which is in the right, the past or the present ? It is important that we should know.

127. Each epoch in philosophy reveals a mental attitude all its own ; its favourite occupations

disappear to give place to new pursuits in the next epoch.   Ancient India devoted most of its speculation to the monistic blending of all things in the region of the real.   Greek philosophy made the relation of the one to the manifold, of the changeable to the stable, the chief engrossing subject of all its meditations and discussions.   The problems which concern us to-day are not exactly those that occupied the attention of our great-grandfathers.   The lapse of a hundred years—three generations of mortals— has introduced a very radical difference between the society of 1789 and that in which we live.   Were a writer of the eighteenth century to reappear amongst us to-day he would be as hopelessly bewildered by current philosophical thought as a labourer of the Empire would be if suddenly dropped down into a modern factory.

So also, the peculiar genius of the Middle Ages will be no longer found in the twentieth century. The mind of the thirteenth century betrayed a peculiar *penchant* for metaphysical and psychological investigations — for metaphysics especially — which represented the culminating point of human knowledge, as being the product of the highest effort of abstract human thought (49).   In fact, certain metaphysical questions had such an all-absorbing interest for the thirteenth century philosophers that they turned up at almost every point in the discussions of the schools : such, for example, the principle of individuation, the multiplicity of individuals in the same angelic species, the questions about essence and existence, about nature and *suppositum*, about matter and form.   Like all the more remarkable and fertile epochs in philosophic thought, the thirteenth century devoted special attention to problems connected with the study of man.   But its psychology was influenced by the metaphysical tendencies of the time : it showed a decided

preference for questions in *rational psychology*, because
these are for the most part closely allied with ontology.
Thus, for instance, the problem of the origin of ideas,
involving the theory of the two intellects, is connected
with the ontological doctrine on *actio* and *passio*
(89); the distinction between the soul and its
faculties, particularly between intellect and will,
is attached to the metaphysical teaching about
operative power in contingent being (85).

In recent times, on the other hand, two entirely
new and original tendencies have asserted themselves
in the treatment of all such problems : towards
positivism and towards *criticism*. The great dogma
of *positivism*—the *positivity*, so to speak, of all human
knowledge—would limit the knowable to the experi-
mentable. This thesis, notwithstanding the error
it contains when formulated in such exclusive terms,
has taught contemporary philosophy to pay the most
scrupulous attention to all facts, and more particularly
to those that lie on the confines of philosophy and
the natural sciences. An emphatic inculcation
of the importance of observation, internal and
external, is the outcome of the tendency in question.
Psychology is the department of contemporary
philosophy in which it has received its fullest application. There, experimental methods of procedure
have been employed in the investigation of conscious
and subconscious states, in studying the neural
concomitant of psychic phenomena, and sensational
and emotional life generally.

Still more marked and widespread is the *critical*
tendency, introduced by Kant into modern philosophy. Before trusting to any natural cognitive
endowment whatever, Kant raised this previous
question : does the structure of our faculties render
at all possible the application of our knowledge to
an extra-mental world ? And we know how the
Critique of Pure Reason enshrouded all our specu-

lative convictions one after another in subjectivism. If we are to believe Kant, the object of our knowledge is a *represented world* and not a *world-in-itself;* for no thing-in-itself is knowable. The genius of Kant has cloven a twofold furrow in contemporary philosophical thought.

In the first place, he has been the direct inspiration of all subsequent systems of " critical " and " neocritical " philosophy, both in the direction of transcendental idealism and of transcendental realism. The idealists—of the type of Fichte and Hegel—reduce all knowledge to a sort of mental poem, a product of *a priori* forms, and pronounce the thing-in-itself to be not merely *unknowable*, but simply *non-existent*. Realists on the other hand, like Schopenhauer or Herbart for example, admit the single fact of the existence of an unknowable, but persist in knowing nothing about it, and in confining all human knowledge to the subjective elaborations of our world of appearances. But be they realists or idealists, followers of Fichte or followers of Schopenhauer, whether they mingle much criticism or little criticism with their systems, and whatever other elements foreign to Kantism they may appropriate—we may safely say that three-fourths at least of our contemporary philosophers have felt the influence of Kantian subjectivism in their studies on epistemology.

Then over and above this first influence on our manner of regarding these problems, Kant has exercised yet another still more profound and far-reaching influence on the world of modern thought. Before *solving* the problem of certitude in the way just indicated, he *stated* the problem, and that in such a fashion, in language so insistent and peremptory, that it has become the problem *par excellence* of contemporary philosophy. Whether his answer be subjectivist or objectivist, every

philosopher of the present day must face the troublesome question : " does the analysis of human knowledge give grounds for human certitude ? "

Manifestly the current of thought in the twentieth
century is not the same as it was in the thirteenth.
Once more, then, what is to be the attitude of the new
scholasticism ?   Can it avoid the new ways where
mind and thought are now in action, and pursue
its solitary course along the beaten—and abandoned
—paths of the Middle Ages ?   No, certainly not ;
for so it might go on interminably, without ever
coming into contact with actual, modern life : a
lonely and unnoticed wanderer, seven centuries
behind its time.

The recognition of modern trends of thought
makes it incumbent on the new scholasticism to take
up new positions without abandoning the old ones.
It is in the doctrinal domain that we must accomplish
the blending of the old and new, of tradition and
innovation, that is to be characteristic of the new
scholasticism—*vetera novis augere et perficere*.   A
cursory glance over the various departments of
philosophy will help to illustrate all this.

SECTION 26.—METAPHYSICS.[1]

128. In the Middle Ages no one doubted the
reality of metaphysics.   To-day, however, even a
slight acquaintance with the various oscillations of
philosophical systems   will suffice to show how
positivists and Neo-Kantians agree in blotting out
of the book of philosophy the chapter formerly
devoted to what was regarded as a department of
the first importance.   Either sense experience is

---

[1] For a full treatment of modern scholastic metaphysics, see fourth
edition of Mercier's *Ontologie* (Louvain, 1905).

the sole criterion of certain knowledge (positivism), or, since the object of our knowledge is disfigured by our own mental structure (Kantism), there can be no possible question of a science that would reach through the phenomenon to grasp the reality beyond, and which would in the forcible language of Aristotle " consider Being as such, and the attributes of Being as such." [1]   Some there are, indeed, who would substitute for the older metaphysic a new metaphysic —of the mind. A new review, established about ten years ago, called the *Revue de métaphysique et de morale*, has repeatedly championed the cause of this new sort of metaphysic.   However, a doctrine does not change or abandon its phenomenalistic tendencies by arrogating to itself an ancient title with a well defined meaning.

To this metaphysic of subjectivism the new scholasticism opposes an objective metaphysic constructed on the fundamental ontological doctrines of the Middle Ages (Section 12).   We have no notion therefore of removing from our programme of ontology the questions so eagerly discussed by the doctors of the thirteenth century : the principle of individuation, the distinction between essence and existence, and so many others in which deep analysis can be easily separated from useless subtleties.   But on the other hand we are well aware that all is not said and studied once we have exhausted the old medieval repertory.   New problems have arisen, attractive problems too, problems which in any case press for an answer from philosophers who live in the twentieth century.   And since the very legitimacy itself of the new scholastic metaphysic is called into question, it is precisely this problem that demands our first and best attention.   To prejudge the whole question instead of meeting the attacks of the Hume-Kant-Comte coalition, or to meet them unprepared

[1] *Metaph.* III., i.

and without counting the cost, would be following an absurd and compromising line of action. Yet such is the conduct of those who proclaim, without establishing, the rights of the Aristotelian metaphysic, or who are content to throw cheap ridicule on the attacks made upon it.

129. What is true of metaphysics in general is also true of most of its fundamental questions. Can we maintain the distinction between substance and accident without meeting the objections of phenomenism ? For Huxley and Taine the *ego* is not a substance, but " a bundle or collection of perceptions bound together by certain relations,"[1] " a luminous sheaf consisting merely of the rockets that compose it,"[2] just as corporeal substance is, in the well-known words of Stuart Mill, " a mere permanent possibility of sensations."

It would be difficult to overrate the importance of the debate between phenomenalism and substantialism. " There are very few notions with which modern thought is so engrossed as that of substance : friends and foes of the idea are alike convinced that the fate of metaphysics depends on the success or failure of substantialism. At first sight the very existence of any such dispute is matter for amazement. Can it be, we may well ask, that so many thinkers of the first order, like Hume, Mill, Spencer, Kant, Wundt, Paulsen, Comte, Littré, Taine, should have really denied, doubted or misunderstood the substantiality of things and of the *ego* ? Would they not have seen that they were running counter to ordinary good sense ? Then, on the other hand, is it credible that Aristotle, with all his genius, was the dupe of such a childish illusion as the phenomenists must needs accuse him of ? Or are we to believe that all those masterly and

[1] Huxley, *Hume* (London, Macmillan, 1886), p. 64.
[2] Taine, *De l'intelligence*, vol. I., pp. 77, et passim.

truth-loving men, who have incorporated the Peripatetic distinction between substance and accident into the scholastic system and kept it there for centuries, were one and all egregiously deceived in the interpretation of an elementary truth of common sense ?   Is there not good ground for suspecting that there must have been misleading quibblings and unfortunate misunderstandings on either side, if not on both sides ; whence undoubtedly originated mutual bandying of arguments and objections that were quite to no purpose ? " [1]   Misunderstandings do, in fact, exist on both sides : wrong notions as to the destructive scope of phenomenism, seeing that inasmuch as it allows an autonomous existence to the object of every perception it thereby admits, in a relative sense at all events, the possibility of self-subsisting realities ; false conceptions, too, of the scholastic theory as involving the gratuitous and erroneous belief that the human mind is capable of intuiting the *specific* determinations of natural substances.   Here, as elsewhere, a careful comparison of theories is all that is needed to dissipate most of the difficulties and diminish considerably the distance that separates conflicting views. [2]

The same applies to the doctrine of relativity or relativism, so ably defended, from quite a number of different standpoints, by Kant and Hegel in Germany, Comte and Renouvier in France, Locke, Hamilton, Mansel and Spencer in England.   The old notion of the *absolute*, which was one of the keystones of scholasticism, will still be found capable of fixing many an archway in the new edifice, provided it be subjected to the limitations necessarily imposed on all human knowledge.

What a crowd of questions may be opened up between the new scholasticism and contemporary

[1] Mercier, *Ontologie* (Louvain, 1902), p. 263.
[2] For solution, see *ibid.*, pp. 267 and foll.

thought! The polyzoistic theories of an Edmund Perrier or a Durand de Gros, regarding the colonies of individual cells in the living organism, must arouse a new and actual interest in the traditional scholastic teaching about individual unity and personality; contemporary pessimism states once more in new terms the old and ever-recurring problem of the existence of evil; the contradictions and inconsistencies of all the modern philosophical offshoots of occasionalism will serve to emphasize once more the profound significance of Aristotle's most fruitful distinction between *potentia* and *actus ;* while recent controversies on determinism, and on the philosophy of the contingent, are sure to bring out anew the ample resources of Aristotelian teleology. A scrupulous testing of the old metaphysical theories in the light of modern facts and enquiries, so far from proving those theories worthless, will only help to show that they still hold their place in human science as some of the most glorious achievements of the Middle Ages. " Their metaphysics is a fully formed science, as was the logic of Aristotle in their own days. We may abridge or simplify or otherwise modify its details; but we may not change either its fundamental principles or its leading conclusions unless we want something else instead of genuine metaphysics, that is to say, the science of the conditions of Being, formally as such."[1]

SECTION 27.—THEODICY.[2]

130. Modern scholasticism can fearlessly proclaim the precious truths bequeathed to it by the Middle

[1] Domet de Vorges, *Essai de métaphysique positive* (Paris, 1883). p. 330.
[2] A neo-scholastic treatise on Theodicy is in course of preparation— coming from the pen of Monseigneur Mercier. [The materials for this treatise are now embodied in the *Compendium* (2 vols.) of the larger *Cours de philosophie* issued by the Louvain Philosophical Institute. We hope that Cardinal Mercier may find leisure to complete and publish the treatise.—*Tr.*]

Ages on the existence and attributes of God.   In
its conception of the *actus purus* natural theology
ascends as far as mortal may ascend towards the
awe-inspiring infinity of the Eternal.

Questions concerning the Deity have been introduced into contemporary philosophy from the two
main centres of philosophical thought outside scholasticism, that is to say, from Kantism and from
positivism.   All the systems born of Kant's philosophy have encountered the " thing-in-itself," the
" unconditioned " : some of them to deny it absolutely, the others to declare our knowledge of it
barren and deceptive.   Materialists and positivists
have found themselves face to face with the same
alternative : some of them, with Comte, have pronounced that Supreme Being inaccessible to
experience to be simply a chimera ; others, with
Spencer, have banished beyond the frontiers of the
knowable and outside the reach of science, that
Absolute Being, to whom, or rather to which they
nevertheless pay solemn homage.

Hence a sort of introductory question that would
have had no meaning in the Middle Ages must now
find its place in the opening pages of the modern
scholastic theodicy : What are we to say of the agnostic
attitude that, *God being unknowable, it is absurd even
to attempt to prove His existence ?*   In other words, we
must nowadays justify the possibility of theodicy
as well as of metaphysics.

131. Perhaps no one has compiled such an imposing
array of difficulties against the *scientific* value of the
traditional proofs for the *existence* of God, as the
author of the " First Principles."   The widespread
influence of the school for which Spencer is spokes-
man, makes it incumbent on the scholasticism of the
twentieth century to examine those new weapons
minutely, and to face the assaults of modern positivism.   It will not now suffice to simply re-edit the

reasonings of the thirteenth century, nor even to reproduce the ostentatious defences formulated in the fourteenth when William of Occam began to question the *demonstrative* force of the Aristotelian arguments (70). Scholastics who would be guilty of adopting such tactics would be like a besieged garrison fortifying the northern side of their citadel while the enemy were actually opening a breach at the south.

Then, too, we must, *at the beginning* of our theodicy substitute for all special conventional or traditional ideas of the Deity a conception derived by way of observation from the universal beliefs of mankind : *that* is the God Whose existence must be proved— postponing for the moment the question as to how or how far that world-wide notion of the Supreme Being accords with the philosophical conception of the Divinity. Studies in the history of religions, and ethnological studies generally, can here be of considerable use to the philosopher ; they will have valuable materials to offer him.

132. Nor are those the only new points to which special attention must be paid. Many of our contemporaries who acknowledge the existence of a God, have substituted for the *transcendent* and *personal* God, an *immanent* and *impersonal* one. Never before were there so many different forms of *monism.* Almost all the German philosophers who acknowledge Kant in any way—as most of them do—are pantheists of some shade or other ; and that even though their several systems are so antagonistic that German post-Kantian philosophy has been not inaptly described as a " civil war of pantheism." Monism has assumed some novel and attractive features in modern philosophy ; it claims to offer a solution of problems heretofore insoluble, such, for example, as the mystery of the transmission of causal influence from an efficient cause to a receptive subject

(Paulsen). Some even go so far as to say that the theory of a transcendent God is unconsciously based on a *petitio principii :* the last " idol " that awaits demolition.

In the face of these facts and accusations the duty of scholasticism is clear : unless it repulses all such attacks it simply cannot and will not count as a *contemporary* system of philosophy. Those who are inclined to entertain pleasant illusions on this point might be just now profitably recommended to learn a little in the school of their own masters : monism of various shades was the dominant anti-scholastic system of philosophy from the ninth century down to the Renaissance, and the war waged against it during all those centuries constantly adapted itself to the needs of the time. The refutation of the ancient Greek monists like Parmenides is not the refutation of the materialistic pantheism of David of Dinant, nor of the emanation theory of Avicebron[*]: nor will the arguments directed by St. Thomas against these latter furnish a fully effective answer to such men as Hegel, Fichte, Paulsen, or Deussen.

An analysis of current theories on the nature and existence of God will introduce the modern scholastic to a number of other questions that are being actually discussed in books and periodicals : controversies on the infinite (so often confounded with the indefinite); the nature and foundations of possibility; the question of exemplarism, etc.

Indeed, there is reason to hope that the clash of the new scholasticism with modern ideas will add a number of important chapters to natural theology ; and the sound and sober teaching of former days will be found to contrast to advantage with the wild and fanciful conceptions of the Deity, unfortunately so common in our own time.

[*]Ibn Gabirol.

Section 28.—Cosmology.[1]

133. Here we are in a department where the new
scholasticism will be busy: firstly, because the
medieval errors in terrestrial and astronomical physics
would seem to have prejudiced most modern scientists
against *all* medieval teaching on the nature and
properties of inorganic matter; secondly, because
we must here allow the phenomena to lead us step
by step, and these seem to be ever growing in number
and complexity according as they are probed and
analyzed under the magic influence of the sciences
of observation.

In fact, the philosophy of nature at the present day
necessarily presupposes a knowledge of physics,
chemistry, geology, crystallography and mineralogy.
" Where the natural sciences leave off there the
domain of cosmology commences."[2]   For, a very
considerable number of scientific *facts* call for some
explanation of the origin, nature and destiny of
material substance.   Such, for example, among
those carefully selected by Professor Nys, are the
atomic weights of the elements, chemical affinity,
atomicity or quantivalence, chemical combinations
and analyses with the thermal phenomena accompanying them, the constant recurrence of the chemical
elements and compounds; the crystalline structure of
matter, isomorphism and polymorphism; all the
phenomena of heat, light and sound, together with
the electric, magnetic and radio-active properties of
bodies; the kinetic theory of gases, the law of
gravitation and the law of the conservation of
energy.

[1] For a full and detailed study of cosmology from the neo-scholastic
standpoint, see the work of Professor Nys, *Cosmologie* (Louvain, 1903,
2nd edit., 1906).

[2] Nys, *Cosmologie*, p. 13.

134. Here, truly, are ample materials for a thorough reconstruction of the ancient physics.   A reconstruction ?   But are the essential principles of scholasticism at all capable of assimilating the new facts, or of offering a philosophical explanation of the conquests of modern science ?   In the face of these facts how will it fare with the theories of matter and form, of substantial change, of specific distinctions between the various bodies and between their various properties, of the rhythmic evolution of forms, and of the finality of the cosmos (Section 14) ? These venerable theories sound all the more out-of-date because neither the great cosmological conception now in vogue—mechanical atomism—nor its less powerful   rival—dynamism—have   preserved   to modern times even a single particle of the ancient scholastic teaching.

And yet what a real surprise there is in store for those who undertake to interpret the new phenomena in the light of the old principles !   Professor Nys, after a careful examination of the various departments of physical science at its present stage of development, has reached a conclusion well calculated to give pause to modern philosophers : the conclusion —which he embodies and supports in his *Cosmologie* —that no hypothesis of the present day has a better interpretation of the facts of physical nature to offer us than scholasticism has.   How, for example, are we to account for chemical affinity, or for the constant recurrence of the same chemical species in nature, without appealing to a finality that must be intrinsic to the constitution and activities of those species ?   Is not the great law of crystallography—that " each chemical species has its own characteristic crystalline form "— a faithful expression of the scholastic principle that in the inorganic world there are specific types which exhibit distinctive and inalienable properties ?   In general, does not an impartial study of the facts of general physics point unmistakably to the existence of *qualities*, in the Thomistic sense of the word ?

135. Nor is that all. Not only is the new scholastic cosmology constructive in the best sense, it is also destructive of rival systems. If it is right, atomism is wrong. There is, no doubt, a seductive charm in the very simplicity of the atomic hypothesis, which would reduce the matter of the whole visible universe to one homogeneous mass, and the vast and ever-varying panorama of its manifold activities to simple local motion. But it would appear that the explicative or interpretative value of the theory must be very considerably discounted. Apart altogether from its philosophical presuppositions, which, as can be easily shown, are not entirely free from latent contradictions and inconsistencies, there are in chemistry, physics and mechanics, certain facts such as the constancy of the thermal phenomena that accompany chemical changes, the phenomenon of universal gravitation and the fact of the conservation of energy, with which mechanical atomism —so far from explaining them—turns out on critical analysis to be really incompatible.

And these failures are felt all the more keenly as natural science progresses. So much so, that they have occasioned among certain men of science—who are also betimes philosophers, and, indeed, necessarily so, we would say, judging from their vast and varied knowledge—a movement of reaction against atomism : a fact whose far-reaching significance scholastics will not be slow to realize. Professor Mansion of the University of Ghent has clearly shown[1] that a series of articles which appeared over the well-known name of Professor Duhem of Bordeaux, may be taken as marking a turning-point in the evolution of cosmological theories, initiating an open and candid return to scholastic conceptions. Professor Duhem has

[1] In the *Revue des questions scientifiques*, July, 1901, p. 50.

since developed and confirmed his views in a remarkable book[1] of a synthetic or philosophical tendency,
many of whose pages will give food for serious
reflection to scientists no less than to philosophers.
The chapter in which the author speaks of *qualities*
is specially interesting and instructive.   Take, for
example, these frank and significant declarations :
" The attempt to reduce all the properties of bodies
to figure and movement must be a futile undertaking,
because not only would it involve unmanageable
if not unimaginable complications, but—what is
far worse—it would be grossly incompatible with the
nature of material things.   We are simply compelled,
therefore, to admit into our Physics something else
in addition to the purely quantitative elements of
which geometry treats ; we must allow that matter
has qualities.   Even at the risk of being reproached
for returning to the old *virtutes occultæ,* we feel
ourselves forced to regard as a primary and irreducible
quality that by which a body is hot, or bright, or
electric, or magnetic ; in a word, we must abandon
the conceptions and hypotheses that scientists have
been incessantly making and unmaking, in the
spirit, and since the time, of Descartes, and begin
to attach our theories to the fundamental conceptions
of the peripatetic Physics."   After which the author
goes on to ask : " Will not this retrograde step compromise the whole vast body of doctrine organized
by physical scientists since they shook off the yoke
of the school ?   Must not the most fruitful methods
of modern science at once fall into disuse ?   Convinced
that everything in corporeal nature was reducible
to figure and movement as conceived by the geo-
metricians, that all was purely quantitative, physical
scientists have long since introduced measure and
number into every department of physical research ;
all the properties of bodies are become magnitudes ;

[1] *L'évolution de la mécanique rationelle,* Paris, 1903.

all laws, algebraical formulas ; all theories, chains
of theorems.   And are we now to be asked to sacrifice
the marvellously powerful assistance we have derived
from the employment of numerical symbols in our
reasoning   processes? "   To   which   questions   he
gives the answer that :   " Such a sacrifice is by no
means necessary.   To give up mechanical explanations does not mean to give up mathematical Physics.
Numbers can be used to represent the various degrees
of a magnitude capable of increase or diminution ;
and the transition from the magnitude to the number
that is made to stand for it we call *measuring*.   But
numbers can also be made to stand for *the various
degrees of intensity of a quality*.   Such extension of
the concept of measure, by which number is made to
symbolize a thing that is not quantitative, would no
doubt have shocked and astonished the peripatetics
of former times.   But that just reveals the real,
genuine progress, the abiding and really fruitful
conquest for which we are indebted to the seventeenth
century scientists and their followers ;   in their
attempt to substitute everywhere quantity for quality
they failed ;   but their efforts were not altogether
without results, for they brought to light this truth
of inestimable value : *That it is possible to deal with
physical qualities in the language of algebra*."   From
all of which emerges this interesting conclusion :
" Physics will reduce the theory of the phenomena
of inanimate Nature to the consideration of a certain
number of qualities ;   but this number it will aim
at making as small as possible.   Whenever a new
phenomenon appears Physical Science will do its
utmost to find a place for it among the known
qualities ;   and only when it has finally failed to do
so will it resign itself to the admission of a new quality
into its theories, of a new variable into its equations."
   The testing of what we have ventured to describe
as the harmony of science with the old scholasticism,

would seem to be specially interesting here in cosmology in its application to this particular theory of *quality* ; it is very likely to throw additional light on the general observations made above regarding the possibility of such harmony : this is our excuse for making such long quotations from the work of Professor Duhem.[1]

SECTION 29.—GENERAL PSYCHOLOGY.[2]

136. The numerous sciences which might be grouped as anthropological—cellular biology, physiology, histology, embryology, etc.—have pushed back almost indefinitely the horizons of this continent which the Cartesian psychologists of the seventeenth century were congratulating themselves on having explored so thoroughly.   Now, as regards the " anthropological " or " human " problems raised by the progress of these sciences, the exaggerated spiritualism of a Descartes or a Cousin—traces of which are still to be found in certain educational centres—must logically disclaim all right to meddle with such problems at all.   And positivism, on the other hand, has been in the habit of claiming a sort of monopoly in these studies ; approaching them, too, with its well-known agnostic prejudices, and confining itself to the mere accumulation of facts and experiments instead of making these latter subservient to the ulterior study of the human *substance.*   The new scholasticism, however, thanks to its fruitful theory of the substantial union of soul and body, " is in possession both of a systematic

[1] As for dynamism, so ably defended by Boscovich, Carbonelle, Hirn, Palmieri, its star has speedily paled.   The denial of formal extension, and the denial of a passive element in corporeal things, are positions more and more difficult to defend as natural science progresses.

[2] We may refer the reader to Mercier's monumental work, *La Psychologie,* already (1903) in its *sixth edition.*

body of doctrines and also of an organic framework
quite capable of receiving and assimilating the ever
increasing products of the sciences of observation."[1]
In truth, when we reflect on the march of scientific
progress, and on the crowds of new and pretentious
theories that are being continually put forward in
explanation of newly discovered facts, we cannot
suppress our astonishment at the reserved and cautious
attitude of the old Aristotelian and scholastic
psychology.   To realize it fully we should have to
explain in detail the position of the new scholasticism
in regard to the problems raised by contemporary
psychology.   For this, however, we must be content
to refer the reader to treatises on neo-scholastic
psychology ; here we can hardly do more than
enumerate in a passing way the questions that are of
greatest prominence and importance.   These have
reference, some to the *activities*, others to the *nature*
of man.

137. The elementary vital phenomena brought to
light by cellular biology have become the starting-
point of psychology.   It is, however, from observing
the manifestations of *sense life* that psychological
science has derived most profit—thanks to the many
remarkable discoveries made by physiology regarding
the structure and functions of the nervous system.
The new scholastic psychology has found in the
medieval teaching a most appropriate framework of
broad, leading principles—made to order, one would
almost say—for the interpretation of the latest facts
in connection with unconscious mental states, with
cerebral localization, with the proper and common
sensibles, and especially with the objectivity of our
muscular and tactual sensations.   The various
phenomena of the association of psychical states,

---

[1][*Op. cit.*, *Preface*, p. 1.—Richet (*Revue scientifique*, t. LI., 1893),
and Döring (*Zeitschrift f. Psych, u. Physiol. d. Sinnesorgane*, 1898,
pp. 222-224), agree in recognizing this vitality in the new scholastic
psychology.

so ably analysed by English psychologists, with its manifold applications to language, to the training of animals, to hypnotism, etc. ; and all the recent minute analyses of instinct, sense memory, the passions, spontaneous vital motions, etc. ; entirely confirm traditional scholastic teaching on the cognitive and appetitive states of sense life. Notably the important scholastic thesis that sense knowledge of whatsoever kind reveals the particular and contingent —is sustained and corroborated by all recent researches.

But as against positivism, it is now more necessary than it has ever been in the past to establish fully and clearly the *essential* distinction between the sensation and the idea. The objections of a Berkeley that the process of abstraction is chimerical, and of a Taine confounding the class-name with the idea and the composite image with what he describes as the so-called universal concept—must be fairly faced, examined and answered at any cost. Therein will the new scholastic ideology show itself more fertile and powerful than either the systems based on sensism where all knowledge is reduced to sensation, or the ultra-spiritualist psychologies (of Descartes, the ontologists, etc.), where the part played by sensation in the genesis of our ideas is either unduly diminished or entirely ignored.

The study of the will involves a discussion of all the arguments urged by determinists against human liberty ; and that of itself implies some degree of acquaintance with practically all contemporary systems of thought. Reason and liberty, so radically distinct from sensibility and instinct, set up an insuperable barrier between man and beast : an assertion which, however, by no means denies that the higher and lower faculties exert a mutual influence on one another ; for the solidarity of sense and reason is abundantly manifest in waking, sleeping and dreaming, in the normal life of the mind as well as in hallucinations and insanity ; and, furthermore, the close union of sense appetite with rational will can alone explain the phenomena of the passions, and the abnormal and morbid states of the will itself.

Modern philosophers should be interested if not surprised to see what a simple and adequate explanation of all these phenomena of interdependence between sense life and rational life the new scholasticism has to offer us in its theory on the constitution of the composite nature of man. We pass, therefore, to the problems regarding man's nature.

138. Neither the recent controversies on the nature of life, like that, for example, between the mechanical organicists and the vitalists of the school of Montpellier, nor the evolutionary hypotheses of a Weissmann or a Darwin, have in any degree discredited the time-honoured definition of Aristotle : " ψύχη ἰστιν ἐντελεχεια ἡ πρώτη σώματος φυσικοῦ δυνάμει ζωὴν ἔχοντος ; anima est perfectio prima primusque actus corporis naturalis organis præditi." [1] The functional unity of the composite animal being, the manifest solidarity of its various forms of energy, confirm the theory of the substantial union of the animal body with the vital principle ; nor is the divisibility of the living organism an insuperable objection against this theory. The psychology of the Middle Ages will be found to be *at least quite as capable* as any other system, of explaining the vital phenomena of the vegetable and animal kingdoms. At the same time it will give a decidedly *better* explanation of the various facts of human life. If man is in substance both corporeal and spiritual he ought naturally to be the seat both of organic and of immaterial or spiritual activities ; and even the highest manifestations of his psychic life should reveal a functional dependence on the

[1] *De Anima,* ii., 1.

nervous system.   Neither the extreme Cartesian spiritualism which makes the body a mere encumbrance to the soul, nor the occasionalism of a Malebranche or the pre-established harmony of a Leibnitz, nor the attempts of positivists to reduce the psychic fact to an obverse or inverse of the nervous phenomenon, nor even the more recent theory of psycho-physical parallelism, can offer us any adequate or satisfactory explanation of the unity of man and the solidarity of his acts.[1]   But the new scholastic teaching will throw an important light on more than one of the leading chapters of contemporary psychology : for instance, the whole doctrine of character, and of personality with its " variations," is subordinate to the main principles concerning the substantial unity of man.

Again, the new scholasticism will have to examine the urgent objections of materialism against the spirituality and simplicity of the human soul : objections drawn from the dependence of even our highest rational activities on the corporeal organism. Besides which there are the questions as to the soul's origin and immortal destiny, etc.   So that on the whole the new scholasticism will have to subject the psychological teaching of the medieval doctors to a careful and thorough process of modern adaptation and enlargement.

139. Nor is this all.   So rapid has been the progress of psychological studies in modern times that the branches of the parent stem have begun to show a vitality of their own.   Of these new sciences some are purely psychological, as, for instance, criteriology.   Others draw more or less from independent philosophical sources, like esthetics ; or from the natural, physical, or social sciences, as is the case with psycho-physics, didactics, pedagogics,

---

[1] Cf. Mercier, *Les origines de la psychologie contemporaine* (Louvain, 1897).

folk-psychology and the numerous other forms of applied psychology.

SECTION 30.—CRITERIOLOGY.[1]

140. Scholasticism has treated the criteriological problem mainly from the *deductive* point of view, deriving a synthetic theory on certitude from divine exemplarism combined with a metaphysical teleology (72, 68). But the present-day scholastic must meet the question of the validity of knowledge in the domain of the *analysis* of that knowledge itself, and must aim at finding an *inductive* solution for it : the critical turn taken by modern philosophy from Descartes to Kant, and even more decidedly since Kant's time, will leave no aspect of contemporary intellectual problems unexamined (127).

Now, the certitude of human knowledge, " being a modality that affects the cognitive faculty, should find its ultimate explanation in the nature of the human soul. Criteriology, therefore, springs naturally from the study of the soul, that is to say, from psychology. It is only confusion of thought and misuse of language that could have assigned to it a place in the logical treatise and designated it by the curious though now familiar title of ' real logic.' "[2]

It is easy to see that nothing less than the whole scholastic system is at stake in the controversy about the objectivity of our intellectual judgments. The traditional scholastic theories on truth (logical and ontological), and notably the division of propositions into those in necessary matter (*per se notæ*) and those in contingent matter (*per aliud notæ*), theories so well known to the doctors of the thirteenth century— can serve as the foundation of quite a new and

---

[1] See Mercier, *Critériologie générale*, (fifth edition, 1906). A volume on *Critériologie spéciale* is promised.

[2] Mercier, *op. cit.*, p. 4 (fourth edition).

complete scholastic criteriology. Our venerable master and colleague, Monseigneur Mercier, who is rightly recognized as the founder of this special department, has admirably shown the latent resources of these old doctrines, and has made successful use of them in vindicating a rational type of dogmatism both against the methodic doubt of Descartes and against the exaggerated dogmatism of Balmes and Tongiorgi.

141. Certain truths (or judgments) have for their object relations between objective concepts, abstracting altogether from the existence of the things conceived : the objective manifestation of these relations to the mind is of the *ideal order*, as in the so-called exact or rational sciences. But these truths are in turn intended to be applied to a *real*, extramental *world ;* by which application the laws of these ideal relations become the laws of things. Hence a twofold epistemological problem : that of the *objectivity* of propositions of the *ideal* order, and that of the objective *reality* of our concepts.

The supreme and ultimate motive for our certitude about *immediate* propositions of the *ideal* order (and consequently about propositions deduced from these) cannot possibly be found in any *extrinsic* test of the kind to which De Bonald, De Lamennais, Pascal or Cousin have had recourse ; neither can it be found in an exclusively *subjective* criterium like that offered by Kant in his second *Critique*, and by the neo-critical theories sprung from that part of the German philosopher's innovations ; those principles of the ideal order must have their final and fundamental motive in an objective, intrinsic criterium, *i.e.* in the evidence of their truth.[1] And that is precisely why the new scholastic criteriology must study in every detail, and encounter point by point those masterful contents of the *Critique of Pure Reason*, in which

[1] *Op. cit.*, p. 201 (fourth edition).

Kant is led to fix upon a blind synthesis, necessitated by the structure of our mental faculties, as the sole explaining reason of the necessity and universality of those propositions which we hold for absolutely certain. Even the first principles of the mathematical sciences, such as $7+5=12$, Kant would hold to be the product of an *a priori synthesis*.

Then, on the other hand, the universality of propositions of the ideal order must also be defended against the attacks of contemporary positivism, which flatters itself that it has demolished the doctrine of the existence of abstract concepts and shown them all to be reducible to mere sense experiences.

142. The second great problem of epistemology is even of more consequence than the first ; for what would it avail to have universal and necessary judgments, motived by objective relations revealed to our minds between subject and predicate, if this whole object were *merely and purely representable*, and corresponded to nothing in the *real*, extramental *order* of actual or possible existences ? The Kantian phenomenism which proclaims our inability to attain, by means of our concepts, to the thing-in-itself, is a logical corollary from the synthetic-a-priori theory of judgment. Kant pronounced himself all at once against the real as well as against the ideal objectivity of judgment.

In this all-important discussion a very vital doctrine of the new scholasticism is at stake : *the legitimacy of the process of abstraction.* What we have to show clearly is this, that in forming our concepts from the data of sense we remain throughout in permanent contact with the realities of nature. For if we do, then " the intelligible forms which become the first subjects of our judgments are endowed with a real objectivity ; in other words, the intelligible object of these forms is not only a representable object but, more than that, it is also a thing-in-itself, actual or possible."

It is obviously upon the real objectivity of our *sensations* that the force of this reasoning depends; and to that point we shall refer again presently. Here we may be allowed to draw attention in passing to the remarkable renewal of interest which the problems of modern philosophy have aroused in the venerable old question of the universals—now having a noble revenge for all the ignorant abuse and ridicule so often heaped upon it. The first great, actual question of criteriology is in very truth none other than that of determining whether the moderate realism of Aristotle and St. Thomas is a sound philosophical attitude as against the nominalism of Hume, Mill, Taine, etc., on the one hand, and the exaggerated realism of the ontologists and of a group of German pantheists on the other. How plain it appears from all this that modern and contemporary philosophy has gradually developed into the one vast and deep criteriological problem of the meaning and value of human knowledge.

143. After the study of certitude in general comes the study of the certitude of at least the more important among our separate and individual convictions. These form the subject-matter of special criteriology. First in importance comes the investigation into the objectivity of our external sensations. Setting out from the incontestible presence in consciousness of a sense *datum* or material—in the shape of a representative impression—of which we are manifestly not ourselves the creators, the earlier Kantists, and after them Schopenhauer and Herbart, inferred the existence of a noumenal world as the cause of those impressions. It is by an analogous application of the principle of causality that modern scholasticism argues from our consciousness of passivity in sense perception to the reality of an extramental object

which engenders in our faculties that peculiar reproduction of itself called a sensation. Consciousness
itself, enlightened by mature reflection and reasoning,
can alone meet the many objections of contemporary
positivism against the existence of an external world.

Each and every distinct source and form of knowledge must find its justification in special criteriology :
there the scientific syllogism as understood by Aristotle and the great teachers of the Middle Ages will
be vindicated against the attacks of such men as
Mill and Bain who make out all deduction to be
either a solemn farce or a *petitio principii ;* induction
will be placed on solid, scientific foundations, and
carefully distinguished from the positivist summing
up of particular facts into a collective proposition ;
neither memory, nor belief in authority whether
human or divine, nor even consciousness itself, can
give us certitude, except with the aid of certain
safeguards and guarantees that need to be carefully
and accurately determined and analyzed in this
department.

SECTION 31.—ESTHETICS.[1]

144. The Middle Ages produced no special treatises
on the study of the beautiful.   The ideas entertained
by the medieval scholastics on the subject are found
scattered through their metaphysics and psychologies,
or in commentaries like those on the treatise of
Pseudo-Dionysius *De Nominibus Divinis.*

Esthetics did not make its first appearance as a
distinct branch of philosophy until after the time of
Leibnitz.   Etymologically, it should be the title
of the philosophical science of sensation (αἰσθανομαι,
sentire), and the term was used in this meaning by

---

[1] A philosophical science of esthetics conceived after the spirit of
the new scholasticism, remains yet to be constituted.   In the present
Section we merely outline the general plan of the questions which we
conceive to fall properly within its scope.

Kant in describing as the *Transcendental Esthetic* his doctrine on the application of the space and time forms to the materials of sensibility. Baumgarten was the first to employ the term " esthetic " to designate the science of the beautiful. Nor was he thereby doing violence to the etymology of the word, for in his time the science of the beautiful meant almost exclusively the science of our sensory and emotional states.

145. But that narrow and inadequate conception of esthetics has nothing to recommend it. For modern scholasticism as for the Middle Ages the idea of the beautiful is complex; it is " an *impression* caused in us by an *object* capable of producing it." Esthetics ought, therefore, to comprise two, or even three, distinct groups of questions : about the subjective elements of the beautiful, about its objective elements, and about the correspondence of the former with the latter. Understood in this way, esthetics would represent a mixed science in the general classification of philosophical studies : it would borrow from psychology the requisite materials for explaining the impression or perception of the beautiful ; and from metaphysics whatever belongs to the constitution of those things to which we attribute the prerogative of beauty. Parallel with this treatment of general questions it would also embrace certain special branches devoted to the study of the great leading manifestations of the beautiful both in nature and in art. Let us take a glance at those various departments.

146. The subjective impression is an element *essential* to the beautiful. This impression is a double phenomenon ; it can be analysed into a cognitive *perception* and a specific *gratification* or enjoyment. Of course, every conscious activity that is exercised within certain limits of intensity and duration can be a source of pleasure ; but not every source of pleasure is esthetic, as the positivists

seem to think and to teach. Esthetic pleasure is the epiphenomenon of a perceptive or cognitive activity (*quæ visa placent*); and if we examine the objective factors (147) of this pleasure we shall find that the perception in question must be of the intellectual order. The enjoyment of esthetic pleasure resides formally in a disinterested contemplation, a "superfluous" activity (Spencer), a "play" impulse without any direct and immediate utility (Schiller). Moreover, in the perception of sensible beauty, the abstraction which conditions intellectual apprehension springs from the *agreeable* feeling in the sensations, and thus the sense pleasure is always closely associated with the intellectual.

The contemplation of the beautiful is the cause of a very special and indefinable sort of tranquility, calm, peace. The esthetic enjoyment of sensible beauty is likewise a *harmonious* pleasure; it diffuses itself over man's whole conscious life: but it could not be harmonious did it not respect the fundamental hierarchy established among man's various mental faculties.

147. The object of this subjective perception is the perfect order of the thing perceived (*unde pulchrum in debita proportione consistit*). But perfect order in a thing implies a multiplicity of parts (*integritas, magnitudo*), the relative importance of each depending on its functional value compared with the whole (*debita proportio, æqualitas numerosa, commensuratio partium*). It is to the formal constituent (the *forma*) of any being or thing that we must refer the factors of its intrinsic orderliness, for the *forma* is the principle of its unity, the thing being then perfect when the arrangement of its parts realizes fully and adequately the constitution demanded by its nature (64).

148. The esthetics of the ancient Greek philosophers investigated almost exclusively the objective elements

of beauty, either confining their attention to objects
which revealed proportion and harmony in their
constitution (Platonic and Aristotelian school), or
considering beauty as a transcendental attribute
of Being as such, and therefore as abiding in
simple as well as in composite things (Neo-Platonic
school).

Modern esthetics, on the other hand, carried to
the opposite extreme by most of its representatives,
would have beauty to be a purely subjective phenomenon, either the outcome of an *a priori* form
(Kantian and post-Kantian schools), or of some
semi-conscious or subconscious activity (Leibnitzian
school), or of any and every agreeable or useful
sensation   whatsoever   (positivism,   utilitarian
esthetics).

The superiority of the new scholastic esthetics
arises from the close correlation it establishes between
the orderliness of the thing and the impression it is
calculated to produce in us.   It completes the
Greek by the modern point of view, and reciprocally.
It also insists that the objective constituents of order
must be *excitants of a kind conformable to the contemplative activity* of the being that apprehends it.

It is only by analyzing this causal relation that we
can mark off the complex notion of *beauty* from the
purely metaphysical notion of *perfection :* a vast
multiplicity of elements may conceivably be necessary
for the objective perfection of a thing, but it would
mar the work of art by fatiguing the faculties of
perception ; for the *objective integrity* of a perfect
thing, the real, physical presence of all its elements
without exception is essential ; for its *esthetic
integrity,* on the contrary, all that is needed is that
the spectator have the " impression " of integrity, and
the deliberate omission or bare outlining of certain
parts is a trick well known to artists, by which they
arouse the contemplative activity of the auditor

or spectator and thus make him a sort of sharer in the creative work itself. The *claritas pulchri*, so often spoken of by the scholastics, is an admirable expression of this comprehensive teaching, for it has in view that " property of things in virtue of which the objective elements of their beauty, that is to say, their order, harmony, proportion, reveal themselves clearly to the intelligence, and so elicit its prolonged and easy contemplation."[1]

149. The efficient agencies productive of the work of art are the creative faculties of man—chiefly imagination and intelligence—subserved by the rules or technique of each particular department. This technique is brought to bear on certain sense materials (the material cause of the work of art) and so fashions them as to realize some ideal (the formal cause of the work of art). This *artist's ideal* is no mere misty dream, but a concrete image in which he has embodied all the objective elements he aims at realizing in his work, and has so embodied them that the functional rôle of each will contribute to the total impression he wishes to produce. This impression will depend on the *resplendentia formæ*, that is, on the " form " made to shine forth from the artist's work (63). Whether it be the " substantial form " of the being, or some " accidental form " that the artist has chosen to body forth (what Taine calls the *caractère dominateur*), the more prominently he makes this unifying principle stand out and " shine forth "—*resplendere*—the fuller, richer and easier will be our knowledge of his masterpiece, and the more powerful the impression it will make upon us. Thus we see the verification of what a scholastic, nourished by the wholesome doctrines of the thirteenth century, has written on this subject : " Pulchrum in ratione sua plura concludit : scilicet

---

[1] M. De Wulf, *Études historiques sur l'esthétique de saint Thomas d'Aquin* (Louvain, 1896), p. 28.

splendorem formæ substantialis vel accidentalis supra partes materiæ proportionatas et terminatas."[1]

If this philosophy of art is to be fruitful it must spring in the first instance from the close study of the best masterpieces. Art criticism and art history contain the materials from which the philosopher of esthetics must abstract his theories ; they are to esthetics what the sciences of inorganic nature are to cosmology, and the biological sciences to psychology. We may here copy the example of positivism, which approaches the study of art problems by the study of masterpieces. The method is entirely in harmony with the peripatetic ideology. It will also prove a valuable test for the new scholastic esthetic, for if the principles of the latter are true they will be able to interpret and to justify the rules and canons followed by the great masters.

Then, there remains the *final* cause of art. Its essential aim is of course the production of the beautiful, but we may inquire whether it has not also some extrinsic mission : Has it a social or educative significance ? Should it come out among the people or remain the exclusive privilege of a coterie of initiated worshippers ? How can we deny it all influence on the moral life of the individual and the community, provided we keep clearly before us the distinction between the *finis operis* and the *finis operantis ?* These, however, are questions of ethics and sociology rather than of esthetics.

150. To conclude : Esthetics has its place clearly marked out in any comprehensive study of the new scholasticism ; it is a natural offshoot from psychology and metaphysics. A thorough and modern scholastic treatment of it should yield an adequate and satisfactory explanation of the many modern problems that have grown up around the concept of the beautiful ; therein shall we find yet another

---

[1] Opusc. *De Pulchro et Bono*, ed. Uccelli, p. 29.

illustration of the striking cohesion and marvellous elasticity of the great organic doctrines of Middle Age scholasticism.

SECTION 32.—OTHER BRANCHES OF A PSYCHOLOGICAL CHARACTER.

151. Psycho-physics, or psycho-physiology, or physiological physiology, or experimental psychology[1] as it is variously called, is a very modern science, based on external as well as internal observation, and having for its object the discovery of the relations between the phenomena of consciousness and their physiological concomitants.   Attaining to a remarkably sudden popularity among men of science, who are naturally partial to those half-psychological, half-physiological forms of research, the new science has already made the rounds of Europe and America.   At the present time it has chairs and laboratories in most universities.

Now, no excessively spiritualist system of philosophy which regards the immaterial soul of man as entirely independent of his body, can consistently give any countenance to this whole department of research ; while, on the other hand it fits in admirably with the spirit of the new scholasticism, and especially with its cardinal psychological doctrine of the *substantial union* of spirit with matter in the unity of composite human nature (137, 138).[2]

The conclusions formulated by Weber and Fechner on the quantitative relation of the sense-stimulus to the intensity of sensation, and their further verification by Wundt ; the results brought to light by

---

[1] A scholastic psycho-physiology is as yet scarcely outlined.

[2] [Cf. art. by Dr. Gasquet in the *Dublin Review*, April, 1882, on " St. Thomas' Physiological Psychology."—*Tr*.]

experiments made with such instruments as the dynamometer and the plethismograph ; the observations made with regard to the duration of psychic phenomena and the limits of conscious sensibility : these, and a whole series of cognate investigations undertaken within the past ten or fifteen years and chronicled in numerous reviews, treatises and monographs, are all quite in accord with the spirit of modern scholasticism, and even amount to a striking vindication of its psychology.

What, then, could be more natural on our part than to extend a sincere welcome to these " new ways " and to contribute our quota to researches that are sure to enrich our philosophy and reflect credit upon it ?

Scientific men of the most widely divergent schools of thought have frequently noticed the remarkable plasticity of medieval psychology.   We need only instance the testimony of one of the well-known founders of the science of psycho-physics, Professor Wundt of Leipzig, who states, towards the end of his *Principles of Physiological Psychology*, that the results of his researches do not fit in with materialism, nor with Platonic or Cartesian dualism ; and that the only theory which attaches psychology to biology and thereby presents itself as a plausible metaphysical conclusion to experimental psychology, is the theory of Aristotelian animism.[1]

152. Very closely connected with psychology we find a large number of problems relating to the education and instruction of the young.   To draw out the intelligence and form the character, we must be thoroughly conversant with whatever in any way influences the normal functioning of the mental activities.   Psychology is, in fact, the very groundwork of didactics and pedagogy.   And as there is

---

[1] *Grundzüge der physiologischen Psychologie*, v. ii., p. 540.

a new scholastic psychology, so will there be new scholastic didactics and a new scholastic pedagogy.[1]

It is customary nowadays to distinguish between *didactics*, or the science of instruction, and *pedagogy*, or the science of education. And such a line of demarcation exactly coincides with the Thomistic theory of the real distinction between at least the higher faculties of the soul—the intellect and the will (62). But, beyond and apart from this, the solidity and reasonableness of the new scholastic psychology stand revealed in all the various departments of didactics and pedagogy ; for it offers an adequate explanation of quite a number of rules and maxims universally held by teachers and educators of experience. Here, then, again, the new scholasticism can rightly set up its principles in opposition to those of the Herbartian and positivist schools of pedagogy. An example or two will prove instructive.

It is the province of didactics not merely to prescribe the sciences and arts to be taught, and the order of teaching them, but also to lay down the right methods for teaching them—the methods common to all and the methods peculiar to each.[2] Now those methods as a whole are an illuminating commentary on scholastic ideology. Why does the master proceed " from the concrete to the abstract " ? Why does he stimulate and sustain attention by employing " intuitive " methods ? Why does he freshen and enliven his teaching by descriptions, illustrations, examples, etc.—if it be not because that great principle which governs our whole psychic life applies in a special manner to the earlier developments of our cognitive faculties : *Nihil est in intellectu quod prius non fuerit in sensu* (89) ? The abstractive

---

[1] Willmann has published a *Didaktik* (third edition, 2 vols., 1903), in keeping with scholastic principles, as well as numerous other writings on pedagogy.

[2] We have touched on *some* of the questions of philosophical pedagogy in Section 21. There are several others, as, for example, that of the order in which the various branches of philosophy should be taught.

process which engenders the universal concept and leads to the formulation of laws, must be constantly nourished by the products of perception and imagination, whatever be the subject-matter of our study. On the other hand, the master is not to spoon-feed his pupils with fully-cooked items of information, but rather to draw out and encourage the exercise of those faculties by which the pupil, through his own *personal* effort, will *acquire* knowledge. The pupil must be *active* in assimilating knowledge : its communication must exert a *formative* influence on his faculties. So the scholastic principle finds its application : " Quando igitur præexistit aliquid in potentia activa completa, tunc agens extrinsecum non agit nisi adjuvando agens intrinsecum, et ministrando ei ea quibus possit in actum exire." [1]

Mere instruction is not an end in itself ; it should contribute to the formation of *personality*, and should therefore have its place assigned to it among the many factors of education proper. Those engaged in the education of youth are well aware of the importance of an equal and well-balanced development of the merely sentient impulses and of the free, rational activities. The full exercise of physical vitality has its influence on the moral side of life ; judicious bodily exercise is an aid to mental activity ; the passions may be made the enemies or the allies of sound moral training. And why all this ? Because, as modern scholasticism teaches, there are not two beings in each of us, a body and a soul, but *one* substantially composite being ; while, on the other hand, rational volition, whether free or necessary, is intimately dependent on the organic appetites (137, 138).

It has been said that education is simply the cultivation of good habits. Nothing truer, if we understand habit in the strict scholastic sense of

---

[1] St. Thomas. *De Veritate*, Q. XI., art. 1, in corp.

habitus or *dispositio.* Since the repetition of any act begets in the faculty a permanent disposition or facility to perform that act (85), the principal duty of the educator will be to guide and watch over the faculties of the pupil in the process of acquiring those good habits. And as the human soul is not a mere loose bundle of independent forces, since the harmony of the various mental activities demands a subordination of the faculties, psychology will place in the teacher's hands this important practical principle : that in the child or youth the ruling faculty must be the rational will. Mistress of itself and of all its energies, the soul ought to guide all these towards the proper end of all. The exercise of the will-faculty, as of any other faculty, demands effort ; and effort begets moral virtue : for the man of character is the man who can direct and control himself in conformity with the exigencies of his end or destiny, that is, of his perfection.[1] Thus man's moral destiny fixes the educational ideal.

Finally, we may note that as the didactics and pedagogy which deal with the formation of the single, separate individual, derive their support from general psychology, so will they need to draw from other sciences when they regard the individual not as isolated, but in his actual social and historical setting. Here the sciences of education will have to address themselves to a group of phenomena concerning the growth and development of the energies of the whole vast, complex social organism. Just in this domain have didactics and pedagogy received a considerable impetus and extension in quite recent

---

[1] Besides intellect and will, many moderns recognise a third faculty, *sentiment*, which, they say, should receive special training. As scholastics consider sentiment, feeling, affection, emotion, etc., to belong mainly to the appetitive faculty [and in some degree to the cognitive], they do not admit this tripartite division into their didactics and pedagogy [though, of course, they fully appreciate and analyze the conscious states referred to].

times.[1]   Education is influenced by political forces,
by the standard of domestic and social morality,
by religion, by the various factors which history
chronicles and criticizes.   The character of the
instruction given to youth will always depend on
the prevailing conditions and conceptions of literature,
science and art.   Educationalists may therefore
expect to find valuable lights and helps from studying
the history of civilizations.   They will also be aided
by ethical statistics, which point to the reciprocal
influences of human liberty and of racial and criminal
phenomena ; by " folk-psychology," with its findings
on the formation of language, on religion, and on
morals.

153. The contact of general psychology with
philology, ethnology and history has given rise to
a new group of psychological researches which
Lazarus and Steindhal have called by the name of
Völkerpsychologie, and which have been more clearly
mapped out and described by Wundt in his great
work bearing that title.[2]   This *folk-psychology*, or
collective psychology as it might be called with greater
accuracy and propriety, studies the *psychological
phenomena of the human crowd, of collective humanity
as such*, abstracting from all particular circumstances
of time and space.   Such, for instance, are the phenomena of language, of public worship or religious rites
and of public morals, to which Wundt has chiefly
devoted his attention.   There are many other
analogous groups of phenomena : the psychological
manifestations of grouping by families, by professions,
by states ; of union on grounds of utility or pleasure ;
of the mere human crowd as such : all these fall
within the scope of the new science.

---

[1] See Willmann, *op. cit.*, vol. I., p. 29, with its interesting introduction,
pp. 1-98.   The full title of the work is : " Didaktik als Bildungslehre
nach ihren Beziehungen zur Socialforschung und zur Geschichte der
Bildung."
[2] Leipzig, 1900.

This folk-psychology has a special bearing on sociology, which studies from a general standpoint the mutual dependence of all social phenomena on one another. The former science does not embrace all the psychic facts which might be assigned to sociological psychology. It leaves the latter science to investigate the influence of the social *milieu* on the mentality of a given individual, as also the influence a powerful personality might wield over a given social state.[1] These two latter questions belong at the same time to what has been called "individual psychology." About the idea that inspires this latter branch, and a few of its applications, a word may be said in conclusion.

154. General psychology deals with the abstract type; it studies *man*, not *men*. But individual differences are so many revelations of each distinct personality, so many factors of the individuation of one common specific nature (66). There are, first of all, characteristics peculiar to certain classes of men. Accurate observation discovers the influences of such factors as age; and notably the science of *child-psychology* (*pédologie*)—itself still in its infancy —traces the development of child-life in the greatest diversity of surroundings: among civilized and uncivilized peoples, in normal and in abnormal circumstances. Other explorers are accumulating the first materials ever collected in view of a sex-psychology; others again are studying the innumerable modifications and disturbances wrought by disease and illness on ordinary psychic phenomena; while investigators in the domain of criminal anthropology are busy comparing the moral type of man with the criminal.

Further still, by analyzing the data of philology,

[1] See some observations by Père De Munnynck, in the *Mouvement sociologique*, published by the "Societé belge de sociologie," 1901, pp. 157 and foll.

ethnography and history, we might build up an ethnical psychology, a psychology of each of the different nations or races of people. And finally, individual biography may be developed in certain cases into a psychology of such types—or exceptions— as Julius Caesar or Napoleon ; a psychology which will analyze those infinitely small perceptions of which Leibnitz speaks, and which stamp on each conscious being the indelible seal of individuality.[1]

155. Whatever be the future achievements of folk-psychology and individual-psychology, the new scholasticism would seem *a priori* to possess certain fundamental doctrines capable of shedding not a little light on these obscure places.   Its theories on the origin of language and on the moral aspirations of man, explain at least as clearly as evolutionism the phenomena of language and religion.   The scholastic ideology offers a satisfactory explanation of the genesis of conscious states in the child ; the mutual dependence of psychical and physiological functions in a being composed of matter and spirit and endowed with substantial unity, will explain the various phenomena of sexual psychology, the strange facts brought to light by pathological psychology, and so on.

SECTION 33.—ETHICS AND NATURAL RIGHT.

156. The century just elapsed has witnessed the rise of the most widely divergent systems of moral philosophy.   Utilitarian ethics are the offspring of the materialism and positivism which would identify happiness either with an exclusively egoistic well-being whose factors may be weighed and measured

---

[1] Under the title of *comparative psychology* or *animal psychology* we may group all investigations into the similarity and dissimilarity of men and animals in regard to their respective states of consciousness.

by a sort of " moral arithmetic," or else with the altruistic well-being of humanity in the lump. Spencer has attempted the reconciliation of egoism and altruism in his imposing synthesis of the evolutionist philosophy : moral conduct has had its first faint, far-away beginnings in the pleasure attending the most elementary processes of conscious life : its evolution runs in a groove parallel to organic evolution : it will finally usher in a social state in which a perfect harmony will be realized between altruistic feelings and egoistic or individual well-being.   The evolution-craze is accountable for some sufficiently wild and fantastic speculations in the domain of ethics as elsewhere.   Most evolutionists, however, have (with Leslie Stephen) abandoned the Spencerian idea of an ultimate state of moral equilibrium, and rather seek the morality of human conduct in its continuous adaptation to the actual exigencies of a social state that is subject to perpetual evolution.   If this be so, there is manifestly no *intrinsic* difference between good and evil ; and the evidences of history, anthropology and ethnography are pointed to as showing that the test of morality has ever and always varied with the time and circumstances. . . . . In other directions the rigid stoicism of Kantian ethics would have us act independently of all self-interest, of all motives extrinsic to duty, and obey the law for its own sake (the categorical imperative).   Schopenhauer's pessimistic ethics, originating in the Kantian concept of the noumenon, regards all nature, man included, as a series of objectivations of will, appearing only for the endurance of struggle and misery.   Pessimism has more recently rid itself of its Kantian associations, and still survives, though more as an attitude of feeling or sentiment than as a philosophical system. These are but a few out of many modern ethical systems, all so utterly defective and unsatisfactory that well-known moralists like Sidgwick have passed through all of them and found rest in none.[1]

Nor has any single theory of scholastic ethics found a place in this chaos of modern systems. Can the time-honoured teachings of scholastics on the last end of man, his freedom and responsibility, on good and evil, law and duty, reward and punishment—be still maintained in the twentieth century ? If they can, it will be by bearing the brunt of modern controversy and emerging successfully from the tests to which positivism and evolutionism will subject them. Our ethical teaching must be submitted to such tests. Instead of starting from stereotyped, traditional principles, which assume precisely what our present-day adversaries call into question, we must carry our analysis some steps farther back ; we must check and supplement the data of consciousness by sociological and ethnographical observations ; take account of the variations and weaknesses and failures of the moral sense or conscience in undeveloped or decadent societies ; and carefully discriminate between the changeable and the unchangeable. The necessity of employing such methods of observation is still more manifest when we pass from the general principles of morals to their applications in the sphere of natural right.

157. And in the first place we must have a proper understanding of the connection between natural or social right and the principles of general ethics. If, with Kant, we are to regard these two departments as entirely separate, the former dealing with man's *interior, autonomous* activity, and the latter with his *external* actions, including the conditions which safeguard the exercise of human liberty—then, obviously, natural right has no connection whatever

---

[1] See some interesting pages from Sidgwick, published in *Mind* (April, 1901, p. 287), under the title : " Professor Sidgwick's Ethical View.   An auto-historical fragment."

with man's last end, nor does it impose any *moral obligation* upon him; its prescriptions in no way surpass the regulations of an ordinary police code.

Against such a weakly and demoralizing doctrine the foundations of our social rights and duties must be clearly shown to consist in the agreement of the known phenomena of social life and intercourse *with the supreme and ultimate end of the individual man.* It may be said with truth that there is a complete and absolute change from the traditional method of dealing with the great leading problems of social ethics: freedom of contract, organization of labour, property rights, education, the family, the origin, forms and limits of State authority, the relations of Church and State, international law, and the rights of war and peace. Not that these questions were unknown in the Middle Ages; but they were dealt with in a rather academic fashion, and solved on almost exclusively *deductive* lines, with only very rare attempts at applying the solutions to actual social conditions. Deduction can, of course, establish certain very general precepts of natural right (the prohibition of homicide, for example); but by itself it is helpless in presence of the highly complex and special ramifications of rights and duties in the various departments of modern life and intercourse. The historical and sociological sciences, so carefully cultivated in modern times, have proved to evidence that social conditions *vary* with the epoch and the country, that they are the resultant of quite a number of fluctuating influences, and that accordingly the science of natural right should not merely establish *immutable* principles bearing on the moral end of man but should likewise deal with the *contingent* circumstances accompanying the application of those principles. Our titles to private property and our methods of production have changed considerably since the thirteenth century; St. Thomas' arguments in justification of the former have not the same convincing force now as they had then. The investment of capital at interest, such a fertile source of production in modern conditions, is something very different from the usury that formed the object of long and bitter controversies in the Middle Ages. Then, also, ethnographical researches have brought to light many elementary forms of family life and domestic relations, differing widely from the type familiar to the Middle Ages. In a word, sociology understood in the wider and larger sense is transforming the methods of the science of natural right.

From all this the new scholasticism stands to gain, if it only avoids preconceived ideas, accepts all facts as they are brought to light, studies *each question* on its merits in the light of these facts, and not merely in its present setting but as presented in the pages of history. Boasting of this experimental method, systems like that of historical materialism have made pretence of revolutionizing natural right : and these must be fought with their own weapons.[1]

SECTION 34.—LOGIC.

158. Of all portions of ancient philosophy, the logic of Aristotle and the scholastics has best stood the shock of centuries. The end of the reign of Aristotle is not yet ; men of the mental calibre of Kant have bowed in homage before him.

---

[1] Writing of the social ethics of scholasticism, M. Charles Gide says : "The renaissance of the Catholic teaching, even in its Thomistic form, renders imperative at the present day a close study of those so-called fossil doctrines ; and when they are brought to light one is astonished at their healthy and promising vitality, at their striking resemblance to many of our modern theories and at the insignificance of our attempts to improve on them." In the *Revue d'économie politique*, 1896, pp. 514-515 (*à propos* of a work of M. Brants, *Les théories économiques au XIIIe et au XIVe siècle*).

The new scholasticism will take up and transmit the best thought of the thirteenth century. But there is such a close connection between ideology and logic that the solutions offered in the former branch will necessarily influence those of the latter. The theory of abstraction underlies the scientific explanation of the mental act of judgment, for it is on abstraction that every intellectual act is based : without presupposing abstraction there can be no proper understanding of the categories and predicables, of the general mechanism of judgment, of the laws of syllogism and induction, of the nature of definition, division and demonstration, nor even of the bare notion of science.

But then, is there nothing new in the new scholastic logic ? On the contrary. Since John Stuart Mill erected his logical system on the basis of a positivist ideology, all the laws of thought have been subjected to a searching analysis. The positivist resolves judgment into an association of sensations ; the syllogism is either declared worthless (143) or reduced to induction ; and the latter is a mere passage of thought from the particular to the particular. Definition, moreover, so far from forming the groundwork of the sciences, becomes a mere description of facts, and science itself is only a catalogue of stable associations between experienced sensations.

By the very fact of its close contact with positivism the new scholastic philosophy must of necessity emphasize and strengthen its vital theories. Thus it is that scientific induction, almost entirely neglected in medieval logic, has been established on a sound basis in order to secure it against the attacks that were being made upon it ; and the inductive methods, so ably outlined by John Stuart Mill, are now commonly adopted by scholastics. Credit is likewise due to him for a new classification of the fallacies.

These are but a few of the points in which the new scholasticism has largely profited by contact with its adversaries.

Nowadays, more than ever, logic is proclaimed to be an *instrument* of knowledge. Scholastics and positivists are at one in thinking that dialectic is not an end in itself. As one of the ancients humorously remarks : " those who stop in logic are like eaters of crayfish, who for sake of a morsel lose all their time over a pile of scales."

159. For some years past scientific method has been the object of such careful and exhaustive study that it bids fair to be no longer a mere chapter in logic but an independent whole. We refer to the *constructive* or *inventive* methods (13), not to the methods of teaching : these latter belong nowadays to *didactics* (152). Under the title of *methodology*, or of *applied logic*, scholars are investigating the constitutive method of each particular science : arithmetic, geometry, the calculus, etc., to mention a few deductive or rational sciences ; physics, chemistry, biology, political economy, history, etc., to instance the inductive sciences of observation and experiment.

As for the method of philosophy itself, the combination of analysis and synthesis must ever remain *a fortiori* the soul of all philosophical effort, since this must ever aim at embracing in one comprehensive view (synthesis) the manifold departments (analysis) on the universal order (4, 48, 120).

CHAPTER III.

THE FUTURE OF THE NEW SCHOLASTICISM.

SECTION 35.—CONCLUSION.

160. Were we to pursue the parallel established in the present volume between medieval and modern scholasticism, we should conclude by comparing the decadence of the former with the future of the latter. (Section 19). It is not, however, the object of the present section to indulge in prophecy, but rather to point to certain general conclusions which emerge from our investigations, and which, so far as we can judge to-day, are destined to influence the philosophy of to-morrow.

To take up the old scholasticism *in globo*, without changing anything, or adding anything, is simply out of the question. It is only the things of to-day that have an interest for the people of to-day : they will give their consideration only to what is modern. Hence, the " scholastic " thought-system must become " neo-scholastic " if it is to have life and influence in the modern world. That is to say, it must undergo a process of overhauling and resetting which will remove its medieval appearance and make it an attractive modern article.

But surely the modern spirit will kill the old philosophy instead of breathing a new life into it ? Can we put new wine into old bottles ? Will they not burst in the experiment ? Well, we can test the tenacity of the old scholastic doctrines by carefully comparing them with their rivals of the present day. And the impartial testimony of enlightened and candid opponents will add some precious information to the results of such a comparison.

Besides the new scholasticism, two other great currents share between them all the philosophical systems of the opening century : Neo-Kantism and positivism. In these two latter currents it is easy to detect the influence of prolonged doubt about the existence of an absolute or noumenal reality. Neo-Kantism especially has exerted quite an extraordinary influence, both in Europe and in America, on the convictions of contemporary thinkers. They are all subjectivists of some shade or other : phenomenism has become a sort of atmosphere breathed by all modern thought.

Neo-Kantism and positivism are both alike met by the rational dogmatism of the new scholastic philosophy—the only one that merits serious attention among contemporary dogmatic systems. Inheriting as it does the traditional spiritualism of a Plato, an Aristotle, a St. Augustine and a St. Thomas, it bases its claims neither on the tradition which it perpetuates nor on arguments from authority—which can be twisted in opposite directions like the nose of a waxen image, to which it is quaintly compared by a thirteenth century scholastic, Alanus of Lille : *auctoritas cereum habet nasum, id est, in diversum potest flecti sensum.* On the contrary, it is after an examination of the facts that are engaging the attention of our contemporaries, after interpreting the results achieved by the sciences, and after testing critically its own principles, that the new scholasticism lays down its conclusions, and invites philosophers of the twentieth century to recognise them and deal with them on precisely the same titles as they deal with those of Neo-Kantism and positivism.

161. That it can rightfully claim to have such consideration accorded to it, its adversaries themselves

admit. Men like Boutroux acknowledge that the system of Aristotle can compare advantageously to-day with Kantism and with evolutionism.[1] Paulsen and Eucken regard the new scholasticism as the rival of Kantism, and describe the opposition of the rival systems as a war between two worlds (der Kampf zweier Welten).[2] " In the presence of such a striking and confident (siegesgewiss) forward march of medieval ideas, writes Mr. Doering, it will no longer suffice merely to ignore them, or to decline or stop short of questions of principles. The time has come for each to deliberately choose his attitude in regard to those principles and to raise aloft his banner."[3] Many, indeed, are the tributes paid by various other adversaries to the new scholasticism, but it would be both superfluous and needless to reproduce all of them here.[4]

162. If we record such testimonies here at all it is firstly in order to show how absurd is the attitude of those numerous sceptics who condemn without hearing and mock at what they do not understand. And it is secondly in order to persuade those of our friends who are impatient for the rapid and sweeping triumph of our philosophy, that success must not be expected from extrinsic factors only, but must always be the crown and the result of real doctrinal superiority. Leo XIII. did not create the merit of the new scholasticism by virtue of a decree, but he understood its merit and saw his opportunity.

---

[1] Aristote, Études d'histoire de philosophie (Paris, 1901), p. 202.

[2] Eucken, Thomas von Aquino und Kant. Ein Kampf zweier Welten (Kantstudien, 1901, Bd. VI, h. 1). Paulsen, Kant, der Philosoph des Protestantismus (ib. 1899). The latter study, being conceived from the religious point of view, is of less importance from the point of view of the present work.

[3] Doering. in the Zeitschr. f. Psychol. u. Physiol. d. Sinnesorgane, 1899, pp. 222-224, in a review of Mercier's Origines de La Psychologie contemporaine.

[4] See, for example, Mercier's Origines, etc., ch. viii : " Le néo-Thomisme " ; and the Revue Néo-Scolastique, 1894, pp. 5 and foll., and under the heading : Le mouvement néo-thomiste.

His energetic words may have hastened the dawn and added to the renown of the new scholastic philosophy; but they could never have given its doctrines an abiding and recognised authority did not these doctrines themselves give evidence and promise of a deep and vigorous vitality.

They will prevail, as the truth prevails; but their growth will be progressive, and always conditioned by the general level of man's intellectual acquirements. In this respect the new scholasticism is self-moving like every living thing; a stop in its evolution would be the symptom of another decay.

APPENDIX.

PHILOSOPHY AND THE SCIENCES AT LOUVAIN.[1]

THE rise and progress of the new Scholastic Philosophy at the Catholic University of Louvain, in Belgium, during the past twenty years, has attracted the attention of philosophers of every school and every shade of opinion.[2] It marks an epoch in the history of Modern Philosophy, and it contains many important lessons for all who take an interest in the progress of thought, especially among Catholics. In the following pages we shall aim at giving a very brief sketch of the spirit that animates the work that is being done at Louvain in the department of Philosophy, and at conveying some idea of the significance and influence of the new movement. We have been already endeavouring to show how Scholastic Philosophy, subsequent to the rise of Cartesianism, became divorced from the Natural Sciences, to the great detriment of both, and of the Catholic religion as well,[3] and how Leo XIII sought, with all the power of a great mind, to repair the damage done, or at least

---

[1] Reprinted, with some minor alterations and omissions, from the IRISH ECCLESIASTICAL RECORD, May and June, 1905.

[2] Cf. *L'Institut Supérieur de Philosophie à L'Université Catholique de Louvain* (1890-1904), by Rev. A. Pelzer, D.Ph. (30 pp. ; Imprimerie Polleunis et Ceuterick, 32, rue des Orphelins). *Le Mouvement Néo-Thomiste* (16 pp.), extrait de la *Revue Néo-Scolastique*, publiée par la Société Philosophique de Louvain. Directeur : D. Mercier. Secretaire de Redaction : M. De Wulf. (Institut Superieur de Philosophie, 1, rue des Flamands, 1901). *Deux Centres du Mouvement Thomiste : Rome et Louvain*, par C. Besse. (63 pp. ; Paris, Letouzey et Ané, 17, rue du Vieux-Colombier, 1902). *Rapport sur les Etudes Superieures de Philosophie*, presenté par Monseigneur D. Mercier au Congrès de Malines, 1891. (Louvain, Librairie de l'Institut de Philosophie, Louvain, 1891, 32 pp.)

[3] I. E. RECORD, January, 1906.

to prevent a continuance of it, by renewing once more the long shattered alliance.[1]

I.—THE PROJECT OF A PHILOSOPHICAL INSTITUTE AT LOUVAIN.

It was Leo XIII himself who conceived the project of founding a special Institute for the study of Scholastic Philosophy in close connection with the sciences in the Catholic University of Louvain. During the time he had been Papal Nuncio in Belgium he had learned to esteem and admire the splendid work done in every department of education by the Louvain professors, lay and clerical alike.[2] He felt that a centre of such scientific renown, such intellectual activity, and such frank and fearless Catholicity, would be just the fittest place in the whole Catholic world to wed once more the old Scholastic Philosophy with the progressive Modern Sciences. The idea of the possibility of such a union gave a severe shock, no doubt, both to timid Catholics on the one hand, and to aggressive infidels on the other. But Leo XIII *knew* Scholastic Philosophy, and knowing it he had confidence in its harmony with scientific truth. Fortunately, too, he found men in Belgium ready to share that confidence in the fullest, to take up his project with ardour, and to carry it through many difficulties and much opposition to the well deserved success which it enjoys to-day. We allude especially to the illustrious Cardinal Archbishop of Mechlin, Cardinal Mercier, founder of the Louvain Philosophical Institute. He was Professor of Philosophy

---

[1] *Ibid.,* February, 1906.

[2] The professors are, of course, all Catholics. They number over one hundred. About two-thirds are laymen. Some priests are to be found in all the faculties. In the appointments—whether of clerics or laics—merit alone is looked to Over 2,000 students—all Catholics—frequent the University.

in the *Petit Seminaire* of Mechlin, when, in 1880, he was called to Louvain to fill the new chair of Thomistic Philosophy established at the University in obedience to the wishes of Leo XIII.[1] The establishment of this chair only prepared the way for a larger scheme. Eight years afterwards, in July, 1888, the Pope evidently considered that the time was ripe for founding a special Institute. In a Brief to Cardinal Goosens, Archbishop of Mechlin, he unfolded his plans. "It seems to Us useful and supremely advantageous," he wrote, "to establish a certain number of new chairs so that from these different departments of teaching, wisely and harmoniously bound together, there may result an Institute of Thomistic Philosophy, endowed with a distinct existence." More than a year afterwards, when some attempt had been made to carry out the Pope's wishes, and want of funds proved the greatest obstacle, Leo XIII came to the rescue with a gift of £6,400 (150,000 francs), exhorting those engaged in the work to use their best efforts to collect the necessary balance from all friends of education in Belgium. That he was determined to have the good project carried out is evident from these further words of his in a Brief of November, 1889 :—

"We consider it not only opportune but necessary to give philosophical studies a *direction towards nature* so that students may be able to find in them, side by side with the lessons of ancient wisdom, the discoveries we owe to the able investigations of our contemporaries, and may draw therefrom treasures equally profitable to religion and to society."

It is easy to recognise in those words the predominant idea that runs through the whole Encyclical *Æterni Patris :* that Scholastic Philosophy must be taught in close conjunction with all the neighbouring

[1] Brief of December 25th, 1880, to Cardinal Dechamps, Archbishop of Malines.

natural and social sciences if it is to come out into the open and vindicate for itself—as it ought—an honourable place amongst the thought-systems that agitate the scientific, social and religious worlds in the twentieth century. That idea was taken up and developed by Mercier and his friends at Louvain, with a largeness and liberality of view and with an amount of zeal and devotedness which we look for in vain even in Rome itself. Speaking of the Institute in those days of its infancy, the Abbé Besse writes :—

" A new force born of the soil, so to speak, gave it life. To its director is due the credit of having first maintained, then emphasized, enlarged and developed the programme and project of the Pope ; and, finally, of having created a Thomism which, while devoid of all Roman initiative and imitation, has nevertheless given to the Pope's ideal a more decided realization than it ever achieved in Rome. " [1]

The appeal for funds to go on with the work met with a response which, if slow at first, was on the whole generous. The Belgian Catholics have to bear a heavy financial burden for the annual upkeep of such a vast university as Louvain. But as they are fully alive to the importance of education, large gifts, often anonymous, unexpected, providential, are usually forthcoming to tide any worthy educational enterprise over its financial difficulties. The foundation and equipment of the Philosophical Institute was not unduly delayed for want of funds.

But there were other difficulties and disappointments, enmities and oppositions, such as are incident to the undertaking of any great and difficult work. To these we shall return later on. They persisted long enough to break the spirit of anyone less hopeful and persevering than Mercier. However, they gradually diminished with time, and the Institute began to show signs of a vigorous and flourishing

---

[1] *Deux Centres, etc.*, p. 38.

life.   God's blessing was with the good work.
Mercier's manifest sincerity, his zeal in the cause
of truth, his many admirable qualities of head and
heart enabled him to overcome all opposition and
win the respect of all.   He enjoyed the fullest
confidence of Leo XIII,[1] and had the pleasure of hearing the holy Pontiff publicly praise and recommend
the work of *his* (Leo's) Institute—the Pope might
have said *their* Institute—as lately as the year 1900.[2]
To-day the Louvain Philosophical Institute wins
the respect and esteem of every impartial visitor.
Not indeed that it is yet quite fully equipped and
organized, or perfect in every detail, but that it is
so far a decided success, an institution that is doing
a vast amount of solid, substantial work of a very
superior and highly creditable sort.   It is training
professors of Philosophy not only for Belgium, but
for many seminaries, colleges and universities all
over Europe and the English-speaking world ; and
it is giving them a training which, it is our honest
belief, cannot be equalled elsewhere.   It is only the
bare truth to say that " if we find engineers who
would wish to have studied at Zurich, doctors who
would wish to have been through the Pasteur Institute, theologians who matriculate in the University
of Tübingen, it seems that it is towards the Institute
of Louvain that our young philosophers ought in
future to direct their steps."[3]

---

[1] We are glad to be able to state that the present supreme Pontiff, Pius X,
is altogether of the same mind towards the Neo-Scholastic Philosophy
and the Louvain School. In a Brief to Mgr. Mercier and the masters and
students of the *Séminaire Léon XIII*, dated June 20th, 1904, and published
in the August number of the *Revue Néo-Scolastique*, the Holy Father
speaks in the highest terms of the Institute and its work. He thanks God
for blessing the project of his predecessor in founding the Institute, and
exhorts teachers and students alike to continue their noble work : "Minime
dubitantes quin in Nobis, apud quos benemeritum Institutum vestrum
plurimum valet, et singularis gratiae et benignae voluntatis ii nunquam
desiderentur sensus, quibus ipse Decessor Noster vos enixe est prosecutus."

[2] Discourse of Leo XIII to the Belgian Pilgrims, December 30th, 1900.
Revue Néo-Scolastique, February, 1901, pp. 84-85.

[3] *Deux Centres, etc.*, p. 38.

With such a general knowledge of the Institute, derived as it were from without, we are now in a position to examine more closely the spirit which, from the outset, animated its inner life and working. What is really most accountable for the remarkable success of the Institute is

II.—THE SPIRIT THAT ANIMATES PHILOSOPHICAL STUDIES AT LOUVAIN.

We can find no more authentic exponent of that spirit than Mercier himself. He was invited by the Cardinal-Archbishop of Mechlin, Cardinal Goosens, to give an exposition of the leading ideas of the projected Papal scheme, before the "Higher Education Section" of the Congress held in that city in 1891. He did so in a very remarkable *Rapport sur les Études supérieures de Philosophie.*

Commencing with the observation that "Catholics live in a state of isolation in the scientific world," he went on to seek the causes of that isolation, fatal alike to science and to religion. Apart from the systematic opposition of some scientists to everything Christian, he set down as a leading cause of the phenomenon the widespread prevalence amongst non-Catholics of a preconceived idea that we Catholics are always engaged in preoccupations subservient to the defence of our faith :—

"Yes [he continues] the idea is widely entertained that the Catholic *savant* is a soldier in the service of his faith, and that, in his hands, science can be nothing but a weapon for the defence of his *credo*. In the eyes of many he would seem to be always under the bolt of a threatened excommunication, or shackled by troublesome dogmas ; and to remain faithful to his religion he must apparently renounce all disinterested attachment to the sciences and all free cultivation of them. Hence the distrust which he encounters. A publication coming from a Catholic institution—Protestant institutions are judged more favourably, no doubt because they have given proofs of their independence by their revolt from authority—is treated as a plea *pro domo,* as an apologetic which can have no right or title to an impartial and objective examination."

Such is the great current misconception of the Catholic attitude towards science in the minds of non-Catholics. To remove this misconception must be our first aim in the future scientific and philosophic education of our Catholic youth. Then, side by side with this misconception, and perhaps to some extent the cause of it and of the consequent ostracism of Catholics from the world of science, there is another misconception—in the minds of Catholics themselves —the mistaken view which a large number of Catholics have about science.

" For them science consists in learning and collecting results already achieved, in order to synthesize them under the conceptions of religious faith or of some spiritualist metaphysic. Contemporary science has no longer such comprehensive aims or synthetic tendencies ; it is, before all, a science of partial, minute observations, a science of analysis.

" From that diversity of point of view in the way of looking at science results this consequence : that Catholics resign themselves too easily to the secondary rôle of mere retailers of science ; too few of them have any ambition to work at what may be called *science in the making ;* too few aim at gathering and moulding the materials which must serve in the future to form the new synthesis of science and Christian philosophy. Undoubtedly this final synthesis will harmonize with the dogmas of our *Credo,* and with the fundamental principles of Christian wisdom ; but while waiting till that harmony shines forth in its full light, the objections raised by unbelief conceal it from the eyes of many, and because our champions are not always there to give back with recognised competence and authority the direct and immediate answers which these objections call for, doubts arise and convictions are shaken; the materials are grouped, arranged, and classified without us, and too often against us, and infidelity monopolizes for its own profit the scientific prestige which should be made to serve only the propagation of truth."

We would fain believe that the above picture is somewhat overdrawn, but we fear it fairly represents what was the real state of affairs when Mercier proposed the remedy which he has been ever since carrying out with such gratifying results. That remedy he outlined in these very explicit terms :—

" To form, in greater numbers, men who will devote themselves to science *for itself*, without any aim that is professional or directly apologetic, men who will work *at first hand* in fashioning the materials of the edifice of science, and who will thus contribute to its gradual construction ; and to create the resources which this work demands : such at the present day ought to be the two-fold aim of the efforts of all who are solicitous for the prestige of the Church in the world and for the efficacy of its action on the souls of men."

So far this one idea stands out prominently : that if the Catholic is to be heard and respected in the world of modern science and modern philosophy *he must be taught to cultivate those studies for their own sake*, and not with any conscious, intended dependence on dogma, nor with any direct subservience to apologetical ends.

But to find the resources for forming Catholic youth on those lines in the sciences is no easy matter. And to give them such a formation in philosophy seems more difficult still ; for the latter presupposes the former discipline : *nemo metaphysicus qui non prius physicus.* Mercier in nowise minimises these difficulties : he gives quite a luminous view of all that such a programme would include :—

" There is question of giving to the Church workers who will break the soil of science as of old the monks of the West broke the virgin soil of Christian Europe and laid the foundations of the material civilization it enjoys to-day ; of showing the respect of the Church for human reason, and the fruit she expects from its work for the glory of Him who has proclaimed Himself Master of the Sciences. . . .

" An immense field is open to scientific investigation. The boundaries of the old philosophy have become too narrow : they must be extended. Man has multiplied his power of vision ; he enters the world of the infinitely small and fixes his scrutinizing gaze upon regions where our most powerful telescopes discern no limits. Physics and Chemistry progress with giant strides in the study of the properties of matter and of the combination of its elements. Geology and Cosmogony reconstruct the history of the formation and origins of our planet. Biology and the natural sciences study the minute structure of living organisms, their distribution in space and succession in time ; and embryogeny explores their origin. The archæological, philological, and social sciences remount the past ages of our history and civilizations. What an inexhaustible mine is here to exploit, what regions to explore and materials to analyze and interpret ; finally, what pioneers we must engage in the work if we are to gain a share in all those treasures ! . . .

" It is imperative, therefore, that in those different domains we should have explorers and masters who, by their own activity, by their own achievements, may vindicate for themselves the right to speak to the scientific world and to be heard by it ; *then* we can answer the eternal objection that faith blinds us, that faith and reason are incompatible, better far than by abstract principles, better far than by an appeal to the past : we can answer it by the stubborn evidence of actual and living facts."

But if it is important for the Church to have Catholics as scientists, it is far more important for her to have Catholic scientists who will be also philosophers :—

" If we must devote ourselves to works of analysis we must remember—experience has only too clearly shown—that analysis left to itself easily gives rise to narrowness of mind, to a sort of instinctive antipathy to all that is beyond observed fact, to positivist tendencies, if not to positivist convictions.

" But science is not an accumulation of facts, it is a system embracing facts and their mutual relations.

" The particular sciences do not give us a complete representation of reality. They *abstract :* but the relations which they isolate in thought *lie together in reality,* and are interwoven with one another ; and that is why the special sciences demand and give rise to a science of sciences, to a general synthesis, in a word, to Philosophy. . . .

" Sound philosophy sets out from analysis and terminates in synthesis as its natural complement. . . . Philosophy is by definition a knowledge of the totality of things through their highest causes. But is it not evident that before arriving at the highest causes we must pass through those lower ones with which the particular sciences occupy themselves ? . . .

" At the present day, when the sciences have become so vast and numerous, how are we to achieve the double task of keeping *au courant* with them all, and of synthesizing their results ? That difficulty is a grave and delicate one.

" Since individual courage feels itself powerless in presence of the field of observation which goes on widening day by day, association must make up for the insufficiency of the isolated worker ; men of analysis and men of synthesis must come together, and form, by their daily intercourse and united action, an atmosphere suited to the harmonious development of science and philosophy alike.   Such is the object of the special School of Philosophy which Leo XIII, the illustrious restorer of higher studies, has wished to found in our country and to place under the patronage of St. Thomas of Aquin— that striking incarnation of the spirit of observation united with the spirit of synthesis, that worker of genius who ever deemed it a duty to fertilize Philosophy by Science and to elevate Science simultaneously to the heights of Philosophy." [1]

We find condensed in the above passages—glowing as they are with the eloquence of one inspired with a noble zeal in the cause of truth—an exalted and true conception of the scope and mission of philosophical training ; a faithful and enthusiastic reiteration of Leo the Thirteenth's bold and outspoken ideas on the close and intimate relations that ought to exist between Science and Philosophy[2] ; a clear understanding of the need to bring together those various studies into one and the same educational centre ; an implicit confidence that true Science and true Philosophy would and should harmonize with each other and both alike with the Catholic Faith ; and a frank and open assertion, based upon that very confidence, that in Schools of Science and of Philosophy those subjects should be taught to our Catholic youth without any view to apologetics, but simply and solely for their own sakes—that the teaching and learning of those branches, to be successful, must be disinterested.

---

[1] The above passages from Mercier's *Rapport* are all translated from the various pamphlets enumerated at the head of this Appendix.
[2] *Vide* I. E. Record, February, 1906.

In order to re-establish more effectually the long superseded alliance between Scholastic Philosophy and the Sciences, Mercier found it necessary to insist most emphatically that this Philosophy was far more than what many Catholics had come to consider it—a mere intellectual discipline subsidiary to Supernatural Theology—that in the presence of that Theology, from which it received such illumination, and to which it could never run counter, it was itself an independent and autonomous science, based upon all the natural sciences of observation and experiment.

" No one [writes the Abbé Besse] could mark off more clearly the respect we owe to theology, from the liberty we retain in science. Mercier here admirably lays down the *a priori* rights of nature and of grace. It is just because he is quite certain that grace never will be wanting to the sincere scientist that he is himself a sincere and disinterested scientist abstracting from grace.[1]

. . . . .

But how were all these views and projects of Mercier received when they were first put forth by him ? Like everything that sounds novel—not without suspicion. Was Philosophy, then, really based on the sciences, and were Catholic philosophers to be obliged to take account of what was going on in the scientific world ? Was not Catholic Philosophy something far above such commerce with the " things of earth " ? Was it not a pure intellectual system subservient only to the noble Queen of Sciences ; *Philosophia ancilla Theologiæ ?* What could it have to do with laboratories and dissecting-rooms ? So argued the Catholic advocates of the *status quo*—philosophers and the scientists alike. There had been already a struggle in Rome between the old ideas and the new before the latter got a *locus*

---

[1] *Deux Centres, etc.,* p. 41.

standi in the schools.   At Louvain the same struggle
was fought over again, only with greater success in
the issue.   The scientists were at first inclined to
look askance at what they considered an unwarrant-
able sort of dilettante dabbling in laboratories on
the part of those young philosophers ; and to hold
aloof rather than co-operate.   Those of the philosophers who were not radically opposed to the new
departure expressed their fears that the neo-Thomists
were going far beyond the Papal wishes, if not in
direct opposition to them.   In reality the disobedience lay with those who, clinging to the letter,
neglected the spirit of the Papal reform :—

"There was no excuse for their having denounced
the work of Louvain as a work of ' discord ' and of
' disobedience,' nay, even of ' treason.'   The truth
is that Mgr. Mercier was . . . the most comprehensive admirer of the idea of Leo XIII.   But
if he has directed it entirely towards the twentieth
century, if he has instinctively put it into the thick
of the contemporary conflict, thus making it actual
and living, if he has transported it into the region
of proof and criticism, giving it that attitude of
confidence and boldness in presence of the revelations
of experience and the warnings of science, all this
was neither a wilful misreading of the Papal wishes,
nor a pretence, nor a betrayal, but the steady march
of a mind that believed the Pope as it did the truth,
and that ennobled and honoured the Papal directions
while submitting to them."[1]

[1] *Deux Centres, etc.,* p. 60.   The writer of the articles reprinted in this
brochure, draws a contrast between the two centres of the Neo-Scholastic
movement,—Rome and Louvain.   He says that Leo XIII. probably never
meant to establish at Louvain anything more than a "Roman College" on the
lines of Cornoldi's school at the Gregorian University in Rome.   That may
be—and certainly such a college would have been a failure at Louvain ; but,
whatever Leo's intention in the beginning may have been, it seems certain
that Mercier's larger and bolder work has been thoroughly in the spirit of
Leo's ideas, and has always had the warm sympathy and support of the late
Pontiff.   Nor is there much room to doubt that Louvain has been hitherto
more successful than Rome in teaching, modernizing, popularizing, propagating the Philosophy of the Schools on the lines indicated by Leo.   In

Mercier succeeded in putting Philosophy at Louvain
"into the thick of the contemporary conflict"
between the various modern systems and sciences,
and he did so because, from a deep and masterly
study of the Scholastic Philosophy in the light of
Modern Science, he was convinced that he saw *a
substantial harmony between the fundamental principles
of the former and the established conclusions of the latter.*

It was in the various non-Catholic camps of modern
Science and modern Philosophy that this vigorous
action of Mercier's, in giving expression to the projects
of Leo, produced the greatest comment and the most
profound sensation.   The idea that Catholics could
be disinterested scientists seems to have been regarded
—then as now—by many unbelieving scientists as
a good joke.   The determination with which Mercier
and his Neo-Scholastic friends kept insisting that
they could and would train disinterested scientists
and disinterested philosophers in the very heart of
a Catholic University ; that they meant to "substitute for the existing patched up peace between
Science and Faith, an agreement that would be
steady and yet progressive, interior and regular ; "[1]
—that determination made unbelievers impatient

that sense the contrast drawn by the Abbé Besse—an earnest admirer of the
Louvain Institute—is quite justifiable.   But it is also only fair to observe
that the success of the Louvain Institute is largely due to a combination
of favourable surroundings which the movement in Rome did not enjoy—
such, for example, as the presence of flourishing faculties of Science and
Medicine, etc., with the ablest professors to give special courses in the
Philosophical Institute ; the presence not only of the best lay professors to
teach, but of the best lay students to frequent the courses of the Institute in
company with the ecclesiastics ; the presence of well equipped laboratories ;
the employment of the vernacular in all their teaching ; the fulness and
variety of that teaching throughout a three years' course ; the superiority
of their staff in numbers and in qualifications ; the life and reality infused
into their studies by their attention to the current periodical literature in the
various departments ; the great intellectual activity and general scientific
prestige of their University.   These circumstances—partly, no doubt, of their
own making at Louvain—have already placed the Philosophical Studies of
the Institute on that higher level which the Roman professors have been
strenuously endeavouring to reach.

[1] *Deux Centres, etc.,* p. 43.

and then afraid, lest after all there might not be some
danger that the Catholics might succeed, and the
infidel monopoly of " Modern Science " and " Modern
Philosophy " be unceremoniously interfered with.

But then the idea of a " Scholastic " revival in
Philosophy, of a " Thomism " that would be " scientific " !   That, of course, appeared nothing short
of ludicrous to the enlightened Moderns in their
blissful ignorance of what Medieval Philosophy was
and what it contained !   For, what was Medieval
Philosophy to them ?   It was a vast fabric of errors
—multiplied and monumental—of errors that were
grotesque in their puerility, and of distortions of
fact that were hoary with age ; such was the idol
that passed for Medieval Philosophy—for Scholasticism—in the minds of " the moderns," and that
stood unassailed until recent critical researches into
the history of that period demolished the idol by
shedding forth a light before which it has crumbled
into dust.   Those historical studies in Medieval
Philosophy—so sadly needed in order to do justice
to Scholasticism in the eyes of the modern world—
were then and are still being carried on partly in
Germany, partly in Paris, and partly in Louvain.
The prominence given to the History of Philosophy
is one of the features of the Neo-Scholastic programme
of studies at the Louvain Philosophical Institute.
Thanks to the very great progress that has been
made in that department, the moderns are now
willing to recognise that Medieval Thomism was
after all something other than a tissue of barren
speculations and empty formalisms ; that the great
scholastics were not " a crowd of dogmatic idealists
trying to construct a world out of the categories of
speech " ; [1] that they were by no means disdainful
of the observation of facts ; that, on the contrary,
they were great men and great philosophers who

[1] *Deux Centres, etc.*, p. 45.

have been much misrepresented ; that their system of philosophy had been travestied and distorted, and then ignorantly ridiculed by the heralds of our " Modern Philosophy " ; that, in fine, its latest presentation to the modern world at the hands of the Neo-Scholastics—in its proper historical setting, and in close contact with the modern sciences— points to this conclusion, that *amongst all the philosophical systems in vogue at the present day, the modern Scholastic Synthesis, on the lines of Aristotelian Animism, is most in harmony with the conclusions and tendencies of modern physical science.* Some of the most distinguished scientists have explicitly avowed that greater harmony between Science and Scholasticism.[1] Catholic scientists can have no difficulty about it—it is only what they should expect —but for many non-Catholic scientists such a revelation must be not a little startling.

In the ranks of the Catholic exponents of the traditional Scholasticism the idea of a close alliance between the natural sciences and their secluded system was looked upon with doubt and suspicion. They could not with any good grace oppose the new project ; for they, too, professed to believe that in Scholasticism there lay concealed in some mysterious way a vast treasure of doctrine that could easily put to flight the impious modern scientist. But they shrank from putting it to the test. They were apparently content to guard their " hidden treasure " and express a pious opinion about its efficacy. They would not ransack it in order to bring forth from it " new things and old."

The fact is that those philosophers did not appreciate the value of the legacy that was bequeathed to them from the golden age of Scholasticism—and that for two reasons : because, firstly, they had

[1] As, for example Wundt in Germany.

followed the tradition of neglecting the history of Philosophy—even of the system they studied; and secondly, and consequently, they had more or less fallen a prey, quite unconsciously, to the ultra-spiritualist views and tendencies of post-Cartesian Philosophy.

In the first place, down to very recent times the history of Philosophy was entirely neglected, even by philosophers themselves. Those most devoted to Philosophy were least devoted to its history. Innumerable errors about systems and doctrines were the inevitable result. False theories and opinions crept into systems and became incorporated with them even in the hands of the traditional exponents of those systems : witness the false doctrine of the migratory *species impressæ*, and other post-Renaissance theories, that vitiated and discredited later-day Scholasticism. It required the work of such recent pioneers in the history of Medieval Philosophy as De Wulf, Baeumker, Ehrle, Denifle, Mandonnet, Picavet, Clerval, to make even a beginning in dissipating those errors. If the traditional exponents of Scholasticism had only attended a little to its history the Neo-Scholastics of to-day would not have experienced so much trouble in giving to the world the authentic philosophical teaching of the thirteenth century—nor so much opposition in proclaiming an alliance between it and the findings of modern science. Unfortunately historical studies had not been in vogue in any department of learning. Even Catholics, though so largely dependent on Tradition in matters of Faith and Theology, which their philosophical studies always subserved, had nevertheless developed no special leaning towards historical criticism of the sources and development of their great deposit of Revealed Truth. One would have expected some such development; for, what is Tradition without History if not a mere empty formula? The Abbé Besse writes some hard things about modern Scholastics who would continue, even in the present age of historical research in every department, irrespective of its history, to teach Scholastic Philosophy as of old.

"Defenders of Tradition, they have become its prisoners, and not a little blindly—seeking to know it only in its official framework. They are destitute of the historical sense. They are unaware of all that is to be gained by an intimate acquaintance with the *milieu* of facts and ideas that accompany each step in the progress of systematization, and each new contribution to clearness of terminology. Their philosophy has neither topography nor chronology. It is of no age. It seems to issue from the night only to plunge into it again. That is undoubtedly the secret of the *ennui* that results from reading their amorphous pages. Fearing, as it were, to disturb the soul in its pure contemplation of ideas they have shut it up in a cavern."

In the second place inattention to the historical sources and growth of Scholasticism left its modern exponents open to the danger of unconsciously misconstruing its whole method and spirit. It was inevitable that the exaggerated spiritualism introduced into Philosophy by Descartes should issue later on in two distinct currents of idealism and materialism. The Scholastics naturally fell under the influence of the former current in opposition to materialism. Then, also, Descartes had unduly emphasized the use of the *deductive method* and created a chasm between Philosophy and the Physical Sciences. Again the Scholastics followed in the same direction; all the more easily because the Physical Sciences soon afterwards claimed a monopoly of the newly "invented" *inductive method*,[1] and

---

[1] Which had been employed by Roger Bacon, Albert the Great and Thomas of Aquin centuries previously.

identified themselves with materialism.   And so
Scholasticism in the second half of the last century
found itself in a condition, of which the following
paragraph gives a striking picture :—

" Catholics for a long time have seen their only
safety in this divorce of speculation from science.
The more Philosophy developed in that direction
the more they felt at ease with it.   They remained
content with the sound of certain familiar words,
such as : God, the infinite, the perfect, the good
and the beautiful, the ideal, etc.   In that effort to
escape all concern in the science of material things
they saw a token of moral elevation, something of
that good taste of which the poet speaks :

> *Coetusque vulgares et udam*
> *Spernit humum fugiente penna.*

What an illusion !   It was thus that Philosophy
came in for the staggering blows of the school of
Taine, and of science in general after him."[1]

Now this false spell of Cartesianism had to be
broken by once more establishing Scholasticism on
the basis of the Physical Sciences ; and the way had
to be cleared for this reform by the historical criticism
that would show how completely such reform would
harmonize with the true spirit of the great Medieval
Scholastics :—

" To historical criticism is due the credit of having
re-established the truth.   On that point doubt is no
longer possible.   Mercier speaks like our best
historians of Philosophy, like Boutroux, Brochard,
Picavet.   Aristotle had the true method and spirit
of science.   With him it was, of course, incomplete ;
even erroneous on many points.   Instead, therefore,
of despising it we should have corrected it.   We
should have freed it from its faults, its limitations,

---

[1] *Deux Centres, etc.*, p. 50.

its shortcomings. We should have completed it.
. . . . Above all, we should have transformed
it according to the new methods of observation and
experiment. And so we should have avoided that
conflict between *science* and *metaphysics* which is
the greatest conflict of modern times.[1]

But yet another obstacle was raised by the defenders
of the old Scholasticism, another attempt to forbid
the banns between Science and Philosophy; a final
fear was expressed by them for the stability and
definitiveness of any superstructure of Metaphysics
reared on the shifting and progressive basis of Physics.
How can such Metaphysics have any pretensions
to finality, if they partake of the nature of hypotheses
based upon the observation of nature? This apprehension for the immutable truth of Metaphysics
was genuine and sincere. But it was an apprehension
for which the alliance of Metaphysics with Physics
could give no grounds; because, in any case, in so
far as Metaphysics is endowed with any positive,
real content, it is dependent, for that content, upon
the domain of Physics where it gets all its "raw
material" so to speak. And it must rest content
with this raw material, such as it is, and take it for
what it is worth.

"It is by the employment of hypothesis that the
philosopher attempts to establish an order and a
hierarchy in that heterogeneous mass. But he
knows that he is quite exposed to see the explanatory
principle he has discovered declared at any time
useless. Hence it is that we cannot exercise too
much patience in waiting before we attempt to open
a parley with that invisible basis of all things, that
hidden god which, like the other God, no doubt,
enlightens the timid and blinds the daring."[2]

[1] The conflict between science and faith is only one particular aspect of it.
(Besse : *Deux Centres, etc.*, pp. 49, 50.)
[2] *Ibid.*, p. 48.

But how long, then, are we to give in to this "timidity"? To content ourselves with the experimental and inductive side of things before attempting any comprehensive synthesis? Are we to postpone our Metaphysical Synthesis of things until we can make it, once for all, absolutely definitive, after the physical exploration of facts is completed—that is, *indefinitely?* Or are we to make it independently of Physics altogether? Or are we to make an incomplete and perfectible working synthesis, based on the actual state of Physics, and progressive as the latter? Not the first nor the second alternative, but the third must be chosen. Not the first evidently, for no matter how men may pretend to despise Metaphysics they cannot and will not get on —it is not in human nature to get on—without Metaphysics of some sort. Not the second, for such a Metaphysic would be nothing better than an empty formalism woven from man's inner consciousness. Therefore the third, imperfect as everything else that is human, must satisfy us in this world of second-bests.

"In short, one or other of two things: either after the scientific progress realized since the time of Aristotle the investigation of facts can be allied with the work of a dogmatic elaboration, or such elaboration will be indefinitely retarded. In the first case some at least of our preconceived errors can be rectified, some at least of our uncertainties settled; in the second case, such elaboration, even though neither definitive nor absolute in its conclusions, should be outlined nevertheless, and in spite of the risks. It would be unstable, like science, but like it, too, progressive. When Metaphysics is made to spring from Physics, Metaphysics has just the same value as Physics. Approximative and provisional as it is, at all events it contains the positive, the real, the actual. But all that—is THE TRUE.

This point of view which surpasses in extension, while interpreting and following, that of Aristotle and the School, is perhaps the only reasonable one." [1]

III.—INFLUENCE OF THE LOUVAIN SCHOOL OF PHILOSOPHY.

It is from that point of view that Scholastic Philosophy has been taught at Louvain for now nearly a quarter of a century. The principles on which their whole method is based at the Philosophical Institute appear to us to be thoroughly sound ; and that they are practical and fruitful is abundantly proved by the ample measure of success that has resulted from their adoption. The Louvain Institute has attracted the close attention of contemporary philosophers of every shade of opinion, not only all over the Continent, but all over the English-speaking world as well. It reflects credit on Catholic Belgium, and deserves well of all Catholics for having renewed, as it were, and re-invigorated Scholastic Philosophy. It is giving that Philosophy a new place—and an honourable place—in the history of Philosophic Thought at the dawn of the new century.

The widespread publications of the Institute have drawn to that Philosophy the serious attention of scientists who had at first been inclined to ask : " Can anything good come out of Galilee ? " Some of them already recognise in that venerable system a *via media*, equally removed from the erroneous extremes of Cartesian Spiritualism and Modern Materialism, and more in harmony than either with the results of modern scientific research. That the Neo-Scholastic Philosophy has to be counted with in the world of modern Philosophical Systems is altogether evident from even a cursory acquaintance with the

[1] *Deux Centres, etc.*, p. 51.

Philosophical periodicals on the Continent. It is not merely in the Catholic reviews but in those of every shade that we find Neo-Scholasticism discussed —favourably or adversely as the case may be. That it should be met with in such publications as the *Revue Thomiste*, the *Divus Thomas*, the *Année Psychologique*, the *Revue de Philosophie*, the *Philosophisches Yahrbuch*, the *Yahrbuch für Philosophie und Speculative Theologie*, the *Beiträge zur Geschichte der Philosophie des Mittelalters*, the *Historisch-Politische Blätter für das Katolische Deutschland*, the *Ciudad de Dios*, the *Revista Ecclesiastica*, the *Era Novella*, etc., is, perhaps, in no way remarkable, for those are Catholic publications; but the large amount of attention it receives from time to time in such Philosophical reviews as the *Kantstudien*, the *Zeitzschrift für Psychologie und Physiologie der Sinnesorgane*, the *Revue de Metaphysique et de Morale*, the *Revue Philosophique*, the *Revue Internationale de l'Enseignement*, the *Revista Filosofica*, the *Revista Critica*, etc. —shows very plainly that the influence of the new school of Philosophic thought at Louvain has made itself felt far and wide. Wherever its tenets are attacked it is not wanting in champions able and willing to defend it in a thoroughly scientific and scholarly manner. Even where it is controverted it is respected and wins esteem for its adherents.

In brief, it bids fair to win, if indeed it has not already won, an honourable *entrée* into the vast arena of Modern Philosophy. Of this providential fact, what the ultimate significance may be, whether for Science, for Philosophy, or for Religion, it would be hard to say. So far at any rate the new Scholasticism has been shedding upon the natural sciences a flood of light which they had been seeking in vain from the competing philosophies; it gives promise of interpreting and complementing them in such an eminently rational manner as to justify its claim to

be not merely *a* philosophy amongst many philosophies, but to be *the* True Philosophy.

We have been living through an age of negative
Philosophy, and have witnessed the spread of
" cowardly " Agnosticism. We have watched that
philosophy confess with false humility that it " could
know practically nothing " : an appropriate anti-
climax to the source whence it had sprung—the
Rationalism that had proudly proclaimed its ability
to " know all things." We have seen the sciences
abandoned by sane philosophy and left to be
misinterpreted by Materialism. Now, at last, in
the new Scholasticism we have a positive philosophy
that gives back certainty and security to the sciences
and offers some positive explanation of the great
Enigma. Man cannot live on negations : by recent
systems of philosophy his soul has been starved and
left desolate, and he is now hungering for positive
truth. If he turns to the new Scholasticism he is
much more likely to find it than elsewhere :—

" There he will find a counteraction and, if I may
say so, an antidote against contemporary Materialism.
There, where science, hitherto interpreted by a group
of materialists, seemed to furnish negative solutions,
the same science on the same problems now furnishes
positive results at Louvain. What will be the outcome of this system in twenty—fifty years ? At
the decline of our critical age, do we not see breaking,
in this direction, a new dawn—that of an organic
age, and of an affirmative philosophy ? If the slow
moral anæsthesia produced by the influential scepticism of the *savant* has long been a source of uneasiness
to every serious mind, will not the certainty now
restored by science and jealously guaranteed by it,
be to the same serious mind a source of strength and
comfort ? People had almost begun to despair of
knowledge. " Science is sad," said Renan ; and in
that little phrase lay hidden and cowering all that

ironical pessimism with which he has, as it were, drugged us. But I expect the opposite effect will be wrought in the long run by metaphysical certainty through science. After a series of reactions, at the end of an important cycle of discoveries and demonstrations, let us hope that men will awake from universal scepticism to find in science a source of joy and peace. Yes, that is the aim of philosophy : to hasten that hour of light for men, to bring it nearer to them. They pine away on empty formulæ so long as certainty appears not in its true form, which is science. We must then force it to appear, and lead back souls to themselves and to God by this sweet violence, as if nothing should be one day more evident than what we shall no longer merely believe but know,—that we have souls acknowledging God no longer merely because He has said that He is, but because we know it and have proved it." [1]

The beneficial results which indirectly redound to Catholicism, especially in Belgium, from this growing prestige of the new Scholasticism, would be hard to overrate. Nowadays, more than ever since the early centuries of Christianity, Religion is attacked by false philosophies, and relies on true Philosophy for her defence. The same is true of Morality and social order in general. And true Philosophy is not any system specially manufactured for polemical ends : it is the Philosophy which is a rational interpretation of the sum total of things :—

> To the solid ground
> Of Nature trusts the mind which builds for aye.

With such a Philosophy the minds of the young Belgian Catholics are formed at Louvain. It is a living and progressive and inspiring discipline. It anchors their minds in Truth in this age of doubt and shifting unbelief. It remains with them in

[1] *Deux Centres, etc.,* p. 61.

after life as an illuminating intellectual heritage, and as a vitalizing force that stimulates to noble action. It fills them with an enthusiasm for the "things of the mind." It puts the highest ideals in religious and social, and civil action, before all in common; and ensures community of interests and activities. It is not surprising, therefore, to find the new Scholasticism making so many proselytes, to find so many young Catholics issue from the University of Louvain, and from the halls of its Philosophical Institute to attain positions of the highest eminence in the parliament, in the courts, in the government, in the schools and universities of the State. With such men as these to leaven society the future of Belgium is full of bright hopes.

What are the causes of this widespread and beneficial influence exerted by the new Scholasticism? How are we to account for the rapid progress it has made and the happy results it has already achieved? Chiefly by the spirit that animates the new movement, and which we have been trying to outline in these few pages. The whole movement is a triumph of the Truth,—an illustration of the proverb: *Magna est Veritas et prævalebit.* Nor should Catholics wonder at that. They know that they possess the Truth in inheriting a philosophy that is in such wonderful harmony with the conclusions of Science, with the demands of Reason, and with the dogmas of Faith. Should we not rather wonder that such an instrument had not been hitherto more powerful in their hands? It was because they did not use it aright. And herein lies the second and equally important reason of the striking success of the Louvain School. They are zealous in the propagation of the Truth. They do not hide their light under a bushel. They come forth fearlessly into the twentieth century with their combined treasures of medieval wisdom and modern science. From those treasures they bring forth the *nova et vetera*. They dispense those intellectual riches to their students and to a wider public in the garb of the living vernacular—and their books are being translated into most of the European languages. They spare no pains in preparing and communicating the most solid doctrine in the most attractive form. Their teaching is a living, organic, vitalizing formation, not in any sense a dry, unreal, academic discipline.

" The work of Mercier offers itself as a vigorous reaction of the scientific spirit against a rigid and anti-scientific formalism. . . .

" In opposition to the old procedure in Metaphysics . . . which was *unilateral*, that is to say, bore exclusively on the data of the understanding, we are here in presence of a *bilateral* procedure, that is to say, one bearing simultaneously on the phenomena of nature and on the phenomena of mind. And each professor, on each question, is expected to observe and to respect this distinction, being officially appointed to show his students the same fact under its two aspects : the experimental and the rational. " [1]

IV.—ORGANIZATION OF COURSES AT THE INSTITUTE.

The Philosophical Institute is called indifferently the *Institut Supérieur de Philosophie* and *École St. Thomas d'Aquin*. It is a special school or department of teaching within the Faculty of Philosophy and Letters. But it is autonomous within its own sphere ; has its own president and professors, its own programme of studies, its own courses and examinations, and confers its own degrees. In this it is like the many other special schools that have sprung up and developed within the other Faculties

[1] *Deux Centres, etc.*, pp. 52, 60.

of the University, and whose existence forms a striking feature of the organization and methods of teaching at Louvain. We may instance the *École des Sciences Politiques et Sociales* and the *École des Sciences Commerciales et Consulaires* in the Faculty of Law, and the *Institut Agronomique* in the Faculty of Sciences. The professors of these various schools belong mainly but not exclusively to the corresponding Faculties; hence the professors of the various Faculties lecture freely outside their own Faculties as well as within the latter.

Although the Philosophical Institute had small beginnings its progress in every respect has been steady since its foundation.[1] We have heard people object to its claim to the title of "higher" or "superior," on the ground that it begins at the beginning, presupposes not even an elementary knowledge of philosophy, and adapts its teaching to the body of its students who are mainly youths commencing philosophy for the first time. But even granting all this we believe that it is nevertheless perfectly justified in its title. This we hope to make sufficiently evident in the course of these pages. Meantime it must be borne in mind that if the students of the Institute are *mainly* beginners in philosophy, *these* consist of a small number of the most talented students selected by competition from the six Belgian diocesan seminaries, and sent to the Louvain Institute for a special training in philosophy. Then, besides these native ecclesiastics, a small number of *lay* students also—chiefly from the Faculties of Law and of Philosophy and Letters—attend the courses of the Institute with the object of getting a special grounding in that philosophy which is at the basis of all true religion, of all sound ethics, of all social and economic progress, and of all

[1] From 1900 to 1903 the numbers of its students each year were 46, 56, 67, and 71, respectively.

individual, domestic and social rights and duties. Moreover, a goodly number of the students at the Institute, from the beginning, have been foreign ecclesiastics—many of them priests already versed in philosophy—sent there from all parts both to pursue their studies as far as opportunities allowed, and to familiarize themselves with all that is characteristic not only of the contents, but of the methods of the new scholastic teaching. Not only the continental countries, France, Holland, Germany, Poland, Switzerland, Italy, Spain, but the English-speaking countries England, Ireland, Canada, the United States, have been sending and are still sending their present and future professors of scholastic philosophy to the University of Louvain : knowing that there they will find scholasticism not merely in the class-halls as a discipline, but in living contact with modern science and in actual conflict with opposing systems in modern philosophic thought.

In 1905 there were about a dozen priests—secular and regular—from various countries, about the same number of foreign ecclesiastics, upwards of thirty Belgian ecclesiastics, and a small number of lay students, following the courses of the Institute.[1] Very many of those who have already passed through its halls are now professors in their various countries, and a large percentage of its present students are intended for the same work.

A glance at the following programme[2] will show how the three years' course is divided, and will help

---

Adjoining the Institute there is a residential College for ecclesiastical students in Philosophy—the *Séminaire Leon XIII.*—consisting of two separate buildings, one for priests and one for unordained students. There is a chapel attached. Every convenience is offered to ecclesiastics ; and with its many obvious advantages for strangers, the terms are very moderate. The pension is 800 francs (£32) for the academic year, payable in three parts ; extras about £2 additional. Opening with the modest number of seven students in 1892, its inmates numbered fifty-eight a few years ago.

[2] The programme given above is that for the academic year 1903-1904. It does not vary substantially from year to year. Cf. last year's programme in the *Revue néo-scolastique*, pp. 339-340.

us to realize the nature and extent of the teaching imparted :—

FIRST YEAR—BACCALAUREATE.

General Courses.

Logic (D. Mercier, and M. De Wulf of the Faculty of Philosophy and Letters), four classes of an hour and a half, or six hours per week, during first half-year.

Ontology (M. De Wulf), four classes, or six hours per week during second half-year.

History of Mediæval Philosophy (M. De Wulf), two years' course, first part, one class per week during first half-year.

Physics (M. Thiéry of the Faculty of Medicine), four classes per week during first half-year.

Psychophysiology (M. Thiéry), three years' course, two classes per week during second half-year.

Chemistry (M. Nys of the Faculty of Sciences), three hours per week during first half-year.

Special Courses.

(FIRST SECTION.)

Trigonometry, Analytical Geometry, and Differential Calculus (M. Sibenaler of the Faculty of Sciences), two classes per week during whole year.

General Biology, Botany, and Zoology, with Practical Exercises (A. Meunier of the Faculty of Sciences), two classes per week during second half-year.

General Anatomy and Physiology (M. Ide of the Faculty of Medicine), two classes per week during second half-year.

(SECOND SECTION.)

Political Economy (M. Defourny, *chargé de cours*), two classes per week during first half-year.

Method of Historical Criticism (A. Cauchie of the Faculty of Philosophy and Letters), two classes per week during first half-year.

Second Year—Licentiate.
General Courses.

Cosmology (M. Nys), three classes per week during first ; four during second half-year.

Psychology (D. Mercier and M. Thiéry), two years' course ; two hours per week during whole year.

Psychophysiology (M. Thiéry), three years' course. *See* Baccalaureate.

Moral Philosophy (J. Forget of the Faculty of Theology), four classes (six hours) per week during whole year.

History of Mediæval Philosophy (M. De Wulf), two years' course, second part.

History of Ancient and of Modern Philosophy (M. De Wulf), two years' course, two classes per week during second half-year.

Anatomy and Physiology (M. Ide), two classes per week during first half-year.

Special Courses.
(FIRST SECTION.)

Integral Calculus (M. Sibenaler), two classes per week during first half-year.

Analytical Mechanics (E. L. J. Pasquier of Faculty of Sciences), two classes per week during first half-year.

Embryology, Histology, and Physiology of the Nervous System (M. Ide), two hours per week during first half-year.

Mineralogy and Crystallography (F. Kaisin, of Faculty of Sciences), two classes per week, second half-year.

(SECOND SECTION.)

History of Social Theories (M. Defourny), two classes per week, second half-year.

Method of Historical Criticism (A. Cauchie), two classes per week, first half-year.

Third Year—Doctorate.

Psychology (D. Mercier and A. Thiéry), *see* Licentiate.

Psychophysiology (M. Thiéry), *see* Baccalaureate.

Natural and Social Law (S. Deploige of the Faculty of Law), four classes (six hours) per week during first half-year.

Theodicy (D. Mercier), one class per week during year.

Theodicy (L. Becker of the Faculty of Theology), two classes per week during year.

History of Ancient and of Modern Philosophy (M. De Wulf), *see* Licentiate.

Apart from the *Practical Courses* and *Laboratory work*, of which we shall speak later on, the above programme represents in faithful outline the amount of work done by professors and students alike. Each student standing for degrees gets a detailed oral examination in each subject from the professor of that subject. In addition, written and original dissertations on philosophical theses are required both for the Licentiate and for the Doctorate. Students who have got their Doctorate with the highest distinction may return afterwards to the Institute to pursue their studies, to write and publish a book on some philosophical question, and to sustain a public defence of a number of philosophical theses. In this way they qualify for the further degree of *Docteur agrégé* of the school of St. Thomas : the *agrégation* corresponding more or less to Junior Fellowship in the Royal University of Ireland.

As will be seen from the programme, the teaching is extended over three years, and during the first two the courses are divided into general and special. The general courses are *obligatory* on all. They comprise all philosophy proper including the history of philosophy, and, in addition, the natural sciences in direct connection with philosophy : physics, chemistry, anatomy, physiology and psychophysiology.

The matter of *all* the general courses of the *three* years, without exception, must be presented at the examination for the Doctorate. The special courses fall into two sections of very different kinds : the first comprising mathematics and the natural sciences, the second comprising economic, social and political sciences. Those special courses are described as optional, but they are optional only in this sense that the student may choose either the first or the second section according to his taste, but *must choose either section.* If he choose the first section he has yet further choice between mathematics and the other courses of that section.

One cannot help being struck by the close alliance thus secured between the sciences and philosophy. Cosmology—the philosophy of matter—can be studied, as it ought to be, in connection with chemistry, physics, mineralogy, mathematics, etc. Psychology —the philosophy of life—in connection with biology, anatomy, physiology and psychophysiology. Ethics —the philosophy of conduct—in connection with the social and economic sciences. And this union is not merely apparent but real. It is not a mere juxtaposition but a living, actual intercourse between philosophy and the sciences. This will be better appreciated when it is understood that chemistry and cosmology are taught by one and the same professor who is specially qualified in each, and that psychophysiology and psychology are likewise taught by one and the same professor similarly qualified. The former, Canon Nys, is Doctor in Sciences as well as in Philosophy, having studied chemistry under Professor Ostwald in Leipsig ; the latter is Doctor in Medicine as well as in Philosophy, and studied psychophysiology under Professor Wundt at the same university. It is hoped that the same principle will be gradually extended as far as may be feasible to the other departments also.

Another feature of the teaching of the Institute is that it is in French throughout. Occasional debating exercises are held in Latin. The works of St. Thomas and some other Latin text-books are in the hands of the students. But that is all. Both the text-books and the teaching of the Institute are in the vernacular. In view of the prolonged controversies that have been carried on in the Continental Catholic reviews relative to this whole question of the advisability of teaching philosophy and even theology to ecclesiastical students in the vernacular, it was not to be expected that the innovation at Louvain would escape opposition. As a matter of fact Leo XIII was for a time so much influenced by the " Latinists " as to order the adoption of Latin in the philosophical courses there. But when it was represented to him that, as a consequence of this mandate, the Institute was rapidly losing its lay students, he at once withdrew it, and allowed the use of French to be continued. Speaking to the Belgian Catholics in December, 1900, he remarked that the studies of the Institute were intended for laics as well as for clerics. " And that," he added, " is why I have decided that while the philosophy of St. Thomas must be studied in Latin the courses there should be given in French." Mercier could soon afterwards point to the brilliant successes of some past students of the Institute, in their theological studies at the Gregorian University in Rome, as a proof that the study of philosophy in the vernacular does not necessarily handicap the student who has to study his theology in Latin.

He would have a very inadequate conception of the professor's duty who would see nothing further in it than the mere oral and passive transmission to his students of the legacy of learning bequeathed to him from the past; and he would have a no less imperfect conception of the student's duty, who would limit it to the mere passive reception and rehearsal of such an irksome load of " learned lumber." Personal, original, scientific work or research in some department, under the direction of his professor, ought to be expected from at least the student who aspires to honours. *A fortiori*, the professor himself is expected to undertake and carry on such work, to study and to write if he wishes successfully to teach. To give him a fair opportunity for doing so, care is taken that he be neither obliged to expend his energies over too wide a field nor unduly over-burdened with class work.[1] A glance at the programme of the Institute will show how they are aiming at such a division of labour amongst the numerous members of an already large and efficient staff at Louvain. We find the teaching of philosophy proper divided amongst *seven* distinct professors— one of whom also teaches chemistry, and another physics and psychophysiology. We find a distinct professor for higher mathematics, a course that is frequented only by a small number of students; and we find four distinct courses in the biological sciences given by two additional professors. These will suffice as examples: a further perusal of the programme will reveal additional indications of the same tendency towards the most liberal staffing of the professorial body, with a view to securing still greater specialization of energy.

The results of this enlightened educational policy in Louvain have been of the happiest. There is no rush or hurry over long programmes in short periods, none of that superficial scampering and cramming without any time to think. The work is well done. The professor can master thoroughly the special branch he has a taste for, has time to write about it if necessary, and to make it interesting to his students—

---

[1] It is difficult to strike an average where there is so much variety. We should say that about six or seven hours' class-work per week would represent the average at the Institute and University.

whose work also, owing to their comparatively small numbers, he can often personally supervise.[1] He discusses any points they submit to him, helps to clear up their difficulties, aids them with his advice and suggestions in preparing their dissertations, and by his own personal example of industry and devotion to his work sets them an example which, perhaps, proves more precious to them in after life than anything else he may have taught them.

A printed programme is often a misleading index to the quantity and quality and character of the work done at an educational establishment. It is not so in the present case : and perhaps we can best show this if we supplement its meagre outline by a few comments based on personal experience.

V.—TEXTBOOKS AND TEACHING AT THE INSTITUTE.

The course of formal logic taught is that comprised in Mercier's *Logique*, which forms the first volume of the *Cours de Philosophie* that is being published by the co-operation of a number of the professors at the Institute. The science heretofore known as Material Logic, or *Logica Critica*, is dealt with by Mercier in his well-known volume on *Critériologie Générale*. This subject is still taught immediately after logic proper at the Institute, although Mercier claims that the proper place for it is immediately after psychology, with which it has undoubtedly an inseparable connection. He has accordingly made it the *fourth* volume of the *Cours*, his *Ontologie* forming the second, and his *Psychologie* the third volume.

There is no doubt about the difficulty of initiating beginners, who are as yet strangers to Psychology, into the various theories of truth and certainty, of

---

[1] This is especially true of those students who frequent the *practical* or *Séminaire* courses, or who undertake *Laboratory* work in any department.

scepticism and dogmatism, of idealism and realism, of the subjectivity or objectivity of human knowledge. It is perhaps even more difficult to deal with those questions in an intelligent way at that early stage than with any of the metaphysical abstractions of general ontology.

In the department of Criteriology the publication of Mercier's *Critériologie Générale* has undoubtedly marked an epoch in the study of questions concerning the Theory of Knowledge. Mercier had made a special study of Psychology and of the Theory of Knowledge, and the appearance of his book on General Criteriology, now in its fifth edition, excited widespread interest in Kantian as well as in Catholic circles. It was only natural that it should, for it was about the first serious and sustained attempt on the part of a representative of scholasticism to examine the numerous questions raised by the Critical Philosophy of Kant, *from the point of view of that system, and independently of any of the scholastic presuppositions questioned or called into doubt by Kantism.* The very first principles of scholastic philosophy had been rejected by Kantism, as indeed by most if not all modern philosophic systems. If these are to be met effectively by the scholastic he must cease to entrench himself behind such dogmatic principles, and come out to meet his adversaries upon their own ground. That is what Mercier has done in discussing the nature of truth, certitude, knowledge, etc. with the champions of scepticism on the one hand and of exaggerated dogmatism on the other; with French traditionalists on the one side and with the psychological subjectivism of Scotch and German schools, and especially of Kant's *Critique of Practical Reason,* on the other. He vindicates the *necessary character* of ideal judgments against the positivism of Taine and Mill and Spencer. But it is especially for its searching and vigorous analysis of the Transcendental Criticism of Kant's *Critique of Pure Reason* that Mercier's book is most noted. He maintains against Kant the *objective character* of the mental act of *judgment*, and the *reality* or extra-mental validity of the universal *concept*. At first his point of view seemed to have been misunderstood by various Catholic philosophers, and perhaps the most enjoyable pages of his thoroughly interesting volume are those devoted to answering the various critics of his definition of truth, and of his teaching as regards the problem of the validity of human knowledge.

Far more significant, however, are the criticisms and controversies to which his attack on Kantism gave rise in the Kantian schools of Germany. A professor in Halle took up Mercier's book as a basis for a *privatissimum* course with his students. Another professor of the same university devoted an article to it in the *Kantstudien*,[1] in which he pronounced it quite a remarkable production that must be taken account of by all Kantists. The concluding words of the article show that Kantists at least regarded the work as something quite different from the ordinary handling of Kant by the scholastics :—

" The Kantist is quite accustomed to see the Critical Philosophy insulted over and over again in Thomist works. . . . Very rarely does he meet with a serious discussion of its problems. But here we have a book which carries on throughout a searching and really scientific discussion of Kantism. A book of this kind is useful, even to the reader who cannot adopt the solutions proposed, for he will be likely to find in it some light thrown on the problems that are engaging his attention."

These are only a few of the many notices taken of Mercier's work in Germany. Needless to say, his critics are no less divided as to the justice or

[1] Vol. i., 1901.

injustice of his appreciation of Kant's Philosophy than they are in interpreting the Kantian system themselves.

The domain of *Ontology* is, of its very nature, abstruse and uninviting to the beginner ; yet even here the clearness of exposition and wealth of illustration so characteristic of the books of the Institute, succeed very largely in making even these nebulous regions attractive to the young explorer. There is a very pleasing contrast between these books and the dry, didactic and dogmatic conciseness of the ordinary text-book on Metaphysics. And it is not that Mercier's *Ontologie* shirks any of the numerous and profound difficulties with which ontology is so abundantly strewn. On the contrary, he faces them boldly and discusses them candidly ; he adopts the views that recommend themselves to him on their merits ; and even when he fails to bring us with him he never fails to make us think deeply and seriously and *understand* the questions better—even though we may not be able to settle them to our own satisfaction. For example, his remarkable view, that in the analytical order an adequate ultimate foundation for *possibles* and their properties is to be had in the abstract concepts derived from actual experience, and that, accordingly, the Augustinian argument for the existence of God, the Infinite Exemplar, based on the properties of possible essences, the "*incommutabilia vera*," is a worthless argument—that view is controverted by very able philosophers. Although we believe that the issue here involved is one of the most fundamental in philosophy, we can at present do no more than note the fact that such a difference of opinion prevails. Throughout the whole volume Mercier is an earnest supporter of Thomistic views regarding the relations of essence to existence, of nature to personality, of the individual to the universal, and of substance to accidents

Particularly worthy of study are the sections on
the existence of substances, on final causes, on the
order of nature, on the beautiful, on esthetics and
notions of art. The study of quantity, space and
time are very properly left to their rightful places
in cosmology ; and the study of "being, finite and
infinite " to theodocy.

The History of Philosophy at the Institute is in the
hands of one of the best authorities at the present
day on the heretofore much neglected Medieval
Period. Professor De Wulf's *Histoire de la Philosophie Médiévale* [1] is unquestionably the best book
of its kind on the subject. It brings together and
utilizes in a masterly way the results of the all-
important researches of Ehrle, Denifle, Chatelain,
Baemuker, Picavet, Rubczinscky, Clerval, Vacant,
Mandonnet, etc. within the past twenty years in
the domain of the Middle Age philosophy ; and it is
no exaggeration to say that these researches have
brought about some revolutions in traditional views
about the scholastic and anti-scholastic systems of
the Middle Ages. The companion volume published
by him under the title of *Introduction à la Philosophie
Néo-Scolastique* gives a luminous presentation of
what Scholastic Philosophy really was and is and is
likely to be, of its genesis, growth and development
in the Middle Ages, of its relations to catholic theology,
to the sciences, and to opposing philosophic systems,
of its method and contents, of the causes of its decay
and the conditions of its successful revival.

Scholasticism thus placed in its proper historical
setting has simply a new meaning and a real attraction
for the student. The studies of Professor De Wulf
have certainly thrown around it for his students an
interest it could not otherwise possess. While the
medieval period naturally receives most attention,

---

[1] 1900, in 8vo., viii. + 480 pp.; 2nd edition, 1905, vi. +568 pp. An
English translation is in course of preparation.

both ancient and modern systems get ample and adequate treatment as well.

Physics is a compulsory subject for the Baccalaureate at the Institute. It is studied there mainly from the theoretic or speculative point of view, as leading up to philosophical theories. Though it is an elementary course—treating of the properties of matter, heat, light, sound, magnetism and electricity, in one term with four classes per week—it is a sufficient if necessary preparation for the study of cosmology, and is insisted on as such.

A good elementary course of *Chemistry* is likewise insisted on at Louvain. Three classes per week for half a year are devoted to it. Specimens are shown and experiments made as far as possible. Special attention is paid to chemical theory and its relations to the scholastic theory of matter and form in cosmology. The field covered embraces organic as well as inorganic chemistry : it is supplemented by the elements of biological chemistry in the special courses of biology, anatomy and physiology.

The prominence given to the course of *Cosmology* at the Institute is significant of the close bond of union which exists between the philosophy of matter and the natural sciences in the neo-scholastic system. Cosmology appropriates three hours per week during the first term and five during the second. As taught at the Institute this course does not touch the questions of the origin and destiny—the efficient and the final causes—of the universe. It leaves these to natural theology and confines itself to a thorough investigation of the ultimate nature—the constitutive material and formal causes—together with the properties and activities, of the inorganic universe. The treatise written by Professor Nys on *cosmologie* —forming the seventh volume of the *Cours de Philosophie*—is a work of an exceptionally high standard of excellence. Out of 575 pages no less than 150 are consecrated to a direct examination—the most searching and powerful we have yet seen—of the modern Atomic or Mechanical Philosophy of the Universe. He subjects its claims to the successive tests of all the physical sciences—especially of chemistry ; and, with his full and intimate knowledge of the latter, he shows by irrefragable reasoning that whatever may be the ultimate philosophical explanation of the Universe, Atomism certainly is not. No idol was ever more thoroughly demolished than that of a " Cosmos built up by inert matter and kinetic energy " is in those masterly pages. To the scholastic conception of the nature and properties of the material universe ; to the doctrine of the double constitutive principle, material and formal, of all corporeal being ; to the essence formed by their union ; to a full and exhaustive study of quantity, mass, volume, impenetrability, etc. ; to the natural *forces* of material things ; to the *qualitative* difference of these forces, and the current theory of their mutual convertibility ; to motion, kinetic and potental energy ; to the harmony of the scholastic conception with the established facts of the various natural sciences—to a full treatment of all those questions he devotes nearly 400 pages. The remaining 40 pages are given to an examination of the pure dynamic and the atomico-dynamic theories. This excellent text-book is supplemented by two additional monographs or special studies, the one on *Space* and the other on *Time*, from the pen of the same author. Both these abstruse subjects are dealt with in a very masterly and attractive manner. The various theories are marshalled and criticized, and the author's clear and incisive reasoning cannot fail to recommend the moderate realism embodied in his views.

Psychophysiology—called by many other names, amongst which " experimental psychology "—is a comparatively new science. It is simply the study of conscious states in their relations to their physiological and physical concomitants. Its method is objective and experimental (physiological), as well as subjective or introspective (psychological). It analyzes our ordinary complex conscious activities into ultimate constituent elements which it calls *impressions*. The study of those from the quantative and qualitative points of view forms the first part of the course. It next passes to the study of these same impressions combined and co-ordinated in time and space so as to form conscious *representations*. Finally, in a third part it examines the *associations* of these representations and the laws that govern such associations. It covers that exceedingly wide and unexplored borderland between physiology and psychology, and seeks by inductive methods to arrive at the discovery of natural laws in that domain. For some time this new science was looked upon with some suspicion by catholic philosophers—partly because they feared that it rested upon materialist presuppositions, and partly because its own early advocates were unduly enthusiastic about its significance and too sanguine in making promises which it could never hope to fulfil. It is now more justly appreciated by both parties, and is recognised by all as a useful auxiliary to psychology proper, and a department of research that may bring to light valuable information about the nature and conditions of conscious organic activities. As a distinct science with a definite field of investigation it has had its origin in Germany—its, first great exponent being Professor Wundt of Leipsig—and it has been followed up with the greatest attention in many of the North-American Universities.[1] Professor Thiéry, who

---

[1] See Mercier's *Origines de la Psychologie Contemporaine*, pp. 284 *seq.*, and Appendix B. There are many recent works in English on Physiological Psychology, and Professor Wundt's classical work is being translated into English.

gives this course at the Institute, studied under Wundt at Leipsig, and is the author of an important and original monograph on the sense of vision : *Optische Geometrische Täuschungen.*

Passing next to the teaching of *Psychology* proper, we find very ample provision made for two distinct courses of a year each.   They are given alternately and are frequented both by the students for Licentiate and by those for Doctorate.   The first is a general course on the nature of living things and the principle of life—*Psychologie Naturelle.*   It follows closely the text of St. Thomas' Commentary on Aristotle's treatise *De Anima.*   The Latin text has been specially edited at the Institute, and a free, modernised exposition and interpretation of the text in French, has been also published by Professor Thiéry under the above title—*Psychologie Naturelle.*   The second course of Psychology is a very full and exhaustive study of the whole subject based upon Mercier's well-known work, *La Psychologie,* which forms the third volume of the *Cours de Philosophie.*

Mercier's *Psychologie* is unquestionably one of the ablest and most remarkable books that has been published on this subject from the scholastic point of view in recent years.   The appearance of its first edition in 1892 attracted considerable attention, and was called, not without reason, " an event in the teaching of scholastic philosophy."[1]   It has now reached its sixth edition in two octavo volumes of nearly 400 pages each, with four excellent lithograph plates in the first volume.   This volume is devoted to vegetative and animal life, and contains the most copious and up-to-date information on the anatomy and physiology, as well as the psychology proper, of living organisms, both vegetative and sentient.   The second volume deals with the higher activities of man, his nature, origin and destiny. The whole is a masterly production, and clearly shows

[1] *Études*, 31 Dec., 1892.

the substantial harmony of the traditional scholastic psychology with the results of modern research.

The importance attached to the study of the *biological sciences*, subsidiary to psychology, calls next for a brief word of comment. A philosophical knowledge of psychology is simply impossible without at least a general acquaintance with the group of natural sciences that deal with living organisms. Hence a general course in *anatomy and physiology* is regarded as the minimum required for all. Three hours per week during a whole term are thus devoted to studying the structure and functions of the various animal tissues, organs, members and systems—skin, bone, blood, circulation, respiration, digestion, internal organs, muscle, nervous system, brain, external senses, sensation, spontaneous and reflex movements, emotions, passions, nervous diseases. It is rightly contended that the student who approaches psychology without the knowledge of those things as a groundwork, and who studies it out of a medieval Latin text-book whose terminology and illustrations are based on the schoolmen's—or Aristotle's—notions and theories of physics and physiology, is practically wasting precious time trying to comprehend, as the elements of a real and *actual* psychological synthesis, much that is *unreal* and without value except to the student of history. If the greatest of the scholastics—St. Thomas of Aquin—were teaching philosophy at the present day, he would introduce his students to psychology through contemporary —not medieval—physiology, thereby merely showing himself as enlightened and progressive in the twentieth century as he actually showed himself amongst his contemporaries in the thirteenth. At Louvain they think they are loyal to the Angelic Doctor's spirit, and they are not deceived. . . . Besides the minimum contained in the compulsory course just referred to, they give their students ample opportunities in three distinct special courses to pursue further this same line of studies. In a *special* course of *anatomy and physiology* the professor of the general course goes more deeply into the histology or microscopic structure and functions, as well as into the composition, physical and chemical, of the various organic tissues. In a second and still more important *special* course on the *embryology, histology, and physiology of the nervous system* he follows step by step, from the fertilization of the *ovum* to the full maturity of middle life, the gradual growth and development of the nervous system which is the immediate organic basis of consciousness, and which is therefore of such prime importance to the psychologist. A third *special* course on *general biology* is devoted to an elaborate study of the basis of all organic life—that marvellously complex unit, the living cell. Its structure, its chemical composition, its functions, its manner of division, its differentiation in plant and animal, its most striking characteristics in the two domains of botany and zoology—such are the main headings of the programme covered by this course. With such admirable opportunities as those there is absolutely nothing to prevent a student whose tastes lie in the direction of psychology from equipping himself thoroughly for a complete mastery of his subject.

Students whose tastes lie rather in the direction of the moral and social sciences can choose the second section of optional courses during their first two years at the Institute. They will thus enjoy, firstly, a series of lectures on the *method of historical criticism* from Professor Cauchie, a distinguished editor of the *Revue d'Histoire Ecclesiastique;* and, secondly, a course on political economy and another on the history of social theories, both given by Professor Defourny, the author of a valuable study entitled *La Sociologie Postiviste: Auguste Comte.* The course on political economy, though elementary, is extremely useful and instructive and much appreciated. It gives a clear grasp of the principles of economics, and deals especially with their application to the actual conditions of Belgium. In a word, it gives the student a fund of knowledge about social and economic principles and problems which will enable him to understand and to deal effectively with those problems when he goes amongst the people afterwards, whether as priest or layman.

The course of *Ethics* at the Institute extends over two years. During the first year three hours per week are devoted to moral philosophy; during the second, six hours per week of the first term are devoted (by Professor Deploige, now President of the Institute in the place of Cardinal Mercier) to natural and social law. Mgr. Deploige is the author of a study on *St. Thomas and the Jewish Question,* and of an original work of considerable value on the *Referendum in Switzerland.* The latter has been translated into English in the *Studies in Economics and Political Science* (London School of Economics and Political Science).

There are, likewise, two distinct courses of *Natural Theology* during the student's third year at the Institute. One class per week during the year is devoted to a full and complete examination of all philosophical systems, directly or indirectly atheistical, and to the establishment of the existence of God. A second course of three hours per week during the year is devoted to the nature, attributes, knowledge, providence, etc. of the Deity.

We have now completed our general analysis of the class work proper. This represents the theoretic side of the Louvain training: though many of the lectures in the scientific department are largely interspersed with experiments and concrete illustrations of various kinds. But there is, in addition to the class-hall teaching proper, a distinct supplementary department of what are called *Cours Pratiques*, namely :—

Laboratory work in psychophysiology under the direction of Professors Thiéry and Michotte—a few hours per week for one term each year.

Laboratory work in chemistry, under the direction of Professor Nys—a few hours per week for one term each year.

Social philosophy conference, under the direction of Professors Deploige and Defourny—once a week during the year.

Seminary of the history of medieval philosophy, under the direction of Professor De Wulf—once a week during the year.

Seminary of psychology, under the direction of Professor Noël.

Professor Thiéry's laboratory was one of the first of its kind established outside Germany. It is well equipped with all the necessary instruments and appliances for psychophysiological research, and a number of students are initiated every year into the methods of investigating and experimenting in this domain. In the chemical laboratory a number of students are trained each year in the elementary practical work of chemical tests and analyses. In addition to these laboratories, the biological class-hall is furnished with a large number of models and specimens to illustrate the various courses. Microscopes are provided, and preparations made and examined by the students under the direction of the various lecturers.

The seminaries of social science and of history are worked with a view to training a small number of students, who evince special tastes for those studies, in the methods of original research and original work in those departments. The students combine their efforts in a certain line of study under the guidance of the director of the seminary, and while they often thus render valuable assistance to him they are being admirably trained themselves to follow up the same sort of work.   It is by means of this *Seminar* system—carried to such a high degree of perfection in the German universities—that the individual student, under the personal guidance of his professor, gets that specialized training which enables him to do sound and useful original work in his chosen branch afterwards.

Besides this official teaching, theoretical and practical, the students of the Institute have two distinct voluntary societies, each with its weekly meeting, under the direction of two of the professors.   At these meetings papers are read and discussions carried on by the students themselves and by strangers.   The subjects—usually philosophical questions of present-day interest—are invariably dealt with in an attractive and pleasing manner. The meetings are very instructive and have an educational value that it would be difficult to exaggerate.

VI.—PHILOSOPHICAL LITERATURE AT THE INSTITUTE.

What contributes, perhaps, most largely to the success of those bi-weekly reunions is the existence of a splendidly-furnished philosophical reading-room at the Institute.   The *Salle des Periodiques* deserves more than a passing mention, for it is a prominent feature of the Louvain philosophical training.   The teaching of neo-scholastic philosophy purports to bring the student face to face with all the philosophical systems of the present day as well as with modernized scholasticism.   And so it does.   In this reading-room the student finds himself in presence of *about one hundred and fifty* of the leading philosophical reviews of the world, of every shade of opinion from all parts, and in many languages. The students have free access to them, are sometimes referred to current articles on the topics discussed in class, often make use of them for their philosophical societies, and oftener still in preparing their yearly dissertations for degrees. When we reflect on the important part played nowadays by the periodical in the advancement of learning we can appreciate the immense educational value of such a reading-room.

Since the year 1895, they have been forming in this same department a very full philosophical bibliography—both according to authors and to subjects—by means of which a person can find out at once all the philosophical literature that has appeared on any subject during those years. The idea is, if we mistake not, to form at the Institute a sort of international *Bibliographical Bureau* for the use of students and professors of philosophy over the world. The system of cataloguing adopted is the decimal system of Dewey, in use at the Brussels International Office of Bibliography. A " *Sommaire Ideologique* " of works and reviews on philosophy is published quarterly as a supplement to the *Revue Néo-Scolastique*—which thus puts its subscribers in possession of a continuous and up-to-date bibliography.

The *Revue Néo-Scolastique* is the principal periodical published by the Institute, and is recognised as one of the leading philosophical reviews of the Continent. It was founded in 1894, and is conducted, under the direction of Mercier and the editorship of De Wulf with the co-operation of the professors and past students who form the *Societé Philosophique de Louvain*. It appears quarterly in numbers of about 200 pages, the subscription being ten francs per year for Belgium, twelve outside Belgium. Each number

contains : (1) articles proper on philosophical subjects ; (2) *Mélanges et Documents*, shorter studies on
current questions, reviews and movements ; (3) a
chronicle of events at the Institute ; (4) reviews of
books ; (5) the *Sommaire Ideologique* already referred
to ; (6) a supplement of forty or fifty pages called
the *Mouvement Sociologique*, conducted by the Belgian
Society of Sociology. The *Revue Néo-Scolastique*
enjoys a wide circulation and is self-supporting.
Practically all the reviews and periodicals that stock
the reading-room of the Institute are received as
exchanges for this review. The *Revue Sociale
Catholique*, founded in 1896 by Professor Deploige,
and M. Legrand of the Agricultural School of Gem-
bloux, is devoted chiefly to labour legislation and to
social and economic questions amongst the masses.
The *Revue Catholique de Droit*, founded in 1898 by
Professor Crahay, of Liège University—a past student
of the Institute—is also concerned chiefly with the
labouring classes. Both of those reviews are issued
monthly from the Institute.

These various publications will convey some idea
of the constant output of intellectual work which the
foundation of the Philosophical Institute has been
mainly instrumental in fostering and developing.
Yet they really represent only a fraction of the total
amount of published matter already to be found in
the *Bibliothèque de l'Institut superieur de Philosophie*
which has been in existence for the past few decades,
and is growing in dimensions and importance every
year. A few years ago the Institute set up
a printing-press, and it now prints and publishes
all its own literature. We have already mentioned
the various volumes of the *Cours de Philosophie*
that have been published up to the present. The
fifth volume is intended by Mercier to deal with
special questions, problems and theories regarding
the validity of knowledge, under the title *Criteriologie*

Spéciale. Volumes are promised on ethics and natural theology ; and a *compendium* of the whole course in two octave volumes of about 500 pages each was published last year.[1] The various volumes of the larger courses are being translated into many languages. All have been done into Polish ; all are being translated into Italian, Spanish and Portuguese. A German translation of Mercier's *Psychologie* has recently appeared, and English translations of Nys's *Cosmologie,* De Wulf's *Histoire,* Mercier's *Logique,* etc. are in preparation. Besides the periodical literature and the volumes of the *Cours de Philosophie,* we must mention two historical collections that are being edited under the direction of Professor De Wulf and M. Pelzer, entitled, *Les Philosophes du Moyen Age.* It will comprise, firstly, a series of folio volumes containing the original texts of works hitherto unpublished or little known on medieval philosophy ; and, secondly, a series of studies (in 8vo volumes) on various medieval philosophers. The first volume of the first series contains the text of the famous treatise, *De unitate formæ,* by *Giles of Lessines,* preceded by an introduction of 120 pages from the pen of Professor De Wulf. The four succeeding volumes—the first of which has already appeared—will contain the *Quodlibeta of Godfrey of Fontaines.* Volumes VI. and VII. (in the Press) will comprise the works of Siger of Brabant, edited by Professor Mandonnet, of the University of Fribourg, Switzerland. This is an excellent collection from every point of view, and no philosophical library should be without it.

The number of isolated publications that have helped to swell the dimensions of the *Bibliothèque* is very large, and some of them of great importance.

---

[1] *Traité élémentaire de philosophie à l'usage des classes,* édité par des Professeurs de l'Institut superieur de Philosophie de l'Université de Louvain (2 vols., 7 fr. net., Louvain, Institut superieur de Philosophie, 1 rue des Flamands, 1906).

Glancing at the catalogue—which may be had on application at the Institute—we would fain bring many of them under the notice of our readers, but we must be content with mentioning two.

De Wulf's *Histoire de la Philosophie Scolastique dans les Pays-Bas* is a valuable work written for a prize offered by the Royal Academy of Belgium, and crowned by that body for exceptional merit.

Mercier's *Origines de la Psychologie Contemporaine*, published in 1898, "has contributed very much towards concentrating the attention of the educated world on what is going on at Louvain."[1] German, English, French, Italian reviews of divers tendencies have greeted this work with words of praise. It is a masterly study—critical, historical and doctrinal— on the rise and growth and various offshoots of Cartesian psychology, and on all the different forces and tendencies observable in the psychology of the present day. It is a work full of light and inspiration for the student of philosophy, and its concluding chapter on "Neo-Thomisme" strikes the keynote to that true scientific method which has won such well-merited repute for the Louvain pioneers of the new scholasticism.

A writer in the *Critical Review*,[2] dealing with Mercier's *Origines*, pointed out to English readers that the new scholastic doctrines form the principal intellectual force actually at work in Belgium, and have a considerable influence in France, Germany, and Italy. He noted as "full of light and progress" those words of the author which are simply a summing up of the programme of the Institute :—

"We avail ourselves of Plato and Descartes and Leibnitz, of Kant and Fichte and Hegel and Wundt, just as fully, perhaps, and certainly just as sincerely as those who count us in the number of their opponents.

---

[1] Professor Dörholt, in the *Theologische Revue*, 1903, p. 292.
[2] 1899, ix., 17-18.

. . . . There is no Catholic philosopher who is not ready to sacrifice ' an idea many centuries old ' the moment it manifestly contradicts an observed fact. For we also are accustomed to take observation as our starting-point, as the origin of all research, the source of truth, and the sovereign mistress of science."

And those words are an unmistakable echo of what we read in the *Æterni Patris* of Leo XIII: " libente gratoque animo excipiendum esse quidquid utiliter fuerit a quopiam inventum atque excogitatum."

VII.—CONCLUSION.

And as to the influence of Louvain teaching, in philosophy as in other departments, upon religious and social and scientific progress throughout Belgium, it would be difficult to overestimate its extent and value. Louvain is to Catholic Belgium what the throbbing heart is to the whole body, sending out its rich warm currents of life blood to stimulate and nourish the entire system. If there are to be found amongst the Belgian Catholic clergy and laity numbers of the best and ablest Catholic writers who uphold and defend Catholic and Christian principles and who attack the Godless tenets of liberalism and socialism in the press and in the pulpit and on the platform, by pen and by voice, without a moment's abatement of zeal, it is to the progressive and militant spirit of thought and action communicated to them at Louvain that such activity is due. If Catholic Belgium has numbers of cultured scholars ready and willing to defend social order, and to point to the true and just solution of complex social problems, and that with all the influence and authority requisite to make their voices heard, Catholic Belgium may thank the training that its youth receives in the various Faculties of Louvain

University. The progress of Belgium in science and industry and agriculture is too well known to need more than a mention : to the scientific achievements and prestige of Louvain this progress is largely due. And material progress has not been accompanied in Belgium, as it often has been elsewhere, by a decadence in religion or morality, or by inattention to the higher and ideal side, the mental and spiritual side of life. Belgium's progress is not abnormal or onesided but wholesome and normal and well-balanced : and this is due above all to the fact that in her philosophy she has rejected the *outré* spiritualism of Descartes—the system that vainly tries to suppress or ignore the material, and thereby allows the senses to run riot and usurp the place of reason—and has espoused the moderate realism of the schoolmen—the philosophy that holds the golden mean between the spiritual and the material, that lays down the true relations between faith, grace and religion, on the one hand, and reason, nature, and morals on the other, thus, as it were, fulfilling the words of a great teacher, to " render unto Cæsar the things that are Cæsar's, and to God the things that are God's."

P. C.

INDEX[1]

A

Abbey Schools, 190.
Abelard, 20, 27, 63, 67, 180, 198.
Absolute, the, 220, 222.
Abstraction Theory, 82, 131, 132, 133, 237, 247.
Accident (*v.* Substance), 100, 101.
Achillinus, 41.
Adelard of Bath, 25.
Adelman of Liège, 22.
Agnosticism, 111, 286.
Agrégation, 294.
Alanus of Lille, 20, 40, 124, 142, 188, 260.
Albert the Great, 20, 76, 77, 87, 102, 105, 201.
Albigenses, 30, 40, 188.
Alchemy, 123, 200.
Alcuin, 29, 79, 80.
Alexander of Halès, 20, 105, 124.
Alfarabi, 57.
Alkendi, 43.
Analytico-Synthetic Method, 21, 144, 205, 272.
Anatomy and Physiology, 307, 308.
Ancilla Theologiæ, 54, 61, 274.
Andronicus of Rhodes, 77.
Angels, Scholastic Teaching on, 103.
Anslem, 20, 25 ; first scholastic, 46, 64.
Anti-scholasticism, meaning, 51, 68.
Aphrodisias, Alexander, 77.
Apologetics, 72, 198.
Appetite, 136 *seq.*
Arabian Philosophy, 111, 129, 133.
Aristotle, 24, 26, 78, 80, 81, 108, 118, 120 ; and Immortality, 126 ; 128, 135, 140, 175, 219, 233, 238, 256, 260, 283.
Aristotelianism, 8, 205, 218, 231, 242, 246, 278.
Arnauld, 134, 147.
Arnold of Bonneval, 66.
Artist's Ideal, 243.

Arts, Seven Liberal, 23 ; and philosophy, 79, 168 ; Paris Faculty of, 81.
Asiatic Philosophy, 43.
Association, Need of, 209, 273.
Associationism, English, 231.
Astral Souls, 121.
Astrology, 123, 200.
Astronomy, 87, 119 ; Discoveries in, 148, 200, 225.
Atomism, 77, 165, 208, 213, 226, 227, 304.
Augustine, 13, 74, 78, 112, 125, 127, 132, 161, 188, 198, 260.
Augustinism, 78, 101, 106, 114, 187.
Authority, Argument from, 78, 260.
Authority, Moral, 140.
Autonomy of Scholasticism, 191, 274.
Averroës, 30, 77, 188.
Averroïsm, and Scholasticism, 40, 41 ; in Italy, 47 ; 65, 74, 126.
Avicebron, 102, 188, 224.
Avicenna, 30, 71, 82, 106.

B

Bacon, Francis, 4, 152, 172.
Bacon, Roger, 50, 86, 201.
Bacteriology, 200.
Baeumker, 6, 8, 186, 279, 302.
Bain, 239.
Baldwin's Dictionary, on Scholasticism, 35.
Balmes, 194, 236.
Barrès, 195.
Baumgarten, 239.
Baumgartner, 6, 20, 29, 124, 135.
Baunard, 205.
Bautain, 193.
Belgium's Debt to Louvain Teaching, 316, 317.
Berenger of Tours, 22.
Bergson, 16, 195.
Berkeley, 232.
Bernard of Tours, 51.

[1] The numbers indicate the *pages*.

Addenda

PHILOSOPHY AND CIVILIZATION IN THE MIDDLE AGES
By Maurice de Wulf

This book does not follow the usual course of compartmentalizing the separate aspects of medieval intellectual life, but shows, instead, how religion, philosophy, science the arts interrelated, and how the entire thought of the period is intimately connected with the whole round of Western civilization.

Here is a discussion of feudal Europe and Catholic influences; the rise of the universities and the establishment of mendicant orders; the new intellectual approach to psychology, logic, metaphysics, ethics and aesthetics, philosophy and national temperament in the thirteenth century; and other topics fascinating to the historian, student of letters and philosophy.

Unabridged. Selected bibliography. Index. viii + 302pp.

T284 Paperbound **$1.60**

THE SYSTEM OF THOMAS AQUINAS
by Maurice de Wulf

One of the leaders of the Neo-Thomistic revival, a most distinguished scholar in the study of Medieval history and thought, here gives a concise exposition of the central doctrines formulated by St. Thomas Aquinas. In his introduction, Professor de Wulf, one of the founders of the University of Louvain, states that it is only through a close study of the historical Aquinas that one may judge the value of his thought today.

The plan of the book follows the classifications set down by the Scholastics themselves. What they called theoretical philosophy is dealt with first, beginning with the theory of knowledge and idea, judgment, reasoning, and consciousness. This is followed by a closer examination of the directing principles of knowledge, and other aspects of the epistemological problem, such as moderate realism versus universals. The problem of desire and freedom is taken up, as well as space and time, the universe of individuals, and Monism. The process of change, involving actuality, potentiality, matter, form, causality, and essence, is dealt with, and this leads into studies on the soul and body. The section ends with proofs of the existence of God, and exposition of the divine attributes.

The second portion of the book deals with "practical" philosophy. This concerns itself with such areas of Thomist thought as morality, the problem of ends or aims, obligation and moral law, and responsibility. The problem of the individual versus the state is dealt with, as well as the uses and methods of science. Also examined are the objective and subjective aspects of beauty, the divisions of philosophy, and such doctrinal characteristics of Scholasticism as the sense of limit, and relations to Catholic theology.

Formerly "Medieval Philosophy Illustrated From the System of Thomas Aquinas." Translated by Ernest Messenger. Introduction. 151pp. 5⅜ x 8.

T 568 Paperbound **$1.25**

ESSAYS IN EXPERIMENTAL LOGIC

by John Dewey

This volume is an unabridged unaltered reprinting of the 1916 edition of this modern classic of philosophy. Written with all Dewey's conciseness and sense for practical application, it contains fourteen of his most influential papers on various aspects of knowledge, reality, and epistemology.

The foundation of these papers on experimental logic is the theory that knowledge about anything implies a judgment, which in turn implies an inquiry or investigation of a sort. The presence of this "inquiry stage" implies that between the external world and knowledge there is an intermediate and mediating stage, which is in turn conditioned by other factors. Expanding upon this basis, these papers consider the relationship of thought and its subjectmatter, the antecedents and stimuli of thought, data and meanings, the objects of thought, control of ideas by facts and similar topics.

Three papers describe various kinds of philosophical realism, in which the thought of Bertrand Russell's OUR KNOWLEDGE OF THE EXTERNAL WORLD AS A FIELD FOR SCIENTIFIC METHOD is closely examined, while two other papers discuss Pragmatism, differentiating Dewey's position from that of James and Peirce. These essays present what is probably Dewey's most easily followed account of his own thought. The section entitled "Stages of Logical Thought" analyzes the role of scientific method in philosophy, while the final essay presents a striking theory of a logic of values.
Index. viii + 444pp. 5⅜ x 8.

T73   Paperbound   **$1.95**

MIND AND THE WORLD-ORDER

by C. I. Lewis

This well-known work by Professor Lewis of Harvard University outlines a theory of knowledge in terms of a new system, "conceptual pragmatism." Building upon the work of Peirce, James, and Dewey it takes into account both recent philosophic thought and the implications of modern mathematics.

Starting with the assumption that there are two systems of truth (abstract mathematical certainty, and secondly, empirical truth—or application of abstract truth to sense experiences) the author demonstrates that the traditional understanding of the a priori must be abandoned.

Chapters are included about philosophy, metaphysics, philosophic method; the given element in experience; pure concepts; common concepts; knowledge of objects; relativity of knowledge; the a priori, traditional conceptions; the nature of the a priori; the a priori and the empirical; the empirical and the problem; experience and order. Appendixes cover natural science and abstract concepts, applicability of abstract conceptual systems to experience, and similar topics.

This book is of interest not only to the specialist in philosophy, but also to the reader interested in the common ground where mathematics and philosophy meet.

xiv + 446pp. 5⅜ x 8.   Paperbound **$1.95**

THE SENSE OF BEAUTY
by George Santayana

It is remarkably appropriate that this work on aesthetics should have been written by George Santayana, who is probably the most brilliant philosophic writer and the philosopher with the strongest sense of beauty since Plato. It is not a dry metaphysical treatise, as is so often the case with works on aesthetics, but itself a fascinating document, as much a revelation of the beauty of language as of the concept of beauty.

This unabridged reproduction of the 1896 edition of lectures delivered at Harvard College is a study of "why, when, and how beauty appears, what conditions an object must fulfill to be beautiful, what elements of our nature make us sensible of beauty, and what the relation is between the constitution of the object and the excitement of our susceptibility."

Santayana first analyzes the nature of beauty, finding it irrational, "pleasure regarded as the quality of a thing." He then proceeds to the materials of beauty, showing that all human functions can contribute: love, social instincts, senses, etc. Beauty of form is then analyzed, and finally the author discusses the expression of beauty. Literature, religion, values, evil, wit, humor, and the possibility of finite perfection are all examined. Presentation throughout the work is concrete and easy to follow, with examples drawn from art, history, anthropology, psychology, and similar areas.

Index.   ix + 275pp.   5⅜ x 8.   Paperbound   **$1.00**

THE PHILOSOPHICAL WORKS OF DESCARTES

This is the definitive English translation and the only comprehensive English edition in print of the important philosophical works of René Descartes.

These two volumes contain all Descartes's revolutionary insights and conclusions, from his famous exposition of "Cogito ergo sum" in the Discourse on Method to his detailed account in Principles of Philosophy of the natural phenomena under investigation in his day. Clearly expressed are all Descartes's key ideas, as the philosophic proofs for God, the separation of mind and matter and their relations, and the astonishingly fruitful concept that all phenomena of the universe (except mind) could by application of mathematical method be reduced to clear and readily formulated laws.

Descartes is frequently called the Father of Modern Philosophy, and his historical influence has been enormous. Many of his philosophic and scientific insights, in addition, are still surprisingly modern. His views on space and matter, the nature of science, the formation of the universe and solar system, the nature of psychology will interest the modern scientific reader.

Contents, Volume One. Rules for the Direction of the Mind. Discourse on the Method of Rightly Conducting the Reason. Meditations on First Philosophy. The Principles of Philosophy. The Search After Truth. The Passions of the Soul. Notes Directed against a Certain Program.

Translated by E. S. Haldane and G.R.T. Ross. Unabridged republication of the last corrected edition of 1931. Introductory notes. Index. vi + 452pp. 5⅜ x 8.   Paperbound **$2.00**

THE PHILOSOPHICAL WORKS OF DESCARTES

This is the definitive English translation and the only comprehensive English edition in print of the important philosophical works of René Descartes.

These two volumes contain all Descartes's revolutionary insights and conclusions, from his famous exposition of "Cogito ergo sum" in the Discourse on Method to his detailed account in Principles of Philosophy of the natural phenomena under investigation in his day. Clearly expressed are all Descartes's key ideas, as the philosophic proofs for God, the separation of mind and matter and their relations, and the astonishingly fruitful concept that all phenomena of the universe (except mind) could by application of mathematical method be reduced to clear and readily formulated laws.

Descartes is frequently called the Father of Modern Philosophy, and his historical influence has been enormous. Many of his philosophic and scientific insights, in addition, are still surprisingly modern. His views on space and matter, the nature of science, the formation of the universe and solar system, the nature of psychology will interest the modern scientific reader.

Contents, Volume Two. This volume contains seven sets of objections propounded by contemporary philosophers and theologians to Descartes's Meditations on the First Philosophy, together with Descartes's replies to each. It is both a first-rate source for the philosophical opinions of such men as Hobbes (Objection Series III) and Arnauld (IV), and Gassendi (V), and for Descartes's defense of his own ideas. It is almost unique in philosophy as a "symposium" of philosopher and critics.

Translated by E. S. Haldane and G.R.T. Ross. Unabridged republication of the last corrected edition of 1931. Introductory notes. Index. iv + 380pp. 5⅜ x 8.   Paperbound **$2.00**

A HISTORY OF MODERN PHILOSOPHY
by Harald Höffding

One of the works most frequently referred to as a source for basic information, this monumental 400,000-word study provides an extremely clear, detailed coverage of modern philosophy from the Renaissance to the end of the 19th century.

Using the historical and comparative methods Professor Höffding analyzes major philosophers and systems in terms of theory of knowledge, logic, problem of existence, nature of man, as well as in terms of individual stresses and contributions. He also provides a valuable coverage of interesting minor systems which are all too often omitted in surveys; these systems include the later Schelling, Hamann, Jacob Boehme, Feuerbach, and over 150 others.

A discussion of the philosophic basis for the ideas of such men as Newton, Kepler, Copernicus, Galileo, Robert Mayer, Charles Darwin will interest philosophers, physical scientists, and readers interested in the philosophy of science.

VOLUME ONE, **partial contents.**

THE PHILOSOPHY OF THE RENAISSANCE. Renaissance and the Middle Ages. Humanism, Pomponazzi, Vives, Bodin, Boehme, etc. THE NEW CONCEPTION OF THE WORLD. Aristotelio-Medieval world-scheme, Nicholas of Cusa, Telesius, Copernicus, Bruno. THE NEW SCIENCE. Da Vinci, Kepler, Galileo, Bacon. THE GREAT SYSTEMS. Descartes, Gassendi, Hobbes, Spinoza, Leibniz, Wolff. ENGLISH EMPIRICISM. Locke, Newton, Berkeley, Hume, Smith, Priestley, Erasmus, Darwin. FRENCH ENLIGHTENMENT. Montesquieu, Voltaire, Condillac, Diderot, Holbach, Rousseau.

Translated by B. E. Meyer. Index. xvii+532pp. 5⅜ x 8.

T117 Paperbound **$2.00**

Catalog
of
DOVER BOOKS

BOOKS EXPLAINING SCIENCE

(Note: The books listed under this category are general introductions, surveys, reviews, and non-technical expositions of science for the interested layman or scientist who wishes to brush up. Dover also publishes the largest list of inexpensive reprints of books on intermediate and higher mathematics, mathematical physics, engineering, chemistry, astronomy, etc., for the professional mathematician or scientist. For our complete Science Catalog, write Dept. catrr., Dover Publications, Inc., 180 Varick Street, New York 14, N. Y.)

CONCERNING THE NATURE OF THINGS, Sir William· Bragg. Royal Institute Christmas Lectures by Nobel Laureate. Excellent plain-language introduction to gases, molecules, crystal structure, etc. explains "building blocks" of universe, basic properties of matter, with simplest, clearest examples, demonstrations. 32pp. of photos; 57° figures. 244pp. 5⅜ x 8.
T31 Paperbound **$1.35**

MATTER AND LIGHT, THE NEW PHYSICS, Louis de Broglie. Non-technical explanations by a Nobel Laureate of electro-magnetic theory, relativity, wave mechanics, quantum physics, philosophies of science, etc. Simple, yet accurate introduction to work of Planck, Bohr, Einstein, other modern physicists. Only 2 of 12 chapters require mathematics. 300pp. 5⅜ x 8.
T35 Paperbound **$1.60**

THE COMMON SENSE OF THE EXACT SCIENCES, W. K. Clifford. For 70 years, Clifford's work has been acclaimed as one of the clearest, yet most precise introductions to mathematical symbolism, measurement, surface boundaries, position, space, motion, mass and force, etc. Prefaces by Bertrand Russell and Karl Pearson. Introduction by James Newman. 130 figures. 249pp. 5⅜ x 8.
T61 Paperbound **$1.60**

THE NATURE OF LIGHT AND COLOUR IN THE OPEN AIR, M. Minnaert. What causes mirages? haloes? "multiple" suns and moons? Professor Minnaert explains these and hundreds of other fascinating natural optical phenomena in simple terms, tells how to observe them, suggests hundreds of experiments. 200 illus; 42 photos. xvi + 362pp.
T196 Paperbound **$1·95**

SPINNING TOPS AND GYROSCOPIC MOTION, John Perry. Classic elementary text on dynamics of rotation treats gyroscopes, tops, how quasi-rigidity is induced in paper disks, smoke rings, chains, etc, by rapid motion, precession, earth's motion, etc. Contains many easy-to-perform experiments. Appendix on practical uses of gyroscopes. 62 figures. 128pp.
T416 Paperbound **$1.00**

A CONCISE HISTORY OF MATHEMATICS, D. Struik. This lucid, easily followed history of mathematics from the Ancient Near East to modern times requires no mathematical background itself, yet introduces both mathematicians and laymen to basic concepts and discoveries and the men who made them. Contains a collection of 31 portraits of eminent mathematicians. Bibliography. xix + 299pp. 5⅜ x 8.
T255 Paperbound **$1.75**

THE RESTLESS UNIVERSE, Max Born. A remarkably clear, thorough exposition of gases, electrons, ions, waves and particles, electronic structure of the atom, nuclear physics, written for the layman by a Nobel Laureate. "Much ·more thorough and deep than most attempts . . . easy and delightful," CHEMICAL AND ENGINEERING NEWS. Includes 7 animated sequences showing motion of molecules, alpha particles, etc. 11 full-page plates of photographs. Total of nearly 600 illus. 315pp. 6⅛ x 9¼.
T412 Paperbound **$2.00**

WHAT IS SCIENCE?, N. Campbell. The role of experiment, the function of mathematics, the nature of scientific laws, the limitations of science, and many other provocative topics are explored without technicalities by an eminent scientist. "Still an excellent introduction to scientific philosophy," H. Margenau in PHYSICS TODAY. 192pp. 5⅜ x 8.
S43 Paperbound **$1.25**

FADS AND FALLACIES IN THE NAME OF SCIENCE, Martin Gardner. The standard account of the various cults, quack systems and delusions which have recently masqueraded as science: hollow earth theory, Atlantis, dianetics, Reich's orgone theory, flying saucers, Bridey Murphy, psionics, irridiagnosis, many other fascinating fallacies that deluded tens of thousands. "Should be read by everyone, scientist and non-scientist alike," R. T. Birge, Prof. Emeritus, Univ. of California; Former President, American Physical Society. Formerly titled, "In the Name of Science." Revised and enlarged edition. x + 365pp. 5⅜ x 8.
T394 Paperbound **$1.50**

THE STUDY OF THE HISTORY OF MATHEMATICS, THE STUDY OF THE HISTORY OF SCIENCE, G. Sarton. Two books bound as one. Both volumes are standard introductions to their fields by an eminent science historian. They discuss problems of historical research, teaching, pitfalls, other matters of interest to the historically oriented writer, teacher, or student. Both have extensive bibliographies. 10 illustrations. 188pp. 5⅜ x 8.   T240 Paperbound **$1.25**

THE PRINCIPLES OF SCIENCE, W. S. Jevons. Unabridged reprinting of a milestone in the development of symbolic logic and other subjects concerning scientific methodology, probability, inferential validity, etc. Also describes Jevons' "logic machine," an early precursor of modern electronic calculators. Preface by E. Nagel. 839pp. 5⅜ x 8. S446 Paperbound **$2.98**

SCIENCE THEORY AND MAN, Erwin Schroedinger. Complete, unabridged reprinting of "Science and the Human Temperament" plus an additional essay "What is an Elementary Particle?" Nobel Laureate Schroedinger discusses many aspects of modern physics from novel points of view which provide unusual insights for both laymen and physicists. 192 pp. 5⅜ x 8.
T428 Paperbound **$1.35**

BRIDGES AND THEIR BUILDERS, D. B. Steinman & S. R. Watson. Information about ancient, medieval, modern bridges; how they were built; who built them; the structural principles employed; the materials they are built of; etc. Written by one of the world's leading authorities on bridge design and construction. New, revised, expanded edition. 23 photos; 26 line drawings, xvii + 401pp. 5⅜ x 8.   T431 Paperbound **$1.95**

HISTORY OF MATHEMATICS, D. E. Smith. Most comprehensive non-technical history of math in English. In two volumes. Vol. I: A chronological examination of the growth of mathematics from primitive concepts up to 1900. Vol. II: The development of ideas in specific fields and areas, up through elementary calculus. The lives and works of over a thousand mathematicians are covered; thousands of specific historical problems and their solutions are clearly explained. Total of 510 illustrations, 1355pp. 5⅜ x 8. Set boxed in attractive container.   T429, T430 Paperbound, the set **$5.00**

PHILOSOPHY AND THE PHYSICISTS, L. S. Stebbing. A philosopher examines the philosophical implications of modern science by posing a lively critical attack on the popular science expositions of Sir James Jeans and Arthur Eddington. xvi + 295pp. 5⅜ x 8.
T480 Paperbound **$1.65**

ON MATHEMATICS AND MATHEMATICIANS, R. E. Moritz. The first collection of quotations by and about mathematicians in English. 1140 anecdotes, aphorisms, definitions, speculations, etc. give both mathematicians and layman stimulating new insights into what mathematics is, and into the personalities of the great mathematicians from Archimedes to Euler, Gauss, Klein, Weierstrass. Invaluable to teachers, writers. Extensive cross index. 410pp. 5⅜ x 8.
T489 Paperbound **$1.95**

NATURAL SCIENCE, BIOLOGY, GEOLOGY, TRAVEL

A SHORT HISTORY OF ANATOMY AND PHYSIOLOGY FROM THE GREEKS TO HARVEY, C. Singer. A great medical historian's fascinating intermediate account of the slow advance of anatomical and physiological knowledge from pre-scientific times to Vesalius, Harvey. 139 unusually interesting illustrations. 221pp. 5⅜ x 8.   T389 Paperbound **$1.75**

THE BEHAVIOUR AND SOCIAL LIFE OF HONEYBEES, Ronald Ribbands. The most comprehensive, lucid and authoritative book on bee habits, communication, duties, cell life, motivations, etc. "A MUST for every scientist, experimenter, and educator, and a happy and valuable selection for all interested in the honeybee," AMERICAN BEE JOURNAL. 690-item bibliography. 127 illus.; 11 photographic plates. 352pp. 5⅜ x 8⅜.   S410 Clothbound **$4.50**

TRAVELS OF WILLIAM BARTRAM, edited by Mark Van Doren. One of the 18th century's most delightful books, and one of the few first-hand sources of information about American geography, natural history, and anthropology of American Indian tribes of the time. "The mind of a scientist with the soul of a poet," John Livingston Lowes. 13 original illustrations, maps. Introduction by Mark Van Doren. 448pp. 5⅜ x 8.   T326 Paperbound **$2.00**

STUDIES ON THE STRUCTURE AND DEVELOPMENT OF VERTEBRATES, Edwin Goodrich. The definitive study of the skeleton, fins and limbs, head region, divisions of the body cavity, vascular, respiratory, excretory systems, etc., of vertebrates from fish to higher mammals, by the greatest comparative anatomist of recent times. "The standard textbook," JOURNAL OF ANATOMY. 754 illus. 69-page biographical study. 1186-item bibliography. 2 vols. Total of 906pp. 5⅜ x 8.
Vol. I: S449 Paperbound **$2.50**
Vol. II: S450 Paperbound **$2.50**

DOVER BOOKS

THE BIRTH AND DEVELOPMENT OF THE GEOLOGICAL SCIENCES, F. D. Adams. The most complete and thorough history of the earth sciences in print. Covers over 300 geological thinkers and systems; treats fossils, theories of stone growth, paleontology, earthquakes, vulcanists vs. neptunists, odd theories, etc. 91 illustrations, including medieval, Renaissance wood cuts, etc. 632 footnotes and bibliographic notes. 511pp. 308pp. 5⅜ x 8. T5 Paperbound **$2.00**

FROM MAGIC TO SCIENCE, Charles Singer. A close study of aspects of medical science from the Roman Empire through the Renaissance. The sections on early herbals, and "The Visions of Hildegarde of Bingen," are probably the best studies of these subjects available. 158 unusual classic and medieval illustrations. xxvii + 365pp. 5⅜ x 8. T390 Paperbound **$2.00**

SAILING ALONE AROUND THE WORLD, Captain Joshua Slocum. Captain Slocum's personal account of his single-handed voyage around the world in a 34-foot boat he rebuilt himself. A classic of both seamanship and descriptive writing. "A nautical equivalent of Thoreau's account," Van Wyck Brooks. 67 illus. 308pp. 5⅜ x 8. T326 Paperbound **$1.00**

TREES OF THE EASTERN AND CENTRAL UNITED STATES AND CANADA, W. M. Harlow. Standard middle-level guide designed to help you know the characteristics of Eastern trees and identify them at sight by means of an 8-page synoptic key. More than 600 drawings and photographs of twigs, leaves, fruit, other features. xiii + 288pp. 4⅝ x 6½. T395 Paperbound **$1.35**

FRUIT KEY AND TWIG KEY ("Fruit Key to Northeastern Trees," "Twig Key to Deciduous Woody Plants of Eastern North America"), **W. M. Harlow.** Identify trees in fall, winter, spring. Easy-to-use, synoptic keys, with photographs of every twig and fruit identified. Covers 120 different fruits, 160 different twigs. Over 350 photos. Bibliographies. Glossaries. Total of 143pp. 5⅝ x 8⅜. T511 Paperbound **$1.25**

INTRODUCTION TO THE STUDY OF EXPERIMENTAL MEDICINE, Claude Bernard. This classic records Bernard's far-reaching efforts to transform physiology into an exact science. It covers problems of vivisection, the limits of physiological experiment, hypotheses in medical experimentation, hundreds of others. Many of his own famous experiments on the liver, the pancreas, etc., are used as examples. Foreword by I. B. Cohen. xxv + 266pp. 5⅜ x 8. T400 Paperbound **$1.50**

THE ORIGIN OF LIFE, A. I. Oparin. The first modern statement that life evolved from complex nitro-carbon compounds, carefully presented according to modern biochemical knowledge of primary colloids, organic molecules, etc. Begins with historical introduction to the problem of the origin of life. Bibliography. xxv + 270pp. 5⅜ x 8. S213 Paperbound **$1.75**

A HISTORY OF ASTRONOMY FROM THALES TO KEPLER, J. L. E. Dreyer. The only work in English which provides a detailed picture of man's cosmological views from Egypt, Babylonia, Greece, and Alexandria to Copernicus, Tycho Brahe and Kepler. "Standard reference on Greek astronomy and the Copernican revolution," SKY AND TELESCOPE. Formerly called "A History of Planetary Systems From Thales to Kepler." Bibliography. 21 diagrams. xvii + 430pp. 5⅜ x 8. S79 Paperbound **$1.98**

URANIUM PROSPECTING, H. L. Barnes. A professional geologist tells you what you need to know. Hundreds of facts about minerals, tests, detectors, sampling, assays, claiming, developing, government regulations, etc. Glossary of technical terms. Annotated bibliography. x + 117pp. 5⅜ x 8. T309 Paperbound **$1.00**

DE RE METALLICA, Georgius Agricola. All 12 books of this 400 year old classic on metals and metal production, fully annotated, and containing all 289 of the 16th century woodcuts which made the original an artistic masterpiece. A superb gift for geologists, engineers, libraries, artists, historians. Translated by Herbert Hoover & L. H. Hoover. Bibliography, survey of ancient authors. 289 illustrations of the excavating, assaying, smelting, refining, and countless other metal production operations described in the text. 672pp. 6¾ x 10¾. Deluxe library edition. S6 Clothbound **$10.00**

DE MAGNETE, William Gilbert. A landmark of science by the man who first used the word "electricity," distinguished between static electricity and magnetism, and founded a new science. P. F. Mottelay translation. 90 figures. lix + 368pp. 5⅜ x 8. S470 Paperbound **$2.00**

THE AUTOBIOGRAPHY OF CHARLES DARWIN AND SELECTED LETTERS, Francis Darwin, ed. Fascinating documents on Darwin's early life, the voyage of the "Beagle," the discovery of evolution, Darwin's thought on mimicry, plant development, vivisection, evolution, many other subjects Letters to Henslow, Lyell, Hooker, Wallace, Kingsley, etc. Appendix. 365pp. 5⅜ x 8. T479 Paperbound **$1.65**

A WAY OF LIFE AND OTHER SELECTED WRITINGS OF SIR WILLIAM OSLER. 16 of the great physician, teacher and humanist's most inspiring writings on a practical philosophy of life, science and the humanities, and the history of medicine. 5 photographs. Introduction by G. L. Keynes, M.D., F.R.C.S. xx + 278pp. 5⅜ x 8. T488 Paperbound **$1.50**

LITERATURE

WORLD DRAMA, B. H. Clark. 46 plays from Ancient Greece, Rome, to India, China, Japan. Plays by Aeschylus, Sophocles, Euripides, Aristophanes, Plautus, Marlowe, Jonson, Farquhar, Goldsmith, Cervantes, Molière, Dumas, Goethe, Schiller, Ibsen, many others. One of the most comprehensive collections of important plays from all literature available in English. Over ⅓ of this material is unavailable in any other current edition. Reading lists. 2 volumes. Total of 1364pp. 5⅜ x 8.   Vol. I, T57 Paperbound **$2.00**
Vol. II, T59 Paperbound **$2.00**

MASTERS OF THE DRAMA, John Gassner. The most comprehensive history of the drama in print. Covers more than 800 dramatists and over 2000 plays from the Greeks to modern Western, Near Eastern, Oriental drama. Plot summaries, theatre history, etc. "Best of its kind in English," NEW REPUBLIC. 35 pages of bibliography. 77 photos and drawings. Deluxe edition. xxii + 890pp. 5⅜ x 8.   T100 Clothbound **$5.95**

THE DRAMA OF LUIGI PIRANDELLO, D. Vittorini. All 38 of Pirandello's plays (to 1935) summarized and analyzed in terms of symbolic techniques, plot structure, etc. The only authorized work. Foreword by Pirandello. Biography. Bibliography. xiii + 350pp. 5⅜ x 8.
T435 Paperbound **$1.98**

ARISTOTLE'S THEORY OF POETRY AND THE FINE ARTS, S. H. Butcher, ed. The celebrated "Butcher translation" faced page by page with the Greek text; Butcher's 300-page introduction to Greek poetic, dramatic thought. Modern Aristotelian criticism discussed by John Gassner. lxxvi + 421pp. 5⅜ x 8.
T42 Paperbound **$2.00**

EUGENE O'NEILL: THE MAN AND HIS PLAYS, B. H. Clark. The first published source-book on O'Neill's life and work. Analyzes each play from the early THE WEB up to THE ICEMAN COMETH. Supplies much information about environmental and dramatic influences. ix + 182pp. 5⅜ x 8.   T379 Paperbound **$1.25**

INTRODUCTION TO ENGLISH LITERATURE, B. Dobrée, ed. Most compendious literary aid in its price range. Extensive, categorized bibliography (with entries up to 1949) of more than 5,000 poets, dramatists, novelists, as well as historians, philosophers, economists, religious writers, travellers, and scientists of literary stature. Information about manuscripts, important biographical data. Critical, historical, background works not simply listed, but evaluated. Each volume also contains a long introduction to the period it covers.

Vol. I: **THE BEGINNINGS OF ENGLISH LITERATURE TO SKELTON, 1509, W. L. Renwick. H. Orton.** 450pp. 5⅛ x 7⅛.   T75 Clothbound **$3.50**
Vol. II: **THE ENGLISH RENAISSANCE, 1510-1688, V. de Sola Pinto.** 381pp. 5⅛ x 7⅛.
T76 Clothbound **$3.50**
Vol. III: **THE AUGUSTANS AND ROMANTICS, 1689-1830, H. Dyson, J. Butt.** 320pp. 5⅛ x 7⅛.
T77 Clothbound **$3.50**
Vol. IV: **THE VICTORIANS AND AFTER, 1830-1914, E. Batho, B. Dobrée.** 360pp. 5⅛ x 7⅛.
T78 Clothbound **$3.50**

EPIC AND ROMANCE, W. P. Ker. The standard survey of Medieval epic and romance by a foremost authority on Medieval literature. Covers historical background, plot, literary analysis, significance of Teutonic epics, Icelandic sagas, Beowulf, French chansons de geste, the Niebelungenlied, Arthurian romances, much more. 422pp. 5⅜ x 8.   T355 Paperbound **$1.95**

THE HEART OF EMERSON'S JOURNALS, Bliss Perry, ed. Emerson's most intimate thoughts, impressions, records of conversations with Channing, Hawthorne, Thoreau, etc., carefully chosen from the 10 volumes of The Journals. "The essays do not reveal the power of Emerson's mind . . .as do these hasty and informal writings," N. Y. TIMES. Preface by B. Perry. 370pp. 5⅜ x 8.   T447 Paperbound **$1.85**

A SOURCE BOOK IN THEATRICAL HISTORY, A. M. Nagler. (Formerly, "Sources of Theatrical History.") Over 300 selected passages by contemporary observers tell about styles of acting, direction, make-up, scene designing, etc., in the theatre's great periods from ancient Greece to the Théâtre Libre. "Indispensable complement to the study of drama," EDUCATIONAL THEATRE JOURNAL. Prof. Nagler, Yale Univ. School of Drama, also supplies notes, references. 85 illustrations. 611pp. 5⅜ x 8.   T515 Paperbound **$2.75**

THE ART OF THE STORY-TELLER, M. L. Shedlock. Regarded as the finest, most helpful book on telling stories to children, by a great story-teller. How to catch, hold, recapture attention; how to choose material; many other aspects. Also includes: a 99-page selection of Miss Shedlock's most successful stories; extensive bibliography of other stories. xxi + 320pp. 5⅜ x 8.   T245 Clothbound **$3.50**

THE DEVIL'S DICTIONARY, Ambrose Bierce. Over 1000 short, ironic definitions in alphabetical order, by America's greatest satirist in the classical tradition. "Some of the most gorgeous witticisms in the English language," H. L. Mencken. 144pp. 5⅜ x 8.   T487 Paperbound **$1.00**

MUSIC

A DICTIONARY OF HYMNOLOGY, John Julian. More than 30,000 entries on individual hymns, their authorship, textual variations, location of texts, dates and circumstances of composition, denominational and ritual usages, the biographies of more than 9,000 hymn writers, essays on important topics such as children's hymns and Christmas carols, and hundreds of thousands of other important facts about hymns which are virtually impossible to find anywhere else. Convenient alphabetical listing, and a 200-page double-columned index of first lines enable you to track down virtually any hymn ever written. Total of 1786pp. 6¼ x 9¼. 2 volumes. T133. The Set, Clothbound **$15.00**

STRUCTURAL HEARING, TONAL COHERENCE IN MUSIC, Felix Salzer. Extends the well-known Schenker approach to include modern music, music of the middle ages, and Renaissance music. Explores the phenomenon of tonal organization by discussing more than 500 compositions, and offers unusual new insights into the theory of composition and musical relationships. "The foundation on which all teaching in music theory has been based at this college," Leopold Mannes, President, The Mannes College of Music. Total of 658pp. 6½ x 9¼. 2 volumes. S418 The set, Clothbound **$8.00**

A GENERAL HISTORY OF MUSIC, Charles Burney. The complete history of music from the Greeks up to 1789 by the 18th century musical historian who personally knew the great Baroque composers. Covers sacred and secular, vocal and instrumental, operatic and symphonic music; treats theory, notation, forms, instruments; discusses composers, performers, important works. Invaluable as a source of information on the period for students, historians, musicians. "Surprisingly few of Burney's statements have been invalidated by modern research . . . still of great value," NEW YORK TIMES. Edited and corrected by Frank Mercer. 35 figures. 1915pp. 5½ x 8½. 2 volumes. T36 The set, Clothbound **$12.50**

JOHANN SEBASTIAN BACH, Phillip Spitta. Recognized as one of the greatest accomplishments of musical scholarship and far and away the definitive coverage of Bach's works. Hundreds of individual pieces are analyzed. Major works, such as the B Minor Mass and the St. Matthew Passion are examined in minute detail. Spitta also deals with the works of Buxtehude, Pachelbel, and others of the period. Can be read with profit even by those without a knowledge of the technicalities of musical composition. "Unchallenged as the last word on one of the supreme geniuses of music," John Barkham, SATURDAY REVIEW SYNDICATE. Total of 1819pp. 5⅜ x 8. 2 volumes. T252 The set, Clothbound **$10.00**

HISTORY

THE IDEA OF PROGRESS, J. B. Bury. Prof. Bury traces the evolution of a central concept of Western civilization in Greek, Roman, Medieval, and Renaissance thought to its flowering in the 17th and 18th centuries. Introduction by Charles Beard. xl + 357pp. 5⅜ x 8.
T39 Clothbound **$3.95**
T40 Paperbound **$1.95**

THE ANCIENT GREEK HISTORIANS, J. B. Bury. Greek historians such as Herodotus, Thucydides, Xenophon; Roman historians such as Tacitus, Caesar, Livy; scores of others fully analyzed in terms of sources, concepts, influences, etc., by a great scholar and historian. 291pp. 5⅜ x 8. T397 Paperbound **$1.50**

HISTORY OF THE LATER ROMAN EMPIRE, J. B. Bury. The standard work on the Byzantine Empire from 395 A.D. to the death of Justinian in 565 A.D., by the leading Byzantine scholar of our time. Covers political, social, cultural, theological, military history. Quotes contemporary documents extensively. "Most unlikely that it will ever be superseded," Glanville Downey, Dumbarton Oaks Research Library. Genealogical tables. 5 maps. Bibliography. 2 vols. Total of 965pp. 5⅜ x 8. T398, T399 Paperbound, the set **$4.00**

GARDNER'S PHOTOGRAPHIC SKETCH BOOK OF THE CIVIL WAR, Alexander Gardner. One of the rarest and most valuable Civil War photographic collections exactly reproduced for the first time since 1866. Scenes of Manassas, Bull Run, Harper's Ferry, Appomattox, Mechanicsville, Fredericksburg, Gettysburg, etc.; battle ruins, prisons, arsenals, a slave pen, fortifications; Lincoln on the field, officers, men, corpses. By one of the most famous pioneers in documentary photography. Original copies of the "Sketch Book" sold for $425 in 1952. Introduction by E. Bleiler. 100 full-page 7 x 10 photographs (original size). 244pp. 10¾ x 8½
T476 Clothbound **$6.00**

THE WORLD'S GREAT SPEECHES, L. Copeland and L. Lamm, eds. 255 speeches from Pericles to Churchill, Dylan Thomas. Invaluable as a guide to speakers; fascinating as history past and present; a source of much difficult-to-find material. Includes an extensive section of informal and humorous speeches. 3 indices: Topic, Author, Nation. xx + 745pp. 5⅜ x 8.
T468 Paperbound **$2.49**

FOUNDERS OF THE MIDDLE AGES, E. K. Rand. The best non-technical discussion of the transformation of Latin paganism into medieval civilization. Tertullian, Gregory, Jerome, Boethius, Augustine, the Neoplatonists, other crucial figures, philosophies examined. Excellent for the intelligent non-specialist. "Extraordinarily accurate," Richard McKeon, THE NATION. ix + 365pp. 5⅜ x 8. T369 Paperbound **$1.85**

THE POLITICAL THOUGHT OF PLATO AND ARISTOTLE, Ernest Barker. The standard, comprehensive exposition of Greek political thought. Covers every aspect of the "Republic" and the "Politics" as well as minor writings, other philosophers, theorists of the period, and the later history of Greek political thought. Unabridged edition. 584pp. 5⅜ x 8.
T521 Paperbound **$1.85**

PHILOSOPHY

THE GIFT OF LANGUAGE, M. Schlauch. (Formerly, "The Gift of Tongues.") A sound, middle-level treatment of linguistic families, word histories, grammatical processes, semantics, language taboos, word-coining of Joyce, Cummings, Stein, etc. 232 bibliographical notes. 350pp. 5⅜ x 8.
T243 Paperbound **$1.85**

THE PHILOSOPHY OF HEGEL, W. T. Stace. The first work in English to give a complete and connected view of Hegel's entire system. Especially valuable to those who do not have time to study the highly complicated original texts, yet want an accurate presentation by a most reputable scholar of one of the most influential 19th century thinkers. Includes a 14 x 20 fold-out chart of Hegelian system. 536pp. 5⅜ x 8.
T254 Paperbound **$2.00**

ARISTOTLE, A. E. Taylor. A lucid, non-technical account of Aristotle written by a foremost Platonist. Covers life and works; thought on matter, form, causes, logic, God, physics, metaphysics, etc. Bibliography. New index compiled for this edition. 128pp. 5⅜ x 8.
T280 Paperbound **$1.00**

GUIDE TO PHILOSOPHY, C. E. M. Joad. This basic work describes the major philosophic problems and evaluates the answers propounded by great philosophers from the Greeks to Whitehead, Russell. "The finest introduction," BOSTON TRANSCRIPT. Bibliography, 592pp. 5⅜ x 8.
T297 Paperbound **$2.00**

LANGUAGE AND MYTH, E. Cassirer. Cassirer's brilliant demonstration that beneath both language and myth lies an unconscious "grammar" of experience whose categories and canons are not those of logical thought. Introduction and translation by Susanne Langer. Index. x + 103pp. 5⅜ x 8.
T51 Paperbound **$1.25**

SUBSTANCE AND FUNCTION, EINSTEIN'S THEORY OF RELATIVITY, E. Cassirer. This double volume contains the German philosopher's profound philosophical formulation of the differences between traditional logic and the new logic of science. Number, space, energy, relativity, many other topics are treated in detail. Authorized translation by W. C. and M. C. Swabey. xii + 465pp. 5⅜ x 8.
T50 Paperbound **$2.00**

THE PHILOSOPHICAL WORKS OF DESCARTES. The definitive English edition, in two volumes, of all major philosophical works and letters of René Descartes, father of modern philosophy of knowledge and science. Translated by E. S. Haldane and G. Ross. Introductory notes. Total of 842pp. 5⅜ x 8.
T71 Vol. 1, Paperbound **$2.00**
T72 Vol. 2, Paperbound **$2.00**

ESSAYS IN EXPERIMENTAL LOGIC, J. Dewey. Based upon Dewey's theory that knowledge implies a judgment which in turn implies an inquiry, these papers consider such topics as the thought of Bertrand Russell, pragmatism, the logic of values, antecedents of thought, data and meanings. 452pp. 5⅜ x 8.
T73 Paperbound **$1.95**

THE PHILOSOPHY OF HISTORY, G. W. F. Hegel. This classic of Western thought is Hegel's detailed formulation of the thesis that history is not chance but a rational process, the realization of the Spirit of Freedom. Translated and introduced by J. Sibree. Introduction by C. Hegel. Special introduction for this edition by Prof. Carl Friedrich, Harvard University. xxxix + 447pp. 5⅜ x 8.
T112 Paperbound **$1.85**

THE WILL TO BELIEVE and HUMAN IMMORTALITY, W. James. Two of James's most profound investigations of human belief in God and immortality, bound as one volume. Both are powerful expressions of James's views on chance vs. determinism, pluralism vs. monism, will and intellect, arguments for survival after death, etc. Two prefaces. 429pp. 5⅜ x 8.
T294 Clothbound **$3.75**
T291 Paperbound **$1.65**

INTRODUCTION TO SYMBOLIC LOGIC, S. Langer. A lucid, general introduction to modern logic, covering forms, classes, the use of symbols, the calculus of propositions, the Boole-Schroeder and the Russell-Whitehead systems, etc. "One of the clearest and simplest introductions," MATHEMATICS GAZETTE. Second, enlarged, revised edition. 368pp. 5⅜ x 8.
S164 Paperbound **$1.75**

MIND AND THE WORLD-ORDER, C. I. Lewis. Building upon the work of Peirce, James, and Dewey, Professor Lewis outlines a theory of knowledge in terms of "conceptual pragmatism," and demonstrates why the traditional understanding of the a priori must be abandoned. Appendices. xiv + 446pp. 5⅜ x 8.
T359 Paperbound **$1.95**

THE GUIDE FOR THE PERPLEXED, M. Maimonides One of the great philosophical works of all time, Maimonides' formulation of the meeting-ground between Old Testament and Aristotelian thought is essential to anyone interested in Jewish, Christian, and Moslem thought in the Middle Ages. 2nd revised edition of the Friedländer translation. Extensive introduction. lix + 414pp. 5⅜ x 8.
T351 Paperbound **$1.85**

THE PHILOSOPHICAL WRITINGS OF PEIRCE, J. Buchler, ed. (Formerly, "The Philosophy of Peirce.") This carefully integrated selection of Peirce's papers is considered the best coverage of the complete thought of one of the greatest philosophers of modern times. Covers Peirce's work on the theory of signs, pragmatism, epistemology, symbolic logic, the scientific method, chance, etc. xvi + 386pp. 5 ⅜ x 8.　　　　　　　　　　　T216 Clothbound **$5.00**
T217 Paperbound **$1.95**

HISTORY OF ANCIENT PHILOSOPHY, W. Windelband. Considered the clearest survey of Greek and Roman philosophy. Examines Thales, Anaximander, Anaximenes, Heraclitus, the Eleatics, Empedocles, the Pythagoreans, the Sophists, Socrates, Democritus, Stoics, Epicureans, Sceptics, Neo-platonists, etc. 50 pages on Plato; 70 on Aristotle. 2nd German edition tr. by H. E. Cushman. xv + 393pp. 5⅜ x 8.　　　　　　　　　　　　　　　T357 Paperbound **$1.75**

INTRODUCTION TO SYMBOLIC LOGIC AND ITS APPLICATIONS, R. Carnap. A comprehensive, rigorous introduction to modern logic by perhaps its greatest living master. Includes demonstrations of applications in mathematics, physics, biology. "Of the rank of a masterpiece," Z. für Mathematik und ihre Grenzgebiete. Over 300 exercises. xvi + 241pp. 5⅜ x 8.　　　　　　　　　　　　　　　　　　　　　　　　Clothbound **$4.00**
S453 Paperbound **$1.85**

SCEPTICISM AND ANIMAL FAITH, G. Santayana. Santayana's unusually lucid exposition of the difference between the independent existence of objects and the essence our mind attributes to them, and of the necessity of scepticism as a form of belief and animal faith as a necessary condition of knowledge. Discusses belief, memory, intuition, symbols, etc. xii + 314pp. 5⅜ x 8.　　　　　　　　　　　　　　　　　　　　　　T235 Clothbound **$3.50**
T236 Paperbound **$1.50**

THE ANALYSIS OF MATTER, B. Russell. With his usual brilliance, Russell analyzes physics, causality, scientific inference, Weyl's theory, tensors, invariants, periodicity, etc. in order to discover the basic concepts of scientific thought about matter. "Most thorough treatment of the subject," THE NATION. Introduction. 8 figures. viii + 408pp. 5⅜ x 8.
T231 Paperbound **$1.95**

THE SENSE OF BEAUTY, G. Santayana. This important philosophical study of why, when, and how beauty appears, and what conditions must be fulfilled, is in itself a revelation of the beauty of language. "It is doubtful if a better treatment of the subject has since appeared," PEABODY JOURNAL. ix + 275pp. 5⅜ x 8.　　　　　　　　　　　T238 Paperbound **$1.00**

THE CHIEF WORKS OF SPINOZA. In two volumes. Vol. I: The Theologico-Political Treatise and the Political Treatise. Vol. II: On the Improvement of Understanding, The Ethics, and Selected Letters. The permanent and enduring ideas in these works on God, the universe, religion, society, etc., have had tremendous impact on later philosophical works. Introduction. Total of 862pp. 5⅜ x 8.　　　　　　　　　　　T249 Vol. I, Paperbound **$1.50**
T250 Vol. II, Paperbound **$1.50**

TRAGIC SENSE OF LIFE, M. de Unamuno. The acknowledged masterpiece of one of Spain's most influential thinkers. Between the despair at the inevitable death of man and all his works, and the desire for immortality, Unamuno finds a "saving incertitude." Called "a masterpiece," by the ENCYCLOPAEDIA BRITANNICA. xxx + 332pp. 5⅜ x 8.
T257 Paperbound **$1.95**

EXPERIENCE AND NATURE, John Dewey. The enlarged, revised edition of the Paul Carus lectures (1925). One of Dewey's clearest presentations of the philosophy of empirical naturalism which reestablishes the continuity between "inner" experience and "outer" nature. These lectures are among the most significant ever delivered by an American philosopher. 457pp. 5⅜ x 8.　　　　　　　　　　　　　　　　　　　T471 Paperbound **$1.85**

PHILOSOPHY AND CIVILIZATION IN THE MIDDLE AGES, M. de Wulf. A semi-popular survey of medieval intellectual life, religion, philosophy, science, the arts, etc. that covers feudalism vs. Catholicism, rise of the universities, mendicant orders, and similar topics. Bibliography. viii + 320pp. 5⅜ x 8.　　　　　　　　　　　　　　　　　T284 Paperbound **$1.75**

AN INTRODUCTION TO SCHOLASTIC PHILOSOPHY, M. de Wulf. (Formerly, "Scholasticism Old and New.") Prof. de Wulf covers the central scholastic tradition from St. Anselm, Albertus Magnus, Thomas Aquinas, up to Suarez in the 17th century; and then treats the modern revival of scholasticism, the Louvain position, relations with Kantianism and positivism, etc. xvi + 271pp. 5⅜ x 8.　　　　　　　　　　　　　　T296 Clothbound **$3.50**
T283 Paperbound **$1.75**

A HISTORY OF MODERN PHILOSOPHY, H. Höffding. An exceptionally clear and detailed coverage of Western philosophy from the Renaissance to the end of the 19th century. Both major and minor figures are examined in terms of theory of knowledge, logic, cosmology, psychology. Covers Pomponazzi, Bodin, Boehme, Telesius, Bruno, Copernicus, Descartes, Spinoza, Hobbes, Locke, Hume, Kant, Fichte, Schopenhauer, Mill, Spencer, Langer, scores of others. A standard reference work. 2 volumes. Total of 1159pp. 5⅜ x 8.　　　　　T117 Vol. 1, Paperbound **$2.00**
T118 Vol. 2, Paperbound **$2.00**

LANGUAGE, TRUTH AND LOGIC, A. J. Ayer. The first full-length development of Logical Positivism in English. Building on the work of Schlick, Russell, Carnap, and the Vienna school, Ayer presents the tenets of one of the most important systems of modern philosophical thought. 160pp. 5⅜ x 8.　　　　　　　　　　　　　　　T10 Paperbound **$1.25**

ORIENTALIA AND RELIGION

THE MYSTERIES OF MITHRA, F. Cumont. The great Belgian scholar's definitive study of the Persian mystery religion that almost vanquished Christianity in the ideological struggle for the Roman Empire. A masterpiece of scholarly detection that reconstructs secret doctrines, organization, rites. Mithraic art is discussed and analyzed. 70 illus. 239pp. 5⅜ x 8.
T323 Paperbound **$1.85**

CHRISTIAN AND ORIENTAL PHILOSOPHY OF ART. A. K. Coomaraswamy. The late art historian and orientalist discusses artistic symbolism, the role of traditional culture in enriching art, medieval art, folklore, philosophy of art, other similar topics. Bibliography. 148pp. 5⅜ x 8.
T378 Paperbound **$1.25**

TRANSFORMATION OF NATURE IN ART, A. K. Coomaraswamy. A basic work on Asiatic religious art. Includes discussions of religious art in Asia and Medieval Europe (exemplified by Meister Eckhart), the origin and use of images in Indian art, Indian Medieval aesthetic manuals, and other fascinating, little known topics. Glossaries of Sanskrit and Chinese terms. Bibliography. 41pp. of notes. 245pp. 5⅜ x 8.
T368 Paperbound **$1.75**

ORIENTAL RELIGIONS IN ROMAN PAGANISM, F. Cumont. This well-known study treats the ecstatic cults of Syria and Phrygia (Cybele, Attis, Adonis, their orgies and mutilatory rites); the mysteries of Egypt (Serapis, Isis, Osiris); Persian dualism; Mithraic cults; Hermes Trismegistus, Ishtar, Astarte, etc. and their influence on the religious thought of the Roman Empire. Introduction. 55pp. of notes; extensive bibliography. xxiv + 298pp. 5⅜ x 8.
T321 Paperbound **$1.75**

ANTHROPOLOGY, SOCIOLOGY, AND PSYCHOLOGY

PRIMITIVE MAN AS PHILOSOPHER, P. Radin. A standard anthropological work based on Radin's investigations of the Winnebago, Maori, Batak, Zuni, other primitive tribes. Describes primitive thought on the purpose of life, marital relations, death, personality, gods, etc. Extensive selections of original primitive documents. Bibliography. xviii + 420pp. 5⅜ x 8.
T392 Paperbound **$2.00**

PRIMITIVE RELIGION, P. Radin. Radin's thoroughgoing treatment of supernatural beliefs, shamanism, initiations, religious expression, etc. in primitive societies. Arunta, Ashanti, Aztec, Bushman, Crow, Fijian, many other tribes examined. "Excellent," NATURE. New preface by the author. Bibliographic notes. x + 322pp. 5⅜ x 8.
T393 Paperbound **$1.85**

SEX IN PSYCHO-ANALYSIS, S. Ferenczi. (Formerly, "Contributions to Psycho-analysis.") 14 selected papers on impotence, transference, analysis and children, dreams, obscene words, homosexuality, paranoia, etc. by an associate of Freud. Also included: THE DEVELOPMENT OF PSYCHO-ANALYSIS, by Ferenczi and Otto Rank. Two books bound as one. Total of 406pp. 5⅜ x 8.
T324 Paperbound **$1.85**

THE PRINCIPLES OF PSYCHOLOGY, William James. The complete text of the famous "long course," one of the great books of Western thought. An almost incredible amount of information about psychological processes, the stream of consciousness, habit, time perception, memory, emotions, reason, consciousness of self, abnormal phenomena, and similar topics. Based on James's own discoveries integrated with the work of Descartes, Locke, Hume, Royce, Wundt, Berkeley, Lotse, Herbart, scores of others. "A classic of interpretation," PSYCHIATRIC QUARTERLY. 94 illus. 1408pp. 2 volumes. 5⅜ x 8.
T381 Vol. 1, Paperbound **$2.50**
T382 Vol. 2, Paperbound **$2.50**

THE POLISH PEASANT IN EUROPE AND AMERICA, W. I. Thomas, F. Znaniecki. Monumental sociological study of peasant primary groups (family and community) and the disruptions produced by a new industrial system and emigration to America, by two of the foremost sociologists of recent times. One of the most important works in sociological thought. Includes hundreds of pages of primary documentation; point by point analysis of causes of social decay, breakdown of morality, crime, drunkenness, prostitution, etc. 2nd revised edition. 2 volumes. Total of 2250pp. 6 x 9.
T478 2 volume set, Clothbound **$12.50**

FOLKWAYS, W. G. Sumner. The great Yale sociologist's detailed exposition of thousands of social, sexual, and religious customs in hundreds of cultures from ancient Greece to Modern Western societies. Preface by A. G. Keller. Introduction by William Lyon Phelps. 705pp. 5⅜ x 8.
S508 Paperbound **$2.49**

BEYOND PSYCHOLOGY, Otto Rank. The author, an early associate of Freud, uses psychoanalytic techniques of myth-analysis to explore ultimates of human existence. Treats love, immortality, the soul, sexual identity, kingship, sources of state power, many other topics which illuminate the irrational basis of human existence. 291pp. 5⅜ x 8.
T485 Paperbound **$1.75**

ILLUSIONS AND DELUSIONS OF THE SUPERNATURAL AND THE OCCULT, D. H. Rawcliffe. A rational, scientific examination of crystal gazing, automatic writing, table turning, stigmata, the Indian rope trick, dowsing, telepathy, clairvoyance, ghosts, ESP, PK, thousands of other supposedly occult phenomena. Originally titled "The Psychology of the Occult." 14 illustrations. 551pp. 5⅜ x 8.
T503 Paperbound **$2.00**

DOVER BOOKS

YOGA: A SCIENTIFIC EVALUATION, Kovoor T. Behanan. A scientific study of the physiological and psychological effects of Yoga discipline, written under the auspices of the Yale University Institute of Human Relations. Foreword by W. A. Miles, Yale Univ. 17 photographs. 290pp. 5⅜ x 8.   T505 Paperbound **$1.65**

HOAXES, C. D. MacDougall. Delightful, entertaining, yet scholarly exposition of how hoaxes start, why they succeed, documented with stories of hundreds of the most famous hoaxes. "A stupendous collection . . . and shrewd analysis, "NEW YORKER. New, revised edition. 54 photographs. 320pp. 5⅜ x 8.   T465 Paperbound **$1.75**

CREATIVE POWER: THE EDUCATION OF YOUTH IN THE CREATIVE ARTS, Hughes Mearns. Named by the National Education Association as one of the 20 foremost books on education in recent times. Tells how to help children express themselves in drama, poetry, music, art, develop latent creative power. Should be read by every parent, teacher. New, enlarged, revised edition. Introduction. 272pp. 5⅜ x 8.   T490 Paperbound **$1.50**

LANGUAGES

NEW RUSSIAN-ENGLISH, ENGLISH-RUSSIAN DICTIONARY, M. A. O'Brien. Over· 70,000 entries in new orthography! Idiomatic usages, colloquialisms. One of the few dictionaries that indicate accent changes in conjugation and declension. "One of the best," Prof. E. J. Simmons, Cornell. First names, geographical terms, bibliography, many other features. 738pp. 4½ x 6¼.
T208 Paperbound **$2.00**

MONEY CONVERTER AND TIPPING GUIDE FOR EUROPEAN TRAVEL, C. Vomacka. Invaluable, handy source of currency regulations, conversion tables, tipping rules, postal rates, much other travel information for every European country plus Israel, Egypt and Turkey. 128pp. 3½ x 5¼.
T260 Paperbound **60¢**

MONEY CONVERTER AND TIPPING GUIDE FOR TRAVEL IN THE AMERICAS (including the United States and Canada), **C. Vomacka.** The information you need for informed and confident travel in the Americas: money conversion tables, tipping guide, postal, telephone rates, etc. 128pp. 3½ x 5¼.   T261 Paperbound **65¢**

DUTCH-ENGLISH, ENGLISH-DUTCH DICTIONARY, F. G. Renier. The most convenient, practical Dutch-English dictionary on the market. New orthography. More than 60,000 entries: idioms, compounds, technical terms, etc. Gender of nouns indicated. xviii + 571pp. 5½ x 6¼.
T224 Clothbound **$2.50**

LEARN DUTCH!, F. G. Renier. The most satisfactory and easily-used grammar of modern Dutch. Used and recommended by the Fulbright Committee in the Netherlands. Over 1200 simple exercises lead to mastery of spoken and written Dutch. Dutch-English, English-Dutch vocabularies. 181pp. 4¼ x 7¼.   T441 Clothbound **$1.75**

PHRASE AND SENTENCE DICTIONARY OF SPOKEN RUSSIAN, English-Russian, Russian-English. Based on phrases and complete sentences, rather than isolated words; recognized as one of the best methods of learning the idiomatic speech of a country. Over 11,500 entries, indexed by single words, with more than 32,000 English and Russian sentences and phrases, in immediately usable form. Probably the largest list ever published. Shows accent changes in conjugation and declension; irregular forms listed in both alphabetical place and under main form of word. 15,000 word introduction covering Russian sounds, writing, grammar, syntax. 15−page appendix of geographical names, money, important signs, given names, foods, special Soviet terms, etc. Travellers, businessmen, students, government employees have found this their best source for Russian expressions. Originally published as U.S. Government Technical Manual TM 30-944. iv + 573pp. 5⅝ x 8⅜.   T496 Paperbound **$2.75**

PHRASE AND SENTENCE DICTIONARY OF SPOKEN SPANISH, Spanish-English, English-Spanish. Compiled from spoken Spanish, emphasizing idiom and colloquial usage in both Castilian and Latin-American. More than 16,000 entries containing over 25,000 idioms—the largest list of idiomatic constructions ever published. Complete sentences given, indexed under single words —language in immediately usable form, for travellers, businessmen, students, etc. 25−page introduction provides rapid survey of sounds, grammar, syntax, with full consideration of irregular verbs. Especially apt in modern treatment of phrases and structure. 17−page glossary gives translations of geographical names, money values, numbers, national holidays, important street signs, useful expressions of high frequency, plus unique 7-page glossary of Spanish and Spanish-American foods and dishes. Originally published as U.S. Government Technical Manual TM 30-900. iv + 513pp. 5⅝ x 8⅜.   T495 Paperbound **$1.75**

SAY IT language phrase books

"SAY IT" in the foreign language of your choice! We have sold over ½ million copies of these popular, useful language books. They will not make you an expert linguist overnight, but they do cover most practical matters of everyday life abroad.

Over 1000 useful phrases, expressions, with additional variants, substitutions.

Modern! Useful! Hundreds of phrases not available in other texts: "Nylon," "air-conditioned," etc.

The ONLY inexpensive phrase book **completely indexed.** Everything is available at a flip of your finger, ready for use.

Prepared by native linguists, travel experts.

Based on years of travel experience abroad.

This handy phrase book may be used by itself, or it may supplement any other text or course; it provides a living element. Used by many colleges and institutions: Hunter College; Barnard College; Army Ordnance School, Aberdeen; and many others.

Available, 1 book per language:

Danish (T818) 75¢
Dutch T(817) 75¢
English (for German-speaking people) (T801) 60¢
English (for Italian-speaking people) (T816) 60¢
English (for Spanish-speaking people) (T802) 60¢
Esperanto (T820) 75¢
French (T803) 60¢
German (T804) 60¢
Modern Greek (T813) 75¢
Hebrew (T805) 60¢

Italian (T806) 60¢
Japanese (T807) 60¢
Norwegian (T814) 75¢
Russian (T810) 75¢
Spanish (T811) 60¢
Turkish (T821) 75¢
Yiddish (T815) 75¢
Swedish (T812) 75¢
Polish (T808) 75¢
Portuguese (T809) 75¢

LISTEN & LEARN language record sets

LISTEN & LEARN is the only language record course designed especially to meet your travel needs, or help you learn essential foreign language quickly by yourself, or in conjunction with any school course, by means of the automatic association method. Each set contains three 33⅓ rpm long-playing records — 1½ hours of recorded speech by eminent native speakers who are professors at Columbia, N.Y.U., Queens College and other leading universities. The sets are priced far below other sets of similar quality, yet they contain many special features not found in other record sets:

* Over 800 selected phrases and sentences, a basic vocabulary of over 3200 words.
* Both English and foreign language recorded; with a pause for your repetition.
* Designed for persons with limited time; no time wasted on material you cannot use immediately.
* Living, modern expressions that answer modern needs: drugstore items, "air-conditioned," etc.
* 128-196 page manuals contain everything on the records, plus simple pronunciation guides.
* Manual is fully indexed; find the phrase you want instantly.
* High fidelity recording—equal to any records costing up to $6 each.

The phrases on these records cover 41 different categories useful to the traveller or student interested in learning the living, spoken language: greetings, introductions, making yourself understood, passing customs, planes, trains, boats, buses, taxis, nightclubs, restaurants, menu items, sports, concerts, cameras, automobile travel, repairs, drugstores, doctors, dentists, medicines, barber shops, beauty parlors, laundries, many, many more.

"Excellent . . . among the very best on the market," Prof. Mario Pei, Dept. of Romance Languages, Columbia University. "Inexpensive and well-done . . . an ideal present," CHICAGO SUNDAY TRIBUNE. "More genuinely helpful than anything of its kind which I have previously encountered," Sidney Clark, well-known author of "ALL THE BEST" travel books. Each set contains 3 33⅓ rpm pure vinyl records, 128-196 page with full record text, and album. One language per set. LISTEN & LEARN record sets are now available in—

FRENCH	the set $4.95	**GERMAN**	the set $4.95
ITALIAN	the set $4.95	**SPANISH**	the set $4.95
RUSSIAN	the set $5.95	**JAPANESE** *	the set $5.95

* Available Sept. 1, 1959

UNCONDITIONAL GUARANTEE: Dover Publications stands behind every Listen and Learn record set. If you are dissatisfied with these sets for any reason whatever, return them within 10 days and your money will be refunded in full.

ART HISTORY

STICKS AND STONES, Lewis Mumford. An examination of forces influencing American architecture: the medieval tradition in early New England, the classical influence in Jefferson's time, the Brown Decades, the imperial facade, the machine age, etc. "A truly remarkable book," SAT. REV. OF LITERATURE. 2nd revised edition. 21 illus. xvii + 228pp. 5⅜ x 8.
T202 Paperbound **$1.60**

THE AUTOBIOGRAPHY OF AN IDEA, Louis Sullivan. The architect whom Frank Lloyd Wright called "the master," records the development of the theories that revolutionized America's skyline. 34 full-page plates of Sullivan's finest work. New introduction by R. M. Line. xiv + 335pp. 5⅜ x 8.
T281 Paperbound **$1.85**

THE MATERIALS AND TECHNIQUES OF MEDIEVAL PAINTING, D. V. Thompson. An invaluable study of carriers and grounds, binding media, pigments, metals used in painting, al fresco and al secco techniques, burnishing, etc. used by the medieval masters. Preface by Bernard Berenson. 239pp. 5⅜ x 8.
T327 Paperbound **$1.85**

PRINCIPLES OF ART HISTORY, H. Wölfflin. This remarkably instructive work demonstrates the tremendous change in artistic conception from the 14th to the 18th centuries, by analyzing 164 works by Botticelli, Dürer, Hobbema, Holbein, Hals, Titian, Rembrandt, Vermeer, etc., and pointing out exactly what is meant by "baroque," "classic," "primitive," "picturesque," and other basic terms of art history and criticism. "A remarkable lesson in the art of seeing," SAT. REV. OF LITERATURE. Translated from the 7th German edition. 150 illus. 254pp. 6⅛ x 9¼.
T276 Paperbound **$2.00**

FOUNDATIONS OF MODERN ART, A. Ozenfant. Stimulating discussion of human creativity from paleolithic cave painting to modern painting, architecture, decorative arts. Fully illustrated with works of Gris, Lipchitz, Leger, Picasso, primitive, modern artifacts, architecture, industrial art, much more. 226 illustrations. 368pp. 6⅛ x 9 ,.. .
T215 Paperbound **$1.95**

HANDICRAFTS, APPLIED ART, ART SOURCES, ETC.

WILD FOWL DECOYS, J. Barber. The standard work on this fascinating branch of folk art, ranging from Indian mud and grass devices to realistic wooden decoys. Discusses styles, types, periods; gives full information on how to make decoys. 140 illustrations (including 14 new plates) show decoys and provide full sets of plans for handicrafters, artists, hunters, and students of folk art. 281pp. 7⅞ x 10¾. Deluxe edition.
T11 Clothbound **$8.50**

METALWORK AND ENAMELLING, H. Maryon. Probably the best book ever written on the subject. Tells everything necessary for the home manufacture of jewelry, rings, ear pendants, bowls, etc. Covers materials, tools, soldering, filigree, setting stones, raising patterns, repoussé work, damascening, niello, cloisonné, polishing, assaying, casting, and dozens of other techniques. The best substitute for apprenticeship to a master metalworker. 363 photos and figures. 374pp. 5½ x 8½.
T183 Clothbound **$7.50**

SHAKER FURNITURE, E. D. and F. Andrews. The most illuminating study of Shaker furniture ever written. Covers chronology, craftsmanship, houses, shops, etc. Includes over 200 photographs of chairs, tables, clocks, beds, benches, etc. "Mr. & Mrs. Andrews know all there is to know about Shaker furniture," Mark Van Doren, NATION. 48 full-page plates. 192pp. Deluxe cloth binding. 7⅞ x 10¾.
T7 Clothbound **$6.00**

PRIMITIVE ART, Franz Boas. A great American anthropologist covers theory, technical virtuosity, styles, symbolism, patterns, etc. of primitive art. The more than 900 illustrations will interest artists, designers, craftworkers. Over 900 illustrations. 376pp. 5⅜ x 8.
T25 Paperbound **$1.95**

ON THE LAWS OF JAPANESE PAINTING, H. Bowie. The best possible substitute for lessons from an oriental master. Treats both spirit and technique; exercises for control of the brush; inks, brushes, colors; use of dots, lines to express whole moods, etc. 220 illus. 132pp. 6⅛ x 9¼.
T30 Paperbound **$1.95**

HANDBOOK OF ORNAMENT, F. S. Meyer. One of the largest collections of copyright-free traditional art: over 3300 line cuts of Greek, Roman, Medieval, Renaissance, Baroque, 18th and 19th century art motifs (tracery, geometric elements, flower and animal motifs, etc.) and decorated objects (chairs, thrones, weapons, vases, jewelry, armor, etc.). Full text. 3300 illustrations. 562pp. 5⅜ x 8.
T302 Paperbound **$2.00**

THREE CLASSICS OF ITALIAN CALLIGRAPHY. Oscar Ogg, ed. Exact reproductions of three famous Renaissance calligraphic works: Arrighi's OPERINA and IL MODO, Tagliente's LO PRESENTE LIBRO, and Palatino's LIBRO NUOVO. More than 200 complete alphabets, thousands of lettered specimens, in Papal Chancery and other beautiful, ornate handwriting. Introduction. 245 plates. 282pp. 6⅛ x 9¼.
T212 Paperbound **$1.95**

THE HISTORY AND TECHNIQUES OF LETTERING, A. Nesbitt. A thorough history of lettering from the ancient Egyptians to the present, and a 65-page course in lettering for artists. Every major development in lettering history is illustrated by a complete alphabet. Fully analyzes such masters as Caslon, Koch, Garamont, Jenson, and many more. 89 alphabets, 165 other specimens. 317pp. 5⅜ x 8.
T427 Paperbound **$2.00**

LETTERING AND ALPHABETS, J. A. Cavanagh. An unabridged reissue of "Lettering," containing the full discussion, analysis, illustration of 89 basic hand lettering tyles based on Caslon, Bodoni, Gothic, many other types. Hundreds of technical hints on construction, strokes, pens, brushes, etc. 89 alphabets, 72 lettered specimens, which may be reproduced permission-free. 121pp. 9¾ x 8. T53 Paperbound **$1.25**

THE HUMAN FIGURE IN MOTION, Eadweard Muybridge. The largest collection in print of Muybridge's famous high-speed action photos. 4789 photographs in more than 500 action-strip-sequences (at shutter speeds up to 1/6000th of a second) illustrate men, women, children—mostly undraped—performing such actions as walking, running, getting up, lying down, carrying objects, throwing, etc. "An unparalleled dictionary of action for all artists," AMERICAN ARTIST. 390 full-page plates, with 4789 photographs. Heavy glossy stock, reinforced binding with headbands. 7⅞ x 10¾. T204 Clothbound **$10.00**

ANIMALS IN MOTION, Eadweard Muybridge. The largest collection of animal action photos in print. 34 different animals (horses, mules, oxen, goats, camels, pigs, cats, lions, gnus, deer, monkeys, eagles—and 22 others) in 132 characteristic actions. All 3919 photographs are taken in series at speeds up to 1/1600th of a second, offering artists, biologists, cartoonists a remarkable opportunity to see exactly how an ostrich's head bobs when running, how a lion puts his foot down, how an elephant's knee bends, how a bird flaps his wings, thousands of other hard-to-catch details. "A really marvelous series of plates," NATURE. 380 full-pages of plates. Heavy glossy stock, reinforced binding with headbands. 7⅞ x 10¾. T203 Clothbound **$10.00**

THE BOOK OF SIGNS, R. Koch. 493 symbols—crosses, monograms, astrological, biological symbols, runes, etc.—from ancient manuscripts, cathedrals, coins, catacombs, pottery. May be reproduced permission-free. 493 illustrations by Fritz Kredel. 104pp. 6⅛ x 9¼. T162 Paperbound **$1.00**

A HANDBOOK OF EARLY ADVERTISING ART, C. P. Hornung. The largest collection of copyright-free early advertising art ever compiled. Vol. I: 2,000 illustrations of animals, old automobiles, buildings, allegorical figures, fire engines, Indians, ships, trains, more than 33 other categories! Vol II: Over 4,000 typographical specimens; 600 Roman, Gothic, Barnum, Old English faces; 630 ornamental type faces; hundreds of scrolls, initials, flourishes, etc. "A remarkable collection," PRINTERS' INK.

Vol. I: Pictorial Volume. Over 2000 illustrations. 256pp. 9 x 12.   T122 Clothbound **$10.00**
Vol. II: Typographical Volume. Over 4000 speciments. 319pp. 9 x 12.   T123 Clothbound **$10.00**
Two volume set, Clothbound, only **$18.50**

DESIGN FOR ARTISTS AND CRAFTSMEN, L. Wolchonok. The most thorough course on the creation of art motifs and designs. Shows you step-by-step, with hundreds of examples and 113 detailed exercises, how to create original designs from geometric patterns, plants, birds, animals, humans, and man-made objects. "A great contribution to the field of design and crafts," N. Y. SOCIETY OF CRAFTSMEN. More than 1300 entirely new illustrations. xv + 207pp. 7⅞ x 10¾. T274 Clothbound **$4.95**

HANDBOOK OF DESIGNS AND DEVICES, C. P. Hornung. A remarkable working collection of 1836 basic designs and variations, all copyright-free. Variations of circle, line, cross, diamond, swastika, star, scroll, shield, many more. Notes on symbolism. "A necessity to every designer who would be original without having to labor heavily," ARTIST and ADVERTISER. 204 plates. 240pp. 5⅜ x 8. T125 Paperbound **$1.90**

THE UNIVERSAL PENMAN, George Bickham. Exact reproduction of beautiful 18th century book of handwriting. 22 complete alphabets in finest English roundhand, other scripts, over 2000 elaborate flourishes, 122 calligraphic illustrations, etc. Material is copyright-free. "An essential part of any art library, and a book of permanent value," AMERICAN ARTIST. 212 plates. 224pp. 9 x 13¾. T20 Clothbound **$10.00**

AN ATLAS OF ANATOMY FOR ARTISTS, F. Schider. This standard work contains 189 full-page plates, more than 647 illustrations of all aspects of the human skeleton, musculature, cutaway portions of the body, each part of the anatomy, hand forms, eyelids, breasts, location of muscles under the flesh, etc. 59 plates illustrate how Michelangelo, da Vinci, Goya, 15 others, drew human anatomy. New 3rd edition enlarged by 52 new illustrations by Cloquet, Barcsay. "The standard reference tool," AMERICAN LIBRARY ASSOCIATION. "Excellent," AMERICAN ARTIST. 189 plates, 647 illustrations. xxvi + 192pp. 7⅞ x 10⅝. T241 Clothbound **$6.00**

AN ATLAS OF ANIMAL ANATOMY FOR ARTISTS, W. Ellenberger, H. Baum, H. Dittrich. The largest, richest animal anatomy for artists in English. Form, musculature, tendons, bone structure, expression, detailed cross sections of head, other features, of the horse, lion, dog, cat, deer, seal, kangaroo, cow, bull, goat, monkey, hare, many other animals. "Highly recommended," DESIGN. Second, revised, enlarged edition with new plates from Cuvier, Stubbs, etc. 288 illustrations. 153pp. 11⅜ x 9. T82 Clothbound **$6.00**

ANIMAL DRAWING: ANATOMY AND ACTION FOR ARTISTS, C. R. Knight. 158 studies, with full accompanying text, of such animals as the gorilla, bear, bison, dromedary, camel, vulture, pelican, iguana, shark, etc., by one of the greatest modern masters of animal drawing. Innumerable tips on how to get life expression into your work. "An excellent reference work,' SAN FRANCISCO CHRONICLE. 158 illustrations. 156pp. 10½ x 8½. T426 Paperbound **$2.00**

THE CRAFTSMAN'S HANDBOOK, Cennino Cennini. The finest English translation of IL LIBRO DELL' ARTE, the 15th century introduction to art technique that is both a mirror of Quatrocento life and a source of many useful but nearly forgotten facets of the painter's art. 4 illustrations. xxvii + 142pp. D. V. Thompson, translator. 6⅛ x 9¼.　　T54 Paperbound **$1.50**

THE BROWN DECADES, Lewis Mumford. A picture of the "buried renaissance" of the post-Civil War period, and the founding of modern architecture (Sullivan, Richardson, Root, Roebling), landscape development (Marsh, Olmstead, Eliot), and the graphic arts (Homer, Eakins, Ryder). 2nd revised, enlarged edition. Bibliography. 12 illustrations. xiv + 266 pp. 5⅜ x 8.　　T200 Paperbound **$1.65**

STIEGEL GLASS, F. W. Hunter. The story of the most highly esteemed early American glassware, fully illustrated. How a German adventurer, "Baron" Stiegel, founded a glass empire; detailed accounts of individual glasswork. "This pioneer work is reprinted in an edition even more beautiful than the original," ANTIQUES DEALER. New introduction by Helen McKearin. 171 illustrations, 12 in full color. xxii + 338pp. 7⅞ x 10¾.
T128 Clothbound **$10.00**

THE HUMAN FIGURE, J. H. Vanderpoel. Not just a picture book, but a complete course by a famous figure artist. Extensive text, illustrated by 430 pencil and charcoal drawings of both male and female anatomy. 2nd enlarged edition. Foreword. 430 illus. 143pp. 6⅛ x 9¼.
T432 Paperbound **$1.45**

PINE FURNITURE OF EARLY NEW ENGLAND, R. H. Kettell. Over 400 illustrations, over 50 working drawings of early New England chairs, benches, beds cupboards, mirrors, shelves, tables, other furniture esteemed for simple beauty and character. "Rich store of illustrations . . . emphasizes the individuality and varied design," ANTIQUES. 413 illustrations, 55 working drawings. 475pp. 8 x 10¾.　　T145 Clothbound **$10.00**

BASIC BOOKBINDING, A. W. Lewis. Enables both beginners and experts to rebind old books or bind paperbacks in hard covers. Treats materials, tools; gives step-by-step instruction in how to collate a book, sew it, back it, make boards, etc. 261 illus. Appendices. 155pp. 5⅜ x 8.　　T169 Paperbound **$1.35**

DESIGN MOTIFS OF ANCIENT MEXICO, J. Enciso. Nearly 90% of these 766 superb designs from Aztec, Olmec, Totonac, Maya, and Toltec origins are unobtainable elsewhere! Contains plumed serpents, wind gods, animals, demons, dancers, monsters, etc. Excellent applied design source. Originally $17.50. 766 illustrations, thousands of motifs. 192pp. 6⅛ x 9¼.
T84 Paperbound **$1.85**

AFRICAN SCULPTURE, Ladislas Segy. 163 full-page plates illustrating masks, fertility figures, ceremonial objects, etc., of 50 West and Central African tribes—95% never before illustrated. 34-page introduction to African sculpture. "Mr. Segy is one of its top authorities," NEW YORKER. 164 full-page photographic plates. Introduction. Bibliography. 244pp. 6⅛ x 9¼.
T396 Paperbound **$2.00**

THE PROCESSES OF GRAPHIC REPRODUCTION IN PRINTING, H. Curwen. A thorough and practical survey of wood, linoleum, and rubber engraving; copper engraving; drypoint, mezzotint, etching, aquatint, steel engraving, die sinking, stencilling, lithography (extensively); photographic reproduction utilizing line, continuous tone, photoengravure, collotype; every other process in general use. Note on color reproduction. Section on bookbinding. Over 200 illustrations, 25 in color. 143pp. 5½ x 8½.　　T512 Clothbound **$4.00**

CALLIGRAPHY, J. G. Schwandner. First reprinting in 200 years of this legendary book of beautiful handwriting. Over 300 ornamental initials, 12 complete calligraphic alphabets, over 150 ornate frames and panels, 75 calligraphic pictures of cherubs, stags, lions, etc., thousands of flourishes, scrolls, etc., by the greatest 18th century masters. All material can be copied or adapted without permission. Historical introduction. 158 full-page plates. 368pp. 9 x 13.　　T475 Clothbound **$10.00**

* * *

A DIDEROT PICTORIAL ENCYCLOPEDIA OF TRADES AND INDUSTRY, Manufacturing and the Technical Arts in Plates Selected from "L'Encyclopédie ou Dictionnaire Raisonné des Sciences, des Arts, et des Métiers," of Denis Diderot, edited with text by C. Gillispie. Over 2000 illustrations on 485 full-page plates. Magnificent 18th century engravings of men, women, and children working at such trades as milling flour, cheesemaking, charcoal burning, mining, silverplating, shoeing horses, making fine glass, printing, hundreds more, showing details of machinery, different steps in sequence, etc. A remarkable art work, but also the largest collection of working figures in print, copyright-free, for art directors, designers, etc. Two vols. 920pp. 9 x 12. Heavy library cloth.　　T421 Two volume set **$18.50**

* * *

SILK SCREEN TECHNIQUES, J. Biegeleisen, M. Cohn. A practical step-by-step home course in one of the most versatile, least expensive graphic arts processes. How to build an inexpensive silk screen, prepare stencils, print, achieve special textures, use color, etc. Every step explained, diagrammed. 149 illustrations, 8 in color. 201pp. 6⅛ x 9¼.
T433 Paperbound **$1.45**

PUZZLES, GAMES, AND ENTERTAINMENTS

MATHEMATICS, MAGIC AND MYSTERY, Martin Gardner. Astonishing feats of mind reading, mystifying "magic" tricks, are often based on mathematical principles anyone can learn. This book shows you how to perform scores of tricks with cards, dice, coins, knots, numbers, etc., by using simple principles from set theory, theory of numbers, topology, other areas of mathematics, fascinating in themselves. No special knowledge required. 135 illus. 186pp. 5⅜ x 8. T335 Paperbound **$1.00**

MATHEMATICAL PUZZLES FOR BEGINNERS AND ENTHUSIASTS, G. Mott-Smith. Test your problem-solving techniques and powers of inference on 188 challenging, amusing puzzles based on algebra, dissection of plane figures, permutations, probabilities, etc. Appendix of primes, square roots, etc. 135 illus. 2nd revised edition. 248pp. 5⅜ x 8.
T198 Paperbound **$1.00**

LEARN CHESS FROM THE MASTERS, F. Reinfeld. Play 10 games against Marshall, Bronstein, Najdorf, other masters, and grade yourself on each move. Detailed annotations reveal principles of play, strategy, etc. as you proceed. An excellent way to get a real insight into the game. Formerly titled, "Chess by Yourself." 91 diagrams. vii + 144pp. 5⅜ x 8.
T362 Paperbound **$1.00**

REINFELD ON THE END GAME IN CHESS, F. Reinfeld. 62 end games of Alekhine, Tarrasch, Morphy, other masters, are carefully analyzed with emphasis on transition from middle game to end play. Tempo moves, queen endings, weak squares, other basic principles clearly illustrated. Excellent for understanding why some moves are weak or incorrect, how to avoid errors. Formerly titled, "Practical End-game Play." 62 diagrams. vi + 177pp. 5⅜ x 8.
T417 Paperbound **$1.25**

101 PUZZLES IN THOUGHT AND LOGIC, C. R. Wylie, Jr. Brand new puzzles you need no special knowledge to solve! Each one is a gem of ingenuity that will really challenge your problem-solving technique. Introduction with simplified explanation of scientic puzzle solving. 128pp. 5⅜ x 8. T167 Paperbound **$1.00**

THE COMPLETE NONSENSE OF EDWARD LEAR. The only complete edition of this master of gentle madness at a popular price. The Dong with the Luminous Nose, The Jumblies, The Owl and the Pussycat, hundreds of other bits of wonderful nonsense. 214 limericks, 3 sets of Nonsense Botany, 5 Nonsense Alphabets, 546 fantastic drawings, much more. 320pp. 5⅜ x 8. T167 Paperbound **$1.00**

28 SCIENCE FICTION STORIES OF H. G. WELLS. Two complete novels, "Men Like Gods" and "Star Begotten," plus 26 short stories by the master science-fiction writer of all time. Stories of space, time, future adventure that are among the all-time classics of science fiction. 928pp. 5⅜ x 8. T265 Clothbound **$3.95**

SEVEN SCIENCE FICTION NOVELS, H. G. Wells. Unabridged texts of "The Time Machine," "The Island of Dr. Moreau," "First Men in the Moon," "The Invisible Man," "The War of the Worlds," "The Food of the Gods," "In the Days of the Comet." "One will have to go far to match this for entertainment, excitement, and sheer pleasure," N. Y. TIMES. 1015pp. 5⅜ x 8. T264 Clothbound **$3.95**

MATHEMAGIC, MAGIC PUZZLES, AND GAMES WITH NUMBERS, R. V. Heath. More than 60 new puzzles and stunts based on number properties: multiplying large numbers mentally, finding the date of any day in the year, etc. Edited by J. S. Meyer. 76 illus. 129pp. 5⅜ x 8.
T110 Paperbound **$1.00**

FIVE ADVENTURE NOVELS OF H. RIDER HAGGARD. The master story-teller's five best tales of mystery and adventure set against authentic African backgrounds: "She," "King Solomon's Mines," "Allan Quatermain," "Allan's Wife," "Maiwa's Revenge." 821pp. 5⅜ x 8.
T108 Clothbound **$3.95**

WIN AT CHECKERS, M. Hopper. (Formerly "Checkers.") The former World's Unrestricted Checker Champion gives you valuable lessons in openings, traps, end games, ways to draw when you are behind, etc. More than 100 questions and answers anticipate your problems. Appendix. 75 problems diagrammed, solved. 79 figures. xi + 107pp. 5⅜ x 8.
T363 Paperbound **$1.00**

CRYPTOGRAPHY, L. D. Smith. Excellent introductory work on ciphers and their solution, history of secret writing, techniques, etc. Appendices on Japanese methods, the Baconian cipher, frequency tables. Bibliography. Over 150 problems, solutions. 160pp. 5⅜ x 8.
T247 Paperbound **$1.00**

CRYPTANALYSIS, H. F. Gaines. (Formerly, "Elementary Cryptanalysis.") The best book available on cryptograms and how to solve them. Contains all major techniques: substitution, transposition, mixed alphabets, multafid, Kasiski and Vignere methods, etc. Word frequency appendix. 167 problems, solutions. 173 figures. 236pp. 5⅜ x 8. T97 Paperbound **$1.95**

FLATLAND, E. A. Abbot. The science-fiction classic of life in a 2-dimensional world that is considered a first-rate introduction to relativity and hyperspace, as well as a scathing satire on society, politics and religion. 7th edition. 16 illus. 128pp. 5⅜ x 8.
T1 Paperbound **$1.00**

HOW TO FORCE CHECKMATE, F. Reinfeld. (Formerly "Challenge to Chessplayers.") No board needed to sharpen your checkmate skill on 300 checkmate situations. Learn to plan up to 3 moves ahead and play a superior end game. 300 situations diagrammed; notes and full solutions. 111pp. 5⅜ x 8. T439 Paperbound **$1.25**

MORPHY'S GAMES OF CHESS, P. W. Sergeant, ed. Play forcefully by following the techniques used by one of the greatest chess champions. 300 of Morphy's games carefully annotated to reveal principles. Bibliography. New introduction by F. Reinfeld. 235 diagrams. x + 352pp. 5⅜ x 8. T386 Paperbound **$1.75**

MATHEMATICAL RECREATIONS, M. Kraitchik. Hundreds of unusual mathematical puzzlers and odd bypaths of math, elementary and advanced. Greek, Medieval, Arabic, Hindu problems; figurate numbers, Fermat numbers, primes; magic, Euler, Latin squares; fairy chess, latruncles, reversi, jinx, ruma, tetrachrome other positional and permutational games. Rigorous solutions. Revised second edition. 181 illus. 330pp. 5⅜ x 8. T163 Paperbound **$1.75**

MATHEMATICAL EXCURSIONS, H. A. Merrill. Revealing stimulating insights into elementary math, not usually taught in school. 90 problems demonstrate Russian peasant multiplication, memory systems for pi, magic squares, dyadic systems, division by inspection, many more. Solutions to difficult problems. 50 illus. 5⅜ x 8. T350 Paperbound **$1.00**

MAGIC TRICKS & CARD TRICKS, W. Jonson. Best introduction to tricks with coins, bills, eggs, ribbons, slates, cards, easily performed without elaborate equipment. Professional routines, tips on presentation, misdirection, etc. Two books bound as one: 52 tricks with cards, 37 tricks with common objects. 106 figures. 224pp. 5⅜ x 8. T909 Paperbound **$1.00**

MATHEMATICAL PUZZLES OF SAM LOYD, selected and edited by M. Gardner. 177 most ingenious mathematical puzzles of America's greatest puzzle originator, based on arithmetic, algebra, game theory, dissection, route tracing, operations research, probability, etc. 120 drawings, diagrams. Solutions. 187pp. 5⅜ x 8. T498 Paperbound **$1.00**

THE ART OF CHESS, J. Mason. The most famous general study of chess ever written. More than 90 openings, middle game, end game, how to attack, sacrifice, defend, exchange, form general strategy. Supplement on "How Do You Play Chess?" by F. Reinfeld. 448 diagrams. 356pp. 5⅜ x 8. T463 Paperbound **$1.85**

HYPERMODERN CHESS as Developed in the Games of its Greatest Exponent, ARON NIMZOVICH, F. Reinfeld, ed. Learn how the game's greatest innovator defeated Alekhine, Lasker, and many others; and use these methods in your own game. 180 diagrams. 228pp. 5⅜ x 8. T448 Paperbound **$1.35**

A TREASURY OF CHESS LORE, F. Reinfeld, ed. Hundreds of fascinating stories by and about the masters, accounts of tournaments and famous games, aphorisms, word portraits, little known incidents, photographs, etc., that will delight the chess enthusiast, captivate the beginner. 49 photographs (14 full-page plates), 12 diagrams. 315pp. 5⅜ x 8. T458 Paperbound **$1.75**

A NONSENSE ANTHOLOGY, collected by Carolyn Wells. 245 of the best nonsense verses ever written: nonsense puns, absurd arguments, mock epics, nonsense ballads, "sick" verses, dog-Latin verses, French nonsense verses, limericks. Lear, Carroll, Belloc, Burgess, nearly 100 other writers. Introduction by Carolyn Wells. 3 indices: Title, Author, First Lines. xxxiii + 279pp. 5⅜ x 8. T499 Paperbound **$1.25**

SYMBOLIC LOGIC and THE GAME OF LOGIC, Lewis Carroll. Two delightful puzzle books by the author of "Alice," bound as one. Both works concern the symbolic representation of traditional logic and together contain more than 500 ingenious, amusing and instructive syllogistic puzzlers. Total of 326pp. 5⅜ x 8. T492 Paperbound **$1.50**

PILLOW PROBLEMS and A TANGLED TALE, Lewis Carroll. Two of Carroll's rare puzzle works bound as one. "Pillow Problems" contain 72 original math puzzles. The puzzles in "A Tangled Tale" are given in delightful story form. Total of 291pp. 5⅜ x 8. T493 Paperbound **$1.50**

PECK'S BAD BOY AND HIS PA, G. W. Peck. Both volumes of one of the most widely read of all American humor books. A classic of American folk humor, also invaluable as a portrait of an age. 100 original illustrations. Introduction by E. Bleiler. 347pp. 5⅜ x 8. T497 Paperbound **$1.35**

Dover publishes books on art, music, philosophy, literature, languages, history, social sciences, psychology, handcrafts, orientalia, puzzles and entertainments, chess, pets and gardens, books explaining science, intermediate and higher mathematics mathematical physics, engineering, biological sciences, earth sciences, classics of science, etc. Write to:

Dept. catrr.
Dover Publications, Inc.
180 Varick Street, N. Y. 14, N. Y.

7379